PENGUIN BOOKS

HEART OF FIRE

Senator Mazie K. Hirono is a graduate of the University of Hawaii, Manoa, and the Georgetown University Law Center. She has served in the Hawaii House of Representatives (1981–1994), as Hawaii's lieutenant governor (1994–2002), and in the U.S. House of Representatives (2006–2013). She became Hawaii's first female United States Senator in 2013, winning reelection in 2018. Hirono serves on the Committee on the Judiciary, the Committee on Armed Services, and the Committee on Energy and Natural Resources, among others.

* * *

Praise for *Heart of Fire*

"A beautiful book." —Trevor Noah, *The Daily Show*

"Absolutely incredible." —Mika Brzezinksi, cohost, *Morning Joe*

"Inspiring and compassionate." —*The Seattle Times*

"[A] multigenerational tale . . . built around [Hirono's] political and feminist awakening . . . Most powerfully, *Heart of Fire* is about Hirono's growing determination to loosen her tongue." —Rebecca Traister, *The Cut*

"Beautiful . . . You can't help but be moved by [Hirono's] book." —*Salon*

"[A] book unique among those by politicians, written more in the tone of a late-night conversation between two close friends, or a journal entry, than a town hall or stump speech." —*Politico*

"With both ferocity and compassion, Hirono chronicles her experiences in Congress, exposing the rampant hypocrisy and illogical behavior she has witnessed. At the same time, warmth and love shine through, as she attributes her success and determination to the example set by her mother. A heartfelt and fiery political memoir and immigrant story."
                                                                    —*Kirkus Reviews*

"*Heart of Fire* is an urgent read for a nation in need of healing, inspiration, and introspection. It vividly captures Mazie Hirono's journey to the Senate, which is both strikingly unique and yet speaks to compelling universal spiritual themes. A profound testimony to the glorious possibility that is our nation, this important book is a gift to the reader, just as Mazie's life of breaking barriers and her leadership as a champion of the people continue to be gifts to all Americans."
            —Cory Booker, United States senator and *New York Times* bestselling
                                                                    author of *United*

"If a life can be called implausible, Mazie Hirono has lived it. In *Heart of Fire*, she tells an astonishingly compelling story. As a child born in postwar Japan, she crossed an ocean with her brother and mother, grew up in poverty in paradisiacal Hawaii, and emerged as a fiery voice and agent of change in the male-dominated, rough-and-tumble world of American politics. Powerful, poignant, and beautifully told, *Heart of Fire* is her inspiring, singular story."
                    —George Takei, *New York Times* bestselling
                                        author of *They Called Us Enemy*

Keiko, age three, Fukushima, Japan

HEART *of* FIRE

*An Immigrant
Daughter's Story*

Mazie K. Hirono

PENGUIN BOOKS

PENGUIN BOOKS
An imprint of Penguin Random House LLC
penguinrandomhouse.com

First published in the United States of America by Viking,
an imprint of Penguin Random House LLC, 2021
Published in Penguin Books 2022

Photo of the author with David Hagino (insert p. 7); Photo of the author canvassing (insert p. 9);
Photo of the author and her mother tending to their garden (insert p. 12); Photo of the author and
Leighton Oshima campaigning in 2018 (insert p. 15) courtesy of Alan Van Etten/Friends of Mazie Hirono.

Photo of the author and Leighton Oshima on the Senate
subway (insert p. 13) AP Photo/Harry Hamburg.

Photo of the author with John Lewis (insert p. 14) courtesy of the
Faith & Politics Institute; © HPM Ltd. Photo by Mark Harrison.

Photo of the author with Senators Richard Blumenthal
and Kamala Harris (insert p. 14) AP Photo/Carolyn Kaster.

Portrait of the author with Betty Friedan's *The Feminine
Mystique* (insert p. 15) Celeste Sloman/*The New York Times*/Redux.

Photo of the author with Supreme Court Associate Justice Ruth
Bader Ginsburg (insert p. 14) courtesy of Vincent Eng.

Cards (pp. xx, 72, 144, and 210) by Laura Hirono.

Cards (pp. xii, 364, and 379) by the author.

All other images courtesy of the author.

ISBN 9781984881625 (paperback)

THE LIBRARY OF CONGRESS HAS CATALOGED THE HARDCOVER EDITION AS FOLLOWS:
Names: Hirono, Mazie, 1947– author.
Title: Heart of fire : an immigrant daughter's story / Mazie K. Hirono.
Description: [New York] : Viking, 2021. |
Includes bibliographical references. |
Identifiers: LCCN 2020053648 (print) | LCCN 2020053649 (ebook) |
ISBN 9781984881601 (hardcover) | ISBN 9781984881618 (ebook)
Subjects: LCSH: United States. Congress. Senate—Biography. |
United States. Congress. House—Biography. | Japanese American
women—Hawaii—Biography. | Lieutenant governors—Hawaii—Biography. |
Legislators—Hawaii—Biography. | Women legislators—Hawaii—Biography. |
Legislators—United States—Biography. | Women legislators—United
States—Biography. | United States—Politics and government—1989– |
Hawaii—Politics and government—1959–
Classification: LCC E901.1 .H57 2021 (print) | LCC E901.1 (ebook) |
DDC 328.73/092 [B]—dc23
LC record available at https://lccn.loc.gov/2020053648
LC ebook record available at https://lccn.loc.gov/2020053649

Printed in the United States of America
1st Printing

Designed by Alexis Farabaugh

To my mother, Laura Chieko,
who dared everything, and
whose compass is my surest guide

To my husband, Leighton,
who makes me laugh, and inspires me
to keep taking copious notes

Contents

Author's Note

As with all memoirs, the dialogue in this narrative has been re-created from the author's best recollection and characterizes the spirit and substance of conversations rather than the precise words that may have been spoken.

Necessary Fire

I n one of my most vivid childhood memories, I am sitting on the curb next to the bus stop with my older brother, Roy, waiting for our mother to get home. Three nights a week, after she leaves her day job as a typesetter at a Japanese-language newspaper, she goes to work as a server for a caterer downtown. Roy is eleven and I am nine. Most days after school, we play in the street and climb trees with boys from the neighborhood until late, and then we wait at the bus stop. A soft evening breeze cools our flushed faces as we sit chewing wads of wax candy, pleasantly tired from our games. In the tree branches above us, roosting sparrows ruffle their wings, their chatter mingling with the occasional rumble of passing cars. I think how different the night noises are here in Hawaii, compared to the stillness of evenings in rural Japan, where I was born.

Roy and I jump to our feet at the sight of our mother's bus turning onto

Kewalo Street. We crowd around the door as it opens, knowing Mom will be the only passenger getting off at this hour. On this night, when Mom steps off the bus, she stumbles and steadies herself with a hand on Roy's shoulder. She pauses, closes her eyes, and sucks in a deep breath. She looks pale and worn, and I realize she's not feeling well. I watch her face closely as Roy and I walk slowly beside her to the white clapboard boardinghouse where we live together in a single small room.

As soon as we are inside, Mom changes out of her white server's uniform and climbs under the sheets. She lies sideways across the mattress the three of us share, feet hanging off the side, careful to leave space for Roy and me. She refuses the bowl of rice that I have saved for her dinner and turns to the wall, a tiny moan escaping her. I touch her face. Her skin is on fire. I gather her clothes from the top of the dresser, where she has neatly placed them, and find that the cloth is soaked through. I try to appear calm, but I'm frightened. Roy stretches out next to our mother, watching her sleep, his forehead creased. I can tell he's worrying, too. Not knowing what else to do, I walk to the communal washbasin at the end of the hall, carrying Mom's uniform. Barely tall enough to reach the sink, I stand on a small step and drape the white cloth over the wooden washboard. I set about scrubbing the sweat stains from her clothes, working vigorously to distract myself from the fear that makes me feel hollow at the center. Mom has only one white server's uniform and will need to wear it again for her next shift, later in the week.

I know how hard my mother works to keep us afloat, and I have already begun looking for ways to help her. Every day during the school year, Mom leaves two quarters on the table for Roy and me to buy lunch. A couple of times a month, she adds a dime for each of us. Roy always spends his dime, but I drop mine into the slot of a metal baseball piggy bank that Mom gave me. It is a cheap thing she picked up for a few cents, but I treasure it. In the evening before bed, I shake it, pleased by the jingle of coins. Some nights, I open the piggy bank and arrange the dimes in ever-lengthening rows on the floor, enjoying the simple fact of them.

One evening a few weeks before, I shook my piggy bank, anticipating its jingle. But it made no sound. "I had to buy food," Mom explained when she arrived home later that night. Where my saved coins had been, there was now only the heaviness of her regret. It chased my own disappointment away instantly. It had taken me many months to save those coins, but I understood that Mom had needed them. A few days later, she pressed a new coin in my palm. She folded my fist around it, smiling at me ruefully. The cool metal in my hand felt like a kind of promise as I pulled my piggy bank from under the bed and dropped the dime into its slot. Hearing its lonely clink, I knew there was nothing else to do but to begin saving again.

Now, I rinse Mom's uniform and hang it to dry on a communal line in the yard. By the time I get back to our room, Mom and Roy are both snoring softly. I sleep fitfully that night, alert to Mom's every movement and sigh. I'm half-awake when she rises before daybreak as usual, dresses quietly so as not to disturb us, and leaves for her day job at the newspaper. After she's gone, I lie there, staring into the darkness. Beside me, Roy rolls onto his back and softly exhales.

Even at that young age, I knew that there was no safety net to catch us should anything happen to our mother. Two years earlier, she had fled her unhappy marriage and brought us to Hawaii. We'd had to leave my three-year-old brother, Wayne, behind in Japan with my beloved maternal grandparents; he was too young to go to school, and there would be no one to take care of him while Mom worked. Wayne and my grandparents would be joining us soon, but in the meantime, our mother was all we had. A single parent, she worked two jobs for low wages, and if she couldn't work, we didn't eat. There was no question of her seeing a doctor, as we had no money for that, and no health coverage.

That childhood insecurity shaped the woman—and the public servant—I would become. It helped fuel my desire to study law and to position myself in rooms where I could advocate for those who were as vulnerable as our family had once been—as I had once felt. When, as a state legislator, I helped to pass laws that ensured safer working conditions and expanded health-care coverage for Hawaii's families, I thought of my mother. When I advocated for public schools to have the resources they needed to serve all different types of learners, I thought of the teachers who had made a difference in my life— and those who hadn't been able to help Wayne. And when, as a U.S. senator, I vociferously opposed the Trump administration's cruel and devastating family separation policy, I thought again of my brother Wayne, who would carry the scars of a much gentler separation for the entirety of his tragically short life.

I have now spent five decades fighting for my constituents while also navigating old-boy networks in the staterooms of Hawaii and in the House and Senate chambers of Washington, D.C., creating a place for myself in political arenas dominated by men. For the vast majority of that time, I strove to be polite and civil, even as I fought tenaciously for the causes I believed in. From my earliest days in the Hawaii legislature, I schooled myself to bite back the snappish retorts that sprang to my lips at the chauvinistic nonsense that remains an inevitable part of American politics, not to mention the hypocrisy of colleagues who speak one way behind closed doors and vote another way on the floor. Though this restrained civility had clear roots in the cultures I was steeped in—that of both Japan and Hawaii—it was not my underlying nature. But, given the expectations placed on women in politics, that we must be reasonable at all costs and never risk appearing to be overly emotional, it had seemed the most pragmatic approach to getting things done.

After the 2016 election, however, I found I could no longer censor myself. I began to let loose my frustration and anger at the forty-fifth administration's appalling practices and policies, from tearing little children away from their desperate, asylum-seeking parents, to unleashing the hateful violence of white supremacists, to disparaging war veterans, to packing the nation's courts with ideologues. As I started publicly decrying in the strongest possible terms the lawless president and those who enabled him, I was heartened to discover that this merging of my private and public personas was embraced by my constituents, as well as by the Democrats and progressives across this nation who shared my outrage. I haven't stopped speaking my mind since.

In bringing us to the United States, my mother radically changed the trajectory of my life, making it possible for a daughter who might have grown up to marry a rice farmer in rural Japan to become the first Asian American woman and the only immigrant serving in the United States Senate. My deep emotional connection to my mother is the current that has driven my entire life. Everything I have achieved is a testament to her fortitude. It was her example that showed me how to stand up for myself, persevere, and not back down from a just fight. And it was her steady, loving presence that provided the secure base from which I could leap. Now ninety-six and mostly bedridden, my mother can no longer bear witness for herself, and so I have chosen to honor her by telling the story of the daughter she inspired to live boldly, and to fight with everything she is to make the promises of this nation a reality.

As of this writing on the eve of the 2020 presidential election, we stand at a crossroads, one that calls each of us to take action to preserve our democracy, to join in the fight against racial injustice, and to support one another through a global pandemic that has brought widespread grief, trauma, and the worst economic collapse since the Great Depression. The past four years have demanded that I become the most vocal and determined public servant I can be. In doing so—in becoming more fully myself—I have had to shed all the expectations others may have placed on me as an immigrant, a woman, and an Asian American. My deepest wish is that my story will inspire you to do the same, to become more fully yourself as you step into your own immense power, regardless of the circumstances into which you were born.

Part One

GOOD GIRL

If you are scorched earth, I will be warm
rain.

—Lady Murasaki Shikibu,
THE TALE OF GENJI

CHAPTER ONE

Tari and Chieko

The sky itself seemed new, a brash fluorescent blue in place of the soft pewter I had known before. And yet this was the same sky that sheltered my grandparents and little brother back in Fukushima, Japan. The thought comforted me. I was grateful then that my first-grade teacher at Queen Kaahumanu Elementary had seated me next to a window. In those early days in Hawaii, as notes of a language I didn't yet understand swirled around me, I would turn my gaze to the sky with its towering palms, their fronds swaying hypnotically. Watching the fronds' stately dance, I thought of my grandmother Tari, my beloved baachan, and remembered the ginkgo and persimmon trees I had dreamed under only months before, when we'd lived with my grandparents in rural Japan.

I was seven and Yoshikazu was nine on the afternoon in March 1955 when we left Baachan, and our home, behind. With our mother's palms resting lightly on our backs, we'd climbed the gangway onto a hulking iron ship that would carry us across the Pacific Ocean to another life. I was already missing my three-year-old brother, Shigeki. It had torn our mother's heart to leave him behind in Fukushima. I could still see Shigeki with his eyes squeezed shut, shaking his head in silent dissent as our mother tried to explain to him that it was only for a little while, until he was old enough to start school.

Baachan had traveled by train with us to the port of Yokohama, determined to see us off. I tasted the salt of my tears even before the U.S.S. *President Cleveland* pulled away from the docks. Standing on deck, my hands gripping the chipped white paint of the railing, I watched my baachan grow smaller and smaller. She kept waving until I couldn't make her out anymore, yet even when the shores of Yokohama slipped from view, I knew she was still there, head bowed as she whispered Buddhist prayers for our protection.

My mother had explained that we were going to live in the place where she was born. At twenty-two, my grandmother, Tari Shinoki, who had been educated through finishing school, had traveled to Hawaii as a picture bride, agreeing to marry my grandfather, Hiroshi Sato, a twenty-six-year-old migrant worker, sight unseen. The carefully raised daughter of a village leader, Baachan had decided to become a picture bride to escape the pressure of too many marriage proposals from men who did not interest her. Her sister had just made a good match with one of Hiroshi's brothers in Fukushima, and when her brother-in-law suggested she marry Hiroshi and live with him in Hawaii, she had judged the arrangement a good bet, with a little adventure thrown in. She would become one of the nearly twenty thousand picture brides from Japan, Okinawa, and Korea who arrived in Hawaii between 1908 and 1924. But when Tari finally laid eyes on the man she was to wed, he looked nothing like the smiling youth in the photograph his brother had shown her. In 1923, as Tari stood on the docks of Honolulu with all the other picture brides with whom she had made the sea crossing, and pledged to have and to hold my grandfather, she swallowed the disappointment she felt on seeing her husband for the first time. He'd arrived to meet her in the same torn, sweaty work shirt he wore to chop sugarcane with the other migrants in the plantation fields.

"I had to clean him up," Baachan would tell me years later. Under the grime, she discovered a tall, handsome, deeply reticent man who knew very little of the world, despite having left his home in Japan when he was just sixteen to join an older brother who was working on Waipahu's sugar plantation, located just north of Pearl Harbor on Oahu. Hiroshi's simplicity exasperated Tari. Worse, she was now obliged to toil in the cane fields beside her husband, a detail she hadn't grasped when she agreed to marry him.

She found the plantation work punishing and the living conditions crude. Migrants were crowded into rustic cabins, usually with no running water, and the pay was meager, barely enough to sustain a single worker, much less a married couple with a growing family. And as hard as the men worked, women put in even longer days. A wife was expected to rise before daybreak to prepare the family's breakfast and pack lunches for herself and her husband. The women would then walk with the men or take the plantation train to the fields in time to begin work by 6:00 a.m. Some wives were assigned to a women's field gang; others worked alongside their husbands. Women did the same hard labor as the men, often with a child growing in their swollen bellies or an infant strapped to their backs.

Working six days a week, my grandmother was paid substantially less than her husband. Always small in body, she somehow managed the heavy physical labor of weeding the fields, stripping the cane of dry leaves, cutting and harvesting the stalks, and carrying and loading the sugarcane for processing. And no matter how weary she might be after ten hours in the field, at night she would have to cook dinner, clean the cabin, and do laundry with water hauled from a nearby well. Not surprisingly, Tari loathed plantation life with every molecule of her being, and began immediately to save for the day when she could move away from Waipahu with her husband.

My mother, Chieko, was born in the west camp of Waipahu on July 11, 1924, a year after Tari sailed to Oahu. By the time my uncle Akira arrived two years later, Baachan was already thinking about buying a bathhouse and moving the family to a little cottage in town. With this concrete goal in mind, she hoarded every penny she could until she was able to purchase the business she had identified. But if my grandmother was unhappy in Waipahu, my mother and my uncle recalled the family's time there as footloose and carefree. Not yet of school age, they roamed the fields, playing with the children of other migrant families while their parents worked. Even after Tari and Hiroshi opened the bathhouse on Beretania Street in Honolulu four years later, Chieko remembered her early years in Hawaii as easy and unencumbered. Not even the chore of helping her parents clean the bathhouse every day after school had marred her sense of life's spaciousness.

Plum Bathhouse catered to an almost exclusively Asian clientele, as Europeans, or haoles as they were called in Hawaii, were unfamiliar with the concept of communal bathhouses or had disreputable notions of what transpired there. On one occasion, a group of haole men came to the premises looking for prostitutes. Baachan explained that nothing of the sort took place there and politely showed them the door. My grandparents ran a highly efficient and hygienic operation. In addition to separate baths for men and women, there were single rooms with showers, as well as more expensive Western-style bathrooms outfitted with bars of soap and towels. Since most plantation workers had no access to indoor baths, hundreds of them took the train into town every week to immerse themselves in the Plum Bathhouse's waters. My grandparents' business prospered. Tari and Hiroshi also worked second jobs, Tari as a seamstress making kimonos to order for a store in

Waipahu, and Hiroshi in a cobbler's shop where he crafted new shoe soles from old tires.

Tari continued to save diligently, now sending regular installments back to Japan to purchase a plot of farmland there. Despite the welcome turn in their fortunes, she had never stopped longing for the place she called home. Her girlhood in Japan had been infinitely more refined than this life of unceasing toil, and she yearned for the familiarity and comfort of being once more among her own people. During her time in Hawaii, she refused to learn English—she hadn't seen the point, given her determination to leave the islands and live out the rest of her days on the farm she had purchased in Fukushima.

As tensions between the United States and Japan escalated in the lead-up to the Second World War, Tari began to suffer from blinding migraines, and some instinct told her that the time had come to leave Hawaii and go home to Japan. Toward the end of 1939, she sailed for Yokohama with Chieko and Akira, then fifteen and thirteen, leaving Hiroshi behind to wrap up the details of selling the bathhouse they had successfully operated for eleven years. Baachan would later tell me that trusting Jiichan to conclude their business arrangements had been a mistake: A con artist swindled him out of the money he had earned from the sale of the bathhouse, after promising Hiroshi he could triple the sum.

Two years after Tari returned to Japan with their children, Hiroshi caught the last ship back to Yokohama before Japanese fighter pilots dropped their bombs on Hawaii's military base at Pearl Harbor. The surprise attack on December 7, 1941, had pushed America off the sidelines and into the Second World War. On the mainland, people of Japanese descent were forcibly relocated to internment camps as a part of a nationwide roundup. Even in Hawaii, where the mandatory relocation was less common, Japanese Americans who were seen as troublemakers were detained in Honouliuli Camp near

Pearl Harbor. By then, the Satos were back in Japan, a family of poor farmers scratching out a living near the border of Fukushima Prefecture, while at a distance, the world raged.

Hiroshi was forty-five and Tari forty-one when they settled into their new lives in Koori, a farming community on the outskirts of Fukushima, the capital city of Fukushima Prefecture in central Japan. Baachan was thankful to be back home, though the reverberations of war were felt even in their farming village, where solemn schoolchildren could be seen marching in orderly lines to the Buddhist temple during weekly mass-evacuation drills.

Unlike Baachan, my mother had preferred life in Hawaii. For her first fifteen years, it was all she knew. Now, she found the customs of Japan to be overly formal, restrictive, and lonely, her routines so predictable that she felt almost numb. She missed the tropical islands where she had been born as much as Tari had yearned for the winter snows of her homeland. But Chieko was a stoic in the deepest sense of the word, and she never complained—though it seems she remained alert for a way to transform her situation, given what happened next.

She graduated from high school in the spring of 1945, just months before American atomic bombs devastated the cities of Hiroshima and Nagasaki, forcing Japan's surrender. I cannot recall my mother or my grandparents ever discussing these events, which happened far to the south of Fukushima, before I was born. I can only imagine how they must have felt, their grief for the tens of thousands who instantly died complicated by profound relief that at last the war was over.

In the fragile peace that followed, Chieko found work as a bookkeeper in a government accounting office in Fukushima City; she had always been skillful with the abacus. It was while working in that office that she met my father, Matabe Hirono, a young veterinarian who took an avid interest in her. My mother shared no stories about how this young man courted her; she said only that he was charming and attentive and had good prospects as a vet for farm animals. But when he proposed to Chieko, Baachan begged my mother not to marry him. Though she never explained to me her opposition to the match, I suspect that Tari might have sensed an instability, a recklessness in the man. But Chieko, a young woman of twenty-one eager to start her life, disobeyed her mother for the first time, and she and Matabe Hirono were wed.

The couple soon moved to a remote part of the prefecture, which felt to Chieko as if she had traveled back in time. "Japanese families are already pretty traditional," Mom would tell me many years later, "but your father's family was the most tradition bound I had ever known. Women, especially daughters-in-law, were to be used, and you could have nothing to say about it." The farmhouse she now shared with her husband, his mother, and several in-laws was a drafty old structure on the edge of a stream, an isolated outpost all but cut off from modern amenities. Alone in that inhospitable place, my mother very quickly realized that her new husband was doubly addicted to liquor and mah-jongg. And he was uncaring, making no effort to ease his new wife's transition. Instead, he stayed away from the farm on "business trips" for weeks at a time, coming home only to recover and to refill his pockets for more drinking and gambling.

Chieko said nothing when he sold her fine silk kimonos, one after another, to pay off his debts. Instead, she tried to understand what had made her husband so neglectful. She knew that his father had died by suicide when he was a boy, and she supposed that her mother-in-law's pattern of excusing Matabe's worst behavior had developed in the aftermath of his father's death. Whatever the reason, Matabe had grown to become an intellectually bright but callous man, completely selfish in the pursuit of his indulgences. My great-grandfather alone seemed to find his grandson's behavior inexcusable. He would eventually disown Matabe for his profligacy and the careless way he treated his wife and children.

The old man is the sole relative on my father's side whose face I can recall, because my mother kept a photograph. "He was the only person in your father's house who did not treat me like a servant," my mother said on the day she showed me the photograph. In the black-and-white studio image, my great-grandfather is sitting in an armchair, round black-framed glasses on his nose, his head perfectly bald. My mother, beautiful and somber, stands behind, and my older brother and I are on either side of the chair. I am two years old in the picture, and my homemade bloomers droop to my knees.

Aside from this man, Matabe's family treated my mother no better than chattel, expecting her to wait on them day and night, and to feed all the farm animals and clean their stalls before serving herself and her children. Despite Matabe's general neglect of his marital vows, my mother was pregnant every two years, and bore four children. Her first child, who she named Yoshikazu, meaning "fortunate and righteous firstborn son," was born in January 1946. Weeks later, she learned that her mother-in-law had changed his name without consulting her, registering him under Matazaemon, an ancient samurai name that to my mother sounded grandiose and old-fashioned. The shock of hearing her son being called by a name she had not given him, and her distress at learning that it was in fact his legal name, caused her breasts to cease producing milk almost overnight.

After a week of waiting for the milk to return, her mother in-law insisted that Chieko's upper arm be branded with a sizzling iron, to shock her body into making her milk flow once more. I will never forget my mother's glazed look as she told me this story many years later, almost as if she were recalling an event that had happened to someone else. The barbaric remedy failed, but

for the rest of my mother's life, the scar on her upper arm would remind her
of the day that her husband's family had treated her as little better than a farm
animal.

But if Chieko had resigned herself to the state of her marriage and the
abuse of her in-laws, when it came to her children, she would not be cowed.
And so she wrote her mother a letter asking her to send money for train tickets so that she could bring her firstborn to visit his grandparents. Once in
Koori, she arranged a trip to the Legal Affairs Bureau in Fukushima City
and changed her son's name back to Yoshikazu.

Soon after Chieko returned home to her in-laws, my father's work forced
the family to relocate to an isolated village near Tadami. The farm on
which they now lived was set in a valley between two mountains, in a region
blanketed by deep drifts of snow for most of the year. The rocky terrain,
pockmarked by ice and water erosion, prone to dangerous avalanches in winter
and floods and rapids from snowmelt swelling the Tadami River in summer,
only made Chieko's outdoor tasks more arduous, while the area's snowbound
seclusion made evenings alone with her in-laws longer than ever.

I was born in that lonely place on November 3, 1947, and was given the
name Keiko by my mother, meaning "celebrated child." There would be no
mother's milk for me either. In fact, my mother's body would never produce
another drop with which to nourish her babies, leaving her four children
with only cornstarch boiled with water and sugar for baby food. The lack of
proper nutrition would prove disastrous for my younger siblings.

My sister, Yuriko, was born in 1949. Before she was a year old, she contracted pneumonia. When Yuriko fell ill, our father was nowhere to be found.
To get my sister to a doctor, my mother would have had to walk through deep

drifts of snow to the village on another mountain. She had done it before, when Yoshikazu was two and suffering from a severe ear infection, one that would leave him with permanent hearing loss. Her mother-in-law had refused to call a doctor, so to reach one, Chieko trudged through the snow for miles along a narrow mountain road, wearing straw sandals, my brother strapped to her back. She did not want to subject another sick child to that cold, unforgiving trek, and had no money for a doctor besides. After asking a sympathetic friend in the village to lend her money for train tickets, she traveled by steam locomotive for most of a day with little Yuriko, along with Yoshikazu and me, to her parents' house. But it was too late.

I will never forget the sight of my mother and grandmother kneeling over the futon on which my sister lay, her breathing stilled. My mother's shoulders shook as she hugged herself and rocked back and forth, her mouth a cavern, wailing without sound. I was not yet three years old, yet I remember an almost annihilating desire to take away her pain. In all my years since, that feeling has never left me.

On our return to my father's house with Yuriko's ashes in a small box, Matabe immediately took the ritual condolence money, known as koden, which had been offered by family and friends. My mother did manage to hide away some additional funds that her mother had given her, which was fortunate, because within the year we would face another crisis.

I was upstairs at my father's house, on my hands and knees wiping the floor with a rag. I wanted to help my mother with her chores. In my earnest effort, I failed to notice how close I was to the edge of the wooden platform, which was open to the house's main floor. I tumbled backward and landed in a heap next to the steps, blood pouring from a gash next to my right eye. My mother, then pregnant with Shigeki, scooped me up, her terror growing at the same rate as the impressive lump on the side of my head.

She cleaned and wrapped my wound before once again boarding a train to her parents' home with her children in tow. By the time we arrived, the swelling had gone down and the gash had begun to knit itself back together, but there was still a fearsome purple bruise covering the upper right side of my face. Having already lost one child, Chieko was taking no chances. She decided I should stay with Baachan for a little while, so that my grandmother could watch over me. I ended up staying with my grandparents for four years.

In that old farmhouse with its thick timbers and thatched roof, Baachan became my world. I would sit with her for hours applying rice paste to strips of newspaper, making small bags to cover budding green apples to protect them as they ripened on their branches. We hardly talked as we worked, but I was perfectly content, my mind roaming everywhere. I did not pine for my mother or my two brothers, because I always knew they would be coming again to visit us soon.

My days at my grandparents' house were easy and untroubled. A flock of chickens gave us eggs; a goat provided milk; and rice paddies, vegetable gardens, and plots of soybeans offered simple but nourishing food. Breakfast usually consisted of a raw egg mixed into hot rice, still a favorite meal of mine. Best of all, I could pick fruit right off the trees. Along with a small grove of apple trees, there was an apricot tree, fig trees, peach trees, and a large, spreading persimmon tree under whose golden canopy I often daydreamed. I would entertain myself by wandering around the farm and collecting things: ginkgo leaves in poetic shapes, smooth rocks, bits of bark, discarded cellophane candy wrappers with interesting designs. I kept these treasures in a cardboard box next to my futon. I would lay them out in rows on the floor sometimes, studying and admiring them—much as I would later arrange the coins from my piggy bank.

After I started first grade at age six, my circle grew. I loved my Japanese school, where students wrote and illustrated stories of what we had done over the summer, put on plays, and held family sports days. Sometimes in the afternoons, Jiichan would take me fishing for dojo at a nearby stream or help me to make kites out of newspaper. Other times, I would join children from the neighborhood in winding cobwebs onto sticks, which we used to catch cicadas and fireflies. And, during Fukushima's snowy winters, my friends and I would gleefully sled down the slope at the back of my grandparents' farm, packing the ice so hard that Jiichan would have to chip away at it to help it melt in the spring.

Unfortunately, things were not nearly so congenial at my father's house. One afternoon, about two years after Yuriko had died, when Shigeki was still an infant, my father stumbled home from a weeklong drinking and gambling bender. Chieko begged him to give up mah-jongg and liquor for the sake of their children, but Matabe laughed with no hint of mercy and shook his head no. Chieko asked him again the next morning, in the brief moment after he'd slept off the stupor of drink and before he disappeared again. This time, he told her clearly and without equivocation that what she was asking would never happen.

That was when she knew that her husband would never change. "I threatened to leave him then," my mother recalled. "I even told my mother in-law that I wanted a divorce. She replied that I was free to leave her son, but I would not be allowed to take her grandchildren. I never mentioned it again."

I was nine years old when my mother told me this. I marveled at the lack of bitterness in her tone, though her eyes searched the high corners of our rented room on Kewalo Street in Honolulu, as if she were seeing again the hopeless young wife she had been. Chieko felt she had no choice but to endure the lot she had cast for herself in foolish defiance of her mother. Her unhappiness was relieved only by her visits to my grandparents and me. But when Yoshikazu turned six and was ready to enter first grade, an important milestone in the life of a Japanese child, there came a breaking point.

My uncle Akira had given my mother money to buy his nephew's first-grade uniform and a new pair of shoes. Akira, who had returned to Hawaii as a young man and served for three years in the United States military during the Korean War, had some sense of the condition of his sister's marriage from her letters. On a visit to my grandparents' farm in Fukushima a few months earlier, Akira had urged Chieko to bring the children and join him on Oahu. Though grateful for her brother's offer, Mom wasn't yet ready to take the fateful step that would mark the end of her marriage.

Her husband happened to be at home when she got back to Tadami. She was careful not to let him see her tuck the money Akira had given her underneath the futon. She thought she would bide her time until he left again before purchasing Yoshikazu's first-grade uniform and school supplies. She didn't have to wait long; Matabe was gone by the time she opened her eyes the following morning. But when she went to retrieve the money, it was gone.

Matabe arrived home several days later sporting a new spring overcoat. Chieko understood immediately where the money for their son's school uniform had gone. Matabe had stolen it just as he had taken the condolence money after Yuriko's death. Chieko swallowed her anger with such force that she thought she would choke, but she was no longer hopeless. That was the evening she began to plot her escape.

The silver tea canister was the first thing my mother tucked into her brown-striped suitcase the day she left my father. She had already decided to move with my brothers to my grandparents' farm in Koori, reuniting all her children. What we didn't yet know was that Chieko was already formulating a plan to take us with her to Hawaii, and she had no intention of leaving Yuriko behind. Unsure whether U.S. customs officials would allow her to carry my sister's remains into the country, she had poured them from the simple black box in which she had received them into a small plastic bag. She placed the bag at the bottom of a plain, cylindrical tea canister, and then filled the container to the brim with pieces of hard candy, their wrappers a colorful camouflage.

Next, she packed her most treasured kimono, an exquisite, shimmering, royal blue garment with a delicate rose-colored lining and floral designs that her grandmother had made using threads from silkworms she had raised herself. One of only three that my father hadn't sold in the village to pay his gambling debts, the kimono had been a wedding gift from her mother. Now, Chieko resolved that, rather than taking the kimono with her to the new country, she would leave it with Tari for safekeeping—at least until she could get settled in the place where she was going.

Along with these two precious things, my mother packed the rest of her clothes and those of my brothers, then seven and two. She informed her mother in-law that she was taking the boys to visit her parents for a few weeks. Matabe hadn't been home in many days, so she was spared the need to explain her departure to him. She dressed her sons in their traveling clothes and walked with them to the train station, where she purchased three tickets using money Tari had sent her. With my two brothers at her side and my sister's ashes in her hard-sided suitcase, she boarded the hissing steam locomotive to Koori for the last time. She did not tell her sons that they were never coming back to that dark, cold farmhouse, or that she hoped never to set eyes on their father again.

A few days later, as she watched her three children playing with stones and prattling happily among themselves in her parents' yard, her heart seized at the thought that at any moment her husband might arrive and demand that they all return home. She decided that she could wait no longer to execute her plan to take the children far beyond his reach.

Over the next several months, Mom made numerous trips to the U.S. embassy in Tokyo, traveling all night by train each time to secure the proper documents for herself and her children. Sitting before the American consular agent and answering his questions, she tried not to show her anxiety that the plan would be foiled, that the embassy might require her husband's permission for her to take the children out of Japan. But in the end, the consular agent determined that Chieko Hirono née Sato had been born in Waipahu in the American Territory of Hawaii, and she had every right to return home. By the time my father came looking for us, we were no longer in the country.

For ten nights, as the U.S.S. *President Cleveland* sliced through an indigo sea, I climbed into my bunk in steerage, turned my face to the wall, and cried for Baachan.

"How many more days, Kaachan?" I would ask my mother each morning, as Yoshikazu and I sat huddled together on a thin mattress in the chilly bunkroom eating the boiled eggs our mother gave us for breakfast. Chieko stood over us, separating us from the press of other passengers moving in and out of the third-class sleeping area.

With one finger she would trace the salt trail on my cheek and smile sadly. Her eyes were always sad in those days. "Not long now, Keiko-chan," she would say, and I would accept that, never wanting to add to her cares.

Yoshikazu's memory of our sea crossing is quite different. He recalls us playing hide-and-seek and running the length of the boat, laughing with the other children. Yet apart from missing Baachan and being seasick, only two other memories have stayed with me from the *President Cleveland*: my first

American-style shower—there had been no indoor plumbing in my grandparents' house; we took baths in a large wooden farmhouse furo, in water heated by firewood—and my first taste of ice cream, a perfect scoop balanced on a crunchy waffle cone. The flavor was strawberry. I loved its cold, creamy texture and sweetness on my tongue, though I couldn't understand the red dots mixed into the ice cream. They were bits of strawberry, of course, but I thought they were specks of dirt, and I picked out every piece before enjoying my cone.

We arrived in Honolulu on March 11, 1955. Our little family was listed on the ship's manifest as Chieko Sato Hirono, a thirty-one-year-old woman born in Hawaii, and her two Japanese children. My uncle Akira met us at the docks. He had invited us to stay temporarily with him, his wife, and their two children. At the behest of my aunt, I slept in an infant's crib, which I found humiliating. I was relieved when, after a couple of days, my aunt asked us to leave, complaining that their house was too small and we disrupted their lives.

Two spinster cousins of my mother's lived in a boardinghouse on Kewalo Street in town. A room was available, so we moved in there. It was a cramped space, poorly furnished, and yet I was happy to sleep next to my mother and brother across the room's only bed. There was also a table, a chair, and a small bench, and, in one corner, a sink anchored to the wall. This was lucky. It meant that we didn't have to use the communal kitchen area to clean our dishes. After several nights curled up in a crib and days spent tiptoeing around my uncle's wife, this small, windowless room felt like a homecoming. Inside its walls we were free.

My mother soon found a job setting lead type for a Japanese-language newspaper, *The Hawaii Hochi*. The position offered no health benefits, and the pay wasn't nearly enough to cover our needs, but the woman who owned the boardinghouse took pity on us and agreed to accept less rent. Mom's next task was to enroll Yoshikazu and me in school. I had almost completed first grade in Fukushima, but now I would have to learn a new language, so it made sense for me to repeat the grade. Yoshikazu, too, would repeat the year, entering American school as a second grader. We knew not a word of English, so our mother would have my brother and me recite the numbers one through one hundred in English nightly. The ritual was almost like a prayer for her, an assurance that we would be okay.

Some nights, when my brother was outside playing with the boys from our street, I would sit with Mom at the small table in our room and listen as she shared the details of her life with my father. As poorly as she had been treated, Mom never shared these stories as if she were a victim. Those years were merely a part of her history, and therefore mine, and she saw no reason to make them mysterious by refusing to tell the truth of them. I understood from her unemotional delivery that she had no interest in turning me against my father, and yet at some point I made a decision never to seek him out or to lament his absence from our lives. My unshakable allegiance was to my mother, and the fact that she had found it necessary to leave Japan and start over with her children in a new country told me all I needed to know about the man she had married.

Still, I collected the details my mother dropped into our conversations like smooth stones slipping into water with barely a ripple. I never pressed her with questions. I simply accepted the odd reminiscence or memory she might offer up, a faraway expression in her eyes. By the time I was ten, I had gathered enough of her stories to grasp the broad outlines of what had transpired between my parents, including the events that had led to their final unraveling. I also began to fathom that for my mother, returning to the Islands where she had lived happily for the first fifteen years of her life had been all but inevitable. Her memories of running barefoot through sun-showered fields and laughing with the other farm children had been an enduring comfort through the cold dark years of her marriage. In the end, these experiences had beckoned her back to the land that had been her first home.

CHAPTER TWO

On Kewalo Street

The final order of business before we began school was our names. On returning to the Islands, Mom had started calling herself Laura, the name she had given herself as a child in Hawaii. She wanted us to have American-sounding names, too. After poring over a baby-name book, she decided on Roy for my brother and Mazie for me. Our Japanese names, Yoshikazu and Keiko, would now be our middle names. While she was at it, she also chose the name Wayne for our little brother, though we would continue to think of him as Shigeki until he joined us in Hawaii almost three years later.

When I asked Mom later why she had selected those particular names for us, she said simply, "I liked the sound of them."

"Really, Mom?" I pressed. "Of all the names you came up with Mazie?"

I had then pointed out that my birthday, November 3, was the same as that of the Japanese emperor Meiji, whose birth date was a national holiday in Japan. I wondered aloud whether this annual observance had prompted Mom to choose Mazie for me, given that the kanji of my Japanese name meant "celebration," and the sounds *Mazie* and *Meiji* were so similar. Indeed, for the rest of my grandmother's life, whenever she said my English name she would pronounce it "Meiji." But my mother merely shrugged in response to my questions.

"Could be," she said.

Whatever her inspiration, I didn't resist my new American identity. Yet for weeks after I started at Queen Kaahumanu Elementary School, I still thought of myself as Keiko. My teacher must have considered me rude or stupid when she called me Mazie and I took too long to respond. It didn't help that I couldn't always understand what she wanted or that my eyes kept traveling back to the palm trees outside my classroom window. But while Mom was banking on our new American names helping us to fit in more easily with our classmates, this turned out to be a less pressing concern than it would have been had we immigrated to the American mainland. Our school reflected the demographics of the Hawaiian Islands in that most of our fellow students were Asian, and the largest group within the Asian student population was Japanese.

Ironically, Hawaii's vibrant multiethnic culture had its roots in the enormous labor needs of an oppressive plantation system. When the United States initially moved to annex the Islands in 1898, in part to ensure favored access to Hawaii's lucrative sugarcane and pineapple crops, a mere 20 percent of the Islands' original Polynesian population remained. After the arrival of the British in 1778, vast swaths of the Native Hawaiian people had been wiped out by smallpox, measles, tuberculosis, polio, and other diseases brought by the Europeans. By the mid-1800s, white planters began importing contract workers to help maintain the sugar industry's labor-intensive operations.

Almost of all the sugar plantations were under the control of haole plant-ers, wealthy white descendants of missionaries whose corporations, known as the Big Five, would control the political and economic life of the Islands through the first half of the twentieth century. These men were responsible for the steady influx of Asian workers, starting with the Chinese. When Ha-waii became a U.S. territory, however, its sugar barons were forced to seek another source of labor due to the Chinese Exclusion Act of 1882, passed in response to complaints of Chinese workers taking American jobs and dilut-ing the nation's "racial purity." Upon the formal annexation of Hawaii, this law effectively prohibited all future immigration of Chinese laborers.

The planters then turned to Japan, luring workers with the promise of more money than they could make back home. These laborers were primar-ily single men. Rather than marry local women, most opted to bring wives over from Japan. As with my grandmother, matchmakers or family mem-bers paired the couples through an exchange of photographs, and soon ship-loads of picture brides were crossing the Pacific to toil alongside their husbands. The married couples started families, which helped to foster stable communities, within which Japanese cultural traditions could be maintained. But the conditions on the plantations remained challenging. Around the time my grandfather Hiroshi landed on Oahu in November 1912, workers labored in sweltering fields for ten-to-twelve-hour days for a mere six cents an hour, which was less than they had been promised.

By then, Japanese migrants were already becoming organized, protesting the deplorable living conditions through walkouts and worker slowdowns, leading the Big Five corporations to start importing labor from the Philip-pines, Puerto Rico, and Portugal. The haole planters also tried to "whiten" the sugar industry's workforce by recruiting from Siberia, but most of the Siberian workers returned home after the first year, unable to tolerate the heat. Meanwhile, the Big Five owners worked to sow division among the various ethnic groups, stoking animosities to keep migrants from banding together to demand better working conditions.

On the mainland, such efforts by a white ruling class to pit one ethnic group against another had been devastatingly effective. In Hawaii, however, perhaps because nonwhite groups were in the majority, and workers of different ethnicities understood their common cause, these hierarchies were less easily maintained. When Japanese, Chinese, and Filipino workers joined with their Native Hawaiian and Portuguese counterparts to stage the Islands' first interracial labor strike in 1920, wages and living conditions for all migrant workers began to improve. Later, workers would organize themselves into labor unions, which would help to further dissolve racial and cultural hierarchies and promote the uniquely Hawaiian spirit of ohana, the idea that we are all one family.

That first mass uprising of workers had taken place only three years before my grandmother landed in Hawaii as a picture bride. Just one year after her arrival, shortly after my mother was born, the U.S. Congress passed a new Federal Immigration Act restricting all migration from Japan and selected other countries, abruptly cutting off the stream of Japanese contract laborers who for four decades had helped to sustain Hawaii's booming sugarcane industry. Japanese migrant communities were already well established throughout the Islands, however, and now the immigrants began to move into other occupations, building Buddhist temples and Japanese schools, establishing their own newspapers, transplanting their festivals to the Islands, and mixing Japanese traditions with local customs. By 1955, when we sailed for Hawaii, the Japanese were the largest ethnic group in the Islands, making up 37 percent of the population, with all Asian groups combined accounting for more than 50 percent of the Islands' residents in the census of 1960.

My mother may have hoped that her children being sent to an elementary school where most of the students were Japanese would help smooth their way. But race was only one strand of my still-unfolding identity. As I would soon discover, the fact that almost everyone in my class shared my ethnic background would not be enough to inoculate a poor immigrant child, especially one who could not yet speak the language, against the feeling of being different.

At Queen Kaahumanu Elementary, when I wasn't studying the palm trees outside, I often found myself watching a boy on the other side of my first-grade classroom. I felt a kinship with him, even though we had never exchanged a single word.

Robert sat in the last row on the far left, diagonally across from me at the front by the window. He was small and skinny like my younger brother, Shigeki, who we had learned was having a hard time understanding where his mother and siblings had gone. In her last letter, Baachan had written that every day my little brother held a grainy picture of us in his hands and asked when we were coming home. I think I first noticed Robert because I was missing Shigeki. But while my brother's hair was black and glossy and fell in a straight line across his forehead, Robert's was wiry and blond, sticking out around his head at wayward angles. His front teeth were chipped—like Shigeki's—and the white shirt he wore every day was crinkled, though always clean.

Outwardly, Robert and I were as different as any two first graders could be. My hair was as midnight black as my brother's, and my flower-print dress was washed every night and neatly pressed. On my feet I wore rubber slippers, or flip-flops, while Robert's feet were usually bare. But it wasn't only our poorly shod feet in a class where most of the other children wore proper closed-up shoes that told me Robert and I were alike. I also knew this to be true because of the way we both dreaded the lunch hour—Robert because he usually had no money to buy food, and me because the unfamiliar smell of butter on our lunch sandwiches made my head swim.

"Robert, where is your lunch?" our teacher would call from her desk at the front of the classroom. "Why aren't you eating?"

There was no free school lunch in those days. Instead, the students bought twenty-five-cent meals from the cafeteria and carried the food back to the classroom on trays. Every day, as my classmates settled down to eat, I forced myself not to look at Robert, knowing he would be hunched low in his seat, his eyes fixed on his hands as he shrugged his thin shoulders in response to the teacher's question. Even though Mom always gave Roy and me a quarter to buy lunch like most of the other students, I knew it was a sacrifice for her, and that had made me very aware of Robert's predicament. It was obvious to me that he didn't have any money, and I couldn't understand why the teacher insisted on humiliating him with her question.

The other kids, almost all of them from comfortable, middle-class homes, were required to eat everything on their lunch trays, unless a classmate was willing to take an unwanted item. And so every lunch hour, kids would stand at the front of the classroom and offer up whatever they didn't feel like eating. Robert seldom volunteered to eat the unwanted food, but some days, I suppose when he was really hungry, he might raise his hand for an apple or a carton of milk.

I concluded that we were both outsiders in that oppressively privileged setting, where glass shards were sprinkled in the flowerbeds to prevent children from running through them. Of course, only the barefoot or rubber-slippered kids like Robert and me would bleed if we dared to forget about the glass shards. This, in addition to Robert's lunchtime embarrassment, forcefully brought home to me that in a room full of children who looked like me, only one other child *lived* like me.

One day, our teacher announced that there would be a class party; what we were celebrating I had no idea. The teacher went around the classroom, assigning food items for students to bring.

"Leilani, I'd like you to make the macaroni."

"Peter, you should bring fruit salad."

"Akemi, pinwheels."

"Joseph, deviled eggs."

"Sandra, pineapple upside-down cake."

As the teacher went up and down the rows of the class, calling out the names of popular American party foods while looking over her glasses at the list she had made, my panic grew. I could not identify most of the dishes she named, and I prayed that when she got to me, I'd at least be able to recognize what she wanted me to bring.

"Mazie, you should bring bread," the teacher said at last. I expelled a long, slow breath. I was one of four kids in the class who'd been assigned to bring in bread. At least I knew what bread was. But that night, when I told my mother about the class party, she was confused.

"Bread?" she asked. "I don't understand. Does she mean sandwiches? Should we put something in it? Or maybe she means rolls? We don't have any rolls."

"I don't know." I shrugged. "She said bread."

"I think maybe she means sandwiches," my mother said. "But we don't have anything to make them with."

"She said bread," I repeated, sounding like a stuck record.

"Well, okay," Mom said dubiously. "Let's go see, then."

I followed her to the kitchen area at the end of the hall, which was really just a rusty old refrigerator and a four-burner stove that all the boardinghouse residents shared. I watched as Mom rummaged inside the refrigerator and came up with our partial loaf of bread. Still suspecting that my teacher meant for me to bring sandwiches, Mom compromised by carefully trimming the crust from several slices and cutting each slice into four quarters. I felt my shoulders loosen as she wrapped the squares of bread in brown paper and handed the little packet to me.

The next day at lunchtime, as all the other kids laid their offerings on the teacher's table, I placed my quarters of bread between a plate of deviled eggs and a bowl of macaroni salad and went to my desk. I watched as our teacher circled the table, unwrapping food, straightening plates, and making approving noises. And then she came to my plain brown paper with its few pieces of bread, and paused. All at once, I realized my mistake. I saw now that the other kids assigned to bring bread had set down little pyramids of sandwiches: egg salad, tuna and cucumber, ham and butter. How was I to know? We never ate such things back in Japan. My heart was skittering as the teacher turned and looked at the class. "Who brought this?" she asked.

I opened my mouth to speak, but no sound came. I just sat there, staring at my feet and begging the floor to open up and swallow me. And then a voice piped up in the space left by the teacher's question. "Oh, I like plain bread," the voice said brightly. It was Robert, and in that moment I felt saved.

Forty-five years later, as I sat in the U.S. House of Representatives and voted on a bill to increase funding for free public-school lunch programs, Robert's face came back to me. Amid the pervasive privilege at my majority-Japanese school, he was the lone haole boy who had made me feel less alone.

On Kewalo Street, Mom left for work before daylight, while Roy and I still slept. If she had requests of us for the day ahead, she would leave us a note, carefully tucked beneath a bowl on the table. At *The Hawaii Hochi*, she spent hour after hour retrieving pieces of movable type with her fingers and lining them up on a letter shelf with a stick. She also worked the clanging rotary relief-printing presses in a room filled with the nauseating aromas of oil and lead. Once, her left pointer finger got caught in the presses, and without the benefit of any medical intervention, it remains crooked to this day. But despite having no previous experience in printing operations, Mom soon mastered the machines.

It was impossible for Roy and me not to notice how hard our mother was working to secure our family. Three nights a week, as her coworkers washed the ink from their hands and went home, Mom would head to her second shift for a luau party caterer that staffed the Royal Hawaiian Hotel in Waikiki. The servers were also sometimes hired out for private events held by some of Honolulu's wealthiest families. These could last well into the early morning, leaving my sleep-deprived mother only enough time to change out of her server's uniform and brew a quick pot of tea before heading straight back out to her day job. She told me later that she had been so tired at work one day that she fell asleep while setting type, only to be jolted awake by the thud of her head smashing into the letter shelf and the sudden laughter of her co-workers.

On the nights that Mom worked as a server, Roy and I would roam until all hours, ducking through yards in games of hide-and-seek with our friends, or playing touch football on the street in front of the rooming house. I was usually the only girl out that late, and though Roy often tried to ditch me, I refused to let him. I was a skinny barefoot tomboy in a hand-me-down dress, hair flying as I climbed trees and clambered over fences with the best of them.

One evening, a neighbor took our mother aside and told her that her children were running wild at night. Mom's solution was to save her pennies and buy a small, used black-and-white television set. Roy and I made our way home earlier after that. We would boil hot dogs or a pot of rice with vegetables on the stove at the end of the hall and take the food back to our room, where we would stretch out on the whitewashed wooden floor, eating and watching *I Love Lucy* and *Gunsmoke* until our eyes grew heavy with sleep.

In the summers, when school let out, Mom would leave Roy and me a dollar on the table each morning to cover our needs for the day. For lunch, we would stop by the corner grocery and buy a can of Campbell's tomato soup to share. Afterward, we would spend the rest of our coins on tickets to whatever was playing at the movie house on our street. One day, we watched the same Mighty Mouse cartoon five times in a row, two latchkey kids escaping the heat for an afternoon inside the air-conditioned theater.

Mom's absence weighed less heavily during the school year, when our days would be taken up with classes and homework and we only had to find ways to occupy ourselves during the evenings. We both missed Mom more during those hot, sticky, seemingly endless summer days, and wished she didn't have to work so hard. We knew money was tight, yet I don't think either of us really understood just how close to the edge of subsistence we were or how it weighed on our mother. Only very rarely did she let it show.

I remember one school night, when I was complaining about a project my teacher had assigned; it required us to bring a washcloth from home to be fashioned into some sort of zoo animal around a bar of soap. Mom had arrived home from her catering job early that evening, and we were in our room eating bowls of rice topped with pickled vegetables for dinner. A work friend of our mother's had recently given us two additional chairs, allowing us to be seated around the table for dinner like the American families we saw on TV. Mom's work friends had also donated a used dresser and bags of clothing that their own children had outgrown.

Now, at the mention of the washcloth I needed for school, Mom's chopsticks hovered midway to her mouth.

"A washcloth?" she asked me incredulously. "To make *zoo animals*?"

"I know! We don't even use washcloths!" I exclaimed, throwing up my hands.

"But why?" Mom said. Her voice was soft and bewildered, as if she were sincerely trying to make sense of my teacher's request.

I didn't understand the point of the washcloth project either, although my English was still somewhat shaky, so it was possible that the purpose of the assignment had been lost in translation. In any case, we didn't own a wash-cloth, and no store was open at that hour to purchase one. Even if one had been, I understood from my mother's obvious distress that we had not a cent to spare on something as frivolous as a square of cloth to be folded into a zoo animal and then, presumably, discarded.

Roy and I began to complain about all the odd requests our American teachers made of us. Our two voices became louder and louder as we tried to outdo each other with the outrageousness of our examples. Occupied by our innocent rivalry, we almost missed the moment when our mother's face crumpled, but we were startled into full attention when her bowl went sailing across the room, rice spilling everywhere as it slammed against the wall. We stared in astonishment as she began to sob. We had never seen her so dis-traught. Mom was our solid ground, the one who could solve every hitch we might confront. But that night, her ferociously marshaled defenses cracked open for one brief, terrifying instant, and we saw with stark clarity the toll it was taking on her to bear so much responsibility alone.

As all the frustration, disappointment, and trauma of the past few years poured out of her in tears, Roy and I sat quietly, looking down at our half-eaten bowls of rice. I made a promise to myself that evening that I would do whatever I could to lighten the load Mom carried as she struggled to provide for us. I think Roy came to a similar resolution. I believe it's why he began working at such a young age, delivering newspapers and later stocking shelves at a supermarket after school.

Mom rallied that evening, as she always would. She wiped the wetness from her cheeks with the back of one hand and rose from her chair to begin cleaning the rice grains and broken shards of her bowl from the floor. Roy and I rushed to help her, none of us saying a word. When Mom had once again composed herself, she sent me to knock on the door of her spinster cousins down the hall. "They might have a washcloth," she said. "Go and ask."

Her cousins didn't have a washcloth either, but another neighbor did, a torn, threadbare piece of material that would have to do. I stuffed the rag into my pocket and took it with me to school the next day, grateful to have avoided the sure humiliation of being called out by my teacher. After that night, I began to save every cent I received in the cheap baseball-shaped piggy bank that Mom had given me. It felt like a mission now, to help Mom through those lean stretches before payday by shouldering some small part of the load she carried. It would be my way of appreciating the quiet courage it had taken for her to leave my father and bring us to America, where we would live in a cramped room with my sister's ashes in a silver canister, looking toward the day when we would be reunited with Wayne and my grandparents.

CHAPTER THREE

Star Spangled

W*on again!* I pumped one fist in victory but held myself back
from cheering out loud. Scrambling to my feet, I wiped my
dusty palms on my shorts, leaving streaks of red dirt down the
front. I smiled at the four boys I'd just beaten at five-hole marbles and winked
at Wayne, who was already scraping up my winnings from the ground. At
seven, he was the youngest among us, while I was one of the oldest, eleven
years old and already a head taller than those scrawny Japanese American
boys. Almost the best part of our games was the way my little brother beamed
with happiness when I won—which was almost always. He was glad to be
included when my friends and I challenged one another on the dirt paths that
crisscrossed the flower fields and pig farms of Koko Head. About two hours
by bus from downtown Honolulu along the Kalanianaole Highway, this

remote agricultural region a few miles inland from the turquoise waters of Hanauma Bay was now our home.

Our number had grown to six, including my grandparents and Wayne, who had joined us in Hawaii eighteen months before. I can still remember the rushing joy of that Sunday afternoon, October 20, 1957, when their ship docked in Honolulu. They had traveled aboard the *President Cleveland*, the same vessel that had brought Mom, Roy, and me to Honolulu in 1955. So many details of their arrival remain fuzzy to me, vague impressions more than actual memories, but the intensity of emotion remains. As Uncle Akira drove Mom to the docks to meet the boat, Roy and I waited at the boarding-house, alert for the sound of our mother's key in the door. Suddenly everyone was swarming into our little room, until there were more bodies and overlapping voices than the cramped space had ever held. I was literally quivering with excitement to see my family, but like many Japanese, we weren't physically demonstrative, so I contained myself, allowing my expansive smiles and eager chatter to transmit my joy.

Wayne was different. His elation at seeing us burst out of him. All afternoon, again and again, he would leap onto Mom or Roy or me, trusting us to catch him as he wrapped his tiny arms around our necks and held on tight. A gleeful giggle shook his little body, as if he couldn't quite believe he was finally here. Wayne's happiness, and my own as I pressed my cheek to his hair, would be my most vivid memory of that day.

I think now that Mom must already have packed up our belongings before leaving for the docks that morning, because I don't recall my grandparents and Wayne sleeping a single night in the rooming house. Uncle Akira must have transported our few possessions in his car, helping us move into our new living quarters on a flower farm in Koko Head that same day.

The creaky old shack on Aku Street was at the end of a long, dusty ribbon

of unpaved road. Surrounded on all sides by pink and yellow chrysanthe-
mum fields, our new home featured two small bedrooms on one side of the
living area, and a punee, or daybed, set against the wall next to the kitchen.
My grandparents took one of the bedrooms, Mom and I set our things down
in the other, and Roy and Wayne shared the punee near the kitchen.

In one corner of the common area, Baachan set up her hotokesama, a Buddhist shrine contained inside a small wooden cabinet. On the shelf of the altar
she placed bowls of rice, water, and a small cut of greenery, which she refreshed regularly. I would grow accustomed to the sight of my grandmother's
tiny figure kneeling on a cushion in front of her hotokesama, her eyes closed
and lips softly chanting *nam-myoho-renge-kyo* as she moved her prayer beads
back and forth between her palms. I did not remember her being quite so
devout when I'd lived with her in Fukushima. When I asked Mom about it,
she explained that after we had sailed to America, Baachan had joined a Buddhist practice called Soka Gakkai and now she prayed morning and night to
call forth our Buddha natures and keep us safe from harm.

The rest of us sat quietly as she chanted, or took ourselves outside so as
not to disturb her. We did identify as Buddhists, though we did not share in
Baachan's practice. For us, Buddhism was a way of life. As my mother explained it, our Buddha natures were continually being revealed in the way we
went about our days and in how we chose to treat other people. Mom expressed the cornerstone of our faith with her usual succinctness. "Be kind,"
she had told us. For my mother, that covered everything.

As we all settled into our new lives on the flower farm, Wayne became
my constant companion. I was responsible for him after school, when
Mom and our grandparents were at work. On the days we met up with kids

from surrounding farms to play marbles, Wayne would eagerly help to dig the required five holes in the red earth and would rush to scoop up any marbles I won before I could.

Now, as Wayne dumped a handful of marbles into my cupped palms, I saw with satisfaction that there were six bumboolas among them, the large pretty orbs with delicate swirls of color inside their globes. Light glinted off glass as I dropped them one by one into the brown paper bag in which I kept my collection. I folded down the top of the bag securely and squinted at the sky. The sun had begun to lower itself, saturating the rows of colorful blooms that fanned out before us as far as the eye could see. "Gotta run, see you tomorrow," I called to my friends as I took off down the dusty road at a sprint. Wayne, his skinny legs pumping, was on my heels like a tracker.

Our unpainted shack, set in the middle of the flower fields, came into view. The way I remember it, at this hour the scene was vintage Americana, all weathered wood and golden light. The reality was more rough-hewn. The dilapidated structure was poorly lit inside, and cramped for six people— though, of course, it was an improvement over our single room on Kewalo Street, where living with six people would have been impossible. The shack, and the farm on which it stood, was the property of the Okabes, a Japanese couple my grandparents had known back when they all worked together on the sugar plantation on Oahu before the war.

As noncitizens, my grandparents had had to be sponsored before they could immigrate to Hawaii. They had written to their old friends to ask if they would vouch for them, and the Okabes had agreed. Ironically, the Okabes had been too poor to return home to Japan when my grandparents did, but after the war they had become successful growers of chrysanthemums and roses, and had offered us the unoccupied shack in exchange for my grandparents laboring on their flower farm six days each week. Tari was fifty-six and Hiroshi was sixty when they became farmworkers for the Okabes. Though we were all eager to be reunited as a family, I have often wondered what they must have felt at returning to the fieldwork they had left behind so many years before.

My grandmother in particular must have dreaded it. Her joints were arthritic and ached almost constantly. Although she never protested, every evening she would cover her thin, frail-looking body with pain-relief patches that she had brought with her from Japan. Sometimes, members of the Buddhist mission temple she had joined would visit the shack to pray with her. On seeing her wince as she got down on her knees, they would admonish that if she only prayed harder, she would be relieved of her pain. Baachan would meet my eyes fleetingly when they said this, and smile with a finger to her lips. She knew how much it annoyed me when her friends from the temple questioned her devotion, but she chose to remain silent rather than argue.

Like our baachan, Wayne was small in stature. My little brother hadn't grown much in our time apart, which was probably just as well, because he had been placed in a class at Koko Head Elementary School with children who were some years younger than he was. Roy and I now attended the same school as Wayne, the two of us having transferred there from Queen Kaahumanu in the middle of our fifth- and fourth-grade years. I infinitely preferred our new school. It reflected the ethnic makeup of Hawaii itself, with a slight majority of the students being of Japanese descent, plus a good mix of Filipino, Native Hawaiian, Caucasian, and Portuguese kids, and a large number of mixed-race children. And while many of my classmates were from farm families like ours, even the wealthier haole kids didn't care one bit that our clothes were hand-me-downs or that our feet were often bare. Nor did the teachers at Koko Head give a rip whether we ate our lunches or gave them away; they were far more interested in what we put into our heads than into our mouths. But perhaps what I most appreciated about Koko Head was that its teachers treated the children from wealthy families and poor families as equals, and were attentive to the needs of each of us.

I cannot tell you the sense of ease that washed over me at our new school. It was as if I could finally start to breathe. No longer was I the odd new girl who couldn't find her voice and barely understood what the teacher was asking. Instead, I was now scoring in the gifted category on standardized tests, and my teachers took pains to assign me extra work so that I would feel challenged. By fifth grade, I was voted captain of the school's campus patrol, a leadership role that required me to wear a red sash with two official-looking white stripes, and to serve as the student MC at assemblies. I was also tasked with helping to enforce school discipline—though beyond occasionally asking students to put their trash in the bin, there were few issues. The kids at Koko Head could be rambunctious in their play, but they were respectful of authority, and they possessed a kindness that revealed itself in the way they readily folded in three dusty immigrant children who showed up in the middle of the year.

Years later, I would look back on my time in Koko Head as my *Grapes of Wrath* period. In that remote farming area, I was usually as scruffy as the Joads, the tattered migrants in John Steinbeck's Pulitzer Prize–winning classic. But Koko Head was also where I first started to see myself as "one of the bright kids." I might have red dust under my fingernails and dirt caked on the soles of my feet, but I was a diligent worker and an ardent reader, and I excelled in school.

The librarian at Koko Head, Miss Petrie, had a lot to do with my newfound enjoyment of reading. She had awakened my appetite for books simply by demonstrating her own love of them. Miss Petrie looked like every librarian in every story I ever read. Tall and angular, with brown hair primly curled around a thin, pale face, she wore white blouses and straight skirts in neutral colors, her no-nonsense glasses perched halfway down her nose. Conscientious and neat, even austere, her eyes were gentle, and her passion for introducing young minds to the magic of books was boundless.

My favorite part of every week was when our class trooped into the library to sit at Miss Petrie's feet and listen to the stories she read to us. Afterward, we would choose books to check out. In that unassuming school library, whole worlds became accessible to me, and I couldn't get enough of them. My nose was always in a book. I read as I walked to school with Wayne. A book lay open on the table next to me as I prepped or ate meals. And when I washed the dishes at night, I'd prop whatever I was reading on the windowsill above the sink, mechanically soaping and rinsing bowls and cups, never lifting my eyes from the page. Many nights, as I tried to wait up for my mother to get home from work, I'd fall asleep with a book still clasped in my hands. But perhaps my very favorite place to read was perched in a purple-blossomed jacaranda tree that grew near our house. On Sundays, while Mom cooked and did laundry, my brother Wayne at her side, I'd fill my pockets with dried, red-dyed squid and walk out to the road. I'd climb the jacaranda tree and settle myself on a smooth L-shaped branch maybe six feet off the ground, and while munching on snacks I would lose myself in stories.

After a while, I started showing up at school early to help Miss Petrie. I was a club of one, the only student who chose to spend her mornings sorting and reshelving books in the school library. As Miss Petrie's self-appointed assistant, I made myself a little construction-paper badge with my name over a drawing of a book with a worm boring its way through. Taking note of my hunger, Miss Petrie began recommending titles for me to read. I started devouring series after series, from Mary Poppins to Beverly Cleary's Ramona stories to the Doctor Dolittle books. With each new series my vocabulary and ability to express myself in my second language grew richer and more nuanced. At a certain point, I began to think in English more than I did in

Japanese. At home, our family now spoke English to one another, with the exception of Baachan and Jiichan, who addressed us in Japanese, though they understood when we responded in English. For the rest of my life, I would continue to relish the escape offered by literature. Miss Petrie had given me an enduring gift, and for that I will remember her always. During mornings shelving books in the library with her, and afternoons playing five-hole marbles with my friends, I was once again as happy as I had been when I dreamed under the persimmon tree on my grandparents' farm in Koori.

With three generations of Hironos and Satos sharing one household, we all contributed whatever we could to the family pot. Roy had secured two paper routes, one delivering the *Star-Bulletin,* one of Hawaii's largest daily newspapers, and another delivering *The Hawaii Hochi,* the Japanese-language paper for which Mom still worked. Yet even with so many of us working, money remained tight. I tried to help out by cashiering in the school cafeteria in exchange for free lunches, and delivering the Japanese-language newspaper for Roy in the afternoon.

After walking Wayne home from school and instructing him to stay inside until I returned, I would straddle an old bicycle that Roy had found in the trash lot behind a supermarket and brought home for me. He and I had set about bringing it back to life, sanding the rust from the steel tubing of the frame before painting it a brilliant blue with a can of enamel paint we found in the toolshed next to our house. The can was almost empty, but it yielded enough color to render my bicycle shiny and new. We both swelled with pride as we stood back and admired our handiwork. I loved riding that blue bicycle to deliver papers to Japanese immigrant women who worked in the lavish ocean-view homes of Portlock, while Roy rode his own bicycle in another direction to deliver the *Star-Bulletin*. Looking back, I find it so fitting that one of my first real jobs was performing a service for those maids, who were exactly the kind of workers I would one day champion.

Once my paper route was done, I would collect Wayne from the shack and head out to play marbles and other games with our friends from the surrounding farms. Toward sundown, with the rest of my family still at work, it fell to me to prepare dinner. Our meals were simple, usually fried bologna or spam with rice and raw vegetables, which my brothers and I would eat with our grandparents as the shadows inside the shack deepened. Our mother would arrive home hours later, the lonely dirt road she walked from the bus stop lit only by the moon.

Toward the end of that year, Mom saw a notice for a job as a proofreader with *The Honolulu Advertiser*. Even though her instinctive language was Japanese and she had no proofreading experience, she decided to apply, because the position paid better than her typesetting job. In the days leading up to her interview, Mom brought home an old manual typewriter and practiced almost nonstop to increase her typing speed. She thought the *Advertiser* might ask her to do a typing test, a requirement for many jobs in those days, and she wanted to make sure that she passed. I was her partner in this effort, clocking her time with Jiichan's ancient pocket watch as she tapped out each exercise from the instruction booklet a coworker had given her. For some reason, our dedication irritated Roy.

"Why are you even bothering?" he snapped at us one evening. "It's not going to make any difference."

Mom and I just stared at him for a beat and then went back to what we were doing. I think now that our mother's continual striving to improve our lot scared Roy. I imagine his heart clutched at the possibility that she would be disappointed, and he wanted to spare her that. What he didn't understand was that disappointment would never destroy our mother. She had a heart of fire, and would always pick herself up and try something else, seek another way forward. Mom didn't believe in feeling sorry for herself or in bemoaning her circumstances. She intended to take care of us, and in that purpose she never wavered. Always looking out for the next opportunity, she would prepare herself to meet whatever challenges it might hold.

Watching my mother, I unconsciously internalized the value that guided her life: We should not be afraid of that which is hard, because struggle builds character. We should always be striving. Though Mom never actually verbalized this, I remember feeling a gust of recognition when I later ran across this very idea, as expressed by the poet Robert Browning, who wrote: "A man's reach should exceed his grasp / Or what's a heaven for?" It captured exactly how my mother approached her life. Looking back now, I can see that her calm, consistent bravery centered and settled me, and made me unafraid to try, even if I might fail.

Mom got the job at the *Advertiser*. The man who interviewed her had been moved to learn that she was a single mother trying to raise and support three children, and decided to give her a chance. His faith was well placed. Despite not having a complete educational background in English and no experience in proofreading, Mom would go on to become the best and most rigorous of proofreaders at the *Advertiser*. She would spend the next twenty-four years making sure their copy was error-free, retiring from the newspaper in 1986, when she was sixty-two. During her years there, she worked eight hours or more a day, struggling at first with English spellings and stylistic conventions. At night, she studied her craft tirelessly, and kept a notebook in which she would record proofreading marks and difficult or tricky words and idioms. Over time, she created a stylebook for herself, which the other proofreaders marveled at. That was my mother. Whatever she had to master, she would do it, and if it took her more time than the next person to get the work exactly right, well, so be it.

Ironically, when I became a state representative years later and my name was regularly in the local newspapers, it was frequently misspelled as "Hirano." Though Hirono was a common name in Fukushima, Japan, there were only two Hirono families in the entire state of Hawaii. Meanwhile, there were numerous Hiranos in the Islands. As painstaking as she was, it exasperated Mom no end when she would correct the spelling of her own daughter's name only to see it appear in print as "Hirano," apparently changed back by an editor. It was my mother's cross to bear.

The best part of the *Advertiser* position was that Mom no longer had to work a second job in the evenings to cover our needs. There was more money now. By the end of her first year as a proofreader, a shiny Sears, Roebuck white washing machine appeared in our unpainted shack, and a split-level coffee table and a standing floor lamp now graced our living room. Our new appliances and furnishings might not be expensive or fancy, but they signified that things were definitely looking up for our family. Still, the *Advertiser*'s offices were in downtown Honolulu, a two-hour bus ride away from Koko Head, requiring Mom to leave as early as she always had. That much had not changed: she still slipped out of the house in darkness each morning while her children were asleep, and arrived home each night long after the sun had given way to a starry evening sky.

I was about to enter sixth grade at Koko Head Elementary when the Territory of Hawaii became the fiftieth state in the union. On the morning of August 21, 1959, when the official call from President Dwight D. Eisenhower was to be placed to Hawaii's governor William F. Quinn, more than one hundred people pressed into the governor's office inside Honolulu's Iolani Palace.

Everyone wanted to be on hand to witness the historic moment. The president's call came through at 10:15 a.m. and the room fell silent as Quinn picked up the phone. Moments later, he replaced the receiver on its cradle and announced, "Ladies and gentlemen, Hawaii is now a state!" The crowd erupted in cheers.

Significantly, the palace in which the governor made this historic proclamation had once been the royal residence of the Hawaiian monarchy. It was on this site that the last reigning monarch, Queen Liliuokalani, had been overthrown in 1893, in a coup staged in part by the white planter class with assistance from U.S. Marines stationed at Pearl Harbor. Yet even as American soldiers facilitated the coup, members of the U.S. Congress were still arguing against annexation, concerned that Hawaii's nonwhite population, in particular Japanese and Filipino migrants and their offspring, far outnumbered local residents of European descent. For the members of Congress, that calculus began to change in 1898, after the naval base at Pearl Harbor was shown to offer strategic military advantages during the Spanish-American War. That same year, a resolution was passed annexing the Islands, and two years later, Hawaii officially became a U.S. territory.

For the next six decades, the Islands' powerful white elite would petition continually to make Hawaii a state. Not only would bringing Hawaii under the banner of U.S. statehood protect mainland markets and secure lower tariffs for the planters' sugar and pineapple crops, the planters pointed out that it could also ensure that Hawaii's large Asian population would be effectively marginalized, given a U.S. federal immigration law stating that only a "free white person" could be eligible for the rights and privileges of naturalized citizenship. Nonwhite immigrants "of good moral character" who had been living in the country for two years were allowed to legally claim permanent residency, but they were denied the right to vote or have any say in the selection of their government representatives. This "free white" requirement had been in place in 1900, when Hawaii became a territory, and had indeed served to consolidate power in the hands of the Islands' wealthy, white planter elite. Though the provision was struck from the law in 1952, officially bringing an end to the systematic exclusion of Asian and other immigrants of color by allowing domiciled nonwhite persons to become naturalized citizens of the United States, the move toward statehood had had undeniably racist underpinnings.

From time to time, nonwhite residents had challenged the "free white person" requirement of the U.S. naturalization law. One case in 1898, *United States v. Wong Kim Ark*, involved a twenty-five-year-old Chinese man born and residing in San Francisco. The young man had traveled abroad to China to visit relatives, and on his return home he was prohibited from entering the United States on the basis of the Chinese Exclusion Act of 1882, which was still on the books and being actively enforced by customs officials. That legislation, adopted to stem the flow of Chinese migrant workers to the United States, also held that Chinese immigrants and their American-born children were ineligible for naturalization. Wong Kim Ark challenged the government's refusal to recognize his birthright citizenship.

In a landmark decision, the Supreme Court ruled in his favor, citing the Fourteenth Amendment, which states in part: "All persons born or naturalized in the United States, and subject to the jurisdiction thereof, are citizens of the United States and of the State wherein they reside." The court argued that this clause granted Wong Kim Ark all the rights and privileges of citizenship, and such rights could not be infringed upon by any subsequent act of Congress.

The Wong Kim Ark decision established the Fourteenth Amendment as overriding existing naturalization law, thereby nullifying constraints on nonwhites becoming citizens. But its effect was hardly a sweeping mandate. In

Hawaii in the first half of the twentieth century, the decision merely allowed Hawaii's Japanese, Filipino, and Chinese residents to sue in court, not always successfully, for recognition of their citizenship rights.

Of course, I was not aware of the profoundly discriminatory history of U.S. immigration law at the time that Hawaii became the fiftieth state. Nor did I learn until much later that 120,000 Americans of Japanese descent had been interned in camps during the Second World War, and that some of my mother's *Hawaii Hochi* coworkers had been detained at the Honouliuli Camp near Pearl Harbor. Japanese American families seldom talked about that painful chapter. Certainly, I could not have guessed that America's long-repealed "free white" naturalization laws would, some sixty years later, undergird the white nationalist aspirations of the most dangerous U.S. president in our lifetime, Donald Trump.

Even before he was elected, Trump had vowed to end birthright citizenship for children born to undocumented immigrants, either through an executive order or congressional legislation. Constitutional scholars repeatedly explained that such actions would be unenforceable under the law, and that ending birthright citizenship could only be achieved by the ratification of a new amendment to nullify the existing provisions of the Fourteenth Amendment. It was stunning, therefore, when in January 2019, my future self—now a United States senator and a member of the Judiciary Committee—asked Trump's nominee for attorney general, William Barr, whether he believed that birthright citizenship was guaranteed by the Fourteenth Amendment and he replied in his usual mumble, "I have not looked at that issue legally." I found it inconceivable that the former attorney general under President George H. W. Bush could have such a feeble grasp of the Constitution. Even after I pressed him on the question, he would not concede that birthright citizenship was settled law. It was obvious that his response was intended to appease the president.

Fortunately, I would be afforded decades during which to cement my belief in America as a land of great potential and a country enriched by its cultural and ethnic diversity, before having to confront the deeply xenophobic imagination of the nation's forty-fifth chief executive. Without a doubt, Hawaii becoming a state helped to strengthen my fundamental political idealism, which was rooted in love for and pride in my new country.

At the time that President Eisenhower signed the proclamation admitting Hawaii to the union, he also ordered that all American flags—which had previously displayed forty-nine stars in seven rows of seven stars—should henceforth feature fifty stars arranged in nine alternating rows of six and five stars. In the spirit of this decree, the administrators at Koko Head Elementary School decided to hold an assembly on the front lawn, during which a student from my sixth-grade class would pin the fiftieth star on our flag to mark Hawaii becoming a state just weeks before our fall term began.

Mr. Yoshinobu Oshiro would be my teacher that year. He was from a Japanese migrant family himself, his parents having worked on the Ewa sugar plantation at around the same time my grandparents labored in Waipahu. He would become the only teacher with whom I stayed in touch throughout my life. Many years later, when I became a state representative, he shared with a reporter that, in his view, I had always been studious and self-possessed, and he'd hoped that I might become a teacher. Perhaps it was the seriousness he saw in me that made him choose me as the student who would pin the new star on our school flag. He made sure I understood this was an honor. "Tell your mother and your grandparents they are welcome to attend the ceremony," he instructed me. "They will be very proud."

We were standing near the flagpole on the front lawn when he told me this. It was the end of September, and he had called out to me just as Wayne and I were about to set off on our walk home. The flag pinning would take place during assembly the following morning, he added, and with that, he smiled, nodded his head, and walked away. I realized he hadn't said anything about where I would get the star that I was supposed to affix to the flag. And how exactly would I secure it to the navy blue cloth? I decided that I would simply need to be resourceful.

"Shigeki, go and play for a bit," I told my brother, whom I still sometimes called by his Japanese name. As Wayne ran off toward the younger children's play yard, I headed back into the school, striding purposefully through the breezeway to my classroom. It was empty at this hour, the afternoon light slanting through a wall of windows. I opened the supply closet and rummaged until I located a sheet of heavy white construction paper and a pair of scissors. Pulling a pencil and a ruler from my book bag, I sat at one of the long tables and began to outline a star, two opposing, intersecting triangles that resembled the six-pointed Star of David that I had seen in my history book.

Before cutting out my star, I went back out to the front lawn to peer up at the American flag fluttering against the blue sky. I was trying to gauge the size of the star I needed, but it was impossible with the afternoon breeze rippling the flag ceaselessly and the sun's rays falling directly into my eyes. I shrugged and went back to the classroom. I'd just have to do my best. I picked up the scissors and cut out the star I had drawn, carefully erasing any pencil lines that still showed. I placed the star for safekeeping in my history textbook, thinking I'd find something to pin it with at home. I swept my paper cuttings into the trash can and left the room to find Wayne.

Mom and Baachan were indeed proud when I told them the news, but of course there was no question of either of them missing work to attend my assembly. Mom helped me pick out what to wear, a light blue, full-skirted dress with tiny white flowers, a ruched, cross-laced top, and puffed sleeves.

Mom lamented that I didn't have proper shoes to wear, but I was unfazed. At Koko Head, I often went to school barefoot, like many of the kids in my class, and was completely unselfconscious about it. On the morning of the assembly, I simply washed the red dirt from the soles of my feet and stepped into my blue rubber slippers. I was ready.

The entire school gathered on the front lawn to watch as the principal lowered the flag. I stepped forward with my paper star and a safety pin Mom had given me clutched in my hands. Solemnly, I secured the star to the cloth, carefully aligning it with the other stars. Even though Mom and Baachan couldn't be there to witness my moment, I felt its import, and I was grateful to Mr. Oshiro for having recognized me in this way. As I crossed the lawn to rejoin my class, everyone began singing "The Star-Spangled Banner," our new national anthem, and I lifted my voice to join them.

One month later, on October 22, 1959, my brothers and I would stand with our mother in a judge's chambers in Honolulu to be sworn in as naturalized citizens of the United States. Roy, Wayne, and I raised our right hands and recited the Oath of Allegiance in unison, led by the justice of the peace:

I will support and defend the Constitution and laws of the United States of America against all enemies, foreign and domestic . . .

As I spoke the words, I could not have imagined how many more oaths I would swear in similar government chambers in my lifetime. Instead, my mind went back to the flag ceremony, and the excitement with which students of so many different backgrounds had sung about the "the land of the free and the home of the brave." Now, as I finished up the oath, my eyes roamed the grand mahogany-paneled room, and landed on a crisp new American flag hanging from a gleaming brass pole. I smiled at the memory of my own makeshift paper star floating proudly against the sky on its billows of blue cloth. In that moment it came home to me that even though I had been born across the sea, I was *here* now, and America was my country, too.

CHAPTER FOUR

The Flower Farm

I drew my forearm across my brow, wiping away beads of sweat before bending to adjust the water hoses. There were four of them snaking along endless rows of pink, yellow, and red blooms on the flower farm. The year I was twelve, Roy and I spent the entire summer moving these green plastic hoses over acres upon acres of Old Man Okabe's rosebushes. Roy would take the first shift, four hours of positioning the unwieldy hoses at opposite ends of each row, then waiting the interminable minutes as the water crawled along earthen trenches that had been dug under the bushes. Only when the two streams of water met in the middle could we move the hoses to the next rows. It was tedious and lonely work, and Roy always hooted with relief when he saw me walking toward him to take over at lunchtime. Roy had given up his two paper routes the year before, and now worked as a stock boy at a supermarket in Kaimuki, thirty minutes by bus from Koko Head. After waving him off to his afternoon job, I would spend the next four hours under a merciless sun, soaking the loamy earth.

That summer, as I counted and recounted the rows of rosebushes still to be watered that day, I entertained myself by imagining the dresses Mom had promised to make for me. She was a skilled seamstress, having sewn uniforms for Japanese soldiers as a teenager in Fukushima during the war. Some weeks before, Mom had brought home a used but serviceable sewing machine, set it in a corner of our bedroom, and handed me a stack of Japanese fashion magazines. "Pick out some styles you like," she told me. "I'm going to sew you four new dresses for school."

As I worked in the hot sun, I could hardly wait to get back to the shack to pore over the glossy fashion magazines some more. The women in their pages looked otherworldly to me, their hair sleek and glistening, unlike mine, which frizzled in the salty breeze that blew up from Hanauma Bay. Sometimes, Mom would run her ink-stained fingers over my hair, trying to tame the strands. "Ah, Mazie, what will we do with this?" she would murmur. But I didn't ever feel criticized. Her touch was soft and her voice gently amused as she braided my unruly hair.

I peered up at the sun for the hundredth time, trying to gauge how many more hours I had to go. Then I surveyed the fields, making sure I was still alone. A few days earlier, one of the farmworkers had approached me as I worked. Lost in my daydreams, I hadn't heard his footfalls on the sodden earth. Suddenly, a squat, sun-browned man in dirty khakis was looming over me, his head and shoulders blocking out the sky. With the sun behind him, his face was in shadow, and I couldn't read his expression as he pulled a scrap of paper from his pocket, tore a hole in the middle, and stuck one finger back and forth through it.

"Little girl, do you know what this is?" he asked me.

I did not, but a cold shiver went through me, and I knew at once that the man's question was creepy and wrong. He grabbed my hand as if to demonstrate what he meant, but I snatched it from his grasp and backed away. He moved toward me, reaching for my hand a second time. I dropped the hose I was holding and took off, running between the rosebushes. I raced through the flower fields until I found a hiding place several rows away. The blood pounding in my ears, I crouched under the bushes for a long time, my chest rising and falling with exertion mingled with fear. I concentrated on breathing, trying to calm myself down, hoping that when I ventured back out the man would be gone. Somehow it didn't occur to me to blow off the rest of my shift with the roses. I had a job to do, and no matter how careful I might need to be from now on, I would finish it.

Sometime later, when I went back to the row where I'd been working, the man was nowhere in sight. I decided not to tell anyone what had happened, especially not my mother. It would only make her worry about me. But now I knew to pay attention, to attune my eyes and ears to the sight and sound of any person who might approach me in the fields. I would make sure the man who had tried to grab me would never again have the chance to get anywhere near me. I wonder now at the sense of duty I felt about watering Mr. Okabe's roses. It wasn't as if the old man ever paid Roy or me for working in his fields. He didn't pay my grandparents any sort of wage for their labor either. As far as he was concerned, allowing us to live in the old, tumbledown shack was compensation enough, but I couldn't help thinking that as hard as my grandparents worked, and as old as they were, he could have treated them more kindly.

While I mostly enjoyed my life in Koko Head, I chafed at living under the thumb of Old Man Okabe. I saw so plainly the pleasure he took in Baachan and Jiichan's reduced circumstances. He lorded it over them, never missing a chance to remind them that they were in Hawaii only because of his sponsorship. I swallowed the resentment I felt at the smug smile he would offer as my grandparents repeatedly expressed their gratitude.

That Christmas, in what I'm sure Old Man Okabe believed was a further display of his benevolence, he presented me with a cheap pink plastic purse, the kind you could buy for pennies at the dollar store. When I opened the purse, I found a single quarter tucked inside. I thanked the old man politely, knowing that to do anything else would have been to embarrass my mother. Yet I couldn't help resenting how he made us all work in his flower fields for free. I couldn't fathom why he seemed so pleased with himself as he watched me discover the quarter inside the little coin purse. *What a puny reward for a whole summer's work*, I thought, though I knew to keep that opinion to myself. I also knew I would never carry or use that purse; it was nothing to be grateful for. Besides, it wasn't as if I had expected any sort of gift from the old man anyway. Our family only nominally observed the usual holidays. Given the long hours Mom worked, and how poor we were, even our birthdays passed without gifts or fanfare.

Christmas Day, however, was a little different, at least when it came to Wayne. Every Christmas, Roy and I would each receive one modest gift from Mom, but Wayne always got several. Mom wanted him to feel special and to be able to answer proudly when other children asked what he'd received for the holiday. If neighbors or schoolmates seemed to judge us for the number of presents we'd been given, Mom knew Roy and I wouldn't care. But Wayne wasn't nearly as secure. When other children taunted him, he would fold in on himself. He didn't have the heart to fight back.

Roy and I understood why our mother wanted to go above and beyond for the child she'd had to leave behind. None of us had realized the lasting psychological injury that our parting would cause him. Indeed, it would be decades before we connected Wayne's struggles in school, his extreme social reticence with strangers, and his watchful clinginess at home with the fear of abandonment that had taken root in him during our time apart. How could we have known how damaged Wayne would be by our departure? After all, Mom had reasoned, I had been perfectly happy to be left in the care of my grandparents at the same age. But Wayne was a more fragile child. And in retrospect, my being a train ride away from my mother and seeing her several times a year had certainly been far less traumatic than the separation Wayne had endured, with his mother an ocean away and unreachable to him for more than two years.

Soon after Mom started working at the *Advertiser*, she had seen a shiny red tricycle in a store window. More than anything, she wanted to get that tricycle for Wayne as a Christmas gift. Picturing his joy when he saw it, she had pushed open the door of the store and put down a deposit that very afternoon, returning with the balance a week later. The tricycle was too bulky for her to transport from downtown Honolulu to Koko Head by bus, so she asked one of Old Man Okabe's sons if he would drive her to the store to pick up Wayne's gift. He graciously agreed. The week before Christmas, they traveled into the city along with his son, a boy about Wayne's age, to collect the tricycle. Back home at the shack, Mom hid the gift in the toolshed until Christmas morning.

Christmas fell on a Sunday that year, so no one had to work; everyone was home to open presents. Wayne was beside himself when Mom walked into the living room carrying his tricycle. "For me?" he asked her, his eyes as large as moons. Mom nodded and set the trike on the floor. Wayne climbed aboard immediately. Every day after that, my brother rode his tricycle all over the surrounding clay dirt roads. I can still see him, a red bandanna tied around his neck, long black hair streaming behind him, skinny legs pumping. But then one day I noticed he wasn't riding his red tricycle quite as often anymore. His bright joy in zigzagging around the dusty roads seemed to have dimmed. What we didn't know until many years later was that Old Man Okabe's grandson, the nine-year-old who had been in the car when his father drove Mom to pick up the tricycle, had seen Wayne happily careening around one afternoon and decided to burst his bubble.

"You know we gave you that tricycle," the boy told Wayne. "We bought that for you, my father and me."

"No, you're wrong," my brother protested. "Kaachan gave this to me."

"No," the boy insisted. "Your mom didn't buy you that tricycle. My father did. I was there."

Even if Old Man Okabe's grandson had truly believed what he was saying, I have often wondered why he felt the need to taunt Wayne like that, effectively saying to him, You have nothing. You *are* nothing. To my mind, the boy's behavior was rooted in the belief that Wayne and the rest of us were beneath him, as if our material need made us somehow inferior to his family. Certainly it was how his grandfather seemed to feel. Sadly, the old man's patronizing attitude appeared to have infected his grandson, too.

Wayne was crushed, but he carried his hurt in silence. It was not until he was in his twenties that he one day mentioned in passing the red tricycle that the Okabes had bought for him. Mom's face fell.

"No, no," she said. "I bought you that red tricycle. It came from me."

To think that for more than a decade Wayne had harbored the mistaken belief that the Okabes had given him his once-beloved tricycle. Mom would never get over the pain she felt at not being able to comfort him all those years earlier, when a boy who seemed to have everything had made her sensitive youngest child feel like a pitiable charity case. The humiliation he suffered stays with me, too.

never invited anyone to our house on the flower farm. Apart from the gloom inside the shack, the bathroom was nothing more than a rough concrete slab with a water faucet on one wall and a rusty commode in the corner. A door on the slatted outer wall opened onto the flower fields, allowing farmworkers access to the washroom throughout the day. Come evening, they rinsed their tools under the faucet and stored them in one corner until the next morning.

I never entered the bathroom until after the farmworkers had all gone home. Some afternoons, as I waited them out, I'd call back the memory of water pulsing on my head aboard the *President Cleveland*, like a cleansing rain. That shower in steerage was still the only one I'd ever taken. On the flower farm, we washed up in our tarai, the large galvanized steel tub that Baachan had brought over with her from Japan. It was the same tub in which she had bathed her children during their years on the Waipahu sugar plantation. She'd shipped that tarai back to Japan when she returned home before the war and then carried it back to Honolulu with her aboard the *President Cleveland*. Like our family, the tarai had crossed the Pacific three times. That old metal tub held our stories.

Though none of my friends ever came to my house, in the summers when I wasn't watering the roses, I spent hours with them, playing marbles, building makeshift forts from discarded wood, or clambering across a rocky ridge and hiking down to Hanauma Bay, where we would swim and splash in the warm sea. Roaming the landscape like that, barefoot and dusty, face to the wind, I felt completely free—not poor, not looked down on, not lacking in anything at all. I imagined this was what my mother's experience of Hawaii must have been before Baachan moved the family back to Fukushima. I understood better now why Mom's time as a farm wife in rural Japan had felt so suffocating to her, and why, when she dreamed of escape, it was this sparkling archipelago of islands in the middle of the Pacific that had called her home.

My best friends at Koko Head Elementary School were Stephanie Berger and Judy Medeiros. As classmates, our friendship had taken root almost without effort. When I look back on those days, Stephanie and Judy were almost always in the picture. Both girls were biracial, as were so many of the kids in our school. Though interracial marriage was illegal in many states until 1967, when the *Loving v. Virginia* Supreme Court decision declared such laws unconstitutional, the blurring of racial lines within families was very common in Hawaii and entirely unremarkable to my friends and me.

Stephanie was a tall, slender girl with dark hair cropped to chin length, gold-brown eyes, and a light spray of freckles across her face. She lived in one of the large oceanfront houses along the highway with her father, who was Caucasian, and her mother, who was part Hawaiian. Stephanie was the niece of Duke Kahanamoku, the world-famous five-time Olympic medalist in swimming who was credited with popularizing competitive surfing as far away as Australia, and whose likeness had been captured in an imposing bronze statue that welcomed visitors to Waikiki Beach.

I once met Mr. Kahanamoku at a Halloween party at Stephanie's house. I went dressed as a boy, wearing my brother's clothes and a black clip-on bow tie, a curlicue mustache drawn above my lips with a black marker. When Stephanie introduced me to her uncle, I strove not to show how starstruck I was. For years to come, and sometimes to my detriment, that would continue to be my default—to greet all circumstances with outward composure, striving never to show myself to be too shaken by events or too obviously impressed. This had less to do with any learned cultural reserve than with the fact that in unfamiliar settings I felt more in charge of myself when I maintained a polite remove.

My other close friend, Judy, was an earnest, bespectacled girl whose father was of Portuguese descent and whose mother was Chinese. Judy's mom ran a burger-and-soda shop in Kaimuki, and her dad was the caretaker of Hanauma Bay. Her family lived in the caretaker's cottage set at one end of that immaculate crescent of white sand beach, now a protected natural reserve.

Judy's upbringing was humble, much like my own. A year younger than I was, she was small in stature and appeared far younger than her age. In my first year at Koko Head Elementary, she had attached herself to me, and before I knew it she was like an ever-present younger sister, so often at my side that I began to feel almost as responsible for her as I did for Wayne.

In seventh grade, another girl, Sandy Kageyama, who was Japanese, joined Judy and me. By then Stephanie, like most of the rich kids from Portlock, had moved on to private school, and I didn't see her after that. Though I missed her, Judy, Sandy, and I soon became inseparable, hanging out on weekends, reading comics and teen magazines or making cutout clothes for paper dolls while sprawled in Judy's or Sandra's bedroom. On summer days, the three of us could often be found in Mrs. Medeiros's burger shop, sitting on stools at the counter, legs swinging as we licked shave ice flavored with fruit syrup. When the shop got busy at lunchtime, we would move behind the counter to help Judy's mom fry burgers and serve customers. But perhaps our very favorite times together were the nights when we stayed over at Judy's house on the beach at Hanauma Bay. Long after the swimmers and beachcombers had gone home, and the gate at the top of the steep cliff path had been closed for the night, Sandy, Judy, and I would lie on the sand counting stars, the only other light in the pitch-black night glowing from the windows of Judy's house. Some evenings, we fell asleep on the beach, to be woken by the sunrise slowly moving over us come morning.

Those enchanted nights under the stars were in stark contrast to evenings in the unpainted shack, especially when Old Man Okabe was practicing his calligraphy in the shed next to our house. We always knew when the old man was in there working with his brushes, rice paper, and inks, because he demanded absolute silence. "Too much noise!" he would yell if we conversed in normal voices or dared to turn on the television. We'd learned to speak only in whispers and to tiptoe around the shack or sit perfectly still when the old man was nearby.

One night, as Mom came through the door from work, Wayne rushed over to her, chattering about some event from his day. As painfully shy and quiet as my brother was, his excitement in sharing a story was a special occurrence to be savored. Mom stooped to listen to him, her hands on his small shoulders. At that moment, we heard Old Man Okabe muttering and grumbling about the little boy being too loud. It was, for my mother, the last straw, one she had had no idea would be so soon in coming.

She straightened up and stalked across the room to the window.

"Shut up!" she shouted at the old man. "Just shut up!"

My grandparents, brothers, and I froze, staring at my mother in stunned silence. Her hand flew to her mouth, because she had shocked herself, too. But now the deed was done, and there was no question in any of our minds that Old Man Okabe would evict us, whether or not we had anywhere to go.

Mom looked at Roy, who was sitting ramrod straight on the punee, and then at me, standing by the sink where I had been washing dishes.

"Start packing your things," she told us.

Calmly, she turned to her parents, who were seated at the kitchen table, looking up at her slack-jawed.

"We can't live here anymore," she told them in Japanese. Her voice was matter-of-fact. "Tomorrow, we'll find a better place."

Years later, I would realize that my mother had offered us a critical lesson that evening. She had shown her children that sometimes you just have to stand up, say your piece, and refuse to be oppressed.

CHAPTER FIVE

Kaimuki Town

Mom learned from a coworker about a house for rent in Kaimuki, a town halfway along the highway between Koko Head and downtown Honolulu. The very next day, after her shift at the newspaper was done, she stopped off on the way home to meet the owner and see the house. When she disembarked in Kaimuki, she realized the address was only two streets away from where she transferred from one bus to another every morning and evening. She allowed herself to be cautiously excited.

The house itself was an unpretentious two-bedroom cottage at the end of a gravelly lane, along which stood six more identical cottages. Three shallow steps led to the front door, and crimson bougainvillea bloomed under the glass-louvered front windows. The rooms inside were smaller than in our unpainted shack, but the place was spotless and the windows large, and the location would cut almost thirty minutes off her daily commute. Mom gave the house's owner a rent deposit on the spot.

I could hardly believe my eyes when I saw our new home. The cottage was as compact as Mom had said, but instead of weathered wood, the walls were painted a clean, airy white. After the dismal old shack, I thought that light-filled space was the most beautiful thing I had ever seen. Even better, there was a full indoor bathroom with a white porcelain tub and a showerhead. So what if Baachan and Jiichan had been forced to find new jobs as part of the grounds maintenance crew at the Waialae Country Club? You could say it was a step up from working on the flower farm for free. And who cared that my brothers and I would have to travel thirty minutes by bus to get to school? As far as I was concerned, our liberation from Old Man Okabe more than made up for the in-convenience. Mom immediately set about making our little cottage home, hanging gauzy curtains at the windows, planting ferns and hibiscus plants along the side of the house, and even digging a small koi pond in our front yard.

What we didn't know at first was that our new home put us outside of the Koko Head school district, which meant that my brothers and I would have to change schools. I was sorry to leave my school friends from Koko Head behind, but I had always been independent, so I didn't agonize. I wasn't pre-pared, however, for the atmosphere of simmering aggression that sometimes surfaced on the campus of my new school, Jarrett Intermediate.

In the early 1960s, Jarrett was a rough place. Many of its students lived in the economically depressed neighborhoods of Palolo Valley, where crime, drugs, and gangs had made their lives a struggle. The student body was di-verse, a mix of Japanese, Portuguese, Filipino, Native Hawaiian, and haole kids, and many of them had learned to present a tough face to their peers. Though I would come to recognize their attitudes as mostly bluster, once in a while I would be confronted by truly intimidating behavior from some of my fellow students.

One morning, for example, soon after I started at Jarrett in the seventh grade, I arrived to find a circle of kids watching two large boys torment a stray dog. The boys were trying to shove the terrified animal into a garbage can and were laughing loudly at its frantic efforts to escape. I paused for a minute, not quite believing that everyone was just standing around, doing nothing to help. Then, appalled by the boys' cruelty, I pushed through the crowd and marched up to them.

"Stop doing that," I said.

I didn't yell, but my feet were planted, my hands were balled into fists at my sides, and my tone was firm. I recognized the tormentors, two eighth graders whom I had seen around the school harassing younger students, taking their lunch or cuffing smaller kids on the back of the head and pushing them around. I was secretly scared of these hulking boys, but not scared enough to walk away. My instinct to intervene had likely been sharpened by my habit of looking out for Wayne, who was sometimes bullied by kids who sensed that, small and shy as my brother was, he would not fight back. My protectiveness of Wayne had given me a heightened response to mean behavior, and I would not let it go unchallenged now.

One of the boys whirled on me.

"This your dog?" he demanded.

"It's not my dog," I said, pulling myself up to my full five-foot-one-inch height. "But stop doing that."

The boy who had spoken glowered at me, while the other studiedly ignored me. I was surprised and relieved when a moment later they dropped the trembling dog to the ground and walked away. The dog skittered away in the other direction, and the crowd slowly dispersed. As I walked to class on that morning, I wondered where the heck the teachers had been.

Fortunately, the teachers at Jarrett Intermediate were not always missing in action. In fact, one of my teachers had a lasting impact on me when she praised my writing. To this day, I remember her saying that she thought my turns of phrase in an assigned book report were "unexpectedly vivid," and she asked where I had learned to write that way.

"I read a lot," I told her. Enthralled as ever by books, at the time I was making my way through the Nancy Drew mysteries, imagining myself as the girl detective.

My teacher looked a little surprised that a barefoot kid like me found pleasure in reading and could write well, but she had given me an A on my book report and that's what counted. That teacher cannot know the effect our small exchange had on me. For one thing, she helped me to make a connection between being an avid reader and writing proficiently. Many years later when I became a public official, I would ask job applicants if they liked to read as a way of gauging their writing fluency. The conclusion I had reached that day at Jarrett—that an enjoyment of reading generally led to good writing—was usually borne out.

Though I did not realize it myself until long after, that teacher's comment had encouraged me to write more surely and boldly. In time, that boldness would extend to how I expressed myself verbally as well, giving me the confidence to run for eighth-grade class treasurer the following year. It was my very first campaign, and I won.

Some months before our family moved away from the flower farm, Mom had called Roy, Wayne, and me into the living room and sat us down on the punee.

"I'm going to be married," she'd said without preamble.

She sounded as if she were merely observing that the sky looked as if it were going to rain. We'd met the man before; he was someone she used to work with at *The Hawaii Hochi*. He was nikkeijin—of Japanese descent—like us, and his two sons were about the same age as Roy and me. Whether he was divorced or widowed I did not know. Mom shared no further details about him. I forced myself to swallow the questions that flooded my mind: How did this happen? When would the wedding take place? Where would we live? How would my mother and this man feed and clothe *five* children? I was acutely aware of how much of a struggle it was to take care of three.

But these weren't the sorts of intrusive questions that Japanese children put to their elders, and so my brothers and I just sat on the punee with our eyes wide, absorbing the news. To say this was an unwelcome development didn't begin to express my feelings. I wanted to shout "No!" and beg Mom not to marry this stranger. I was sure it would upset our family's hard-won peace. Even with the curmudgeonly Old Man Okabe as our landlord, we had found a kind of serenity in Koko Head, with all of us together again under the same roof. If my mother got married, the dynamic would change, and I wasn't sure whether I'd like the new shape of things. I felt as if the ground were shifting beneath me, in danger of falling away.

The man's courtship of our mother had happened out of our sight, but after her announcement, they introduced the families to each other. We must have shared picnics or beach days with the man's sons, because I can still muster a dim image of those two skinny boys. But I seem to have blocked all memory of the man himself.

What would it be like to have a father like other children? I wondered. The thought only made me fretful, because surely if Mom were married I would no longer be as close to her as I'd always been. I feared, too, that my grandparents might no longer be allowed to live with us. That idea alone made me ache with missing them, as if they were already gone. Whenever I started to ruminate on these unknowns, my throat would grow tight and my stomach would churn, and I'd quickly push the thoughts away.

Now we were living in a small painted cottage, and Mom had still not spoken of a wedding date. One Sunday about a month after we moved to Kaimuki, she again gathered her three children together and had us sit side by side on the daybed. Baachan was out of the house, attending services at her Buddhist temple, and Jiichan was working his gardening shift at the Waialae Country Club—but I'm sure both my grandparents already knew what Mom was about to share.

"I will not be getting married after all," she stated. She then told us that the man to whom she had been engaged had gotten cold feet at the prospect of taking on the care of her children in addition to his own. Mom betrayed no emotion as she said this. My brothers and I sat very still and waited for more. Seeing our expectant faces, Mom made a sweeping gesture with her hands, as if to say "Go, go," shooing us back to whatever we had been doing before she called us in. Our mother would never be accused of being long-winded.

I was ecstatic. My heart flip-flopped with wild joy as I turned back to the book I had been reading, and it took great effort not to let the elation show on my face. I didn't want to be selfish. Even though Mom had not expressed it, I knew she might be upset that the marriage had been called off. If there was disappointment, however, she showed little sign of it in the days and weeks that followed, and she never mentioned the man with the two sons ever again.

Many years later it occurred to me that my mother may have thought of marriage as a way to get us out from under the thumb of Old Man Okabe. When she ultimately freed us herself, perhaps the marriage no longer seemed necessary. Whether my speculation was correct, I will never be sure. My mother would have told me the truth of it had I asked her, but since she volunteered nothing more on the matter, I took that as my cue and never posed the question.

Always seeking to improve our situation, Mom moved our family two more times before I graduated from high school. We lived in different rental houses around Kaimuki, pooling our earnings and efforts to afford homes with incrementally more space. Mom was still employed by the *Advertiser*, my grandparents were still part of the grounds crew at the Waialae Country Club, Roy still worked after school at the supermarket; my responsibilities centered around the home—cooking dinner for everyone, cleaning the house, taking care of Wayne, while also finding time to study. With Mom and my grandparents working such long hours, I was glad to be able to contribute in this way.

The year I started tenth grade at Kaimuki High School, we were living in a three-bedroom house on Sixteenth Avenue, a very central location. Though swarms of termites flew around us as we sat on the small veranda on summer nights, living in a house with a front porch was a step up for our family, and we liked it there. Four doors away from us, a popular high school band called the Dimensions rehearsed on weekends. Though the band's drummer was a boy I would one day grow to love, I never once noticed him back then. Not that I ever would have pictured myself with someone as frivolous as a drummer in a rock band anyway. I was a sober-minded sixteen-year-old who wrote essays about the evils of apartheid in South Africa for my history class and was the page one editor for my school's award-winning biweekly student newspaper, *The Bulldog*. I might have some fun with alliterative headlines—"Sock Hop Set for Saturday"—and I even attended some of the interschool dances where the Dimensions played. I also went to school foot-ball games and joined a girls' social club, but I definitely wasn't a part of the popular crowd. I often joke that one should never peak in high school—I certainly never did. Back then if I thought of dating anyone at all, I imagined that person would be a hardworking, studious type like me. Somehow, it didn't occur to me then that a boy who played drums in a band could also possess such qualities.

Outside of schoolwork and my chores at home, my days were almost completely taken up with putting out the school newspaper. Perhaps in praising my writing my English teacher at Jarrett had helped set me on the path to joining the *Bulldog* staff. And, of course, my mother had worked as a typesetter and then a proofreader, which had made newsroom operations familiar to me. By eleventh grade, I could usually be found in Room F202, the newswriting classroom, where I edited and laid out stories and pasted-up pages between classes, after school, and into the evening when the paper was due to the printer. When I was named editor in chief at the start of my senior year, I considered it a position I had justly earned, especially given that I'd almost lost out on the opportunity when our family moved to a new neighborhood yet again, putting me outside the school district for Kaimuki High.

My brothers and I had already changed schools every two to three years, but this time was different. Transferring to another high school would have meant giving up my chief editorship of *The Bulldog*, and I wasn't going to let that happen without a fight. And so the summer before senior year, I re-searched my options and took it upon myself to call the state's Department of Education to request a district exemption. "I am going to be the editor in chief of my school newspaper," I explained to the person on the other end of the line. "I've worked hard for this for two years, and don't want to miss this chance." I added seriously that if department officials insisted on my changing schools, they would need to arrange for me to be the editor in chief of the newspaper at my new school. I was relieved when the faceless bureaucrats granted me a district exemption later that summer, and I returned to Kaimuki High in the fall, excited to take on my new role. Imagine my chagrin when, during the first week of school, the newswriting adviser took me aside and told me that I would need to share my chief editorship.

She explained that my coeditor in chief would be a boy recommended to her by the school's English department head, who said he was a talented writer. There was a catch, however. This boy would only agree to join our newswriting class if he were named chief editor of *The Bulldog*. I found it infuriating that a student who had never shown any independent interest in working on the paper had the gall to demand that he run the whole thing. Our adviser had explained to him that the paper already had an editor in chief, and he would have to settle for being coeditor. Meanwhile, I'd been toiling in the newswriting trenches for two years and was an active member of the student journalism honor society, Quill and Scroll. I doubted the boy now being foisted on me even knew what that was. But, as the adviser put it to me, bringing in a strong writer like this boy would help us retain our national award. I swallowed my pride, well aware that refusing to share my chief editor position was not an option. I resolved to be gracious to my coeditor, whose name was Allison Lynde.

He came into the newsroom the next afternoon so that I could give him a rundown of the editorial operation. He was coolly distant as I described our procedures, as if he felt himself above it all. And yet I sensed right away that the boy with a girl's name was socially self-conscious. As conceited as he seemed, and as good-looking as he was, he carried himself with a guardedness that made me suspect he was insecure. Six feet tall and slender, he was hapa, a person of mixed Asian and Caucasian heritage—in his case, the son of a Japanese mother who was a social worker and a haole father who, I would learn, had died in a house fire when Allison was very young.

My new coeditor had a reputation as one of the smartest boys in our school. Certainly he was the only student to have read the Honolulu city charter in middle school just for kicks. Yet I quickly discovered that when it came to the newspaper, he routinely shirked the grunt work, leaving me to do the layouts with the page editors and get the paper to the printer by myself. His lack of responsibility annoyed me. I grew to resent what I saw as his condescension in leaving the challenge of putting out the paper to me. Even our newswriting adviser accepted that I did most of the work. In the mornings before school, as I sat in the newsroom trying to finish my homework, she would pepper me with queries about the paper's progress.

"Are the page layouts ready?"

"Did the head counselor's column come in?"

"How soon can I see the lead story?"

Her micromanaging annoyed me. She should have figured out by then that I was diligent and organized and would get everything done in time. But what really bothered me was that while she constantly pestered me, she demanded nothing of Allison, though she was the one who had saddled me with his coeditorship. Frustrated, I went home one night and asked Mom for advice on how to handle her constant harassment.

"Here is what you do," she told me. "The next time your teacher questions you, say nothing. Just ignore her."

I stared at her in disbelief and she smiled sympathetically. She knew full well that a polite, studious kid like me would find it difficult to just ignore a teacher, yet here she was giving me explicit permission to do exactly that. Having seen my mother stand up for herself and her fellow workers during a recent newspaper strike, when she had risked her very livelihood to walk the picket line and support the call for a union, I trusted that she knew what she was talking about. And so I decided to try things her way, to nurture my own quiet fire, uncomfortable as it might make me.

The next morning, as I sat finishing my homework before class, the news-writing adviser came out of her office, which opened into the newsroom. She walked across the room and stood next to me.

"Are all the stories in?" she asked. "How many stories do you have left to paste up?"

I hunched lower over my notebook and kept working, as if I hadn't heard her.

"Mazie, I'm talking to you. Do you have all the stories laid out?"

I still refused to look up. I forced myself to keep working on my history paper. The adviser hovered over me for a few moments more before finally snorting with exasperation. "Honestly, Mazie, talking to you is like pulling teeth!" she said before marching back to her office.

Mom was onto something, because the newswriting adviser never both-ered me again. That didn't mean, however, that she now expected Allison to step up to the plate. She seemed to assume that I would continue to do what was necessary to get the paper out. But she was wrong. One night, as I la-bored alone in the newsroom, once again pasting up pages without his help, I'd had enough. The adviser had already left for the evening, and her office door was open. I picked up the phone on her desk and called Allison at his home.

"Why aren't you here?" I demanded. "You know we're on deadline."

"I have a lot of homework," Allison protested.

"Homework, my eyeballs," I blurted. "You think I don't have homework, too? You get yourself over here right now."

I had known from the start that my coeditor wasn't interested in doing the work, and for a long time it had seemed easier for me to persevere and do everything myself. But that time was now over. There is a Japanese word, "gaman," which means "to put up with it" or "to endure the seemingly unbearable with patience and dignity." This was very much a character trait that ran in my family—but only to a point. Allison did return to the newsroom that evening, and from then on I insisted that if he was going to carry the title of coeditor, he had to do his job. I was my mother's child after all.

Part Two

REVELATIONS

Who knows what women's intelligence will
contribute when it can be nourished without
denying love?

—*Betty Friedan,*
THE FEMININE MYSTIQUE

CHAPTER SIX

Tinderbox

I n the summer of 1966 I graduated from Kaimuki High with honors, keenly aware that when I started at the University of Hawaii at Manoa in the fall, I would be the first in my immediate family to attend a four-year college. Roy had earned a two-year degree from the Electronics Institute of Hawaii after high school, graduating in 1965, all while continuing to work part-time as a manager at the supermarket where he had once been a stock boy. There had been no question of either of us attending mainland schools; there was no money for such grand dreams. Even my modest local tuition would need to be funded through the federal work-study program, requiring students to find part-time jobs, in my case assisting a botany professor with his research on trumpet plants at the university's Lyon Arboretum.

As I was mulling over what major to pursue, it occurred to me that my mother, in executing a clandestine plan to flee my abusive father and bring her children to America, had completely transformed our futures. For her, seeing Roy and me prepare through study for a more secure livelihood than she had ever known must have felt like a fulfillment of the promise all immigrant families make—to give their children a better life.

Though I didn't know it when I began my freshman year of college, my expected future would be altered once again just two years later, in 1968, which would turn out to be the deadliest year for American troops in the Vietnam War. A moment of great turbulence in our nation's history, that year would also bring the assassinations of Dr. Martin Luther King Jr., sparking riots in cities across the country, and two months later, Democratic presidential candidate Robert F. Kennedy, who had campaigned on a civil rights platform. Before their deaths, both leaders had denounced the Vietnam War. Now, the violent ends of these two charismatic and widely beloved men poured gasoline on the flames of the civil rights and antiwar movements.

As protests ramped up, college students everywhere took up the cry. At the University of Hawaii, young activists from the mainland joined with local students to form a chapter of Students for a Democratic Society, or SDS, which was at the forefront of demonstrations against the continuing military action in Vietnam. As I entered my sophomore year at UH Manoa, I did not support their views, as my education up to that point had not encouraged me to question deeply the decisions of our country's leaders. I kept myself occupied with classes, my research assistant job, and my volunteer hours as a reading tutor for middle-school students at the campus YWCA. When I wasn't in class, working, or tutoring, I took myself straight home to study. I still lived with my mother, my grandparents, and my brothers in a house Mom had purchased for $37,000 the year before I started college. The house, the largest we had ever lived in, was part of a planned residential community developed in the early 1960s by American industrialist Henry J. Kaiser. Built on top of the razed pig and flower farms, dredged waterways, and landfilled wetlands of Koko Head, the area had since been renamed Hawaii Kai. For my family, moving to that newly constructed, three-bedroom tract house marked our definitive entry into the American middle class.

A few days into the spring semester of my sophomore year, I was surprised to see Allison Lynde walking across campus. I knew he had won a full scholarship to Colgate, a prestigious private institution in Upstate New York, because I had interviewed him for an article about the few students from my high school who had earned places at mainland universities. It was far more typical for students from Kaimuki High to enroll at UH Manoa.

"You?" I said quizzically as I fell into step beside Allison. "What are you doing here?"

"I transferred," he told me. "I go here now. Colgate wasn't for me."

Despite the many hours I had spent putting out the school paper with Allison, I hadn't gotten to know him very well, and after all the hoopla surrounding his departure to Colgate, I was mystified as to why he had returned. He shared that he'd felt out of place on that sprawling, bucolic campus two hundred miles north of New York City, and that the winter snows had been relentless. After freshman year, he had elected to come home.

I knew he had always been a solitary sort, and as we walked together, catching up on our year apart, I sensed his loneliness. Before parting ways, he asked if we could meet up at the library the next day.

Sitting across the table from Allison the following afternoon, and on countless afternoons after that, it dawned on me that we were slowly becoming a couple, unlikely a pair as we were. Though we did not formally acknowledge it to each other, Allison now frequently introduced me to other people as his girlfriend. That spring, we spent most of our free time in each other's company. We were both studious outsiders, so our rhythms were well synchronized.

What most people didn't know about Allison was that, for all the con-

fidence he projected, a core of self-doubt haunted him. It was rooted perhaps
in an emotional wound he had sustained as a young boy, when his alcoholic
father had gone to bed with a lit cigarette and failed to awaken from his
drunken stupor to save himself from the fire it started. As a fatherless child
myself, I felt a strange, almost karmic desire to protect Allison, to allay his
insecurities, to hold up to him a vision of himself that he could tolerate. It
helped that I respected his intellect; we often engaged in animated discussions about politics, books, and issues in the news, and were both voracious
readers. And, of course, one could not help noticing that Allison was also
very attractive. Even so, he held himself aloof from almost everyone but me.
If he was attracted to other women on campus, the ones who were taller,
thinner, more stylish than me, he never acted on it. I often wondered what
Allison saw in me, a short, understated Japanese girl in simple capris and
button-front blouses, rubber slippers on my feet. I eventually decided that it
was my measured steadiness that appealed to him: I was practiced in pulling
myself back from expressing my own extremes of emotion, which perhaps
allowed him room to give free rein to his every mood. Looking back, I suspect, too, that after his time on the mainland, it was comforting to be with
someone who had known him before.

During our college years together, I began to notice that Allison also felt
very competitive with me. In our senior year, for example, he questioned
how it was that I had been chosen for the high academic honor of joining the
Phi Beta Kappa society when he had not. Sorely disappointed, he could not
bring himself to congratulate me. He was later chosen to join the Phi Kappa
Phi honor society, but he saw it as a less prestigious accolade and never mentioned it. Ridiculous as it sounds, I had also bought into the idea that Allison
was smarter than me, and I found myself wondering along with him why the
Phi Beta Kappa society had not selected him, too. It wasn't until much later
that I grasped how badly Allison needed me to believe in his superior

intellect. Belatedly, I realized that his reluctance to affirm me was an unconscious effort to bolster his own self-esteem, as if he could elevate himself by subtly putting me down. Sad to say, even when I recognized this pattern, I often failed to call him on it.

To be fair, Allison was generous toward me in other ways. He had moved out of his mother's house and now lived in a tiny, run-down one-bedroom apartment near campus. I spent most of my weekends there, the two of us studying together, going to dinner, the movies, and sometimes to the beach. By this time, Roy had been transferred to Vietnam as a civilian contractor for the electrical company that employed him. About a year before being stationed abroad, he had bought a used 1957 Chevy. This coveted American model was the first car our family ever owned, and Roy had spent many weekends restoring its wide chrome-front grille, swooping stainless-steel side moldings, and silver tail fins to their original glory. He had finished the car off with a gleaming Pacific blue paint job that reminded me of the bicycle he once found discarded in the trash, which we had refurbished together.

Now, with Roy stationed overseas, someone had to make sure his car was kept in good driving order. Since I was the only other person in our family with a driver's license, that responsibility fell to me. Oh, I was a sight, pulling into the campus parking lot before my morning classes, my head barely visible above the dashboard, my foot barely reaching the pedals. In truth, I didn't particularly enjoy driving my brother's boat of a car. The Chevy was bigger than I could confidently maneuver through the heavy traffic around the university, and without Roy being there to constantly service the car, its engine would sometimes conk out without warning.

Allison quickly realized my difficulty and offered to drive me wherever I needed to go. Soon, he was picking me up in the mornings and driving me home on the nights when I didn't stay over at his apartment. He even tried to teach me to handle the white Volkswagen Bug his mother had given him, in case I ever needed to use the car when he was busy, but I never got the hang of the stick shift. To this day, I can hear the gears grinding as I tried to operate the vehicle. Whatever my talents might be, Allison observed dryly, driving certainly wasn't one of them.

On a Monday toward the end of our sophomore year, Allison and I were strolling across campus, the two of us discussing what majors we intended to declare. He thought he might become an English major, though he was also drawn to theater, while I had ultimately decided on psychology. At the time, the human potential movement was sweeping the country in ubiquitous EST and PSI weekend seminars, promoting the idea that by developing our inner resources, we could tap into unparalleled joy in all our undertakings, even as we unleashed our potential to foster social change. Unlike many of my peers, I did not endeavor to "find" myself through these consciousness-raising seminars, though I was not unmoved by the idea that we might elevate our own engagement with what it meant to be human through working to uplift others.

I shared with Allison that I was hoping to enter a helping profession like social work or counseling. As obvious as it seems now, I had not yet fully connected this ambition to my own childhood, or to the deep longing I had always felt to make life less painful for my younger brother. Though I did not realize it at the time, surely Wayne's unending difficulties in school were at the root of my decision to spend one afternoon each week as a volunteer tutor for economically disadvantaged children.

From kindergarten on, Wayne had floundered in school. In all likelihood, had he lived in another era, my brother would have been diagnosed as a special-needs child and might have received proper accommodations. Instead, he was shunted from class to class, scolded by his teachers, teased by peers, and eventually simply ignored. I was hurt by the way Wayne's teachers dismissed him, not a single one of them ever helping him to achieve even the smallest measure of academic success. Finally, during my freshman year in college, Wayne had been expelled after he was found smoking on school grounds. He was only sixteen. Mom had appealed to the principal, to no avail. "I'm really glad I didn't raise a kid like that," she told my mother during their meeting. Imagine an educator saying such a thing to a parent! When Mom later recounted the principal's words to me, I was just as furious as she was. "She has no idea what Wayne and our family have gone through," Mom said bitterly. We both knew the principal had made not the slightest effort to understand my brother, perhaps, I thought now, because Wayne and children like him forced her to confront her failure as an educator. Her unforgivable response had been to abandon him, making it plain to my mother that she was glad to be rid of Wayne.

My brother eventually found work in an auto mechanic shop. When business was slow, he would pack his fishing rod and tackle and climb down to his favorite spot in a craggy area along the coastline called the Lanai Lookout, near where we lived. Wayne would fish there for hours on end, lulled by the hypnotic murmur of the ocean. He loved nothing more than to have Mom cook his catch for dinner the next day. He knew how hard our mother had always worked to support us, and the fish he caught became his proud contribution to the family pot.

As Allison and I walked across campus, reflecting on our ambitions, we noticed hundreds of students gathered in front of the university's main administrative building, Bachman Hall. As we moved closer, we could read the homemade placards they held aloft:

GIVE US PEACE IN VIETNAM!

I DON'T GIVE A DAMN ABOUT UNCLE SAM!

WE WON'T FIGHT YOUR RICH MAN'S WAR!

The protesters milling about in the courtyard in front of Bachman Hall represented a diverse cross section of students from the Islands—Chinese, Japanese, Korean, Caucasian, Filipino, and a few Native Hawaiians and African Americans—but the young man holding the microphone was from the mainland. Allison recognized him as a transplanted New Yorker who was one of the haole leaders of SDS on campus.

"We demand President Tom Hamilton reconsider tenure for Dr. Lee!" he was shouting. A cheer went up from the demonstrators, who waved their fists and posters in solidarity. The professor the young man had mentioned, Dr. Oliver Lee, was a popular member of the political science department and a vocal opponent of the war. After he had been promised tenure, the university's Board of Regents had revoked the offer, presumably due to his outspoken views. Students had rallied to his defense. Now the crowd began chanting:

"Justice for Oliver Lee!"

"Bring our troops home!"

"Make love, not war!"

Allison and I were used to encountering these protests, though neither of us had ever taken part. In fact, at the time we were both *in favor* of the war, each of us having bought into the idea that if communism was allowed to take root in North and South Vietnam, it would have a domino effect across Southeast Asia, with Cambodia and Laos following in its wake. In high school, I had been a member of the Pacific and Asian Affairs Council, or PAAC, a national organization founded in 1954 to help students develop a global consciousness. In the mid-1960s, PAAC was still fairly conservative in its philosophy, which had likely undergirded my pro-war views. Indeed, I was so convinced back then about the rightness of the war that I had learned all the words to "The Ballad of the Green Berets"—Fighting soldiers from the sky / Fearless men who jump and die—which played regularly on local radio.

My teachers had certainly never taught us to examine much less challenge actions undertaken by our government, or to question the opinions of adults in our lives. Given that I was also Japanese, born into a culture that encouraged conformity and deference to authority figures, being the politically passive young woman I was at the start of 1968 was perhaps to be expected. Yet I remember being intrigued in high school that a teacher at a nearby school had actively encouraged her PAAC students to think critically about the war; many of those students had marched in antiwar protests even before they got to college. At the time, I had judged that teacher guilty of unduly influencing her students' views, failing to realize the extent to which our teachers, through their omission, had also helped to shape ours.

Now, as we paused to watch the demonstrators in front of Bachman Hall, Allison made a clucking noise of disapproval.

"Just look at them," he scoffed. "What do they think they're doing? They should all be arrested."

I looked up at him, dumbfounded. Though I supported the war, it did not occur to me to object to my fellow students' right to express a different view.

"They're doing what they think is right," I responded, my voice sharper than I had intended. "They're just acting on what they believe."

"If you really think that, why don't you go join them," Allison snapped.

Now I was irritated. "I can have sympathy for what they're doing without having to adopt their beliefs," I retorted. With that, we continued on to our respective morning classes, neither of us saying anything more.

The Bachman Hall protests would be all over the local news by the end of that week. Soon after Allison and I walked away, the demonstrators had marched into the administrative building, occupying the second-floor landing outside the president's office. On the lawn outside, more antiwar demonstrators gathered, as did a small cadre of students who had come out to support the administration's position on tenure for Dr. Lee. As the afternoon wore on, a delegation of student leaders met with university president, Tom

Hamilton. Emotions were running high as it became clear that a resolution would not easily be reached. A contingent of students hunkered down for the evening, refusing to decamp from the second-floor landing. Police swarmed the building the next afternoon, arresting all the protesters who remained inside. The arrests further inflamed the mood on campus, and for the rest of that week, up to one thousand students occupied the courtyard outside Bachman Hall, giving speeches, raising chants, and singing "We Shall Overcome" and other protest songs.

In the end, the student demonstrators would achieve at least a partial victory. The university's president stepped down in the wake of the protests, and although the school's Board of Regents initially refused to reverse its position on Dr. Lee, a court overruled the decision, and he was ultimately granted tenure. Administrators also embraced a national campaign to offer more support to underrepresented and historically marginalized groups. This led to the university launching a number of social initiatives to benefit Native Hawaiians, and the eventual creation of an Ethnic Studies program.

The sit-in had ended with mass arrests, but even this would turn out to be a win, because the police action only served to radicalize ever-increasing numbers of students. And, though I didn't yet realize it that spring, my own political awakening was at hand.

CHAPTER SEVEN

Waimanalo

few weeks after the Bachman Hall protests, the YWCA posted a
notice inviting students to apply to live in Waimanalo and help develop a summer program for indigenous at-risk youth. I marched
straight into the main office and filled out the application. The position
seemed perfect for me. During my time tutoring at the Y, I had participated
in a number of sensitivity-training sessions intended to increase awareness of
race and gender stereotypes. As a psychology major, I found that these sessions complemented and deepened my classroom learning. Now, eager to
have a real-world experience that would allow me to help young people, I
hoped to be among the students chosen to spend the summer in Waimanalo,
an economically disadvantaged community on the windward side of Oahu.
In the 1920s, the area had been designated as Hawaiian Home Lands, tracts

of property set aside for those who were at least 50 percent Native Hawaiian. Though much of Waimanalo consisted of these homestead lands, the area was bordered by Waimanalo Beach, along which haole residents had built stately oceanfront homes.

A couple of weeks later, as I sat helping a middle-school girl with homework in the common room, the director of the Y tapped me on the shoulder. "Mazie, come and see me in my office before you leave," she said before walking away. An hour later, I learned that I had been selected for the Waimanalo program. The director also told me that the Y had rented one of the beachfront houses as our residence for the summer. I was thrilled, but my elation was quickly tempered by the director's next words.

"I should tell you, Mazie, we're a little worried about you," she said, as I stood in her small airless office, my hands clasped in front of me. My smile died, my brow furrowed, and I looked at her, perplexed. "All the other students are antiwar activists," she went on. "Most of them were arrested at the Bachman Hall sit-in. We know you aren't involved in all that, but the selection committee felt we had to include you because you do so much volunteering with our kids. But frankly, we aren't sure how you'll fit in with the other counselors."

I wanted to laugh. *So I've never been arrested*, I thought. *Why is that a big deal?* The director clearly perceived me to be a mild-mannered, self-contained Japanese American girl. She had no idea that, having changed schools numerous times, I was used to holding my own in new and unfamiliar settings, among people who might seem to be very different from me. "I'll be fine," I assured her. "Don't worry about me."

Two weeks later, my clothes and a few favorite books sliding around in the brown hard-sided suitcase my mother had brought from Fukushima thirteen years before—it was still the only suitcase we owned—I moved into a large, two-story house with the other nine students. The executive director of the summer program, John Von Gnechten, was already in residence. He and his wife and their two elementary-school-aged children occupied the bedrooms on the ground floor, while the students settled into two dormitory-style rooms on the upper floor. We were five women and five men; most had come to Hawaii from the mainland; and all were white but for a part Native Hawaiian girl and three Japanese American students, including me.

The upstairs rooms had been outfitted with bunk beds, and from my perch on one of the top bunks, I could see crystalline blue waters lapping against a wooded shore. In that moment, I imagined that the summer ahead would be as sustaining as that view, a flawless convergence of purpose and need. My naivete didn't last. At the end of the very first day, the ten of us went swimming. Afterward, I hung my bathing suit to dry on a clothesline at the side of the house. The next morning, my swimsuit was gone.

"The thieves of Sherwood Forest strike again," John said, shaking his head. He didn't seem at all perturbed or surprised. Seeing my frown, he explained that some people referred to the wooded area that ran along the beach as Sherwood Forest because local youth stole from the rich under cover of night. John noted that some of the teens responsible could well be in our summer program. As we got to know these kids over the next few days, the word went out that the college students who had just arrived in town were only trying to help. Soon after that, my swimsuit reappeared, slung over the same line from which it had be taken.

The theft of my bathing suit was my first intimation of the scarcity that marked the lives of the people of Waimanalo. In time, we would get to know some of the area's gang leaders, who began coming to the youth center to see what we were up to. One of them, who I will call Samuel, was a baby-faced nineteen-year-old with an affable demeanor; he was said to be far more vicious than he seemed, a fact that was borne out when he was arrested for a violent crime later that year. Samuel's family was apparently locked in a power struggle for control of the area with members of a rival gang, whose leader had recently been convicted of shooting someone at a party after the victim complained that he was making too much noise. Since the rival gang leader was now in jail, we never met him. However, Samuel and his younger brother, call him Jimmy, started showing up at the teen center almost every day. They were unfailingly friendly and cheerful with the staff, and apart from occasionally smoking pot on the front steps of the porch, they left their alleged criminal activities outside our door.

The recreation center was located in the middle of town, inside a green-painted wooden building that the Y had rented. We shared the space with VISTA, which stood for Volunteers in Service to America, a domestic program modeled on the Peace Corps. I would forge a lifelong friendship with one of the VISTA volunteers, Kate Stanley. In her midtwenties, she had traveled from her home in Upstate New York to do antipoverty work in Waimanalo for a year. She helped us understand the lay of the land, informing us as to what issues certain kids in our program might be grappling with. By the time we met, Kate had fallen in love with the vibrant diversity of the Islands. She would ultimately decide to stay on in Hawaii after her VISTA year was done, and I would one day, many years in the future, introduce her to her current husband.

My other close friend that summer was Steve Carter, a skinny haole guy with a curly tangle of red hair and the scraggly beginnings of a beard. Steve had grown up in Shreveport, Louisiana, and ended up in Hawaii after joining the navy straight out of high school and being stationed at Pearl Harbor. His two years as a sailor had converted him into a staunch opponent of the war in Vietnam, though he had never been deployed there. After his discharge, he had enrolled at the UH Manoa campus on the GI Bill. He'd been arrested that spring for lying down on a road to stop a National Guard transport of soldiers being shipped to the front lines.

I admired the way both Steve and Kate were able to build trust with the teens in our respective programs. With wry humor, they drew the kids out and got them talking about the most desperate circumstances of their lives— relatives who had beaten them, parents in jail or on drugs, friends in gangs who were bent on recruiting them. The stories tumbled out as the teens slammed Ping-Pong balls back and forth across the scuffed green table at one end of the recreation space, or played a board game at the rickety card table, or sat with Steve or Kate on the battered couches next to the kitchen.

At the youth center, three walls of wooden shutters were propped open with sticks to let in light and fresh air. Along the fourth wall was a galley kitchen with a sink, a cooktop, and an old refrigerator that we kept stocked with soda, bread, peanut butter, and fresh fruit. A low shelf next to the couches held board games, books, craft supplies, and brochures for soccer or basketball clubs, water sports, medical care, community colleges, and academic tutoring. Our main objective was to keep the kids occupied and off the streets—safe from the petty lawbreaking and casual drug use that might otherwise claim them. In one sense, we were fighting an uphill battle, as many of the kids and some of the counselors, too, could often be found out on the front steps smoking joints with Samuel and Jimmy. It was the sixties, after all, and weed was everywhere. All the cool kids smoked it—or ate brownies laced with it.

A cool kid I definitely was not. To this day I have never once inhaled, injected, or swallowed an illegal substance. Because of the devastating effect of my father's drinking and compulsive gambling on my mother and my family, I'd decided at a young age never to risk developing that kind of dependence. In the freewheeling sixties, however, my resolve wasn't always appreciated. One night in Waimanalo, a girl in our group passed around a tray of brownies after dinner, neglecting to mention that they had been made with hash. It was only when another student joked that he was already high after just one bite that I realized what they were. Incensed that the girl who'd made them hadn't bothered to disclose that they had been spiked, I jumped up from the dining table and bolted from the room. I don't know what would have come out of my mouth had I stayed.

Steve followed me out of the house and down to the beach, where I had gone to vent my anger. We all knew that the girl who had made the brownies had brought a virtual pharmacopoeia of illegal substances with her that summer. Until that night, she had kept them out of my sight, though I was well aware that some of the members of our group did not refrain from sharing her stash. I realized now that I was upset with them, too. They had sometimes teased me for being so straitlaced, as though they thought I was silly for objecting to a little harmless fun, rather than respecting that I had my own reasons for my abstention.

"I'm leaving," I blurted to Steve as he approached me. I was standing with my back against one of the tall, slender ironwood trees, my eyes fixed on the waves as they caught the pink iridescence of the sunset. "What is she *thinking* bringing drugs here?" I huffed. "How are we supposed to set an example for the kids?"

Oh, I was rigid and righteous, but Steve decided to befriend me anyway. "Mazie, you can't quit," he said. "Think about the kids. They need us. They especially need people like you, who take what we're doing here seriously."

I didn't respond. I just kept staring out to sea.

"Look," Steve continued, "we'll talk to John and he'll make sure this kind of thing never happens again. And that will be the end of it. But you have to stick out the summer. You can't quit on those kids."

I knew he was right. My breathing was already growing calmer, and I was thankful he'd come to the beach to talk me down. I shrugged and plopped myself down on the powdery sand, and Steve sat down beside me. In silence, we watched as vivid pink streaks along the horizon dipped slowly into the water, until the night got so dark we couldn't see anymore. Only then did we rise and head back to the house. We never actually said anything to John, but the pot brownies never made another appearance.

See him?" Samuel said one afternoon. Several of us were with him on the front porch of the youth center. Our eyes followed where he was pointing, landing on a large, fearsomely tattooed, copper-skinned man with a mass of waist-length black hair. He was standing on the road outside the youth center, as if waiting for someone. "If you ever see that guy walking toward you on the street," Samuel said, "cross to the other side or he'll kill you." A generally jovial sort, Samuel didn't flash any hint of a smile, which told us he was being deadly serious.

Some teens at the center believed that Samuel's and Jimmy's daily presence in our midst offered us a measure of protection. In fact, the opposite was true, as we realized one afternoon when Jimmy ran up the front steps and yelled that some rival gang members were marching toward us, and they intended to shoot up the building. The fact that our center had become a hangout for Samuel's crew had apparently made us a target.

John quickly hustled the summer workers and the kids out the back door. We crouched in the bushes behind the building, bracing for the worst. We were afraid for John, who, instead of leaving with the rest of us, had joined Jimmy on the front porch, waiting for the rival gang. We all knew John could handle himself—he was a tall, burly man who, before becoming a social worker, had served as a U.S. Marine—but that didn't make him any match for gang members with guns.

Hiding in the shrubbery, we waited for what seemed like an eternity. My heart was beating so hard I could hear it like a drumbeat in my head.

Everything else remained quiet. In the absence of shouting or sounds of gun-fire, we took a chance and sent the kids home before making a run for it ourselves. We didn't stop until we got back to the beach house, where we assembled in the living room and waited some more. I remember John's wife and kids were away that week. I was glad they weren't there, so we wouldn't have to tell them that John might be in grave danger. We stayed awake all night, waiting up and fearing the worst.

John finally staggered in bleary-eyed at six the following morning. He told us that he'd been drinking whiskey all night with some of the homestead men, and that they had come to an agreement that from then on, the youth center would be off-limits for gang action. We all stared slack-jawed at our executive director, dubious about just how safe we would really be when we returned to the center.

"No, I'm telling you, it's okay to go back," John insisted, his words thick and his eyes at half-mast. "Besides," he added sleepily, "you've got to be there today. The kids are expecting you. Remember, you're taking them to that Taj Mahal concert. I guarantee you, they don't plan on missing it." With that, John swayed into his bedroom and left us to carry on with our commitments for that day as though nothing had happened.

As he predicted, all the teens showed up in anticipation of the Taj Mahal concert at the university campus that afternoon. We often arranged outings like this for the kids. Earlier in the summer, I had allowed two of the girls I worked with to spend the weekend at Allison's apartment in town. Allison and I had cleaned the place from top to bottom, and then turned the keys over to them, encouraging them to go out and wander in the city. It was my way of exposing them to a world beyond the one they already knew. And when we had heard that the popular blues singer Taj Mahal would be performing on the UH Manoa campus, we decided we had to take the teens; not only would it be fun for them, but it would also allow them to experience the feeling of being on a college campus. We wanted them to aspire to such a setting, to imagine that they could belong there as much as any of us. We were trying to sell them on the notion that an education would open doors for them. But later that night, a campus security guard caught one of our boys throwing rocks at birds, killing them. My heart sank. It was clear to me, not for the first time, that we were barely scratching the surface of what these kids needed.

That summer would upend every idea I had held about my future. It forced me to confront the fact that even though I had grown up poor, my mother and grandparents had taught and sheltered me in ways that had made me far more middle class than I had imagined. Often, my relative privilege was revealed in the most mundane ways. One day, Steve and I bought hot lunches for the kids, for example, and when we got back to the recreation center, we discovered that the restaurant hadn't packed any forks.

"What we need forks for?" one of the girls asked. The fourteen-year-old wrinkled her eyebrows at us, then took a container of food and proceeded to use her fingers as utensils, scooping gravy-soaked rice into her mouth. I thought of my first-grade teacher at Queen Kaahumanu and her failure to fathom that a boy in her class was so poor that he couldn't afford a quarter for lunch. I remembered how that teacher had called Robert out, embarrassing him with her ignorance, and now here I was, ignorant myself of the realities of these kids' lives, little better than my teacher had been.

In truth, ten college do-gooders were hardly the best counselors for these at-risk teens. We were hardly more than children ourselves, and our judgment was sometimes poor. One of the counselors in our group had even started an affair with a local boy who had recently been released from jail. I was relieved when the young woman's parents sent her away to put an end to the relationship.

But even those of us who would never have crossed such lines were ill-equipped to truly help kids whose homes had been fractured by gang violence, crime, drug addiction, and sexual assault. I did my best to help, but I knew I was out of my element. What could a sheltered young college student like me say to a thirteen-year-old girl whose uncle had raped her? How was I to convince a boy bent on some violent act of gang initiation that staying in school offered him a better future? Who was I to judge the thieves of Sherwood Forest, when they possessed so little? Many of the homestead kids saw no path forward for themselves other than a continuation of their current circumstances. They had few role models for how to climb out of the stickiness of poverty. And yet their families had welcomed us warmly. At no point did the people of Waimanalo hold our middle-class privilege against us, even when it was painfully obvious that they needed so much more than what a few college students could provide in a single summer. Almost the worst part was knowing that at the end of the summer, we would say aloha and mahalo to these kids and return to our comfortable, middle-class lives.

For me, Waimanalo had been a culture shock in another way as well. Being Japanese, I was unused to physical expressions of affection. Within my own family, we had always been restrained about touch, but now I was immersed in Native Hawaiian culture, in which everyone wrapped me in bear hugs or kissed my cheeks on greeting, and friendly contact like throwing an arm around someone's shoulders was routine and expected. Though I would grow more comfortable with it as the weeks went on, I still felt like an interloper.

By the end of the summer, I was forced to admit that the highly individualized and unending challenge of being a social worker, or even a counselor, might not, after all, be the right path for me. It seemed that for every problem I managed to resolve, a succession of even thornier issues would lie in wait. In working with the youth of Waimanalo, I had been quietly heartbroken by their need and overwhelmed by my inability to offer little more than what felt to me like Band-Aid solutions.

Many years later, Steve Carter would insist that I had done more for the

Waimanalo teens than I'd realized. "You were an example to them," he told me. "You were a local girl who, like them, had grown up poor, and yet you were in college. By your very presence there, you showed them what was possible." Steve, who had gone on to become a licensed mental health counselor, working with people in low-income communities, reminded me about Bernice Akamine, a teen mother in our program. Bernice had enrolled in college at UH Manoa after raising her daughter, eventually earning a master's degree in fine arts, and teaching ceramics at the prestigious Punahou School in Honolulu. Steve shared that Bernice had credited a visit to a professor's home that summer, arranged by the counselors, with exposing her to a whole new world of possibilities. Now a sought-after Native Hawaiian multimedia artist, with pieces in illustrious collections around the world, Bernice had described her art as a way to highlight her roots in Waimanalo and preserve cultural knowledge. Her journey was proof, Steve argued, that our efforts that summer had not been in vain. "You helped those kids," he reflected. "And they helped you, too."

The latter part of his statement, at least, rang true, because that one summer spent in the company of those teens had changed everything for me. It showed me that I would need to find ways to help them and their families that were more suited to who I knew myself to be. As I asked myself how I could fight for them in a manner that would address the whole barbed field of their challenges, my mind was already turning to other possibilities, such as politics, which as I understood it then, could mandate sweeping community-wide change with the stroke of a pen. Clearly, I still had a lot to learn.

CHAPTER EIGHT

Rich Man's War

When I returned to campus for my junior year in the fall of 1968, Steve and I continued our friendship. In between and after classes, I sometimes hung out at his apartment on the edge of campus, where I got to know his other friends, most of them active in the antiwar movement. Though only four or five people actually lived in the cramped two-room apartment—with the exception of Steve, all were Japanese American—there were often some ten or twelve people there at any given time. The single beds lined up in the living room made the place look like a soldiers' barracks. We would sprawl on those beds, or on windowsills, the floor, wherever we found a perch, as the group engaged in ardent debates about the deadly toll of the Vietnam War. For a long time, I was mostly silent, taking in arguments that were completely new to me.

One of Steve's roommates was a short, fiery senior named David Hagino.

Among the activists at the forefront of the SDS movement on Oahu, David was one of the few local leaders. I had seen a picture of him in the campus newspaper the year before, wearing Vietcong pajamas. David was easily the most ambitious and charismatic of the group. The son of an undertaker's assistant from Hilo, he spoke so vividly and persuasively about the young American soldiers whose lives would never be the same that we could not be unmoved.

Sitting in the midst of these students as they held forth on so many afternoons, I had slowly become convinced that our leaders had plunged us into an unwinnable conflict that amounted to nothing more than American imperialism—because what else is it called when a powerful nation invades another to dismantle its system of government? It was increasingly clear to me that we had entered the war in 1965 not to free the South Vietnamese people from the scourge of communism, as our government claimed. Rather, the primary motivation was to maintain America's influence and interests throughout Southeast Asia.

As I listened to Steve, David, and the rest of their antiwar friends, one of the protest signs from the Bachman Hall sit-in the previous spring kept coming back to me: WE WON'T FIGHT YOUR RICH MAN'S WAR. I was beginning to understand the piercing accuracy of that statement, because most of the young men being conscripted were from economically disadvantaged communities, while the sons of the wealthy and powerful remained for the most part untouched by the draft. In a sense, it seemed to me now, all wars were rich men's wars, entered into by the privileged and protected, and won or lost on the backs of the poor. In the case of Vietnam, when many of the soldiers returned home, if indeed they were lucky enough to do so, they were less likely to hold meaningful employment, and many would be forever traumatized by the violence and death they had witnessed, broken in body and soul. At the time, the suicide rate among veterans was already climbing, though definitive studies of PTSD among Vietnam vets came later. It was a travesty that those "fighting soldiers from the sky" to whom I had once sung praises, those "fearless men who jump and die," were in fact sacrificing themselves and their futures for an unjust cause.

To put it mildly, my evolving views grated on Allison, who still supported the war. "You're different," he would say. "You're letting them change who you are."

Given this attitude, I kept him away from my new friends at first. But about halfway through the year, David remarked, "Mazie, we know you have a boyfriend. How come we've never met the guy?"

I laughed at the question, though in truth I had lately been considering introducing Allison to my antiwar circle. I was sick of him criticizing them, and felt confident that once he heard their arguments, he could not fail to see the merits. He was the smartest person I knew, and was sure to follow up with his own research. I finally decided that, no matter how awkward I feared it might be, bringing him into the group would help him understand how and why my thinking had changed.

A week later, Allison reluctantly agreed to accompany me to Steve and David's apartment after classes. That afternoon, he listened attentively as everyone dissected how the Tet Offensive had revealed the true hideousness of American involvement in what should have remained a sovereign nation's civil conflict.

Tet referred to Vietnam's observance of the Lunar New Year at the end of January. In 1968, the allied forces expected a cease-fire during this period and so were completely unprepared when the North Vietnamese stormed the U.S. embassy in Saigon and launched surprise attacks on more than one hundred cities and military garrisons in the South. It took the allied forces several months to fight off the North Vietnamese attacks, with enemy deaths reported to run as high as fifty-eight thousand. The allied losses, too, were devastating. In March 1968, *The New York Times* estimated that close to four thousand Americans had been killed since the start of the offensive in early January, along with fourteen thousand South Vietnamese men, women, and children. The bloodiest and most prolonged fighting to date, the Tet Offensive more than any other military action had helped to harden American hearts against the Vietnam War.

One year after Tet, toward the end of our junior year, a photo essay in *Life* magazine ran headshots of 242 young soldiers who had lost their lives in a single week of combat. The effect of seeing all those young men staring out from page after page, full of promise in their crisp dress blues, their lives needlessly cut short, was shattering. That *Life* photo essay would help to convince Allison, and indeed most of America, that the cost of the war was too unbearably high.

His approval ratings in tatters over his handling of Vietnam, President Johnson had declined to run for a second term, and in November 1968, the Republican nominee, Richard Nixon, had been elected president. Though Nixon had made campaign promises to end the war, once in office, he appeared to be in no rush to bring the troops home. Antiwar protesters called for the Selective Service draft to be abolished in favor of armed forces that were entirely voluntary, but Nixon knew that an all-volunteer military would be insufficient to maintain troop levels.

The new draft lottery system Nixon signed into law in November 1969 was billed as a cure for the inequities of the old system, which had resulted in a combatant force that was disproportionately poor and African American. In the new system, all men born between 1944 and 1950 would have to report when the randomly selected number that corresponded to their birth date was called, with the lowest numbers being called first. However, in a significant change from the previous draft system, which had conscripted older men first, nineteen-year-olds would now be the first ones called, followed by twenty-year-olds and on upward. Psychological studies would reveal this to be a disastrous policy, as it resulted in a preponderance of young draftees whose frontal lobe pathways, governing higher reasoning, memory retention, planning, and impulse control, had yet to be fully developed. In men, these dopamine connections aren't fully mature until age twenty-four, which meant the new lottery would end up sending to the front lines boys whose neurological wiring could only be ravaged by the hell of war.

As the first step in their induction, draftees would be ordered to report for physical examinations. Those who passed their physicals but did not want to enlist were given ten days to present a case for deferment. If they were enrolled in a college full-time, they would be removed from the pool until they graduated or were no longer making progress toward a degree. Many men with low numbers would choose to continue in full-time degree programs until they had passed the age of twenty-six and were therefore no longer eligible for conscription.

There were several other ways to avoid serving in Uncle Sam's army, some legal, some not. Many fled the country, taking up residence in Canada, and were unable to return to the United States until President Jimmy Carter granted them amnesty on his first day in office in 1977. Others gained exemptions by arguing that their families would suffer undue hardship if they were removed from the home. Some draftees showed up for their physicals wearing women's underwear, claiming to be gay, which at the time prohibited them from serving. Many more argued that they were against the war for religious or philosophical reasons; these arguments could be presented in an essay that, if persuasive enough, would allow them to be exempted from military service as a conscientious objector, or C.O. They would, however, be required to serve the country for two years in another capacity.

By the time the new lottery system was announced, both Allison and I were already solidly against the war. Allison had even marched alongside me in numerous protests, the two of us singing protest anthems and spirituals, including my favorite "We Shall Overcome." Many months before, Allison had also resolved to become a conscientious objector, and he had spent many late nights doing intensive research to prepare his arguments. This was greatly relieving to me when I first learned about the new draft lottery. At least I knew that Allison would not be going to Vietnam, nor would my anti-war friends, who were all in degree-granting programs. Nor did I have to worry about Roy, who some years before had been ruled ineligible to serve due to the hearing loss he had suffered from his severe ear infection as a young child. Wayne, too, was not in danger, as he was still too young to be drafted. I suspected that even if he had been old enough, his emotional fragility might have disqualified him.

On the night of December 1, 1969, Allison and I sat on his living room floor, watching the CBS News broadcast of the draft lottery on his small black-and-white TV. Even though I did not have to be concerned about the immediate safety of those I loved, I knew that millions of other families were not so fortunate. All across America, young men waited anxiously to hear their fates. On the TV screen, a dour-looking man reached into a water-cooler-size glass jar containing oblong blue capsules. Inside each capsule was a piece of paper on which a birth date had been printed, three hundred and sixty-six dates in all, including February 29 for leap-year babies. We

instinctively held our breath as the grim-faced man—New York congressman Alexander Pirnie, the ranking Republican on the House Armed Services Committee—pulled the first blue capsule apart and unrolled the paper
scroll inside. "September fourteenth," he intoned. "September fourteenth is
0-0-1."

Beside me, Allison released a sharp breath. "This is ridiculous," he mut-
tered with plain disgust at the prospect of yet more of his countrymen fighting and dying in Vietnam. On-screen, the congressman now stepped aside to
allow Selective Service youth delegates to draw the rest of the numbers.
Nixon had apparently insisted that young people be involved in the drawing
to improve the optics surrounding our government sending teenage boys to
war. The first of these youth delegates stepped forward and reached into the
jar, handing the capsule he selected to an older, white-haired man.

"April twenty-fourth," the older man announced. "April twenty-fourth is
0-0-2."

We kept watching in silence as more blue capsules were pulled from the jar.

"December thirty-first," the announcer continued. "December thirty-
first is 1-0-0."

Hearing his birth date called, Allison sighed and let his body roll backward onto the floor. For the rest of the drawing he lay there, gazing at the
ceiling as he listened to the monotonous calling of numbers on the TV. I
imagined he was mulling over the various arguments he would make in his
C.O. essay.

Finally, the last scroll was unrolled. "June eighth," the announcer said, his
voice a robotic drone. "June eighth is number 3-6-6."

We both knew that with a draft number of 100, it was likely Allison would
be called to serve. As I got up to turn off the TV, a ripple of dread ran through
me. *What if the draft board refuses to grant him C.O. status?* I thought suddenly.
I glanced down at Allison, who was still lying on the floor. The brooding

look on his face told me that the thought had occurred to him, too. I reminded myself that going all the way back to our *Bulldog* days, Allison was the strongest writer I knew, and he would bring all his talent and intellect to bear in making the clearest arguments possible for C.O. status.

Starting the following January, young men were called at a rate of roughly thirty numbers per month, and by the end of February, some 29,500 men had been drafted. In August, the Defense Department announced that it would conscript 163,500 men that year, which meant that potential draftees with numbers above 195 would likely not be called.

When Allison's number was announced that spring, he was prepared. Indeed, his essay explaining his practical and philosophical objections to the war was so convincingly written that the draft board granted his alternative service proposal: to counsel other young men on Oahu on how they, too, could qualify for C.O. status. For the next few years—until the North Vietnamese army wrested the city of Saigon from allied control on April 30, 1975, marking the official end of the war—Allison would do his part to keep those draftees who did not support the war from becoming one of the 58,220 American soldiers killed in action, the 150,000 wounded in combat, or the 1,246 who went missing, most of them never to be found. It was, for Allison, important and purposeful work, and he dedicated himself to helping those young men, with more commitment and drive than I had seen him bring to any previous endeavor. Watching him do his part for the antiwar movement, my admiration for him deepened.

CHAPTER NINE

Betty Friedan and Me

I f my experiences in Waimanalo and the antiwar movement on campus had served as my political awakening, it was not until the spring of 1970, around the time Allison was granted C.O. status, that my actual involvement with politics began. I was a senior at UH Manoa that year, set to graduate with my bachelor's degree in December. That was also the year that David Hagino decided to run for the State House from the 12th District of McCully-Moiliili, and he was determined to draft me as his campaign manager.

"What do I know about running a campaign?" I protested. "I'm still in college." But David was adamant. He wanted a woman to run his campaign and he insisted that that woman was going to be me. I had to admire David's forward thinking. The Women's Liberation movement was gaining momentum across the country, and choosing a woman as his campaign manager was a clear and clever way for him to separate himself from the "good old boy" politics of the past and signal his embrace of feminism. I ultimately agreed to run his campaign, thinking that it would force me to grow, much as my summer in Waimanalo had done.

Running from a working-class district of densely packed apartment dwellings and small homes, David wanted to tackle such issues as affordable housing and the preservation of open spaces for the use of the community. During the campaign, we even gathered together a group of residents to plant grass and trees to create a small park, which is still there today. As I recall, David referred to our burgeoning political activation as "the Hagino Generation." Even back then, I could hear how presumptuous his slogan sounded, but that was David, and the rest of us went along.

His race would be an important training ground for me, as we would have to be creative. We had no experience and hardly any budget, but we did have a handful of volunteers, and I was their taskmaster. In Hawaii, all political races were grassroots campaigns. People we knew who had previously run for office had advised us to buy "walking cards"—three-by-five-inch index cards listing registered Democratic and Independent households—from a local company. The candidate could then use these cards to go door-to-door and talk to people in their homes. We also printed up campaign brochures with artwork and haiku. After painstakingly drawing up routes on district maps, I would give our volunteers stacks of these brochures and send them out to canvass.

"Don't come back until you've knocked on every door," I would say. I had anticipated that each person would complete their route in a couple of hours, but many streets in McCully-Moiliili were lined with modest two- and four-story walk-ups, which took far longer to canvass than a street with single-family homes. Based on our volunteers' feedback, I was constantly redrawing our maps to give each canvasser roughly the same amount of time in the field. But as we had only five or six volunteers on a good day, some of our crew would inevitably have to do more than one route. I can still remember them straggling in well after nightfall, exhausted from hours of climbing stairs.

Sometimes, in addition to brochures, we handed out our eye-catching posters featuring a half-moon on an orange background and the slogan: IT'S ALREADY TOMORROW. One day, when I was out knocking on doors with the volunteers, I handed a young man this poster, and he took it with a puzzled look. "It's already tomorrow?" he said. "You mean the election is tomorrow?" Obviously, we hadn't quite nailed the political messaging.

Veteran advisers had suggested that we also send out mailers. "You'll reach more people than going door-to-door," they told us, so we diverted most of the funds we had raised from supporters to paying for postage. Our budget was so tight that I learned how to expertly bundle our brochures by bulk-rate routes to qualify for the lower postage. Day after day, as our volunteers canvassed in person, I sat in the cheap, windowless backroom we had rented as our headquarters, *The Forsyte Saga* playing on a fuzzy TV as I affixed address labels to envelopes stuffed with our brochures. When the volunteers got back from their routes, I drafted them to help me with the mailers. I noticed one guy, a longtime friend of David's, slapping the labels crookedly on the envelopes. I held my tongue for a while until I couldn't take it anymore.

"Look," I said, "when people get these mailers, it might be the only thing they're going to know about David." I held up one of his envelopes with its cockeyed label. "This makes a bad impression. You can't just slap the label on. It's going to make people think we don't care, so can you please put the rest of the labels on straight?"

"If you don't like how I do it, then I can leave," he replied. No doubt he thought I should be grateful that he was giving any time at all to our shoestring operation. I didn't blink.

"Then leave," I said, which he did.

That November, despite our efforts, David narrowly lost his race. However, by the time I graduated from college one month later, he and I were fully immersed in the processes of grassroots Democratic politics. Our strong support for populist causes such as workers' rights and affordable housing would eventually pull us into the orbit of a cadre of rising stars in the Democratic Party, including John Waihee, who in 1986 would be elected the first Hawaiian governor of the state, and Carol Fukunaga, one of the few other women in our fledgling political group, who would be elected to the State House in 1978.

It became an article of faith within our circle of activists that we would be the generation to reimagine the political priorities of the state. Though the Democratic old guard had done important work and earned popular support by championing workers, we had the fervor and idealism of youth, and the conviction that we were the ones with the vision and drive to create a government that would be more responsive to our state's evolving needs. For one thing, unlike the old guard, we were passionate about protecting the environment and advocating for clean energy sources such as wind, hydro, and solar power—in this we were definitely ahead of our time. We all knew that if we meant to achieve such goals, it would not be sufficient to march around and sing "We Shall Overcome." And so, with David and John as the acknowledged leaders of our group, we gathered regularly to discuss how best to prepare ourselves to take seats at the tables where decisions were made. We were so sure of our high purpose. Our young hearts burned to change the world.

Two years after his failed bid for the State House in 1970, David would convince me to manage yet another campaign, this time for his friend Anson Chong. Anson and I knew each other from when he had been a volunteer in David's earlier race. "I'd run his campaign myself," David told me, "except I'm heading to law school in St. Louis in the fall. The only other person who can do this is you, Mazie. Anson needs you." He pointed out that Anson was a champion of workers and labor unions, just as we were, and that he supported access to better education, housing, and health care for struggling communities, as we did. He then sang my praises for how I'd handled his campaign, and insisted that no one else could bring as much as I could to Anson's race. The tack he took was quintessential David; he would flatter, cajole, and hound people until they fell in with his plans, if only to get him off their backs. And so, despite my suspicion that Anson lacked a certain discipline, I agreed.

Anson was a candidate straight out of central casting. Handsome, charismatic, and self-assured, he was older than David and me by almost ten years and his credentials were impeccable: He had graduated from Colgate University, worked as a White House Fellow, earned a master's in economics from Columbia and a postgraduate certificate in urban administration from Yale, and served in the Peace Corps in Nigeria. He was also a natural campaigner who enjoyed walking into laundromats and coffee shops in the middle of the night and talking to the people he found there. Not surprisingly, this time my candidate would prevail, with Anson becoming an elected representative from the multimember Manoa district in 1972.

After his win, Anson hired me to run his legislative office, a job that would mark the start of my many years in the State House. Our partnership was not entirely successful, however. For one thing, we were both still learning the personalities and procedures of the legislature. For another, as much as I appreciated Anson's warmth as a person, I quickly realized that he found the job of assessing constituents' needs, drafting legislation to meet those needs, and doing the consensus building necessary to get the bills passed to be a tedious process, while I believed that this was where the real gold of politics lay. This meant that the nitty-gritty of our day-to-day work fell mostly on my shoulders.

Back then, only a few women had been elected to the fifty-one-member House, and I was one of a handful more among the office chiefs. The men barely took note of me when I walked into meetings. Granted, I was just out of college and looked younger than my twenty-three years. I was also still very reserved. The fact that most elected officials in the State House were from male-dominated Asian cultures may have also inclined the men to dismiss me. Whatever the cause, I was clearly of little consequence to them. It was during this period in the legislature that I decided that if I wanted to effectively navigate the political arena as a woman, my bachelor's degree would not be enough. I would have to go back to school and get some kind of graduate credential. Choosing what degree to pursue was another matter.

Since the legislature was only in session from December through May, for the rest of the year I pieced together a living as an office temp. One client, Madelyn Dunham, the first woman vice president of the Bank of Hawaii, would call the temp agency and specifically request me every time she needed extra hands to type legal documents. Dunham's grandson was Barack Obama, who at the time was thirteen years old.

Forty years later, I would run for the U.S. Senate and be elected to that body in 2012, the same year that Obama won his second term as the nation's first African American president. In January 2015, then majority leader Chuck Schumer asked me to introduce the president at a Democratic Senate retreat. *What more can I say about this historic president that we haven't already heard?* I wondered. And then I remembered there was one story that only I could tell.

Backstage, I told President Obama, "I'm going to share something about you."

"Will it be embarrassing?" he asked me. I laughed and assured him that no, it would not, before walking out to the podium.

"You know, President Obama, you and I share something more than our love for the state of Hawaii, which in itself puts us on the same team," I began. "We were both very close to our grandmothers and we learned some of our most important life lessons from them." I went on to share that my own grandmother had raised me from the time I was three years old, and that I had once worked with his grandmother, who had overseen much of his upbringing, and who I knew had not always been fairly treated as a woman at the Bank of Hawaii. People she had trained had been promoted ahead of her, ostensibly because she didn't have a college degree. But she had persevered, rising through the ranks and setting an example of tenacity, determination, and hard work for her grandson. "I believe we know from our grandmothers how important education is," I continued, "and how to rise above unfair treatment."

The president was moved by my memory of the woman who had played such a significant role in his life. "I had no idea you knew her," he said wistfully, as I came off the stage. A little while later, addressing the audience, he pivoted to humor, reminding those gathered that despite my saying he and I were on the same team, when he first ran for president in 2008, I had been one of the last members of Congress to endorse him.

"My sister from Hawaii," he teased. "What's up with that?"

In fact, I had initially been inclined to support his opponent, Hillary Clinton, in the Democratic primary. Apart from the solidarity I felt toward her as a woman in the bruisingly macho world of politics, I knew how hard she worked, and that in the Senate she was usually among the most prepared. I had also noted that while she sometimes struggled to connect with voters, she was animated by a bedrock commitment to improving their lives. And yet I had held back, waiting to see how the race unfolded, because Barack Obama had impressed me as well. He, too, seemed sincere in his desire to uplift and serve, and he possessed a charisma on the campaign trail that couldn't be taught. Even so, I had been on the verge of endorsing Hillary Clinton when former President Bill Clinton went negative. One report alleged that in trying to convince Massachusetts senator Ted Kennedy to support his wife over Obama, Bill Clinton had stated, "A few years ago this guy would have been carrying our bags." *Hmm, that is totally inappropriate*, I remember thinking. It was one more remark in a pattern of race-tinged comments that the former president had made in an effort to diminish Obama's candidacy. Ultimately, these comments were my tipping point, the reason I decided to throw my support to the candidate from my home state.

As I learned the ropes of the legislative procedure in the early seventies, my brother Roy took a somewhat dim view of my political work. Ever since returning from his time as a civilian contractor in Southeast Asia in 1972, he had been employed by Hawaiian Electric. Steady and conscientious as ever, he would remain with the company until he retired. To Roy, my six-month stints with the state legislature seemed impractical and self-indulgent, given how poorly I was paid. "When is Mazie going to get a real job?" he would ask our mother.

Mom only smiled. She knew I found the work I was doing meaningful, and that was enough for her. I was aware that many Asian mothers of her era had pushed their daughters toward more traditional occupations for women, jobs like teaching, secretarial work, or nursing, which were perceived to be compatible with what were still seen as women's primary pursuits—taking care of husbands and raising children. Not my mother. She held no preconceived notions about the life I should lead. "Why should I try to tell you what to do?" she had said to me. "Look what happened to my life." Her unwavering support and willingness to let me make my own choices would make it all the more disconcerting when my eyes were opened to the unconscious expectations I had placed upon myself.

I was still dating Allison, who was then working for a social services agency that protected Native Hawaiian children. He was also becoming increasingly involved with a local theater group, but had avoided introducing me to his new friends, explaining that he wanted to keep them completely separate from the all-consuming political world I was in. "I need some space," he told me, and perhaps because it had taken me some time to introduce him to my activist friends, I accepted this. I even agreed to cook a meal for a party he was throwing for his theater group, despite not being invited.

At the time, I was still in the midst of the daily grind of running Anson Chong's State House campaign, and after our long days, Anson and I would often have dinner with his mother. She was of Chinese descent, a bright and erudite college professor and a wonderful cook. One night, she served us a mouthwatering baked chicken that she had marinated in vermouth and sage. I requested the recipe, thinking this would be the perfect dish to cook for Allison's party. When Anson's mother learned exactly why I wanted her recipe, she didn't mince words. "You're doing this and you're not even invited?" she asked pointedly.

I laughed ruefully, realizing how stupid I must seem. I went ahead and cooked the meal anyway, because I had already said I would. But a week later, I ended it with Allison. "This isn't working for me," I told him. "Go be with your scintillating theater friends."

He didn't seem particularly upset by our breakup or by my snarky comment about his theater friends, perhaps because he and I had already broken up and gotten back together several times. We declared these separations whenever we began getting on each other's nerves, and then, as the weeks went by, we would slowly fall back into spending time together until it was obvious even to us that we were dating again. I suspected that Allison's equanimity revealed his expectation that this breakup would be as short-lived as the ones before, and maybe I assumed the same. Still, I was starting to see that our on-again, off-again relationship did not bode well for the future.

It was during this period that I happened to pick up and begin reading *The Feminine Mystique* by Betty Friedan. A light bulb exploded. I saw with sudden and overwhelming clarity that despite being raised by a single mother, I had assumed that I would marry after college and have children, and that my husband would be our family's main breadwinner. Why on earth had I subscribed to this dominant cultural narrative, when two strong and capable women had been my primary role models and my own father had never been around? I hadn't seen the man who gave me half of my genetic code since the day I went to live with my grandparents when I was three, and I had remained resolutely uncurious about how his life had unfolded after my mother put an ocean between us. I had long considered it a betrayal of my mother to wonder even for a moment about Matabe Hirono, and yet his long absence from my life had not inoculated me against cultural stereotypes about the kind of woman I should be.

Jolted at how deeply I had absorbed society's expectations of my gender, I immersed myself in Betty Friedan's manifesto, allowing her searing arguments to shatter my regressive notions of womanhood. Why should we wait for a man to come and take care of us, she challenged. Why couldn't we take care of ourselves? As I waded deeper into the book, it dawned on me that I actually felt no driving desire to be a wife and mother. My larger goal, I saw now, wasn't to marry Allison, or anyone. I was far more interested in forging a path to my own freedom and personal agency, and in exploring how I might help to transform a nation in which women, and indeed everyone who hadn't been born straight, white, and male, were routinely judged as less deserving of the rights and privileges of full citizenship.

My journey to feminist empowerment would not be a straight line, how-ever. Despite my consciousness having been so forcefully raised, the domi-nant culture's hold on my thinking would still make stealthy incursions now and then, leaving me to question my capabilities. Fortunately, I always had my mother's example to fall back on. Laura Sato Hirono never allowed doubt about the outcome of a thing to stand in her way.

Five decades later, after the election of a record number of women to the U.S. House and Senate in the November 2018 midterms, *The New York Times* would commission portraits of the one hundred and thirty-two women serv-ing in the historic 116th Congress. In documenting this high-water mark for women, the photographer had requested that we each bring to the photo shoot an item that had been meaningful on our journey. I chose to bring a copy of *The Feminine Mystique*, the book that had broken some of the chains of convention that I hadn't even known had bound me.

CHAPTER TEN

Young Democrats

was still running legislative operations for Anson Chong in the summer of 1974 when a young lawyer named Leighton Kim Oshima returned to Oahu and took a job in the attorney general's office. Leighton had worked on George McGovern's 1972 presidential campaign, and McGovern's loss, which led to Richard Nixon's second term and the subsequent Watergate scandal, had made Leighton want to get involved in Democratic Party politics. Whether this meant running for office himself or supporting lawmakers, he hadn't yet decided. When he asked his friend Bob Miller, then a left-leaning legislative aide to Governor John Burns, how he might get connected to the Hawaii Democratic Party, Bob told him, "There are two people you have to get to know: David Hagino and Mazie Hirono." Leighton thought: *Who the hell are they?*

Like Leighton, I had worked with a group of McGovern volunteers to get the candidate elected in 1972. Though our efforts failed, I had stayed in the fight, lending support to candidates in local races who shared my views. By the time Bob Miller recommended me to Leighton, I was familiar with many of the emerging young leaders of the Democratic Party in Hawaii. As the president of the Honolulu Young Democrats, I was in charge of setting meetings and advancing our agenda, which included holding forums with candidates and elected officials and providing advice to young people who wanted to run for office. At the time, David was not involved with any of these activities as he'd left the Islands two years before to attend Washington University School of Law in St. Louis, Missouri.

"These Young Democrats aren't your fly-by-night young upstarts," Bob had told Leighton. "They're serious about what they're doing, and I guarantee you, they're going to be running things one day." Bob had then suggested that Leighton attend the next Young Democrats meeting, which would be held the following week at the Waikiki-Kapahulu Public Library.

The way Leighton remembers it, he was sitting on a metal chair in the library one week later, waiting for our event to start, when he noticed a young Asian woman in pedal pushers and rubber slippers, carrying an armful of binders, tablets, and yellow legal pads. To hear him tell it, I marched around the room, talking to people and taking copious notes. *This is a Young Democrats meeting*, Leighton thought, watching me with some amusement. *It really shouldn't be that serious.* He quickly surmised that this officious young woman must be Mazie Hirono.

Meanwhile, I had asked a few people about the unfamiliar young man sitting at the back of the room. I was completely unaware that years before, I had heard him rehearsing drums for the popular high school band the Dimensions, in a house in Kaimuki four doors up from my own.

Eventually, I made my way over to him. Surveying him coolly—or, as he remembers it, witheringly—I remarked, "So, I hear you're a lawyer."

Apparently, I made it sound as if being a lawyer were a most disreputable thing. In truth, I felt just the opposite; Leighton was the first attorney I had met who was my own age, and that interested me. But never liking to appear overly impressed by anyone, I gave no outward sign of it. What Leighton saw was a short Japanese girl regarding him with her nose in the air.

"Yes, I'm a lawyer," he responded, his tone almost apologetic. He looked at me briefly and then looked away. Stung by his seeming indifference, I quickly turned to greet another attendee. It was an inauspicious beginning.

Leighton told me later that he had been intrigued by me as I'd marched around the room, until my cool approach made him think that getting to know me might not be worth the trouble. But over the course of the next year, we kept running into each other at the State Capitol, where we both worked. It seemed that every time I encountered him, Leighton was laughing with someone. He was so unlike the serious types I was normally drawn to and yet I was increasingly curious about him.

The following May, we happened to be leaving the building at the same time on the day the legislature was going on recess until December. The usual closing-day celebrations had wound down, and now Leighton offered to drive me home. He didn't actually own a vehicle but was driving his mother's car that day. Though Allison and I had recently agreed to see other people, he still sometimes picked me up after work, but he was nowhere in sight, and I wasn't sure if he would be coming. Rather than risk having to ride the bus all the way out to Hawaii Kai, I took Leighton up on his offer. On the drive home, out of the blue, he asked if I wanted to see a movie with him. I wondered why on earth this happy-go-lucky young attorney was suggesting a date with sober, sensible me. But I said yes, because he made me laugh, too.

We decided on the Steve McQueen and Dustin Hoffman prison drama, *Papillon*. He picked me up for the movie a few days later. Afterward, as the closing credits rolled, Leighton leaned over and asked, "So what do you want to do next?"

I was at a loss. I had assumed that after the movie we would just go home. "We could get coffee and discuss the movie," I suggested.

"Coffee?" Leighton scoffed. "Let's go to a nightclub and get a drink."

I wasn't a drinker, much less a nightclub goer. In fact, no one in my family consumed alcohol, not even beer. But not wanting to seem like a total square, I went along with the plan. Leighton was lighthearted and spontaneous, and I found myself laughing more with him than I ever had.

A few weeks later, he took me to my first rock concert, the Doobie Brothers.

"How do you like them?" he asked me a few minutes in.

"It's pretty loud," I observed as Leighton, the former drummer, pulled me closer to the stage. I let myself be carried along by his exuberance, hardly believing that I could be falling for this impulsive, fun-loving man. I hadn't pegged him as the sort who would choose to date opinionated, unfussy types like me, yet here he was, unabashedly acting as if he were as smitten with me as I was becoming with him. Leighton told me later that I was the first woman he had ever met who cared so much about politics. He admired my level of commitment, even though he had decided by then that he was content to support candidates and issues from the sidelines without running for office himself.

Leighton was the only son and middle child of three children born to a strict Korean mother, Rosemary Kim, and a hardworking Japanese father, James Oshima, who had angered their parents by eloping. The long-simmering animosity between Koreans and Japanese dated back to Japan's colonization of Korea from 1910 through the Second World War. Even today, the relationship between the two nations remains prickly. The Korean side of Leighton's family had gone so far as to disown the young couple, but only briefly—just long enough to register their displeasure. Leighton remarked wryly that in his mother's family, if you hadn't been disowned at least once, you weren't truly a Kim.

I knew from my own experiences as an Asian person in Hawaii that Koreans tended to be much more direct in their approach than the Japanese: If Koreans thought you were in the wrong, they would usually let you know in a manner that left no ambiguity as to their feelings. By contrast, we Japanese would find a way to be obliquely polite. We were masters of the deviously mild comment, the kind that left you nicked with blood, though there were no sharp implements in sight.

These were broad generalizations, of course, and Leighton and I were among the many exceptions that challenged these cultural norms. Despite being 100 percent Japanese, I was the more volatile of the two of us, though I had learned to contain this side of myself. Compared to me, Leighton was more measured, tending toward laid-back equanimity like his father, never getting too worked up about anything—except when he played pickup basketball at the Nuuanu YMCA. Leighton loved the game and was very aggressive on the court. Having earned his bachelor's from the University of Michigan, he always showed up in full Michigan Wolverines regalia and was known to other players simply as "Michigan." Once, in the crush of play, his nose was accidentally broken, and the wild man of basketball calmly drove himself to the emergency room to get his face mended.

After college, Leighton had gone straight on to law school at George Washington University in Washington, D.C. There, he had interned for U.S. representative Patsy Mink. The first Asian American woman to practice law in Hawaii, the trailblazing Democrat had in 1964 become the first woman of color and the first Asian American woman elected to Congress. I was intrigued to learn that Leighton's parents had paid for him to attend both college and law school on the mainland. Leighton's father had considered it important for his children to have time away from the cocoon of Hawaii, where argument and debate, even when useful in resolving a problem, were discouraged by a culture in which the adage "The nail that protrudes gets hammered" was prevalent. In the Islands, people often went along to get along, allowing situations to unfold along a path that avoided confrontation. While this was perhaps less true for Koreans and haoles who grew up in Hawaii, even for them the success of a more aggressive approach might be limited, forcing them to find more agreeable ways to achieve their ends.

As much as he appreciated the easygoing sociability of the Islands, Leighton's father wanted his children to experience being on their own, and to hone their critical-thinking skills in settings where active inquiry was not only encouraged but also required. Perhaps because of his immersion in mainland academic settings, Leighton was never defensive when I challenged his perspective and offered another view. In fact, he relished interrogating an issue and coming up with unconventional solutions to a problem. Yet unlike David and Allison, who were both also deeply creative thinkers, Leighton approached problems with good-natured amusement about the world in general, and me in particular.

Still, I didn't know anyone else whose parents had been able to afford to pay the tuition for a mainland school. And James Oshima had sent not just Leighton but also his sisters, Lynette and Lauren, to prestigious Big Ten colleges on the mainland. Since I had funded my own local college tuition, and would have to pay my own way through any graduate program I wanted to pursue, I assumed that Leighton's family must be financially more comfortable than mine. But Leighton insisted they weren't rich, and that his father simply worked very hard to provide for his children through the three bars he owned in downtown Honolulu—the Wonder, Tahiti, and Midway-Manila on Smith Street, Nuuanu Avenue, and King Street, respectively, in Chinatown. One of his bars, Midway-Manila, had been used in a scene in the original *Hawaii Five-O* television series.

At the time I met Leighton, my mother was working at the *Advertiser* from 4:00 p.m. to midnight, known in newspaper parlance as the lobster shift. She had earned her driver's license when she was in her forties, and had recently bought our family's first new car. Now, we developed a routine. Mom would leave home at around 2:00 p.m. and drive to the newspaper. When I finished work, I would pick up her car from the parking lot and, using my own set of keys, go to meet Leighton. Leighton and I would spend most evenings together, having dinner at a restaurant in town and often going for a drive afterward, exploring far-flung neighborhoods and talking about everything. We would end the evening at his parents' condo in Waikiki, where he'd lived since returning from Washington, D.C. There, ensconced on his couch, we would watch television until it was time for me to pick Mom up at midnight and drive her home.

I quickly realized that Leighton's mother didn't much like me. She was civil but distant toward me, her lips often pressed together in a stern line. I knew why, too. I wasn't warm and fuzzy like some of Leighton's other girlfriends. I made little effort to ingratiate myself with her or to play the part of the nice Asian girl she had likely envisioned for her son. When we did converse, I was way too opinionated for her taste.

Fortunately, Leighton didn't share that view. In contrast to his mother, he applauded my engagement with politics, yet he was able to temper my prickly self-righteousness. His wry wit softened the stridency of my opinions, even as he welcomed the opinions themselves. He was so unlike Allison, with his strange contradictory habit of both supporting me and putting me down, as if he were most comfortable in my company when he could keep me off balance. It was a refreshing change to be with someone who didn't feel a need to compete with me and who wholeheartedly encouraged my goals. The truth was, I needed that sort of reinforcement more than I let on.

A few months into my relationship with Leighton, I began to think about applying to law school, but was I worried that I wasn't smart enough. Never mind that I had graduated Phi Beta Kappa with my bachelor's in psychology and had already taken the LSAT and earned a strong score. Perhaps because no one else in my immediate family had gone to college, much less earned a graduate degree, I had a hard time visualizing myself in law school. But despite my doubts, I had already decided that I needed more than a bachelor's degree if I wanted to stay in politics, so I kept turning the idea over in my mind.

I knew that the University of Hawaii had recently opened its own law school on the Manoa campus, with the stated mission of creating a new generation of not just attorneys but also political leaders and public servants. The inaugural class had already been filled with my activist friends, but I still hadn't fully made up my mind about going to law school. All I knew was that if I did go back to school, I wanted to attend a program on the mainland. Like Leighton's father, I thought the experience of navigating an unfamiliar setting would stretch me in ways that might not be possible if I stayed at home.

Of the mainland programs I'd researched, I was particularly interested in Georgetown University's law school, mainly because it had a top-notch clinical program that offered real-world experience in public interest law, with upper-level students paired with attorneys to represent clients who were underserved or marginalized, such as persons with disabilities. Given my political activities, no one was surprised that public interest law was the area that most appealed to me, or that I had no desire to pursue corporate law. At the time, I was also playing with the idea of getting a master's degree first, thinking that after five years away from academia, it would "warm me up" for the rigors of law school. I went to talk to one of my former professors, Dan Boylan, to get his advice on graduate programs in American Studies that I might possibly pursue.

"Why are you even bothering with that?" he asked me. "Go straight to law school, Mazie. It's what you really want. Don't waste your time and money in a master's program." His words gave me the extra push I needed to fill out my law school applications. Always frugal with money, I had some savings to put toward a portion of the tuition, and I would take out loans to cover the rest. I knew money would be tight, but I had no intention of asking my mother to help, even if she could have afforded it.

Leighton, who knew I was concerned about being able to afford mainland tuition, asked me at one point: "Why don't you go to law school here? All your political friends are here, and it's much cheaper."

"No," I said decisively. Leighton's brow knitted with puzzlement at the doggedness of my tone, so I explained that my friend John Waihee, one of Oahu's leading young activists, was already a student there. John had a big, charismatic personality; I had noticed how the other students at the law school circled around him, in much the same way that we had all circled around David Hagino before he left to attend law school in Missouri. Working in the State House, I knew what it was like to operate in the shadow of ambitious men who took it as their due to call the shots without a second thought. As bright and politically creative as I believed John and David both were, I had decided that it was time to chart my own course. As I said to Leighton, "I have no intention of becoming a moon to John Waihee's sun. I'm going away to school and that's that."

Leighton accepted my reasoning and did not pressure me to stay. We were both aware, of course, that John Waihee was a student representative on the admissions committee of the UH Law School. Even as a first-year law student, John was very influential in the school. In his charming way, he had shared with me that the admissions committee was eager for me to enroll there, given my experience. The prevailing wisdom was that if I wanted to continue in local politics, it would be good for me to attend law school with the other members of my activist cohort, as it would strengthen our alliances and ensure a network I could count on later on. While that may well have been true, I resolved to take my chances on admission to a mainland school.

For students in the contiguous United States, the decision to attend out-of-state schools wasn't particularly complicated, as the schools were often only a road trip away. But for me, choosing to go to a mainland school came with significant considerations, not just of distance and expense but also questions about how I would navigate a setting where, as an Asian American, I would experience myself as a minority for the first time.

Leighton had often talked to me about how much he valued his own experience of attending mainland schools and how grateful he was that his family had encouraged him to go. "People on the mainland are very different than we are in Hawaii," he had told me. "I'm not talking about intellect; it's just a different level of conversation and discussion.

"In Hawaii, we're more reticent," he went on. "Asian cultures tend to be nonconfrontational to begin with, and our public-school teachers never really encouraged us to ask questions or engage in discussion, except, of course, in debate class. On the mainland people are more outspoken. The discourse is different. I would sit in classrooms and be amazed at how confidently my fellow students would argue with the teachers, and how energetically students would raise their hands, wanting to be called on, wanting to be heard. In Hawaii, we are more hesitant to speak up, and we definitely don't want to be called on. We just want to take copious notes." With that, he winked at me, a subtle tease about the day we had met at the Young Democrats meeting, when he had watched me making copious notes myself. I laughed, because I still took copious notes—and in fact I always would, decades later filling an entire notebook during Donald Trump's impeachment trial.

I reminded Leighton that he had also told me that his time on the mainland was the loneliest period of his life. "Oh, definitely," he agreed. "I always tell people to prepare themselves for personal and social deprivation. But it's the sort of deprivation that makes you really appreciate what you have at home—plus, you learn to fend for yourself. You adapt and acclimate and you develop fortitude, especially if you find yourself in a place where you are the only one—the only person from Hawaii, the only Asian, the only person of color, in your case the only woman. It builds character. It broadens your perspective and forces you to grow up and believe in yourself in a way that isn't possible when you stay home."

Listening to Leighton, I recognized that, as independent and as self-sufficient as I considered myself to be, going away to school would present challenges I hadn't even thought about. But having never previously visited the mainland, I was excited by the prospect of new experiences. After another moment, I asked Leighton, "What about us?" I knew that whatever his answer, it wouldn't change my plans. I only wanted to gauge his commitment to whatever it was that we had been doing together for the past year. "I will wait for you," he told me, and I believed him.

I n the end, not wanting to close off a strong opportunity, I applied to the University of Hawaii Law School, along with five law programs on the mainland. My local school became the first to admit me, followed by

Leighton's alma mater, George Washington. I sent in my deposit of fifty dollars to hold a spot at GW, only to then have every other mainland law school accept me as well. When I got that most coveted of acceptance letters from Georgetown University's Law Center, I knew I would be heading to Washington, D.C., in the fall of 1975. It didn't matter that the substantial loans I took out to afford the tuition would take some fifteen years to pay off. To my mind, that was simply the price of my ticket to being taken more seriously by the men who still ran legislative and party politics in my state.

David Hagino arrived back in Oahu with his law degree the summer before I was due to leave for law school. At the time, I was just finishing up helping with a successful House district election campaign for a mutual friend of ours, Carl Takamura. When I next ran into David at a friend's home, he congratulated me on getting into Georgetown and then proceeded to unveil his newest goal—to run for the U.S. House of Representatives.

Are you insane? I thought, but I kept that to myself. "Well, good luck with that," I said instead. It was so like David to come up with such an outrageous plan, to put himself forward with supreme confidence. His political aspirations had often far outpaced anything the rest of us had yet dared to dream, but a race for Congress without any preparation was quixotic, even for him. I sincerely hoped he would succeed, though it seemed to me that he hadn't begun to set the stage or pay the sort of dues most people still believed needed to be paid before mounting such a big race. He hadn't served a day in government, yet he didn't question his ability to represent the state of Hawaii in Congress. He exhibited his usual rock-solid belief in himself, which had often helped him convince others to follow his lead.

"Of course, I don't expect you to stay back and help me with the race," he said at one point. I was taken aback that he would even contemplate such a thing. The thought of putting my own future on hold to help him in his campaign had never entered my mind.

"You're right," I responded dryly. "I'm going to law school."

As a show of support, I was at the airport along with several of David's friends to wave him off later that summer. With a fresh haircut and a sharp suit, David flew to Washington, D.C., to pitch his campaign there.

In the fall, I flew to Washington, D.C., myself, to begin classes at Georgetown. My family bid me goodbye with no trace of sentimentality. I knew my mother would miss me, but she said nothing of this, and was completely supportive. As I saw it, I was going away for three years to bolster my credentials, after which I would return home to Hawaii—Mom could count on that.

I had arranged to stay with a friend from home, Stephen Kohashi, then a Senate committee staffer, while I looked for a place to live in D.C. It was late afternoon when I landed at National Airport. Traveling to Stephen's home in a cab, I was surrounded by urban canyons of concrete and stone, with very little greenery to relieve the hard, cold feel of the city. *What a grim, cheerless place*, I remember thinking, though I would soon learn to appreciate the city's art museums and architectural charms.

Over the next few days, before classes started, I made obligatory visits to the offices of my state's congressional delegation, Senators Daniel Inouye and Spark Masayuki Matsunaga and Congresswoman Patsy Mink—it was what people from Hawaii did when they came to the nation's capital. We saw it as showing respect. I had met each member of our delegation before, back when I was a legislative chief in the State House, though of course they didn't remember me. But they welcomed me warmly, and their staff showed me around. Noting all the young aides strutting around the Capitol officiously, I resolved never to seek work as a government staffer. Only later did I laugh ruefully at the recognition that the self-important demeanor of these young staffers reflected exactly my own demeanor when I first met Leighton at the Young Democrats meeting. Little did I know that after law school I would one day return to the Capitol as a member of Congress myself.

A month later, I moved out of Stephen's place and into a two-bedroom apartment that I shared with two male law students. I lived in those cramped quarters until I found a spacious four-bedroom, $600-a-month, three-story house on Capitol Hill, where I would live with three other students from Hawaii. Once classes began, I realized that by far the most difficult adjustment I would have to make was to Georgetown's Socratic teaching method. Designed to encourage critical thinking and debate, this approach insisted that students vigorously challenge one another as well as the teacher to root out underlying assumptions and biases when making legal arguments. In a Hawaii classroom, this sort of engagement likely would have been viewed as showing off or calling attention to oneself. I wasn't about to start overcoming that early indoctrination in a law school auditorium filled with one hundred and fifty students, the vast majority of them white males who were assertively verbal and competitive. Instead, I sat quietly in my seat, took my usual copious notes, and hoped not to be called on. I needn't have worried. So many of my classmates were clamoring to be heard that few professors ever singled me out. As part of the dominant white male culture, most of my peers had never doubted their right to command attention. Not surprisingly, some studies have found that the Socratic method tends to reinforce society's existing race, class, and gender biases while creating a platform for the most privileged.

I did recognize that my unease in putting myself forward was not helpful, and it occurred to me that the public-school system back home was failing students by not encouraging them to speak out in class. While I never missed a lecture, I was concerned that my reticence would undermine me when it came to my grades. That first semester, I joined a study group, stayed on top of my readings, and participated in moot court to defend my briefs. If I felt at a disadvantage when it came to verbal arguments, I knew I was a good writer and could show my mettle on paper. I was greatly relieved when I received a grade of B-plus on my first final exam. *Okay, I can do this*, I decided. And for the next two and a half years, I did.

While I continued to struggle with the Socratic method of instruction, my first experience of being a racial minority was less daunting. I was five years older than most of my classmates, and didn't spend much time being social with them. When I wasn't studying, I was likely to be found wandering through art museums, strolling under the cherry trees along the Tidal Basin, and baking bread at home. I was never lonely. As a child on my grandparents' rice farm back in Fukushima, I had learned to be content in my own company. And because I kept mostly to myself, I had few interactions with classmates, which would have allowed me to notice how they might be perceiving me, or what notions they might have about me as an Asian American woman. I wasn't aware of being treated differently than anyone else, but the deeper truth was, I didn't really care.

I did have friends in the city, however. I socialized primarily with a handful of college friends from home. Among them were Stephen Kohashi; Bob Miller, who had left Oahu a year ahead of me to attend Georgetown Law; and his girlfriend, Stephanie Agnew, a California native who lived with Bob for the three years he was in law school and later became his wife. For fourteen years, Stephanie would also serve as my campaign treasurer, though at the time we had no idea that such a future lay in store for us.

Stephen Kohashi would eventually start dating one of my roommates, Wendy Ikezawa. The first time I introduced Stephen to her, he had commented under his breath, "She's really loud, isn't she?" Opposites attract, I suppose, because a year later Wendy announced that she and Stephen were moving in together and I would have to find a new roommate. Stephen and Wendy would go on to marry and live happily with their two beautiful children in Washington, D.C., and we would all become lifelong friends.

During my first year at Georgetown, a letter arrived from David, who by then was back in Honolulu. In his letter, he shared that he had decided to drop out of the congressional race. What followed was so unexpected and spiteful that I eventually threw the letter away, and so I am forced to reconstruct its bitter contents from memory. To paraphrase, David had written that I was nothing but a silly girl who had glommed on to him and the antiwar movement, thinking it was the cool thing to do. He said I was shallow and of little substance, a mere hanger-on. It was the nastiest letter I could have imagined coming from a person I considered a friend, and I couldn't understand why he had felt the need to say those terrible things.

Allison came to visit me in D.C. shortly after, and I showed him David's letter. Allison had applied to study law at the same time as I had, and he had also been admitted to Georgetown. He ultimately decided it would be better for us to be in different cities, and enrolled at New York University's law school instead. I knew that some part of him was intent on proving that despite his short stint at Colgate as an undergraduate, he could survive in New York. The city's thriving theater scene was also an attraction, as his love affair with acting and theater people continued. Still, he and I remained friends, and with both of us now on the East Coast, we visited each other occasionally.

Allison's mouth fell open as he read David's words. "I don't blame you for being upset," he said. "This is horrible."

"But why?" I asked him. "Why would David write such things to me?"

Allison thought for a moment, his lips pursed. "Maybe he feels as if he's lost control of you," he said finally. "You've always been on hand to help execute his grand schemes before. Except this time, you're in D.C., where he wants to be, and maybe he's trying to put you back in his corner."

"By insulting me like this?" I said. "I don't think so."

I wondered if there might be some truth to Allison's remarks, however. I tried to imagine David's disappointment at his stalled congressional campaign, and the resentment he may have felt, consciously or not, that his usual cadre of supporters had not been there to help him.

The crazy thing was, I never did confront David about that letter. I should have sought him out and waved the sheets of paper in his face, demanding, "What the *hell*, David?" Certainly, it is what I would do today. But in the midseventies I was still under the sway of a cultural triple whammy—I was a woman; I was of Japanese descent; and I had been raised in the nonconfrontational atmosphere of the Islands I called home. All three aspects of my identity had taught me to sidestep conflict and to let unpleasantness simmer in the hope that it might eventually fade away. This unwillingness to engage in uncomfortable conversations, I saw later, too often led to passive-aggressive behavior in conflict-averse cultures.

What I didn't yet know was that during that first year of law school, an even greater disappointment lay in store. By December, I began hearing from friends back home that Leighton was seeing another woman. Although I had decided against confronting David about his letter, I felt infinitely more connected to Leighton—besides, he had promised to wait for me. So I dared the uncomfortable thing. I picked up the phone and asked him if the rumor was true.

"Yes," Leighton said quietly. "What you heard is true."

"Well, then, this relationship is over!" I declared and slammed down the phone.

I stood there for several moments, trying to breathe through my wrath. Then, very deliberately, I went through my room, gathering up all Leighton's letters and photographs. Dumping them into a glass bowl, I set a match to the whole pile. I watched as blue and orange flames licked and curled the letters and swept across the photographs, obliterating Leighton's mischievous eyes and playful smile. When the fire burned itself out, I stuck the bowl under a faucet and washed the ashes of our relationship down the drain.

Afterward, waves of fury and sorrow, resignation and regret took their turns with me, until at last I pulled righteous anger around myself like a protective cloak. *Leighton Oshima is dead to me*, I vowed as I slumped into a chair.

CHAPTER ELEVEN

The Quiet Fisherman

When I opened my eyes on the morning of March 24, 1978, nothing in the play of light at the open window, or the feel of the cool spring air, or the rumble of New York City traffic on the street below gave any hint that I was waking to the very worst day of my life. I was in my final year at Georgetown, with graduation just three months away. The weekend before, I had taken the train to New York City, thinking it might be fun to spend some time with Allison during our last spring break. As had long been our default, he and I had slowly drifted back together, and now we were officially dating again. Our dynamic hadn't changed much. Allison was still always eager to one-up me, and yet it had been all too easy to fall back into our relationship, which had the familiar comfort of a well-worn shoe.

That afternoon, after Allison left for a session with his study group, I met my friend Mark Borenstein for coffee and a walk through Central Park. Mark had been a staff attorney during my rotation with Georgetown's Institute for Public Interest Representation. The legal clinic provided opportunities for students to hone their lawyering skills by writing briefs and conducting research for a wide range of pro bono clients who were fighting for community, environmental, and civil rights causes. The clinic had been the main reason I had wanted to attend Georgetown. Though my attention often wandered during theoretical classroom presentations, when a real person's destiny was on the line, I was at my most painstaking, resourceful, and tireless. As my supervising fellow, Mark had worked with me on an amicus brief I wrote for the Eighth Circuit, relating to a case in which a hearing-impaired student had been denied acceptance to college and was suing to have the college accept her and provide accommodations for her disability. The Eighth Circuit ruled in our favor, and it had been exhilarating to see portions of my brief quoted in the decision the court handed down.

While putting in long days and sleepless nights on this case, Mark and I developed a warm friendship that continues to this day. He was a native New Yorker, and when we met up in the city that afternoon, he was in town visiting his parents before heading to Europe and then to a kibbutz in Israel for the summer. When he returned, he would take a job with a large Los Angeles law firm, eventually becoming a state court judge. Mark had shared with me that he wanted to bring change to people's lives through his work as a litigator, while I had told him I sought to do the same through politics. He was sure that we would both succeed, and had predicted I would one day be the governor of Hawaii. *Yeah, right*, I had chuckled inwardly. I had yet to imagine myself attaining such a high office—or any office, for that matter.

Yet as close as Mark and I had become during my clinical semester, I had never once spoken to him, or anyone else I met in Washington, about my family, and especially not about Wayne. I felt protective of my little brother, and was reluctant to share the degree to which he had struggled in life, lest others judge him without knowing him. And yet, on this day, I found myself describing to Mark how Wayne loved to spend his afternoons fishing while perched on the craggy rocks of a high cove. Wayne was so strongly in my heart that day, the image of him sitting on those rocks vivid in my mind. I even reflected to Mark that those rocks might be the only place on this earth where Wayne had truly found peace.

"But fishing off the rocks," Mark had said. "Isn't that dangerous?"

"Oh, he does it all the time." I shrugged. "He'll be fine."

At around the same time in Hawaii, my mother was dropping Wayne off at his favorite fishing spot at Lanai Lookout. She waved him goodbye and then sat watching as he strolled away, her youngest child now a handsome twenty-six-year-old man in a yellow T-shirt and jeans, his fishing pole resting easily over one shoulder. Mom felt a vague sadness rising inside her, the way it often did when she contemplated him. She sighed, turned the key in the ignition, and pulled onto the highway.

Wayne was the one who made all our hearts ache. My mother in particular had never gotten over having to leave him behind in Japan. While Wayne staying with our grandparents had been necessary, Mom hadn't realized the lifelong damage it would cause him. But his abandonment trauma wasn't the only challenge Wayne had faced. His nutrition as an infant in rural Fukushima had been so deficient that his teeth were pocked by cavities, and by the time he was twenty, he had needed a full set of dentures. Of course, Wayne had also struggled in school. He had a hard time concentrating, perhaps because he had difficulty learning to read and therefore could not follow the lessons. I can remember my mother meeting with his teachers on several occasions when he was disruptive in class. Perhaps because I had always been so attuned to my mother, I shared her crushing guilt and sorrow at how hard everything was for her youngest child. I had already decided that when she could no longer care for Wayne, I would be the one to look after him.

Most days after Mom dropped Wayne off at the lookout, she returned home to prepare dinner for the family. She would leave the covered dishes in the refrigerator for my grandmother to warm up when Wayne returned from his fishing. Roy no longer lived in the house in Hawaii Kai. He had moved into his own home with his wife, Emi, née Shimahara, who had been a classmate of his at Kaimuki High.

After she finished cooking, Mom liked to work in her garden until it was time to get dressed for her evening shift at the newspaper. She was a gifted grower of orchids and other exotic plants, and her yard was the most beautiful on our street. She had single-handedly erected a hothouse in which she raised thousands of orchids, some of which she would package and send to family and friends back in Japan for their various celebrations. Others she gifted to people on their birthdays or as a gesture of thanks. Far away on the other side of the American continent, I liked to picture Mom's absolute concentration as she tended her plants in the early afternoon, and then to imagine Wayne sitting down with Baachan and Jiichan to eat the dinner she had made for them.

On the day I met Mark for coffee in New York, my mother remembers that at around noon Hawaii time, her mood turned dark. She had just finished watering the flower beds and was inside the Sears, Roebuck aluminum toolshed that she had constructed in the backyard, returning the coiled garden hose to its hook behind the door. Suddenly, there was a loud bang, like a large rock slamming against the side of the metal shed. Startled, Mom dropped the hose and ran outside. Nothing seemed out of place. She circled the shed twice, three times, surveying the ground, but found no sign of an object that could have made the crashing noise. Feeling strangely unsettled, she hung the hose, locked the shed, and went into the house.

Minutes later, she heard a convoy of ambulances and police cruisers screaming past outside. Her uneasiness only deepened as she dressed for work. As she sometimes did before driving to the office, she stopped by Lanai Lookout to see if Wayne wanted a ride back to the house, but on this day, he wasn't there. He must have already finished his fishing and decided to walk home via a different route, she thought. As she pulled up in front of the *Advertiser*'s office, she tried to push down the bad feeling that wouldn't leave her alone. She had been at her desk for twenty minutes when a report came over the wire that an unidentified person had been swept off a rock by a surging wave while fishing, and had drowned. Mom stiffened, the hairs on the back of her neck prickling. One of her coworkers, a woman who knew that Wayne was a fisherman, knelt in front of my mother and asked her softly if her son had been out on the rocks with his fishing pole that day. Mom nodded wordlessly.

"Laura, what was he wearing?" the coworker asked gently.

"Yellow T-shirt," Mom whispered. "Jeans."

Mom's whole body turned cold as she read the truth in her coworker's eyes. This was how she learned that her youngest child, the quiet boy whose hurt places she had spent his whole lifetime trying to soothe, had come to wish her goodbye with a bang on the side of her toolshed as he passed from this world.

have often thought it strange that the first time I ever talked about Wayne during my years in law school was the day we lost him. I like to think that his spirit had come to say goodbye to me, too, insisting on my attention, my sweet younger brother more assertive in death than he had ever been in life.

Mom didn't cry at first. She was too much in shock at losing yet another child. The sheriff who came to inform her of what had happened had shared that Wayne's body had been recovered from the rough seas by two police officers, who would later be recognized for their service. It was my uncle Akira who identified Wayne in the morgue. When I imagine my family later that night, I see Mom hunched over in our living room surrounded by her parents, Roy, and Emi. A nurse by profession, Emi was a born nurturer. I can still picture her and my baachan holding Mom's thin, sturdy hands as the tears finally flowed.

For several days, Mom couldn't bring herself to tell me that our beloved boy had died. She feared the news would disrupt my studies. When she did finally call, I got on a plane at once and flew home to be with the family for my brother's funeral. After the service, which we held at the Jodo Mission temple where Baachan and Mom were members, we brought Wayne's ashes home in a brass urn. We set down the urn on our hotokesama, our family shrine inside a small armoire of dark wood. In a few days, Wayne's remains would be moved to a niche at the Jodo Mission, where our sister Yuriko's ashes had already been placed. In the meantime, Baachan put containers of rice and water beside Wayne's ashes and refreshed the bowls each night. Mom added a framed photograph of my brother, handsome in a gray suit and tie, his eyes as gentle as they had been in life.

Wayne's short life and premature death once again filled my thoughts when, in the spring of 2018, it became the official policy of the Trump administration to separate the children of asylum seekers at our southern border from their desperate parents. The cruel and appalling so-called zero-tolerance policy was meant to deter immigration to the United States by people from countries that the president deemed undesirable. Under Trump and his then attorney general, Jeff Sessions, those seeking refuge from poverty, gang warfare, domestic violence, and other dangers in Central American nations—many of which had been destabilized by the policies of our own government—would now be incarcerated as lawbreakers, despite the fact that they were acting in accordance with international law. This meant that their children, even breastfeeding babies, would be forcibly removed from parental custody and detained separately.

By May, more than two thousand children were reported as having been separated from their parents. Other estimates ran much higher. Some of the children had been herded onto planes and flown to foster care agencies several states away. Many more were being held in the chain-link-partitioned areas inside abandoned strip malls and big-box store warehouses, while still others were transported to hastily erected tent cities on military compounds. In June, Associated Press reporters discovered three "tender-age internment camps" at which infants and young children ripped from their parents were being held. Medical and legal advocates who had visited the camps described youngsters under the age of five sobbing hysterically or staring vacantly. The plight of those babies tore the hearts of millions of Americans, including some of our most seasoned journalists, with Rachel Maddow breaking down in tears while trying to report on the South Texas camps where the youngest detainees had been warehoused.

Watching the news reports, my own heart was in shreds. My younger brother had sustained lasting psychological damage from being separated from our mother—and he had been left with loving family members, not locked in a cage without adequate nourishment or access to basic hygiene products, as so many children now were. Every day, new images showed empty-eyed children staring out from what looked like large dog kennels or curled under silver foil blankets on bare floors. Perhaps most wrenching of all was the sight of seven- and eight-year-old girls trying to comfort wailing babies in sodden diapers that had not been changed for days.

One detail in particular brought home to me the true horror of these detention camps, and it was the fact that border officials routinely removed the laces from children's shoes before taking them from their parents. The only explanation was that the agents were aware that the children's distress would be so extreme that they needed to remove any means of self-harm.

Meanwhile, Trump defended his racist immigration policies by referring to the migrants as "an infestation" and saying, "These aren't people. They're animals." In the Senate, Democrats proposed one bill after another to end the brutality. But as the minority party in the Senate, we could not force Majority Leader Mitch McConnell to bring our legislation to the floor. Gone were the days when both sides of the aisle could work together to pass legislation for the greater good of our nation. With Trump in the White House, that door had been slammed shut. But this was no time to wring our hands and moan about Republicans' indifference to human suffering. Families were being destroyed before our eyes, and so we did the next best thing—shone a ferocious light on what was happening at the border so that no one in America would be left in any doubt about the atrocities being committed in our name. We held public hearings at which experts testified about the conditions in detainment camps and the psychological damage being done to the migrant children. We also met with immigration advocates, spoke out at rallies, and held press conferences, all to pressure the White House to end the policy.

Across the nation, demonstrators mounted their own resistance, thronging the streets to protest the family separations. Through it all, I continued to reflect on the ways in which my own brother's temporary separation from his family had irrevocably marked him. Finally, on June 20, 2018, in a Senate floor speech calling for Trump to revoke his zero-tolerance executive order,

I decided to speak about Wayne. As a public servant, I had seldom gone to this raw place, never wanting to seem to use my brother's pain to score a political advantage. But after many conversations with my staff, I had come to believe that, as the only immigrant then serving in the Senate, it was my responsibility to offer a firsthand perspective on an experience that none of my colleagues had likely shared.

"The president appears to take pleasure in the chaos he sows," I told my Senate colleagues. "But this chaos causes real damage to real people. These misguided, shoot-from-the-hip decisions of his have already caused significant harm to thousands of children who will face a lifetime of trauma after being separated from their parents." And then, haltingly, I told Wayne's story.

"My mother always had deep sorrow about having to leave her baby behind," I said, my voice quavering with emotion. "What's happening to these children feels personal to me. . . . These children have already been traumatized, yet the president's executive order does not prioritize reuniting these children with their parents. . . . I will continue to fight against this president's reprehensible actions that dehumanize immigrants, tear families apart, and undermine our country's moral leadership."

A day later, bowing to national outrage in the wake of the revelations of the "tender age" camps, Trump signed an executive order reversing his family separation order, but it was mostly for show, because the ink was barely dry before he was doubling down on his policy of criminalizing migrants at the southern border. In the weeks following, the true scale of the administration's inhumanity would become even clearer. Though judges had ruled that separated children be immediately reunited with their parents, border officials had maintained no system of tracking the children. Hundreds of parents had been deported back to their home countries while their children remained lost in the detention system, ensuring that a heartbreakingly high number of the migrant families would remain broken forever. Even in cases of children who were eventually returned to their parents, irreparable physical and psychological damage had already been done.

The hard truth was, despite Trump's claim to have ended the child separation policy, children were being detained away from their families on an even more massive scale throughout the following year, with the AP reporting that a record 69,550 migrant children had been held in custody during 2019. I would witness for myself the ongoing misery on three different visits to detention centers. Even on these carefully staged tours, the migrants stared at our Senate delegation with hollow eyes. At a desert encampment of tents on a military base in Tornillo, Texas, I witnessed children in gray regulation sweat suits being marched single file from one activity to another, and was reminded of nothing so much as the internment camps that held Japanese American families during the Second World War. Yet even in that painful chapter of our nation's history, children had been allowed to remain with their parents.

Dr. Jack Shonkoff, director of Harvard University's Center on the Developing Child, would provide the scientific underpinning for the trauma of separated children when he testified before Congress in February 2019, in connection with our goal of setting clear guidelines for the care of the detained children and establishing a protocol for their release either to relatives or to foster care. "Early experiences are literally built into our brains and bodies," he explained. "Stable and responsive relationships promote healthy brain architecture. If these relationships are disrupted, young children are hit by the double whammy of a brain that is deprived of the positive stimulation it needs, and assaulted by a stress response that disrupts its developing circuitry."

As a result, he continued, the child may become withdrawn and socially reticent, and his or her foundation for learning, feelings of security, and health may be irreversibly compromised. It was a lesson my own family had learned in the hardest way possible—that a secure parental bond during the critical years of a child's life can stave off the damaging effects of poverty and other deprivations, while the toxic stress that children experience at being separated from their parents can permanently rewire the brain at a critical moment in its development.

My brother Wayne never did recover from being separated from his mother and siblings. On the day that he was swept out to sea, more than two decades had passed since we were all reunited in Honolulu. His happiness at seeing us had burned like the sun, and yet he never again trusted that he would not wake up one day and find us gone. His emotional health remained fragile, his schooling painful, and his life mostly solitary, save for his connection to us. And this was a boy who had been left in a loving home, who became a man on whom my mother lavished unconditional care. Wayne had received more restorative attention in his twenty-six years than the thousands of migrant children still separated from their families might ever again know.

On the morning I was to return to Washington, D.C., for my final weeks of law school, I stood in front of our family's hotokesama, staring at my brother's picture. I felt a profound sadness at how difficult life had been for him, and yet I was grateful, too, that he had found a reprieve through his love of fishing. Though I hadn't fully understood it before, Wayne had been a part of every decision about my future that I had made up to then. He was the one I had most wanted to protect, this quiet, wounded boy who had never for a single day of his abbreviated life felt adequate to the rigors of this world. I often wonder now about the karmic reverberations, because just as our family had traumatized Wayne by our leaving, the loss of him to a churning sea had broken us all.

Part Three

A VOICE FOR ALL

Let everything happen to you: beauty
and terror.

Just keep going. No feeling is final.

—*Rainer Maria Rilke,*
"GO TO THE LIMITS OF YOUR LONGING"

CHAPTER TWELVE

Stew and Rice

As I poured myself into finishing up the last few weeks of law school, everything felt at a strange remove, as if I were looking out at the world through a pane of glass. My body was in the room with everyone, but all sound and sensation was muted. I couldn't get past the dislocating fact that I would never again see my brother.

After my last final exam, I arranged to have the school mail my law degree home to Hawaii, then I packed up my belongings, said goodbye to my classmates, and took the train to New York to help Allison finish a paper for one of his nonlaw classes. Predictably, when he had called to say he was struggling to get all his final projects done, I had rolled up my sleeves to help him. A week later we flew home to Honolulu, where I had already secured a position in the antitrust division of the state attorney general's office.

That summer, I worked during the day and spent most evenings studying with Allison for the bar. Staying busy helped me to manage my still-fresh grief at losing Wayne, though holding down a full-time job while preparing for the bar exam was challenging. Thankfully, both Allison and I passed on the first go. Our swearing-in celebration was documented in a photo of the two of us with lei piled high around our necks, beaming on the steps of the State Capitol as my mother and grandparents looked on proudly.

Afterward, Allison took a job with a corporate law firm, while I continued my antitrust work, counseling business owners on how to avoid illegal practices such as price fixing, and filing lawsuits against corporate entities that had violated laws intended to protect the rights of consumers. I was also eager to get back into the political mix, but having been away in Washington, D.C., until recently, I had not run to become a delegate in the 1978 Constitutional Convention, as so many of my friends who had already graduated from law school had done. Delegates to ConCon proposed amendments to the state constitution that, if taken up, would be put on a ballot for voters to approve or reject. At that year's ConCon, which had convened in July and would last through the fall, John Waihee, as one of the delegates, would emerge as a rising political star, a young gun who had forged all the right connections to help him become the state's first Native Hawaiian governor just eight years later.

At ConCon, John would be centrally involved in developing proposals to secure bargaining rights for state and county workers, as well as the creation of an Office of Hawaiian Affairs (OHA), to protect the rights of indigenous people and redress injustices long suffered by Native Hawaiians. Most significantly, the constitutional amendments that came out of the 1978 ConCon would codify the liberal values of Hawaii's Democratic Party and help to ensure a politically progressive future for the state.

Though I wasn't a delegate to the convention, I slowly began to reestab-

lish contact with some of my former activist circle. I even resumed my friendship with David, neither of us ever mentioning the nasty letter he had sent
me in my first year at Georgetown. I had no intention of mending fences
with Leighton Oshima, however. My old flame had recently married, and
was now head of the attorney general's litigation section, which meant that
he and I worked for the same boss. But our offices were in different buildings,
so I seldom ran into him. If I did happen to encounter him in the lobby of the
State Capitol, or riding in an elevator, or occasionally in a meeting, I would
look through him with such iciness that, as Leighton himself would tell me
many years later, he sorely wished he could disappear.

There was the time, for example, when I was walking with John Waihee
at a Democratic State Convention, the two of us talking about David Hagino's bid to unseat the old guard party chair. John and I were lieutenants in
this effort, and we were intently strategizing when we turned a corner and
bumped into Leighton. He and John greeted each other, and then we continued on our way. Once we were out of Leighton's earshot, John chuckled and
said, "I have to say, Mazie, if looks could kill, that guy would be *dead*." I was
so done with Leighton that I didn't even crack a smile.

After returning from the mainland, I had moved back in with my mother
and my grandparents. I knew it would help Mom to have me there. She
was still numb from losing Wayne, and my grandfather's health was failing.
Never much of a talker, Jiichan had become a pale ghost of himself, sitting in
front of the television for hours on end, his clouded eyes staring without
comprehension, his hearing almost gone. To complicate matters, Baachan
had recently declared that she was done being his helpmate. After that, it was
as if Jiichan had ceased to exist for her.

My grandparents' marriage had never been particularly warm; it had seemed transactional at best, an agreement that my grandmother had committed her life to honoring—until now. Growing up, I was aware of the educational gulf between Tari and Hiroshi Sato, and of my grandmother's unspoken wish for a partner who was her intellectual equal. I had seen how Jiichan's slowness, gullibility, and lack of curiosity annoyed Baachan, and it had made me sad for them both. Later, I came to believe that this dynamic had disposed me to highly value, and perhaps overvalue, people of high intellect. Now, Baachan literally washed her hands of any further responsibility toward the simple but quietly faithful man she had married. From then on, the care of Jiichan would fall to his daughter. Mom carried on with her usual fortitude, but I could tell that my grandfather's gradual decline weighed heavily on her.

After a year, I began to think about getting back into public service, which would require me to move out on my own. This was not an easy choice for me. I worried about hurting my mother, though I knew she would never say as much. And yet I also knew that Mom wanted nothing more than for me to live as I chose, and so when my friend Carl Takamura stopped by to tell me he would not run for reelection from the two-member 12th House District at the end of his term, I was intrigued. I knew the district well; it was the same one David had run for back in 1970 in his first failed campaign, and of course I had also supported Carl back when he first ran for the seat he was now planning to vacate.

Standing in my living room, Carl encouraged me to consider running to replace him, noting that he was giving me a year's head start to gear up my campaign. "You've helped so many people to run for office," he told me seriously. "Don't you think it's time you ran yourself?" I decided that it was.

Running for office required that I live in the district, however, and I wanted to reside there for at least a year in order to reestablish myself in the community. The 12th District was an area of small businesses, where many people worked in minimum-wage jobs and lived in one-bedroom rental walk-ups and small middle-class homes. David Hagino was already serving as the other representative from that district, and he joined Carl in encouraging me to run for the soon-to-be available seat. As always, David was brimming with policy ideas and anticipated that his former campaign manager would be the perfect person to help him execute them. Our friend Bob Miller, who now worked with me in the antitrust division of the attorney general's office, wasn't so sure about this plan. He reminded me that I was only two years out of law school, and tried to convince me that I should spend more time practicing law before launching a State House campaign. But I knew that in politics timing was important. I was definitely eager to help support the 12th District's residents, who struggled with poor schools and low wages, and I was optimistic about collaborating with David again. We had worked together well on his first race in 1970, and I believed that, ten years later, we could be a strong team once more.

First, I needed to find a campaign manager for myself, someone to organize events, coordinate volunteers, oversee canvassing routes, and everything in between. I asked Allison to take on that role. It would not be his first time at the helm of a political campaign, as he had run Anson Chong's successful State Senate race in 1974. Allison's initial response was no surprise.

"You know, Mazie," he said, "I could run for a district seat, too, if I wasn't always so busy supporting you."

"Why don't you run?" I asked him sincerely. "I would certainly support you."

"Maybe next time," he told me. "First, let's get you elected."

Understanding that his tendency to measure his accomplishments against mine was rooted in his own insecurity, I let his initial comment go.

Next, I sat Mom and Baachan down and let them know that I would need to move out as I had decided to run for office. I explained to Mom that I wanted to be elected from a district with more pressing concerns than those faced by our planned housing development of Hawaii Kai, where perhaps the worst problem at that time was snarled traffic. My leaving home for any other reason so soon after Wayne's death would have caused Mom pain, but my desire to make a difference through politics she understood. By the time I rented a small walk-up apartment in the 12th District, much like the ones my prospective constituents lived in, Mom and Baachan had already pledged to help with the campaign, as indeed they had helped with every campaign I had ever worked on. I accepted their support gratefully, though I explained that their involvement in this race was likely to be far greater now that I was the candidate, and not simply a volunteer.

Back then, and still today, grassroots political races in Hawaii revolved around fundraising gatherings in school cafeterias, for which volunteers cooked huge pots of beef stew and rice, and other local foods. Everyone who ponied up twenty-five dollars to hear from the candidate received a hot meal, bumper stickers, and if the campaign could afford it, T-shirts with the contender's name. Given my shoestring budget, Mom and Baachan spent many days with my volunteers and me in their Hawaii Kai garage, silk-screening my name onto hundreds of white T-shirts, bumper stickers, and signs. To honor my grandmother, we also printed her Mon, her Japanese family crest, on all my campaign materials, including my brochures.

Despite having managed and volunteered in so many previous political races, I found being the candidate to be a new and somewhat disorienting experience. Once, standing on a woman's doorstep, I completely forgot what office I was running for. For several uncomfortable moments my mind was a complete blank as I tried to gather myself. The pace was unrelenting, requiring many exhausting hours of going from house to house, knocking on doors, introducing myself, and asking for votes. In the days before smartphones and tablets, I carried index cards printed with the names and addresses of registered Democratic and Independent voters. I had many shoeboxes of these cards, sorted by streets. As I met with voters at their homes, I would take careful notes on our conversations, even jotting down what TV programs they had been watching when I knocked on their door and the names and descriptions of the dogs in their yard so I'd have the information handy the next time. I canvassed my district so many times that I came to know the stories of many of my constituents and their families.

Aside from fundraisers and canvassing, the other necessary ingredient in Hawaii's grassroots political campaigns was roadside sign holding. The candidate and volunteers would stand with our signs in strategic places and wave to drivers as they passed by. Voters expected us to hold up signs during the early morning and late afternoon rush hours, even in baking heat and driving rain. If we failed to reach out to constituents in this way, people assumed we didn't really care about getting their vote.

A signature look of mine while sign holding was my haku lei, a wreath of flowers worn on the head. When Mom realized I would need fresh haku lei regularly, she sought lessons from one of the Islands' premier haku lei makers. Soon, she was creating all the beautiful floral headdresses I wore while campaigning, and even began to grow the flowers she used for them herself. During the many hours I spent sign holding, I always felt her with me, her love infused into the circlet of flowers I wore on my head.

It took time for a reserved person like me to become comfortable with the close contact that grassroots campaigns required of us. I was much happier outside of the spotlight, but my desire to represent people who weren't in a position to advocate for their own interests pushed me forward. Fortunately, constituents sensed my sincere wish to bring their concerns into the legislative

chamber. They also appreciated the small businesses and local families I featured in my brochures, as well as the photos of my mother and grandparents.
In truth, so much of the success of my race depended on the emotional support I received from Mom and Baachan. They were all in, two generations of
devoted Japanese women with lei around their necks, supporting an immigrant daughter's dream.

The efforts of my family, as well as volunteers like Allison and other
friends and supporters, would carry me to victory in the 12th District in
1980. David was enthusiastic about having a partner in the House who could
help him turn his big ideas into reality. I didn't mind his presumption. I had
always respected David's creativity and commitment as a public servant, so
it didn't matter to me whether a bill or policy agenda had originated with him
or with me. While I was well aware that David considered me his protégée, I
also knew that I had been elected to office just as he had been, which made
me every bit his equal. And having served for two years as Anson Chong's
legislative chief before law school, I was no neophyte regarding House procedures.

I was sworn in the following January, becoming one of only ten women in
the fifty-one-member state legislature my first year. Though a minority in
terms of gender, as an Asian American I was in the majority. The strong
Asian American influence in Hawaii politics had begun during what was col-
loquially known as the Democratic Revolution of 1954, when Hawaii was
still a U.S. territory. The territorial election that year had sent an unprecedented number of Democrats to the State House, breaking the decades-long
hold of the Republican Party and the Big Five haole-run corporations. The

seeds of this revolution had found fertile soil when Asian Americans like Daniel Inouye and Spark Matsunaga returned to the Islands after fighting for the United States during the Second World War. Seeking to establish themselves in postwar Hawaii, they found the business class closed to them and had turned to politics instead, joining with powerful labor unions to put their preferred candidates in office. Asians in Hawaii quickly coalesced into a dependable voting bloc for the Democratic Party, electing Japanese, Filipino, Chinese, Native Hawaiian, and mixed-race candidates in ever-increasing numbers, and eventually sending both Inouye and Matsunaga, as well as Patsy Mink, to the U.S. Congress in the 1960s.

If race played a minor role in my interactions within the State House, my gender was more of a factor. Aware of how few women there were in the House, I was determined not to allow male colleagues to dismiss me, behave flirtatiously with me, or treat me as anything less than a peer. I soon earned the nickname Ice Queen thanks to the chilly demeanor I adopted to defend against the nonsense that came my way from some of the men. The Democratic chairman of the powerful Finance Committee, for example, wanted everyone to call him Uncle Tony, but I steadfastly refused. His seat in the tiered House chamber was in the last row, a position from which he could survey everyone else. I sat several rows in front of him, and he sometimes tried to get my attention using what we referred to locally as a "love call." "Pssst, pssst," he would hiss at me from his seat at the back of the chamber. I assiduously ignored him, much as my mother had once advised that I ignore my high school newswriting adviser when she kept hassling me. Yet the chairman kept using the call. Finally, I'd had enough. I turned in my chair and fixed him with an icy stare, an expression my staff had learned to refer to as "the look."

"I don't answer to that," I said.

"What?" he said, his eyes dancing with mischief. I could see this was all a big joke to him. "Well, what do you answer to then?"

"Try Mazie," I said.

He laughed at my audacity. He was a powerful senior member of the House, after all, and I was in my first term. But he never again addressed me by anything other than my name, and we went on to forge a cordial working relationship.

Another way in which men took the women in the State House for granted was in the giving of lei to people who were being honored for their service to the community. In Hawaii, women traditionally present lei to men, and men present lei to women. Since most of the honorees were men, our male colleagues would simply leave a pile of lei on our desks with a list of honorees and expect that when these men entered the chamber, we would jump up happily and present them with the lei. But they never asked us directly. It was this presumption, and the fact that so few women were similarly honored, that made me decide I wasn't going to participate in the presentation of lei. And so the first time I saw a male colleague about to leave a lei on my desk, I told him, "I don't do that."

He looked at me with surprise. "You're supposed to give the lei to our honoree," he responded, assuming I hadn't understood the procedure.

"I don't do lei," I repeated.

He took the lei away, and he must have spread the word, because no lei was ever left on my desk with the idea that I would spring up and give it to the man being honored. Sometime later, David came over to me during a break in session, chuckling about my refusal to present lei. "Mazie, you can stop now," he said. "You're getting a reputation as a hard-ass."

I only laughed. I did not mention that our male colleagues had now started *asking* the women to present the lei for them rather than merely dropping the pile on their desks. *Point taken*, I thought.

My approach as a legislator was to focus on the issues that had inspired me to become a public servant in the first place: workers' rights, women's concerns, public education, and consumer protections. My goal was to help the most defenseless among us, and for me, these vulnerable ones had faces: the youth of Waimanalo; the residents in that rooming house on Kewalo Street; farm families in Koko Head and maids in Portlock; and children like my own brother Wayne, who might need special teachers and schools. Unfortunately, however, the men in the State House routinely voted down legislation put forth by the women, such as bills designed to protect domestic violence and sexual assault victims. Since women members were in the minority, we needed the support of the men to get such laws enacted.

Some of the other House women and I proposed a Women's Caucus to help get our bills to the floor. The men tried to dissuade us. "Why do you want to create your own caucus?" the leaders cajoled. "We should all be working together." But the bills of particular interest to women continued to routinely be held in committee, never coming to the floor for a vote. Refusing to be deterred a second time, the women legislators joined together to form our Women's Caucus, which exists to this day. Our strategy was bipartisan unity. At the start of each legislative season we would work with advocacy groups to develop a package of bills to benefit women and children, and then hold a press conference to unveil our initiatives. Not only were we a formidable group of women legislators, but also going public with our policy agenda at the outset made it harder for our male colleagues to overlook or vote against our proposals, because now they would appear to be misogynists.

Among the first bills I got passed was an amendment to the Hawaii rape law that forced the court to focus on the conduct of the attacker rather than on the response of the victim. Prior to passing the bill, defense lawyers were allowed to ask rape victims questions like "What were you wearing?" and, perhaps most pernicious of all, "Did you resist?" If rape victims could not prove they had resisted, then the court deemed that to mean consent, even in statutory cases where the victim was twelve or fourteen years old. With our amendment, defense lawyers now had to refrain from asking these kinds of questions. They were no longer allowed to revictimize the victims.

I also introduced legislation to provide resources to train prosecutors in the sensitive handling of sexual assault cases, with a goal of promoting greater understanding of the psychological trauma of the victims. Our Women's Caucus also helped to create a rape victims fund; increase childcare tax credits; pass job security provisions for employees who took unpaid family leave; and provide tax credits to employers who offered childcare. Protecting the rights of women and children and improving the chances that justice would be done in sexual and domestic assault cases would remain enduring commitments for me; thirty-seven years later, I would welcome the women-centered #MeToo movement as a long overdue drive for gender equity and fairness under the law.

Another top priority of mine was education. I introduced several bills aimed at ensuring that public schools had the resources to reach and secure all the children in their care. An important initiative that I was glad to support was Native Hawaiian language–immersion programs. The Native Hawaiian population had been decimated by diseases carried by the first Europeans to arrive, and they had continued to be disproportionately affected by new diseases brought by waves of immigrants to the Islands. Christian missionaries had also discouraged or outright banned important cultural practices such as the hula. Later, led by descendants of these same missionaries, the provisional government had banned teaching the Hawaiian language. By the late 1970s, the Native Hawaiians were on the verge of losing their language entirely, and with it a critical part of their culture. The creation of language-immersion schools to teach the Hawaiian language has gone a long way toward restoring their social traditions, centering their history, and recognizing their importance to the state.

My own experience had shown me that language was a cornerstone of cultural identity and must be actively preserved. When I'd first arrived in Hawaii, I was discouraged by my teachers from using my first language, Japanese, and had lost my ease with speaking it as a result. I hadn't thought much about this as a child, because as an immigrant, the goal was to assimilate, which meant learning to speak English and using it at virtually all times. To regain familiarity with my first language, I had enrolled in Japanese-language courses in both high school and college. But when in adulthood I traveled to Japan with my mother to visit relatives, though I could understand much of what was said, I could not respond in Japanese with any fluency. With a pang, I realized that in failing to maintain my first language as a spoken habit, I had allowed a crucial piece of my identity to be stripped away. As a state legislator, I resolved to hold the line in some small way against the same loss of identity for Native Hawaiians. As so often happened for me, it was the faces of the Waimanalo teens that came back to me as I spoke in favor of legislation that would restore Hawaii's original language to its pride of place within our Islands.

During my first term in the State House, Hawaii's nine-member reapportionment committee, a bipartisan body charged with overseeing the boundaries of congressional and legislative districts, redrew the Islands' electoral map. This redistricting occurred every ten years on completion of the U.S. Census, and was required by federal law. Though we all know partisan gerrymandering runs rampant across the country these days, local redistricting was originally intended to account for demographic shifts by creating voting areas that were roughly equal in population, that kept communities intact, that would not advantage any party or candidate, and that did not discriminate against any constituents on the basis of ethnicity or race.

The redistricting ultimately resulted in multimember districts being eliminated in favor of single-member representation. This meant that in the next election cycle—which was fast approaching—David and I would either have to campaign against each other for our district's single seat, or one of us would be forced to run for reelection from a different district, forgoing the advantages of being the incumbent candidate. That person would also have to find a new place to live, as house representatives were obliged to reside within the boundaries of the district they served. Since David and I had no desire to run against each other, we agreed to meet and decide together which one of us would stay put for the upcoming election and who would move to a new district.

Some of my colleagues in the State House took me aside and warned me not to trust David. "You know he's going to stab you in the back," one of them told me.

"No, no, he wouldn't do that," I insisted. "We're going to sit down and decide who's running from where."

"I don't know, Mazie. I think you should watch him."

It never occurred to me to doubt David's word. After all, he and I had forged a strong alliance within the state legislature and had done important work together for going on two years. As I saw it, we had built trust in each other during a friendship that dated back to our college years, and I had all but forgotten the unpleasant letter he had sent me while I was in law school. My guard was down, so it came as a shock when, a week later, one of my staff members burst into my office with the news that she had just seen David in the lieutenant governor's office, filing paperwork to run from our current House district in the next election.

For the first time in my life, I understood intimately the meaning of the expression "shaking with rage." I stormed down the hallway to David's office and marched straight in. He was on the phone, but seeing my expression, he hastily ended the call.

"Why did you do this?" I demanded, voice quivering with fury, my hands curled into fists so tight my fingernails dug into my palms. "I thought we were going to talk about this! What made you close down any discussion? People warned me you would stab me in the back and I defended you. After all the work we've done together, David, how could you betray me in this way?"

He jumped up from his chair and came around to the front of his desk to try to appease me. "Mazie, you have to understand," he implored, "my wife would have left me if I'd made her move to another district."

"And you don't think you could have come and told me that?"

I didn't bother to wait for his answer. I was through indulging him. I turned on my heel and stalked out of his office, slamming his door behind me for good measure.

I ultimately decided to run from the neighboring 20th District, where constituents struggled with low-paying jobs and the high cost of living. While David ran unopposed from our old district, cakewalking to victory, my race was hotly contested. In the end I prevailed, and would go on to serve in the Hawaii House of Representatives for twelve more years. During that time I would chair the Consumer Protection and Commerce Committee for six years, becoming known as a defender of workers and protector of consumers, earning yet another nickname—the Consumer Crusader. As a legislator, I was also able to get more than one hundred and twenty of my bills enacted into law. Some of these bills were easy to champion, such as expanding health-care coverage, but many others were highly technical and often boring, even to my colleagues. These involved such initiatives as re-forming no-fault auto insurance laws, rewriting condo rules, and overhaul-ing banking regulations, the last requiring more than one thousand pages of proposed legislation. While some of my fellow members' eyes generally glazed over at the details, if such a bill would help to make life better or easier for working people and consumers, it had my full attention and support.

Over the course of my second term, I came to appreciate that David's duplicity had had a silver lining, because I no longer felt I owed him the kind of allegiance I had offered in the past, and if we worked on anything together, now it was on an equal footing. Indeed, after my reelection, I refused to set foot in his office for a year. David continued to come to my office regularly, however. "Mazie, I have an idea," he would say, and I would look up from whatever I was doing and regard him evenly. While he might still have con-sidered himself my mentor, the scales had definitely fallen from my eyes. *Why on earth would you think I'm still willing to act as your lieutenant?* I thought. *I have my own priorities.* To make my point, I put a box on a shelf near the door, and every time David barged in with some new plan, I would point to the box. "You know what, David, just drop your ideas in there," I told him. "I'll take a look when I have time."

Even though David and I continued to work together in the State House, his betrayal had been a gift. In the end, it had freed me to pursue my own agenda—to stand fully in my purpose as a public servant and know it as my own.

CHAPTER THIRTEEN

Lost and Found

Allison and I were in his condo near Waikiki one Sunday morning when, in the midst of making himself a cup of coffee, he asked me to marry him. I was on the couch in his living room, legs pulled up under me, drafting a measure that would require auto insurers to increase their minimum coverage. I hoped to present the bill at the next convening of the state legislature. It was the middle of November 1985. I had turned thirty-eight one week before. Now, at Allison's question, my pen stopped moving and I stared at him, speechless.

"Well?" he prodded, walking toward me, sipping his coffee. Irrelevantly, or perhaps not, it occurred to me that he hadn't asked if I might want a cup of coffee, too.

"I have to think about it," I said at last.

After eighteen years together, it wasn't the answer he had been expecting.

Yet as much as I had always cared about Allison, and as protective as I felt toward him, something stopped me from giving him an immediate *yes*.

In the days that followed, as I tried to envision a future with Allison, I cast my mind back over our time as a couple. One memory stood out. In my midtwenties, I had been in a car accident—not my fault, and not a terribly serious one in that no one sustained lasting injuries, but I had received a small insurance settlement. I decided to use the money for a long-dreamed-of back-packing trip around Europe with Allison.

At that time, the Watergate scandal had been playing out in the news ever since five men broke into the Democratic National Committee headquarters during Nixon's 1972 reelection campaign. The entire country knew that the men had ties to the Nixon administration, and that the president had ordered the CIA to obstruct the FBI investigation. Several White House aides had testified that tape recordings of Nixon's Oval Office conversations existed, which would offer evidence of the president's involvement in the cover-up. But Nixon refused to turn over the tapes, going so far as to fire the special prosecutor who had demanded he do so.

Finally, on July 27, 1974, around the time Allison and I left for Europe, the Supreme Court ruled that the president could not decline to turn over the tapes. When Nixon still refused, the House Judiciary Committee voted to impeach him for obstruction of justice, abuse of power, and contempt of Congress. On August 8, 1974, before the articles of impeachment could be transmitted to the Senate for a trial, Nixon resigned. As I recount the broad outlines of the Watergate scandal here, I am struck anew by the stark similarities to events leading up to the December 2019 impeachment of President Donald Trump for abuse of power and obstruction of Congress, and by the ominously different outcome—but we'll get to that later.

Allison and I listened to Nixon's resignation speech on a five-dollar transistor radio we had bought in Germany. We could hardly believe our ears. At first, we'd thought that the European press had gotten the story wrong. Could the president we both intensely disliked actually have opted to step down voluntarily and spare the country a Senate trial? It was too good to be true. We had seen the screaming headlines that he planned to resign shortly after our arrival in Munich, and it had prompted a vigorous debate about whether we should purchase the small radio so we could follow the news on the BBC. I'd devised a budget that allowed us to spend twenty-five dollars a day in Europe. That had to include meals, train tickets, local street maps, and accommodations, so even a five-dollar radio had to be carefully considered. Allison argued that what was happening back home was history being made, and we would never have another chance to follow such a political moment in real time. In the end, I agreed. We were both longing to hear the news in English, and besides, Allison was right—Nixon's resignation was monumental.

That summer, as we backpacked through England, Spain, Portugal, Germany, and France over the course of six weeks, there were other small spats. Occasionally, as with the radio, these had to do with whether or not a particular expenditure was truly necessary, but more often we argued over what sights to see and what to do in whatever city we were in. I wanted to spend hours strolling through the Continent's great art museums, but Allison insisted such places bored him silly. For me, seeing the works of the masters in person, and not just on slides in the many art history courses I had taken in college, was magical, but he would grow impatient and begin to grumble long before I was ready to leave the museum or gallery.

This fundamental conflict in our traveling styles came to a head in Paris. I had proposed an evening tour of the Louvre, but Allison wanted no part of that plan. I asked him to indulge me, suggesting that he might find something there to enjoy. On a Parisian sidewalk high above the Seine, our discussion became heated. Allison accused me of being inconsiderate, and then, to my shock and dismay, he stomped off angrily. He knew my sense of direction was notoriously poor, yet he had left me alone to find my way back to our hotel near the Sorbonne, an area full of restaurants and cafés catering to the student crowd. Night was already falling, and I didn't even know the direction of our hotel or how many street corners I would have to turn to find it. For the next hour I tried to retrace our steps, meandering up and down unfamiliar streets and reflecting on the fact that Allison had a mean streak, and I was on the receiving end of it far too often. I found it unforgivable that on a trip for which I paid, he should desert me like that. Later, I would discover that he had been sitting in a café and had seen me wandering past several times, obviously lost, and he had not intervened.

By the time I finally made it back to our hotel, something in me had shifted, though I didn't speak of it. I remembered wondering: Why had I put up with such petty cruelties? Why was I so willing to excuse Allison's selfishness, and his tendency to put me down? Perhaps it was because, even now, I could see his vulnerabilities so clearly, his loneliness, his hunger for affirmation. I empathized, too, with his sense of being different. We were both the children of alcoholic fathers who had essentially abandoned their families, fixing deep in each of us a yearning to be of consequence. But while my own mother had given me the freedom to chart my own course and pick myself up from hard landings, Allison's mother had labored to make life as cushioned as possible for her only child, finding and renting his apartments, buying him a car, doing his laundry, even bringing him several days' worth of cooked food every weekend. Though I had never put it together before now, I suddenly saw that my father's mother back in Japan had done the same thing, pampering and spoiling her son in the wake of his own father's death when Matabe, like Allison, was still a small boy.

And there was something else: Allison's overdependence on prescription pain pills in recent years worried me, though he remained functional and brushed off my concerns. Given my own father's history of alcoholism and compulsive gambling, and my own aversion to addictive substances, this was perhaps the detail about our present relationship that troubled me most of all.

Now, as I considered Allison's proposal of marriage, I reflected that perhaps he and I had each channeled our early psychological injuries in different ways. In a sense, Allison had gone inward to guard and disguise his insecurities, and tended to fault others when things didn't go his way. In contrast, I had looked for healing in the world outside myself, taking my cue from a mother who had refused to be a victim, who took control of her life without blaming others for her circumstances. While Allison believed that people had often been unfair to him, blocking his success, I was of the mindset that you had to squarely meet life's obstacles and work toward the outcomes you wanted.

At the same time, I knew what it was like to scrabble for survival outside the umbrella of privilege. It was why I related so deeply to those who felt as marginalized as I had once been, those who had never known the security of feeling completely valued. Maybe this helped to explain why Allison and I had clung to each other—and had held on for eighteen long years. But now I had been forced by his proposal to make a clear-eyed assessment of how a marriage between us might unfold. I knew that Allison would expect me, as his wife, to make it my primary responsibility to steady him, encourage him, soothe his moods, and smooth his way. Indeed, from the start of our relationship, he had craved from me exactly the kind of coddling and self-sacrifice that his mother had given him.

"Why haven't you pushed me to greater heights?" he had once asked me.

I stared at him gape-jawed.

"Because that is not my job," I had told him.

And yet I had to admit that I had played the role of cheerleader to some degree, defending him to other people, even during those stretches when we had considered ourselves to be officially broken up. But the long history of our relationship had shown me that were I to marry Allison, I could anticipate little of the same in return. I remembered something my mother had told me when I was still a child: "Never marry someone thinking he will change. He will only get worse." I took that advice to heart now, reminding myself that getting married and having children had never been my chief objectives anyway. I was committed to my job as a state legislator and, with a grateful nod to Betty Friedan, had long ago liberated myself from the idea that I needed a husband to validate my existence.

Two weeks later, I still had not given Allison an answer. In fact, I found myself avoiding him, slow to return his calls and citing other commitments as an excuse not to spend time with him. Finally, he waited for me outside the State House one evening and offered to give me a ride home. One the way, he again broached the question of our getting married.

"You've had enough time to think about it," he said. "So, Mazie, what will it be?"

His eyes were steady on the road, but his hands gripped the steering wheel so hard that the ridges of his knuckles stood out bony and white. I knew then that he was unsure of me, and I felt some sadness because I knew very clearly what my answer would be.

"No, Allison," I said quietly. "I will not marry you."

I did not add that as much as it pained me to hurt the vulnerable boy inside him who had perhaps never gotten over his father's death—and who was always trying so desperately to build himself up, to see himself as bright and worthy—in saying no to him now, I knew I was saving my own life.

This time, there was no going back for Allison and me, and we both knew it. We had been each other's touchstones for so long that we both felt vaguely adrift in the new state of things. However, after a couple of months of not speaking, we resumed our friendship, and both began to see new people. I wasn't entirely surprised when, sometime later, Allison announced that he was moving back to New York to pursue his acting aspirations in earnest. He had a new girlfriend, an attractive young woman in her early twenties who was a part of his theater circle. She would be moving to New York, too, he told me, and they had decided to rent an apartment together. Around this time, he also legally changed the name he had always disliked, Allison, to Allen. I never could get used to calling him that, and so I compromised and called him Al, though he always remained Allison in my head. I wished him all the best, and was even at the airport on the day he left to wave him off to a brand-new chapter—for him and for me.

During this period, in addition to serving in the state legislature, I had begun working as a plaintiff's attorney for one of Hawaii's premier law firms: Shim, Tam, Kirimitsu, Kitamura & Chang. We brought suits on behalf of people who had been physically or financially harmed due to the negligence of others, winning them settlements mainly from insurance companies that provided coverage for the entities we sued. As our main goal was to support the interests of ordinary people who might otherwise not be compensated for their injuries, the firm was a perfect complement to my political work because I was still fighting for "the little guy." Ray Tam, the principal partner who had recruited me, allowed me time off from December to May, when the House was in session. He knew that I would work ferociously to catch up on my cases when the legislative calendar closed. I remember one year I had eight cases back-to-back, waiting to be tried. Somehow, I managed to settle them all.

November 3, 1987, was my fortieth birthday. The following month, I walked into my legislative office one morning and announced to my staff, "Okay, I think I'm ready to get married now."

Everyone laughed along with me, and someone observed that I would actually have to seriously date someone to make that happen.

"Well, I'm just going to put it out there," I countered, feeling oddly light-hearted.

I had recently decided I was at the point in my life where I could handle being a legislator and being a wife. I was very clear, however, that the person I chose to marry would have to be at peace with me never assuming a traditional wifely role. This meant that my partner would have to be very low maintenance, in contrast to Allison, who had always been decidedly high maintenance.

I remembered now that years before, one of my friends at the law firm, Paula Nakayama, had questioned me about my romantic history. "Mazie, you'll have to explain something to me," she said, "because this has always confounded me. Of all the people you have dated, when you weren't going out with Allison Lynde, that is"—she winked knowingly—"there's one person that I just don't understand. How could you ever have dated Leighton Oshima? Don't you know he's the enemy?"

"Beats me," I rejoined. "That was more than a decade ago. What did I know back then?"

Paula was jokingly referring to the fact that Leighton was now a defense lawyer who often represented the insurance companies on the other side of our injury cases. After leaving the attorney general's office, he had started his own firm. With several partners, offices on each of the neighbor islands, and a building they had bought in downtown Honolulu to serve as their headquarters, the practice was highly successful. Leighton was a devilishly good lawyer, too, which was why Paula was teasing me about having dated him.

I had run into Leighton only occasionally over the years, which was something of an achievement on my part given that the legal community in Hawaii was a fairly small circle. The previous year, however, he had shown up for the celebration that kicked off the opening of the new legislative session, and he had even brought me a lei. As he courteously slipped the lei around my neck, he shared that he had recently driven past me in his gold Mercedes as I stood alone on a street corner, sign holding early one morning.

"Oh, really?" I retorted. "It's a good thing I didn't see you."

I had always harbored a reverse prejudice against what I judged to be ostentatious displays of privilege, and Leighton's gold Mercedes definitely qualified.

"I didn't toot my horn and wave as I drove by because I didn't think it would be appreciated," he commented good-naturedly.

"You're right," I agreed. "I would have given you the finger."

We both shared a good laugh, and I realized that enough time had passed since our breakup that I no longer harbored open animosity toward Leighton. Perhaps it had begun to melt away the year he had donated fifty dollars to one of my early district campaigns, a more substantial amount than the ten- and twenty-dollar donations I usually received. That onetime contribution meant that every year afterward when my campaign treasurer and I went through the donor rolls, she would say, "Leighton Oshima, he didn't give last year. Should we remove his name?" For some reason, I always responded, "No, let's keep him. Maybe he'll give something this year."

One day in 1988, I received a phone call from my old friend Bob Miller, who had insisted on keeping me apprised of Leighton's doings over the years. It was Bob who had told me that Leighton had gotten married around the time I returned from law school, and that he had a daughter, Malia. More recently, Bob had shared with me the news that Leighton and his wife were getting a divorce. "Why do you keep telling me about Leighton?" I had replied testily. "As if I care." All these years later, a line from Shakespeare's *Hamlet* comes to mind: "The lady doth protest too much."

Now, Bob was calling to let me know that Leighton's divorce had just become final. "Leighton was asking me about you," he went on. "He wants to ask you out to dinner. He wanted to know if I thought you'd be open to that, but he told me not to warn you." Bob chuckled. "Of course, here I am, calling you right away, and I'm willing to bet Leighton knew I would do that. So, Mazie, what would you say if he called you?"

"I mean, seriously, Bob, why on earth would I go to dinner with him?" I said sharply, thinking that if I hadn't been Leighton's type thirteen years ago, I would be even less so now.

"Oh, I don't know," replied Bob. "Just don't be surprised if he calls you." Before hanging up, almost as an afterthought, he added, "You know, Mazie, I always remember that when you were with Leighton, you both laughed a lot."

Leighton did indeed call me the following week. By then I had had a change of heart. *Why not see him?* I thought. *He's divorced now, so there's nothing wrong with our being friends.* Besides, my other former boyfriends contributed regularly to my campaigns and maybe Leighton would, too. In the business I was in, one couldn't have too many friends, and I was nothing if not practical. And so, with no hint of the chill of the past decade, I agreed to meet him for dinner.

Over our meal, Leighton shared that since his divorce, his main priority was his relationship with his fifteen-year-old daughter, Malia, who was then a tenth grader at Punahou School, the same exclusive private school that Barack Obama had attended. Though Malia now lived with her mother, Leighton fully intended to be there for her in all the ways in which she might need her father. I thought: *Why is he telling me this? Is he trying to fend off designs he thinks I might have on him? How presumptuous.* Yet even as I framed these thoughts, I felt my guard slipping. Listening to him speaking so lovingly about his commitment to his daughter, I couldn't help but think of the

In 1923, my grandmother Tari Shinoki traveled to Hawaii as a picture bride to wed my grandfather, Hiroshi Sato, a migrant worker on the Waipahu sugar plantation there. Before boarding the ship in Japan, twenty-two-year-old Tari sat for a formal studio portrait.

Born in Hawaii on July 11, 1924, my mother was named Chie by her parents, who called her Chieko. Eight years old in this photograph, she had already adopted for herself the name Laura.

Baachan posed on the docks of Honolulu with my uncle Akira, then thirteen, and Chieko, fifteen, before sailing for Japan in 1939. My grandfather stayed behind to wrap up the sale of the bathhouse the family had operated for eleven years. In 1941, he caught the last boat back to Yokohama before bombs fell on Pearl Harbor.

My older brother Yoshikazu (Roy) and I playing outside our father's house in 1950. That year, our baby sister Yuriko would die of pneumonia, and I would tumble from the second-story loft of the farmhouse, badly bruising my right eye against the wooden stairs.

My mother and me in rural Fukushima Prefecture, circa 1949.

With my father away gambling and drinking much of the time, my paternal great grand-father (seated, with Yoshikazu on the left and my mother and me on the right) was the only in-law who treated Chieko kindly. This is the sole image Mom kept of any member of my father's family.

Uncle Akira (in uniform, with my mother, my younger brother Shigeki, Yoshikazu, and me, circa 1951) had moved back to Hawaii as a young man and served in the Korean War. When my father stole the money that Akira had given Chieko for Yoshikazu's first grade uniform, it was, for my mother, the final straw. She left the marriage soon after, and resolved to move with her children to America. Roy and I would travel with her to Hawaii in 1955, with Shigeki and our grandparents following two years later.

This photograph of Mom and Wayne, taken days before she sailed to Hawaii with Roy and me, reflects the deep sadness she felt at leaving her youngest child behind. Wayne would be forever marked by the trauma of that separation.

Soon after arriving in Hawaii in 1955, Mom (with me at eight years old) found a job as a typesetter and went back to calling herself Laura. She selected new names for my brothers and me as well—Roy, Mazie, and Wayne.

In 1957, Shigeki, whom we now called Wayne, traveled with my grandparents to join us in Hawaii. They sailed aboard the *President Cleveland*, the same ship that had brought Mom, Roy, and me to Honolulu two-and-a-half years before.

My sixth grade teacher, Mr. Oshiro, (left, in white shirt) selected me (standing second from right) to pin a new star on the school flag when Hawaii became a state in 1959. Fifty-two years later, as a U.S. House Representative, I would present my former teacher with a congressional gold medal, awarded to Japanese Americans who served with distinction in World War II.

Finally together again, our family moved from a rented room to a weathered shack on a flower farm. I refer to our three years in Koko Head as my *Grapes of Wrath* period, because we were always as dusty as the Joads. For this photo, we stood outside our living quarters, the Koko Head volcanic crater behind us.

In a photo from the early 1990s, Mom points to our old tarai, in which Baachan bathed her children during their years in Waipahu. That tarai had traveled back to Japan with the family in 1939, and was shipped back to Hawaii when our family was reunited. The galvanized steel tub is now part of an exhibit on plantation life at the Waipahu Cultural Garden Park.

In Koko Head, we all worked to contribute to the family pot, except Wayne, who was too young. Mom (holding sign) found a better-paying job as a proofreader for *The Honolulu Advertiser*. She later risked it all to walk the picket line during a strike in support of a newspaper workers union.

After we moved to Sixteenth Avenue, Roy bought and restored a 1957 Chevy, our first car. When Roy's job transferred him as a civilian contractor to Vietnam, I would drive myself to and from college in that classic car.

As a student at the University of Hawaii Manoa, I became friends with a circle of activists, with whom I marched in protest against the Vietnam War. One member of the group, David Hagino, would draft me to be campaign manager for his State House race during my senior year in 1970. Though David lost, he would win his next race in 1978 and go on to serve in the State legislature.

While working as a legislative aide in the State House after college, I was accepted to Georgetown University's law school in 1975. Allison Lynde, whom I had dated on and off since college, started at New York University's law school the same year and sometimes visited me in D.C. On one occasion, we toured the Lincoln Memorial.

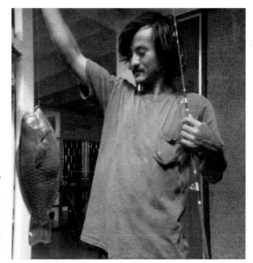

As a young man, my brother Wayne found peace fishing from the rocks of Lanai Lookout, proudly contributing his catch for the family's dinner. He was with his fishing pole at his favorite spot on March 24, 1978, when a surging wave washed him into the sea.

A few months after Wayne's death, Allison and I returned to Hawaii with our law degrees. We studied for the bar together, and after passing, we were officially admitted on the same afternoon. As beaming family members looked on, we stood draped with lei on the steps of the State Capitol.

Having volunteered in numerous campaigns, I became a candidate for public office myself in 1980. Canvassing door to door, I got to know my constituents' stories and concerns. That fall, I would be elected to represent the 12th District.

My mother (with balloons at my campaign headquarters during my 1994 race for lieutenant governor) helped with every aspect of my political races, as did my grandmother.

Leighton Oshima and I were married on August 8, 1989, with our immediate families in attendance, as well as Governor John Waihee and his wife, Lynne, pictured here with Leighton and me. A friend from my young activist days, John had graciously consented to our holding the ceremony on the grounds of the Governor's official residence.

Long-serving Hawaii Congresswoman Patsy Mink (next to me, in white blouse) offered strong encouragement during my 2002 race for governor. First elected to the U.S. House in 1964, Mink was again running for reelection. We both marched in Kailua's Fourth of July parade that year and later posed with volunteers. My friend died unexpectedly three months later, ending her trail-blazing life of public service.

In 1994, I won the race for lieutenant governor, my first statewide campaign. Given that some of my party's old boys had doubted my chances, I felt vindicated as I greeted supporters with Leighton at my side. Four years later, I would be reelected, serving a second term with Governor Ben Cayetano.

My mother pressed flowers from her garden and used them to make exquisite cards that I would send as thank yous to my supporters. Her cards—and my own—are featured throughout this book.

I have been blessed with singularly supportive mother figures: Laura Sato Hirono (left), Rosemary Kim Oshima (center), and Tari Sato, my baachan. One of my most personally meaningful acts as lieutenant governor was to legalize the names my mother and mother-in-law had used for most of their adult lives, filing the paperwork to make official their self-chosen English first names.

After Mom and Baachan moved with Leighton and me to Waialae Nui Ridge, Mom set about beautifully landscaping our yard. Until she was well into her nineties, planting and tending her garden brought her great joy.

Having occupied Patsy Mink's former House seat since 2006, I ran for and was elected to the Senate in 2012, becoming the first Asian American woman and the only immigrant currently serving in that chamber. During orientation, I traveled with Leighton to scheduled events via the Senate subway.

I was honored to serve in Congress alongside the late civil rights hero, Congressman John Lewis of Georgia. I'm pictured here with my friend and colleague during a Faith and Politics Institute congressional trip to Ireland in 2014.

Our nation suffered a crushing loss when Supreme Court Associate Justice Ruth Bader Ginsburg passed away at sundown on September 19, 2020, at the start of Rosh Hashanah. In the Jewish faith, one who dies on Rosh Hashanah is a great and righteous soul. On social media, many posted the same refrain: "May her memory be a revolution."

In the Senate, I have served on the Judiciary, Armed Services, and Energy and Natural Resources committees, among others. During confirmation hearings for Supreme Court nominee Brett Kavanaugh in 2018, I joined Senators Richard Blumenthal of Connecticut, Kamala Harris of California, and Sheldon Whitehouse of Rhode Island (not pictured) in walking out of the Judiciary Committee proceedings in protest of Republicans ramming through a vote without first allowing a thorough investigation of sexual assault allegations against the nominee.

Leighton volunteered for sign holding during my 2018 Senate reelection campaign. I won the general election by a large margin, earning a second term and joining a record number of women voted into Congress in what would become known as the Second Year of the Woman.

The Feminine Mystique

With an unprecedented one hundred and thirty-two women elected to House and Senate in 2018, the *New York Times* assigned a photo portfolio to mark history being made. Asked to bring to the shoot an artifact that had been meaningful on my journey, I chose a copy of Betty Friedan's *The Feminine Mystique*.

In homage to my mother, I now create my own cards, making the paper from scratch using bits of nature and the card stock used for my daily Senate schedule.

In 2009, my mother Laura stood on our lanai overlooking the Koolau Mountains, wearing the kimono that her grandmother made using the threads of silkworms she had raised herself. This beautiful garment has now been in our family for more than one hundred years. For me, it represents the unquenchable spirit of the women who made me who I am today.

lifelong absence of my own father, and I was reminded that, at his core, Leighton was a good man.

We began spending time together again, with Leighton often staying over at my condo, as he had been couch surfing with his younger sister, Lauren, and her husband after his divorce, as well as with friends. That Christmas, his older sister, Lynette, an education professor at the University of New Mexico, returned home on vacation, and Leighton invited me to dinner at a local restaurant with the family.

"You know your mother wasn't really fond of me," I reminded him. "I think you should at least let her know that you're bringing me."

"Of course," he said, but apparently he didn't say anything, because his mother's mouth fell open when Leighton walked into the restaurant with me at his side. It was my turn to be shocked when she rushed to greet me with a warm hug, and expressed how lovely it was that I could be there. All that night, she was so solicitous of me that you would have thought I walked on water. "Your mom sure has mellowed," I whispered to Leighton.

"She said the same about you," he said, his eyes twinkling. "Besides, you're pretty accomplished now. All your political talk, she can see it meant something. You did exactly what you said you would do."

It turned out that Leighton's mother had followed all my State House races. Now she warned him: "Don't forget Mazie is in the state legislature. You have to behave yourself and not drink in public so you don't embarrass her. And you can't be just shacking up together. Mazie has a reputation to maintain."

"What about my reputation?" Leighton asked her.

"You have none," she said.

Leighton and I chuckled over this, and everything else. He was as much fun as I remembered. I quickly realized just how much I had missed his humor, and the way he could always gentle my severity and lighten my mood. Five months later we decided to get married.

"Isn't this rather fast?" Lauren's husband asked when he heard the news.

"You don't know my brother," Lauren said, by which I think she meant that Leighton Oshima had a talent for embracing life's flow.

For the wedding, I chose the auspicious date of August 8, 1989—8889—hoping the lucky repetition of 8s would not only bestow good fortune but would also help us remember our anniversary. I even designed our wedding rings and had them engraved with the date, a convenient reminder given that neither Leighton nor I had much of a memory for such things. There was the time that he and I met some friends for dinner, and after the meal, one of them had raised her glass.

"This is for the birthday person who is with us today," she had announced.

"Oh, who is that?" I asked.

"Leighton," she said.

We all laughed, me most of all.

Leighton understood that growing up, my brothers and I had never celebrated birthdays. There just wasn't any money for gifts or parties or any of the middle-class trappings of birthdays. Now, as Leighton and I planned our wedding, making guest lists and discussing possible venues, I realized that I didn't want a showy reception to which hundreds of people would be invited.

"I've held those kinds of events many times before," I told Leighton, "and they're called fundraisers. I don't want that kind of wedding. I just want something simple in somebody's yard, with just our families there."

Thinking about it some more, it occurred to me that my old friend John Waihee, now governor of Hawaii, and his wife, Lynne, had a very nice lawn that would be perfect for our small gathering: the grounds of Washington

Place, the governor's official residence. I decided that it couldn't hurt to call and ask him if we might use his garden for an afternoon.

"John, do you have anything scheduled at your house for Tuesday, August eighth?"

"No, I don't think so," he said. "Why?"

"Well, I'd like to get married to Leighton in your backyard."

John paused, weighing the wisdom of setting such a precedent. Would other couples now flood him with requests to hold their nuptials on the grounds of Washington Place, too? He decided to take the risk because his next question was: "Can Lynne and I join you?"

"Of course," I assured him. "If you're going to be home, we would be delighted."

This is how Leighton and I came to be standing on the manicured lawn of the governor's mansion exchanging vows in a simple ceremony officiated by my friend Bambi Weil, a district court judge who had once been my colleague at the law firm. Around us were our immediate families, including Malia, and no one else save Bambi, John, and Lynne. It was just right.

"This better be good," I told Leighton as we toasted our union afterward. "I don't have time to do this again."

"I'm not worried," my husband said, smiling.

I had not formally announced that I would be getting married, but the news trickled out after a local gossip columnist got wind of the fact that a wedding had taken place in the governor's backyard, and published a small piece in the newspaper the following week. As Leighton and I embarked on our life together, I made two promises to myself: First, I would not interfere in decisions regarding his daughter, Malia, who already had two parents who were devoted to her. I wanted to avoid creating any friction for Leighton or Malia by giving unasked-for advice. Second, I would not nag my husband. Remembering my mother's wisdom about not trying to change a partner, I reasoned that if Leighton was willing to deal with the relentless demands of my political life, why would I add to that by hassling him? Besides, he was already considerate to a fault. One Sunday soon after we were married, for example, I was walking through the living room and noticed him watching his beloved football games with the sound muted.

"You know, you can turn up the sound," I said.

"Oh, I don't want to disturb you," he responded.

"It won't disturb me," I assured him.

Leighton might be selfless and self-effacing, but I was learning that he was also perceptive. As I grew to rely on his instincts and insights about people and events, I saw that he possessed more depth and nuance than I had previously realized, and that he was as canny as he was witty. When five years into our marriage I threw my hat into the ring for lieutenant governor, John Waihee commented to a reporter, "Leighton Oshima is Mazie Hirono's secret weapon." It would become one of my favorite stories, because the reporter had followed up by asking my husband whether it was true that he was my "chief political confidant and adviser."

"Oh, no," Leighton replied. "Mazie has much smarter people whom she hires to be that." His eyes were alight with mischief as he added, "But I say the last things to her at night and the first things to her in the morning."

CHAPTER FOURTEEN

Made with Aloha

After fourteen years as a state legislator, I was ready for a new challenge. I had recently lost the chairmanship of the powerful Consumer Protection and Commerce Committee after coming out on the short end of an internal leadership battle. As I assessed my next steps, I considered running for the State Senate, but that year reapportionment lines had again been redrawn, diminishing my chances of winning the Senate district seat I had in mind. Staying in the House was not an appealing option, yet I wanted to continue in politics, to be of service to people who needed someone like me to fight for them. And so, in 1994, I decided to take a risk and run for lieutenant governor. It would be my first statewide race. If successful, I would become the second-ranking executive in the Islands, and the second person to win a statewide race from a State House seat. The only person ever to achieve this unlikely leap had been John Waihee, who had been elected lieutenant governor in 1982 and governor in 1986.

Unlike many other states, Hawaii has only four statewide elected officials—the governor, the lieutenant governor, and the two U.S. senators. Another difference is that in Hawaii, gubernatorial candidates do not pick their running mates; the voters make that choice. This means that all candidates for lieutenant governor have to organize and run their own primary campaigns. After the primary, the winning candidates for governor and lieutenant governor from each party run together as a ticket.

I had never had to fundraise more than modest sums in my State House races, but now, to launch a statewide campaign, I would have to pull in at least half a million dollars. My closest supporters were concerned about the challenge, but once I definitively made up my mind to enter the big ring, they rallied to my cause. I knew I could do the job, but some people doubted my chances. I represented a small House district and my statewide name recognition was almost nil. One of the doubters was Ben Cayetano, the sitting lieutenant governor, who was mounting a run for governor. Ben had a Democratic primary opponent, Dr. John Lewin, the state's health department director. Lewin had never held elected office before, but he had the tacit if not overt support of John Waihee, who was leaving office after being term-limited out. Everyone knew that John Waihee and Ben Cayetano were not exactly close, but Ben fully intended to beat Lewin in the primary, and he wanted a lieutenant governor who he felt could help him win the general election.

When he asked me to meet him for coffee one day soon after I announced my intention to run, I had a pretty good idea of what he wanted to say. As soon as the server took our order, he told me bluntly that I should quit the race.

"You don't have the name recognition," he said. "You won't help the ticket, Mazie. We would appeal to the same base. Trust me on this."

Ben himself had run for lieutenant governor from a State Senate seat, a position with a higher profile and a much larger voter base than that of a State House seat. Of Filipino descent, he had grown up in the blue-collar neighborhood of Kalihi and had pitched himself to voters as a street kid with a hard-scrabble story who had clawed his way up in politics. As a state legislator, he had been famously combative and disdainful of the status quo, and he was known to appreciate people who didn't hesitate to tussle with him. Now, as he gave his unsolicited opinion on my lieutenant governor race, I was more than willing to wrangle. For one thing, I thought Ben was wrong in his assessment of our chances if he and I won our respective primaries and became the Democratic ticket. I would actually strengthen his ticket in the general election, as I could draw in the largest Democratic voting bloc in the Islands, the Japanese.

"I hear what you're saying, Ben, but frankly it's all bullshit," I told him. "I've seen the same polling you have. I know my name recognition right now is low. But making sure people know my name is the whole point of a campaign. By the time we get to the primary, people will know who I am."

I would soon learn that Ben's lack of confidence in my candidacy was shared by David Hagino. At the time, David was serving what would turn out to be his final term in the State House, after which he would leave legislative politics altogether and practice law full-time. In the years since we had parted ways over his 12th District reelection betrayal, our relationship had become more distant, so I found it curious when he stopped by my office wanting to talk to me about the race.

"I think you're out of your depth," he told me with conviction. "You're not going to get elected."

"Why would you say that?" I asked him.

With friends like you, who needs enemies? I thought.

"Only one other person has ever gone from being a House rep to winning a statewide race, and that's John Waihee," David said. "And if you remember, he planned everything out. He was front and center at the 1978 ConCon, and he made all the right political connections. Everybody knew him. His ground game was flawless. You haven't laid any of that groundwork. Nobody knows who you are outside your district. How do you expect to win?"

"Well, first of all, that's my problem, not yours," I replied coolly. "And second, I don't need you to come in here giving me advice I didn't ask for."

After David left my office that afternoon, I sat marveling at how often in politics women are told by men that it's not their time, that they're not ready, and that they should content themselves with waiting in the wings to be chosen. Too often, women themselves buy into this fiction. Research has shown that we have to be asked seven times before we will consider running for office, while men need to be asked only once. Indeed, many men don't even need to be asked; they come up with the idea that they are perfect for a particular political office all by their lonesome. I remembered how the summer before I left for law school in 1975, David had announced his intention to run for Congress, despite never having held elected office. Having no record to speak of did not seem to hinder men the way it did women. But Ben's and David's objections had only strengthened my resolve. If I waited around for men of my party to choose me, I was fairly sure it would never happen. Besides, I was perfectly capable of choosing myself. So what if the men believed I didn't have the mettle to compete in the big arena? Their opinions did not factor into my decision at all.

I hadn't yet selected a campaign manager, but now I saw that I would need someone I could trust to be unequivocally on my side, and who would help me push back against all the doubters. When Allison called me from New York soon after, confiding that his efforts to break into the theater world had met with little success, I asked if he would consider returning home to head up my campaign. He and I had partnered on my very first district race back in 1980, and I was counting on bottling that magic again—though this time, it would have to be on a much larger scale. I exhaled when Allison agreed.

But as relieved as I was to have someone I knew so well leading the charge, I was soon forced to admit that placing him in such a pivotal role had been a mistake. My senior advisers, including former Hawaii Supreme Court justice Ed Nakamura and Irwin Tanaka, another prominent political figure, balked at what they viewed as Allison's haughty, know-it-all demeanor.

One day, a few months into the campaign, they put it to me bluntly: "Either he goes or we go." This was serious, as Ed and Irwin had already recruited a number of influential people to support my campaign on the neighbor islands, including former Kauai mayor Eduardo Malapit, the first Filipino American mayor of any U.S. municipality. Ed's and Irwin's departures would severely undermine my campaign—which meant Allison had to go. He accepted my decision graciously, and even pledged to continue supporting me from the sidelines.

After Allison stepped aside, Irwin Tanaka took over as my campaign manager. I also relied more on Bob Toyofuku, who had long been a part of my kitchen table cabinet, my informal advisory team. Bob and I had met when I was still with the attorney general's office, and had gotten to know each other well starting with my first term in the legislature, when he was working as a lobbyist for the state trial lawyers' association and other groups. He had testified many times before the Consumer Protection and Commerce Committee while I was chair. I had also worked with Bob on several pieces of legislation, including fighting back against so-called tort reform efforts that would prevent injured people from being compensated for their injuries by the parties responsible.

For the lieutenant governor's race, it was Bob who came up with my campaign slogan. When I had first contemplated running, he had visited Leighton and me at our condo to help us strategize. At a certain point in our conversation, I found myself sharing how my mother had brought Roy and me to Hawaii with no idea how she would make a life for us. "She worked so hard at low-wage jobs," I told Bob, "long hours every day, and yet it was years before she could put together a living wage. We worried all the time that she'd get sick; my stomach was always in knots over it, because we couldn't afford even the most basic health care. And she had no way to plead her case with the people who could have made things better for her. My mother had no voice at all when she came to this country. That's why I want to serve—to be a voice for people like her."

Bob leaned forward in his chair, his face suddenly alight. He lifted both hands above his head as if he were standing beside a freeway holding an imaginary sign. "That's your campaign slogan!" he exclaimed. "Mazie Hirono: A Voice for All."

Throughout the months of the race, my mother and mother-in-law came to my headquarters daily to supervise volunteers in the making of campaign mementos. I can still see that line of patient and steadfast workers, most of them senior citizens, sitting at a long table, creating bookmarks with the most intricate pressed-flower designs. Laura Sato Hirono and Rosemary Kim Oshima, both of whom I now called Mom, would pass out the card stock preprinted with my name and image, and provide the craft materials—dried petals, leaves, paper cutouts, glue sticks, and a design template. They would go from table to table, guiding the makers and helping to assure quality. I would sign each card when it was done, after which my mother would run it through her laminating machine, which she had brought from home, and set the card aside to be handed out to my supporters.

Over time, more and more people joined us in making the bookmarks, and they became treasured keepsakes. The bookmark-making sessions also captured the essence of my campaign: they brought people together in an endeavor in which the contribution of each individual mattered, in a space that was filled with the Hawaiian spirit of ohana, the welcoming sense of being part of a family.

I had also formed a volunteer group of women tasked with raising small donations of less than one hundred dollars. We decided on the name Mazie's First, since they were the first organized group of women in Hawaii ever to fundraise for a woman candidate. Their efforts eventually helped me qualify for close to one hundred thousand dollars in state matching funds for my race. Although I, too, had run against a primary opponent, a fellow woman legislator, I felt vindicated when I ended up with fifteen thousand more votes in my September primary race than Ben Cayetano did in his. That November, our joint Democratic gubernatorial ticket would go on to win the general election handily.

I wish I could say that my victory in the lieutenant governor's race put an end to the men in my party chronically dismissing my chances. It did not. In fact, one of my friends later confided that she had heard some of the old boys saying, "Well, if Mazie can win, then anybody can." I remember thinking: *How easy it must seem from the cheap seats, when you haven't actually put in the work.*

In Hawaii, the lieutenant governor's responsibilities are not spelled out by statute, which meant my work was designated by the governor or through my own initiative. Having seen how fractious the working relationship between John Waihee and Ben Cayetano had been during their tenure as chief and second executives of the state, I made an early decision to be as supportive of the governor as I could, and to present a united front by not openly disagreeing with him. This wasn't always easy: Ben's reputation for being difficult to work with carried over to his term as governor. As a result, several public-sector organizations, including labor unions, would try to go around Ben by coming to me for help. The governor was often unaware of these arrangements, as the organizations devised ways to make him think our working together had been his idea. For example, unbeknownst to Ben, I ended up becoming very involved in his civil service reform initiative in order to protect the rights of workers.

As lieutenant governor, I also oversaw the creation of Hawaii's Pre-Plus Program, which aimed to build preschool classrooms on elementary-school campuses. I knew the foundational importance of quality early childhood education; I had read all the studies showing that it made students less likely to ever become involved in the criminal justice system, less likely to grow up in poverty, and less likely to need remedial help over the course of their academic career. What most people never saw as I advocated for these programs was my quiet regret that this sort of early intervention had not been available for my own brother Wayne.

Another major initiative was to significantly overhaul our state's workers' compensation laws. Two years into my first term, I proposed a brand-new insurance company, one that would be collectively owned by small-business owners who were having difficulty getting and affording this kind of coverage for their employees through their regular insurance carriers. Given that the law required all employers to obtain workers' comp insurance, my idea was to create a mutual insurance company that would make it more cost effective for small businesses.

At first, banks hesitated to underwrite my idea of an employer-owned insurance company. Not having any experience with this kind of carrier, they were unwilling to take the risk of providing funding. This did not deter me, though Ben seemed to think it should. Not only was he unsupportive of the initiative, he totally dismissed the idea. "Mazie, I don't know why you keep pushing this," he told me. "It's never going to work." I wondered when he would learn not to underestimate me.

Before proposing the new company, I had flown to Maine to consult with then-governor Angus King, who I had learned had successfully implemented a similar program in his state. Running as an Independent, King would later be voted into the U.S. Senate in the same year as me. At our orientation, he asked me: "Mazie, do you remember when you came to Maine to see me about workers' comp?"

"How could I forget?" I replied. "You're the only governor I ever met who rode a Harley-Davidson."

Back in Hawaii after that information-gathering visit to Maine, I made the rounds within our business community and labor unions, presenting them with facts and figures to illustrate how this new kind of insurance company could work to their benefit. The Hawaii Employers' Mutual Insurance Company, or HEMIC, was created by the legislature later that year, and issued its first policy in 1997. It is now the largest workers' compensation insurer in the state, serving some seventy-five thousand workers. I consider HEMIC to be a signature achievement of my tenure as lieutenant governor. I was so proud of the program's success that when Leighton and I adopted a cat months after its launch, we named him Hemic and called him Hemi for short.

We brought Hemi to our new home on Waialae Nui Ridge in the hills above Diamond Head, where we now lived with my mother and grandmother. My grandfather had passed away seven years before, on Valentine's Day 1989, leaving Mom and Baachan alone in the house that had once held the six of us. Given the pressing nature of my work, my visits to Hawaii Kai had become less frequent, and I knew Mom was lonely. The solution, I decided, would be to replicate my experience growing up, when the three generations of my family had all lived under one roof. Taking nothing for granted, I asked Mom if she and Baachan would be willing to come and live with Leighton and me. "Yes," she replied simply, and without hesitation.

In my current position, I was no longer tied to living in any particular district, so Leighton and I went looking for a new home that would be large enough for all of us. We zeroed in on the area around Diamond Head. We had discovered the neighborhood years before, back when we were in our twenties and used to drive up into the hills, exploring. The houses were attractive but not extravagant, more like an upper-middle-class developer's standard build, with three or four design choices. But the views—oh, they were spectacular. I remember the first time we drove up there, I had been awestruck by this rarefied enclave, swept by fresh hillside breezes that made the area at least five degrees cooler than the lowlands. *Who gets to* live *up here?* I wondered.

Fast-forward twenty years. Leighton and I had looked at several homes in the area before we saw the one that would be ours. All the houses we had toured were beautiful, and yet none was quite right. And then our realtor took us to a split-level white house with massive, custom, bronze double doors depicting the ornate trunk of a willow tree and a stylized fan of leaves. I knew at once that this house had possibilities. The previous owners had installed a small plaque on the exterior wall on which appeared the words "The House of the Setting Sun" in Swahili. The whole house was angled toward the setting sun, and had a distinct Eastern flair. Leighton and I agreed that the energy of the place felt right, but it was those bronze double doors that caught my eye. They were one-of-a-kind works of art, and a lovely entry to the living area.

Leighton, meanwhile, was attracted by the panorama of the Koolau mountain range from the lanai at the back of the house. It reminded him of the mountains that had been the setting for one of his favorite World War II movies. "*Objective, Burma!*" he exclaimed happily as soon as he saw the view. As a sweet bonus, the house had front, back, and side yards that Mom could plant and cultivate to her heart's content, with the mountains as a majestic backdrop. Japanese people refer to this kind of relationship between a planned garden and the landscape beyond it as shakkei, meaning "borrowed scenery." I could easily imagine Mom strolling among the flowers and plants she would bring to our yard, looking up at that view and feeling at peace.

The next weekend, Leighton and I brought my mother and grandmother to see the place. To my surprise, Mom had a problem. Leighton and I were in the midst of negotiating with the owners when she called me and said, "You can't buy that house. The driveway is too steep. I won't be able to reverse down to the street."

My first thought was: *This is crazy.* I didn't say that, of course. I knew that Mom never raised an objection unless something was really bothering her. And so, instead of arguing, I tried to address her concerns. I understood that her issue with the driveway arose from her need to be independent, which required that she be able to drive herself wherever she wanted to go. It was a freedom she was understandably loath to relinquish, especially given that she hadn't earned her license or been able to afford her own car until she was well into her forties.

"Here's what we'll do," I said, after reflecting on my mother's dilemma for a few moments. "Every time you come home, Leighton or I will turn the car around for you, so it's always facing the street. That way you never have to worry about reversing down a steep incline."

"Okay," my mother said. "That should work."

The very next day, Mom listed her home in Hawaii Kai with a realtor. "Don't you think you should live with your daughter for a while and make sure it goes well before you sell?" a neighbor asked her.

"No," Mom replied. "It will go well."

Given the selfless resilience that lay at the core of my mother's character, I was not surprised when, two weeks after she and Baachan moved in with us, Mom said to me one morning that it was no longer necessary for us to turn the car around for her. "I can back my car out now," she said. "No need to bother you and Leighton anymore." This small moment pierced me anew with the power of her example. Her whole life, my mother had modeled the idea that if one only persisted, there was no challenge or circumstance that could not be worked out.

I was sure some people wondered how Leighton felt about having to share his home with his wife's mother and grandmother, but it was never a problem for him, or for us. Mom was seventy-one when she moved with us to that house in the hills, and she had retired from the newspaper with a small pension almost a decade before. During the days, while Leighton and I worked, she busied herself with landscaping our yard, including supervising the delivery of truckloads of topsoil to even out the grade of the back lawn, and planting trees and shrubs everywhere. The yard was her domain, and she would tend it daily until she was well into her nineties.

My mother had also taught herself how to press and dry flowers using methods that would maintain their original color and vibrancy. At a card-making station set against one wall of her bedroom, Mom would sit, snipping and gluing for hours, matching her dried flowers to the exact right background, adding gold foil borders or patterned accents, assembling a puzzle of petals and leaves and delicate cuts of paper with subtle motifs. Hemi, our cat, was her faithful companion. When he settled himself on top of her art materials, she would merely work around him. It was a pleasure for me to give her painstakingly handmade cards to people as thank-you notes, and to offer packets of them to my friends and supporters. Many of the recipients of the cards would save and display them, aware that they had been gifted with Laura Sato Hirono originals.

Mom had once offered to teach Leighton's sister Lauren and me her card-making methods. Though I did not take her up on the proposal, Lauren had accepted her invitation, sitting with her for many hours to learn her techniques, the two of them fully absorbed in their joint artistic endeavor. Soon

Lauren, too, was making her own beautifully crafted cards, and it comforted me to know that she would one day carry on my mother's tradition.

Leighton and my mother also got along brilliantly. Their favorite topic of conversation was how hard I worked and how late I arrived at home each evening. The two of them were unfailingly considerate and accommodating of each other. If some small thing arose between them, they refrained from vocalizing it to each other but would bring the appeal to me. Mom asked me, for example, if I thought Leighton might be willing to wear a regular T-shirt to the dining table instead of sitting down to meals in his undershirt. Leighton always joked that left to his own devices, he would be as scruffy as a frat boy in the movie *Animal House*, but after learning that my mother would prefer he wear a T-shirt, he never again came to the table without one.

For his part, Leighton had but one concern when it came to his mother-in-law. "Mazie," he began, "you know that I work six days a week, and on the seventh day, I'm just going to veg out and watch football."

"I do know that," I assured him.

"And you know they say if your husband watches more than three football games at a sitting, you can pronounce him legally dead," he continued.

"Okay," I said, not quite sure where he was going with this.

"You know your mom likes to work in the garden," he went on. "She knows how to use power tools and she has made the yard so beautiful for us, planting, pruning, trimming—"

"Yes, Mom is a yard person," I agreed.

"Well, I'm not," said Leighton, arriving finally at his point. "So I just want you and your mom to know that if I hear the lawn mower or the chain saw start up on a Sunday, I'm not going outside to help her, and I hope she won't mind."

"I think we're both aware of how important your Sundays are," I said, my lips twitching with amusement. I knew, even if Leighton did not, that it would not have occurred to Mom that he should leave his football game to go out and help her in the yard. In fact, if he had made a habit of doing that, Mom would have stopped working in the garden on Sundays so as to ensure that he would not feel obligated to assist her. Still, I appreciated his concern. "Mom understands how hard you work," I promised him, "and she will be perfectly happy for you to be a vegetable on Sundays."

One of the particular treasures in my mother's garden was the guava tree in our backyard. We all enjoyed guava jelly, and it had long been a staple on our grocery lists. One morning, as I was spreading store-bought guava jelly onto a slice of toast, there was so much pectin in the jar that my spoon bounced off the translucent red substance, and when I bit into my toast, I tasted barely a hint of guava. I thought of the guava tree in our yard and the fruit that fell to the ground only to be picked at by birds.

"Mom," I asked, "do you think you could figure out how to make guava jelly from the fruit on our tree?"

That was all it took. She used no recipe. She relied on intuition, imagination, experimentation, and her green thumb to create what would become her famous guava jelly. Under her care, that guava tree began to offer up such an extraordinary abundance of fruit that I had to buy Mom an enormous freezer in which to keep her guavas. The freezer was crammed year-round, as Mom made batch after batch of jelly, boiling the guavas slowly all day, adding just the right amount of sugar at just the right time, simmering and tasting and testing until she had produced her own divine concoction.

Over the years, we created many different labels for her canning jars. Our last was my favorite. It featured a photograph of the two of us, on which were printed the words "Hirono's Homemade Guava Jelly" and "Made with Aloha by Mazie's Mom, Laura." I gave away hundreds upon hundreds of jars of Mom's jelly to my supporters in Hawaii, and later to my colleagues in Washington, D.C. Congressman Joe Courtney of Connecticut sent a heartfelt thank-you note expressing how privileged he felt to have been gifted a jar. I saved the note to show Mom. And Senator Elizabeth Warren of Massachusetts, after she sampled Mom's secret recipe, had called to ask whether my mother sold jars of her jelly because she had found it absolutely delicious. I had laughed apologetically and explained that Mom's guava jelly wasn't for sale. It was for love.

For me, my mother's guava jelly—like her greeting cards, her orchids, her proofreading expertise, her toolshed construction skills, and her learning to back her car out of our steep driveway—revealed so much. Sometimes we take for granted what is right before us—in this case, Laura Sato Hirono's ability to master literally *anything* she decided to undertake. Even now, my mother's patience and perseverance in creating her guava jelly, simply because I had asked her, stirs me deeply. It was one more way in which she showed me her devotion, not with words, but through quiet deeds.

Baachan's days on Waialae Nui Ridge were more sedentary than Mom's. Ninety-four years old when she moved in with us, she was growing frail. She spoke almost exclusively in Japanese, and spent hours at a time watching her Japanese soap operas or sitting on the lanai, our roofed open-sided veranda, gazing out at the view. Since Leighton spoke very little Japanese, he and Baachan communicated mostly through smiles and nods, but sometimes my grandmother would say to him in slow, careful English, "Thank you for buying this nice home for us." She had lived in so many different kinds of houses through the years, starting out as a young wife and mother in a rough plantation cabin. I liked to think that she was content with where she had landed in the final years of her life, in the company of her daughter and granddaughter.

Baachan had wanted to live to be one hundred years old. Born at the dawn of a new century, she was well on her way to achieving her goal when, at ninety-six, she began to develop dementia and, at ninety-eight, had to be moved to a skilled nursing facility, where Mom visited her daily. A little more than a year after that, she contracted pneumonia and was hospitalized. Mom sat at Baachan's bedside every day, staying late into the night before heading home to rest so that she could return bright and early the next morning.

The last time I visited my grandmother at the hospital, on a night when the staff had urged Mom to go home and get some much-needed sleep, I found my grandmother curled into a tight ball under a single sheet, her rail-thin body shivering with cold. Baachan no longer spoke either Japanese or faltering English, and so she could not ask the attendants for a blanket. I knew Baachan liked to stay warm, so I went down the hall and secured a blanket for her. As I wrapped it around my grandmother's tiny body and stroked silvery stands of hair back from her forehead, my heart ached that I could not do more for this beloved woman who had done so much for me.

Two weeks after she was admitted to the hospital, a call came in the middle of the night that Baachan had stopped breathing. The date was November 2, 2000, one day before my fifty-third birthday, and three short months before my grandmother would have achieved the one-hundred-year mark. It is a lasting heartache that neither Mom nor I were with her in her final moments. One nurse tried to comfort us by sharing that, in her experience, those who are close to the end often wait till loved ones are out of the room to take their leave.

We held a small family funeral for Baachan at the Jodo Mission temple. Then we placed the urn with her ashes inside the family niche, next to the remains of Wayne and Yuriko, and her husband, Hiroshi, all of them together again in the unseen world.

CHAPTER FIFTEEN

Daruma Doll

Having served fourteen years in the state legislature and eight years as lieutenant governor, I wanted to continue advocating for the people of my state, especially its women and children, workers and consumers, teachers and labor unions—all the constituents I had championed throughout my life as a public servant. I ultimately decided that running for governor was the next logical step. Just as Ben had ascended to the governorship after serving as John Waihee's lieutenant governor, I was marshaling my forces to run as Ben's successor when it occurred to me that this would be my first political campaign in which my grandmother would not play a major part. She and Mom had been my pillars for so long, I felt a dark, yawning space beside me where Baachan's small figure had once been.

Fortunately, Mom was still as vigorous as ever, and I was grateful for her steady presence. Her hair was fully white now, and the lines on her face made her appear serene and regal, a small, knowing smile often on her lips, as if she had figured out a few of life's secrets. Watching her step into the fray for me one more time, I was struck by just how far we had come.

I have often wondered how it was that a quiet, watchful Asian American immigrant girl who had grown up desperately poor could one day aspire to become the chief executive of her state. The closest I've come to an explanation is this: My mother had lived as if nothing was truly impossible, and her determination—the heart of fire she carried within her, despite her calm demeanor—had set a powerful example for us. She had worked tirelessly to make it possible for me to become a woman with outsize dreams. "Nothing I can do will ever be as difficult as what my mother did . . . coming here with three kids to start a new life, not knowing how it would turn out," I had reflected to a reporter from Honolulu's *Star-Bulletin* newspaper a few years prior. This remained true, even as I geared up for the toughest run of my life.

No woman had ever been elected governor of Hawaii. This fact alone would hamper my candidacy from the start, because the old-guard Democrats, led by the grand master of Hawaii politics, Senator Daniel Inouye, didn't believe that I could carry our party to victory. Political insiders knew that Senator Inouye—who had first been elected to the U.S. Senate in 1962, and who would be returned to office by the electorate every term until his death in 2012—had thrown his support behind Jeremy Harris, the mayor of Honolulu. Word had it that his support was the fulfillment of a promise made when Harris had agreed not to challenge Ben Cayetano in the primary during his reelection bid for governor in 1998.

While the backing of the old-boy network had not been much of a factor in my prior races, running for governor was a different order of magnitude, and without the support of the Democratic old guard, winning would be hugely challenging. But as I saw it, a governor with heart and fortitude, who would be willing to work collegially with others—an approach sorely lacking in Ben Cayetano's tenure—could achieve much for the people of Hawaii. I believed I was that person. Convinced I could deliver results for my constituents, I mounted a campaign and struggled for months to gain traction. Finally, the realist in me took stock and decided to change course, dropping out of the governor's race to run instead for the position Jeremy Harris was vacating. I reasoned that as mayor of Honolulu I could still serve as a countervailing force on whoever won the governorship, as I didn't trust the leading candidates to support the issues and the communities that mattered to me.

I met with Senator Inouye personally to tell him of my decision. Months before, he had strongly urged me to get out of the governor's race, telling me I couldn't win and showing me polls to try to convince me. Now, on learning that I planned to run for the mayor's seat instead, and that I was asking for his support, he gave it willingly. Then he grew animated. "You, me, and Jeremy should go out and eat soup together in a public place," he said. I immediately said no, but the senator kept insisting. I already knew that in the months that I had been running for governor, Senator Inouye had met with the unions to encourage them to support another candidate—everyone knew he meant Harris. Now, for more than twenty minutes he urged me to "have soup" with him and Harris where everyone could see us.

"If we do this, everyone will think we made a deal," I told him.

"They'll think that anyway," he said.

I became even more adamant in my refusal, until at last, like a light switch abruptly turned off, the senator let it go, and we moved on to discussing my mayoral race.

A few months later, news broke that the Campaign Spending Commission was investigating Jeremy Harris for campaign-fund violations and had referred the investigation to the city prosecutor. Harris dropped out of the governor's race, stating that he would not after all be vacating his office as mayor but would stay on to finish out the last two years of his term. Although Harris denied any wrongdoing and was never indicted, after he ended his mayoral term in 2004, the onetime golden boy of the Hawaii Democratic Party would leave politics entirely, never to be heard from again.

The mayor's team had let me know of Harris's decision just forty-five minutes before his press announcement. My mayoral candidacy no longer viable, I tossed my hat back into the ring for governor. But Jeremy Harris's late flip-flop on running for chief executive cost me crucial momentum. By the time I reentered the governor's race in May, the other contenders had already ramped up their campaign operations into high gear. The move also drew public criticism from some, who painted me as shamelessly opportunistic, a career politician in the market for any race she could win. Nothing could have been further from the truth. I knew that achieving victory was going to be the longest of shots for me, given that my Republican opponent would be Linda Lingle, who had previously run for governor against Ben Cayetano in 1998 and lost by only a small margin.

Perhaps even more problematic, I was tied to an unpopular governor. During his second term, Ben had not only battled with the largest public-sector unions, he had alienated the hugely influential Hawaii State Teachers Association (HSTA) when he refused to negotiate a contract aimed at giving the state's teachers higher wages and other benefits. His standoff with the union the year before had provoked a weeks-long statewide teacher strike. Even after the governor finally signed off on a contract that the union members felt they could ratify, Ben remained public enemy number one for Hawaii's teachers, which meant that my two terms as his lieutenant governor could hurt me badly. Despite all the bills I had introduced and passed to

benefit educators during my time in the State House and as lieutenant governor, I was told that many of the newer members of HSTA's endorsement
committee absolutely refused to support Ben Cayetano's deputy.

Never acknowledging that he had left me with a severely pitted road, Ben
once again tried to get me to step down from a big race. "Mazie, how would
you like me to nominate you for the Supreme Court of Hawaii?" he asked.
"I'm sure the State Senate would confirm you." He didn't mention that before
he could nominate me, the state's independent judicial selection commission
would have to forward my name to the governor as a potential nominee. Obviously, Ben thought that was a hurdle that could be managed.

With no hesitation, I declined his offer. I recalled that years before, John
Waihee had obliquely dangled a judicial appointment to get me not to run
against someone close to him in a State Senate race I had been contemplating.
I wasn't interested in being a judge then, and I wasn't interested now, especially as an incentive for stepping aside.

Ben was silent for a moment, his brow knitted. I saw that he was sincerely
trying to offer me a parachute, even though I had not asked him to come to
my rescue. "You know I want to help you," he said at last. "You're not going
to win the governorship. Things aren't going your way."

*Why don't you try to help instead of sitting here trying to talk me out of run-
ning?* I thought with some irritation. It frustrated me that my party, not just
in Hawaii but also across the country, routinely failed to support women for
top state offices like governor. It seemed to me that Republicans were more
willing to back women candidates in the big races and to bring them the resources and endorsements needed to win. Of course, for both parties, if the
choice was between a good old boy and a good old girl, the party would go
with the good old boy every time.

Despite the challenges that lay ahead, I jumped headlong into campaigning. My longtime friend and supporter Bob Toyofuku had agreed to be my campaign manager, having suspended his lobbying activities until the legislature came back in session in December. I trusted Bob's integrity, work ethic, and knowledge of the nuts and bolts of statewide campaigns. The fact that he would cast his lot with a candidate who was decidedly the underdog spoke volumes about his loyalty and belief in me.

Jadine Nielsen, a fiercely efficient organizer whose serene demeanor and genial laugh belied her immense personal power, would work hand in glove with Bob on all aspects of the campaign. Jadine, the eldest of three daughters born to a Chinese immigrant grocer father and seamstress mother in San Francisco, had been active in California politics since her early twenties. She had served as U.S. Senator Alan Cranston's state director, and had later been appointed assistant to the chairman of the Federal Deposit Insurance Corporation (FDIC) under the Clinton administration.

I had met Jadine in 1996 at a San Francisco luncheon for activist women that had been organized by Caryl Ito, a mover and shaker in the Bay Area who would become my good friend. Jadine impressed me immediately. Having left her FDIC position in 2001, when she heard that I could possibly become the first Asian American woman governor in the country, she flew to Hawaii to be a keynote speaker at a luncheon on my behalf and stayed on to volunteer with my campaign. I was grateful to have the help of an experienced political operative with such finely honed instincts, but the even greater gift was the deepening of our personal friendship. From that campaign on, Jadine would become an invaluable member of my brain trust, a brilliant, tough, clear-sighted woman who understood intimately the machinery and gender traps of American politics.

I was going to need her toughness in the race I had undertaken. My main competition in the Democratic primary would be State House majority leader Ed Case, who had tried to position himself as the reform candidate while casting me as tied to my party's old-boy network—a ludicrous notion given that I had spent much of my political life working independently of that patriarchal cabal. In response, Bob proposed that I film a campaign ad comparing my record in the State House with Ed Case's. Up to then, my preference had always been to stand on my own achievements without going negative on my opponents. But Bob insisted that I had to draw the comparison in a very stark way or Ed Case would continue to falsely associate me with a number of old-line Democrats who at the time were facing possible indictments for campaign-funding violations and kickback schemes. In the end, I agreed to a television spot highlighting the fact that my own record had always been squeaky clean, and that I had also been the most productive member of the legislature to date, passing more bills during my tenure than any other State House representative—one hundred and twenty compared to a paltry eight passed by Ed Case.

The ad had the desired effect, opening many voters' eyes to just how effective a representative I had been on behalf of workers and marginalized people. It made constituents who had grown disenchanted with politics as usual take a second look at me. It also taught me a valuable lesson: People wanted to see that you were willing to fight hard to win. It assured them that you would fight just as hard for them once elected.

Unfortunately, I was facing yet another major challenge during the primary, because after Jeremy Harris dropped out of the race, some of the Democratic Party leaders had recruited a new favorite, former Republican Party chair D. G. "Andy" Anderson, whom they had convinced to switch parties and run as a Democrat. It infuriated me that they had so little faith in my chances that they had actually reached across party lines to draft a man who had previously run for governor as a Republican. The state's two biggest labor unions, the Hawaii Government Employees Association (HGEA) and the International Longshore and Warehouse Union (ILWU), also were prepared to back the newly minted Democrat, leaving me out in the cold despite the fact that I had a long track record of working with both unions.

Worse, these men now expected me to just roll with their punches, as was made clear by a revealing comment from one of the union leaders, who had reportedly said: "Mazie is so fair-minded, she won't hold it against us if we back her opponent. She will always side with the workers." I was disappointed—and yes, hurt—by the faithlessness of men with whom I had worked collegially and effectively for so many years. But there was no time to lick my wounds: I had to get busy accepting one of the most painful truths of my political career, namely, to assume absolutely nothing from those you might have once counted as allies, whether they were fellow Democrats or union leaders. Just because you had stood up for people in the past didn't mean they would rally to your cause in the future. It was a harsh lesson, and I would learn it well. Never again would I expect loyalty for loyalty given. Rather, I would have to fight like hell for every endorsement, in every race, and now, I intended to do just that.

I made appointments to meet with the neighbor island labor leaders. I was angry, and I meant to confront them about their disloyalty. I was beyond tired of being taken for granted and I was ready to kick ass and take names. However, on the night before I was to fly to the island of Hawaii—which we call the Big Island—for the first of these meetings, I received a call from Alvin Shim, a well-known union attorney and one of the leading partners in the firm where I had worked before leaving to serve as lieutenant governor. "Mazie," he said, "I know you're very upset, and I don't blame you, but before you sit down with these union leaders, I hope you will take a moment to think about why you do what you do. Because you can go in with guns blazing, or you can walk in centered in your true purpose for getting into politics to begin with."

Considered a wise, Yoda-like guru, Alvin Shim had counseled many of the Islands' union and political leaders over the years; however, his previous attempts at bringing me under his wing had been unsuccessful. But this call, out of the blue, caused me to stop and reconsider. I realized that what that union man had said about me was in fact true: I would never hold the decisions of the unions' top brass against its rank-and-file workers. And so, instead of walking in and lambasting union leaders across Hawaii, I decided to take Alvin Shim's advice.

In my meeting the next day, I began by pointing out to the union leaders that we both shared a goal of uplifting working people. I reminded them that Andy Anderson had spent most of his political life as a Republican whose policies the labor unions had stridently opposed. Then I came to my main message. "I'm not here to drive a wedge between you and your state leadership," I told them. "I just want you to know that no matter whom you decide to endorse, I will always fight for the workers."

One of the ILWU leaders I met with that day, Richard Baker, told me later that he had been all in for Andy Anderson, because that had been the directive from union leadership. But my sincerity had given him pause. While he kept his word to support Andy, he would thereafter become one of my most ardent supporters. Another ILWU stalwart and former state representative, Yoshito Takamine, went so far as to resign his leadership position so that he could campaign for me, a move necessitated by the ILWU's stricture that union leaders could not publicly support candidates whom the union had not endorsed. I would spend many hours on the Big Island campaigning with Yoshito, who would drive me wherever he had decided I needed to go until late in the evening. Often at the end of a long day he would rally me to keep going by teasing, "What? You tired? We not pau yet!"—meaning we weren't yet done.

In the end, because I had made the effort to meet with them, union leaders on each island voted on the question of who to endorse for governor. This break from the usual top-down decision making yielded a split outcome, with the result that the ILWU ultimately chose not to endorse any candidate in the primary, while the HGEA ended up endorsing both Andy Anderson and me. I had avoided a total wipeout by not taking things lying down.

At the annual Fourth of July celebration in Kailua that year, I marched in the parade with veteran congresswoman Patsy Mink, who was up for reelection. Patsy had always been a pacesetter. In 1972, she had sponsored the groundbreaking Title IX legislation to ensure gender equity in federally funded education programs, a bill that would later be renamed the Patsy Takemoto Mink Equal Opportunity in Education Act. And she was a firecracker—she'd had to be, having come up in politics at a time when the men in our party had tried to block and bypass her at every turn. As I was finding in my own race for governor, not very much had changed in that regard, but I also knew that it was Patsy's dogged determination that had helped pave the way for me to be walking beside her on Independence Day, my sights set on the highest office in our state.

Patsy invited me to have lunch with her after the parade. As we ate together in her Kailua headquarters, we talked about our shared commitment to the people of Hawaii and the fact that women in politics had to be tough and resilient, and willing to risk everything to pull out a win. Of course Patsy knew, without my ever having to mention it, that I was running with no backup from the old-boy network in our party. At a certain point, the petite congresswoman put down her fork, leaned forward with a fierce expression, and held my gaze intently.

"Mazie," she said, her tone low and urgent, "you have to win this race. You just have to win."

We were both silent for a long moment, and I knew she was remembering all the times the men had failed to back her, too, forcing her to swim uphill. When she'd first declared her intention to run for Congress in the early 1960s, for example, Daniel Inouye had been persuaded to run as well, and had defeated her. Two years after Inouye moved over to the Senate in 1962, Patsy Mink had again run for the House seat, and this time she won. Now, thirty-eight years later, no one had the slightest doubt that she would be victorious once more.

I felt buoyed by her encouragement, knowing that if the old boys in our party might not have my back, this undaunted survivor surely did. She and I took a photograph together that day, two resolute women in politics surrounded by campaign volunteers in Patsy Mink T-shirts. As the long-serving congresswoman and I said our goodbyes that afternoon, I had no idea that it was the last time I would ever see my friend.

In the Democratic primary on September 21, 2002, I eked out a close victory over my closest competitor, with 41 percent of the vote to Ed Case's 40 percent; Andy Anderson was a distant third with 18 percent. As the Democratic nominee, I would now go up against the Republican former mayor of Maui, Linda Lingle. For the first time in Hawaii, the two major parties would field women in the gubernatorial race. This would be only the second time this had happened in U.S. history, the first when Nebraska state treasurer Kay Orr defeated Lincoln mayor Helen Boosalis in the Nebraska governor's race in 1986.

With only six weeks to go until the general election, I knew that the battle would be hard fought. During his term as governor, Ben Cayetano had angered a number of loyal Democratic bastions, including Japanese Americans, whose support had helped propel me to victory in my race for lieutenant governor. In the summer before the general election for governor, Ben had decided to rename the Tetsuo Harano Tunnel, which ran through the Koolau Range, a dormant shield volcano in eastern Oahu, the John A. Burns Tunnel. Instead of honoring a Japanese American highway engineer who had served in state government for some fifty years, Ben Cayetano had unilaterally determined that it should honor former governor Burns. His move drew vocal opposition from constituents of Japanese descent. Linda Lingle saw an opportunity and seized it, announcing that if elected governor, she would reinstate the original name of the tunnel. I knew that Ben's ill-considered and unnecessary action would cost me a margin of votes, as I had heard from many of my Japanese American constituents that they planned to support Lingle because of her promise.

But my trials in the 2002 governor's race went well beyond Ben's renaming a tunnel and angering the public-sector unions over collective bargaining. The fact was, I had stepped into the arena in the worst possible year to be a Hawaii Democrat. The state's economy was faltering amid a national recession, and the political scandals playing out in the local news had only made things worse. With each new revelation of impropriety by Democrats, constituents grew more dismayed. Once-loyal Democratic voters were turning away from the party that had dominated Hawaii politics ever since the first Constitutional Convention of 1954.

My party sank into further disarray when Patsy Mink contracted viral pneumonia and passed away unexpectedly on September 28, just shy of her seventy-fifth birthday. Amid our shock, dismay, and grief at the loss of this legend of Hawaii politics, no fewer than thirty-eight candidates jumped into the race to replace her in Congress, my former primary challenger Ed Case among them. With little more than a month before the general election, the House race became an unseemly free-for-all. "The Democratic Party is imploding," Ira Rohter, a political science professor at UH Manoa, told *The New York Times* during the chaotic run-up to Election Day. "Right now, there is no Democratic Party here, just a lot of feuding factions. It's like watching a Three Stooges skit." In what I considered to be a beautiful irony, every candidate would ultimately lose to Patsy Mink, whom loyal constituents reelected posthumously. Ed Case would go on to win the seat in a special election two months later.

My own race continued to be challenging, though when it became clear that I would be the Democratic nominee, Senator Inouye and the unions finally rallied behind me and I began to gain steadily on Lingle in the polls. Then, just before the general election, Bill Clinton came to Hawaii to pay his respects to Congresswoman Mink. A secondary hope, at least among the Democratic leaders, was that he would help to bolster my chances of beating Lingle. Clinton was his usual gregarious self as we flew to all the neighbor islands in a single day, talking to voters and even eating ice cream at Tasaka Guri Guri Shop in Kahului, Maui. The Tasaka family's century-old secret recipe, rumored to include guava juice, lime soda, and condensed milk, yielded a delicious frozen dessert that was famous across the Islands. To this day, the shop still displays a photo of President Clinton and me enjoying the treat during the 2002 governor's race.

Clinton's presence in the final weeks of the race may have both helped and hurt me, however. A number of constituents let me know that while they had voted early for me, they would not have done so had they known Clinton was endorsing me. Among some of the people of my state, the former president still had not shaken off the taint of impeachment in the wake of the Monica Lewinsky scandal.

Going into the home stretch, Lingle and I were in a dead heat. I was so close to possibly pulling off the win that, in the final weeks of the race, scores of local officials and business owners who had cast their lot with Lingle began calling my office to see if they could schedule an eleventh-hour meeting with me or contribute to my campaign. I knew they were hedging their bets in case I won. But when all the votes were counted, Lingle would win by 4.54 percentage points, becoming the first woman governor in the state's history and its first Republican governor since 1962.

I was acutely aware that my opponent had defeated me with a sleekly professional team that included highly qualified people from the mainland and twenty full-time salaried staffers. My grassroots campaign had long been the tried-and-true approach for Democrats running for office in my state, and it had carried me and other statewide candidates to victory many times in the past. But now I had to face the reality that, as committed as Bob Toyofuku and Jadine Nielsen had been to my success, and as dedicated as our local supporters were, my scrappy volunteer operation had been no match for Lingle's expensive and sophisticated modern campaign.

Most of my volunteers, unless retired, had to hold down day jobs, which meant that the attention they could give to the daily grind of campaign work was always going to be limited. Indeed, only two members of my campaign team had drawn modest salaries—the cook who made giant pots of beef stew and rice for our supporters, and the person who organized our statewide volunteers. To really level the playing field, I would have had to pay for a core team of experienced campaign operatives, including a full-time campaign manager, which would have meant raising more money than I had ever seen in my political life.

And then there were the very real questions about where I had personally fallen short. If I was being brutally honest with myself, I had to acknowledge that it hadn't been enough to give my all *during* the campaign. Perhaps I could have spent more time setting the stage—calling up contacts and polishing relationships—during my time as lieutenant governor. But unlike many of my colleagues in politics, I did not look ahead to my next race and allow those considerations to guide my legislative agenda. I had long ago decided to simply do the best job I could for the people who needed it in the here and now, letting the future take care of itself. I knew that some considered me shortsighted for not having laid the groundwork years in advance, and maybe they had a point. However, I had never been opportunistic in that way, and it had made my path in the governor's race that much harder. Still, this was the approach I had consciously chosen, and I understood the criticisms that would now come my way because of it.

I mulled over other ironies: For one thing, I had always found my interactions with the ordinary people I met while campaigning infinitely more enjoyable than the effort to cultivate those who could be helpful to my political future. For another, my public persona seemed to be a mutable thing in the minds of voters. When I had first run for lieutenant governor eight years before, for example, advisers had suggested that I soften the Ice Queen persona I had acquired during my time in the State House, with the result that people now wondered if I was tough enough to lead the state. In the end, my decision to be a supportive teammate to Ben Cayetano during his terms as governor had not served me well. Had I been more outspoken, calling Ben out when I disagreed with him instead of playing the loyal deputy, voters would have seen my independence and known that I would fight for them.

I remembered Senator Inouye telling me when I was lieutenant governor that I was a lawmaker at heart, better suited to the legislative rather than the executive branch. At the time, I had seen his remark as being unsupportive, but now, though convinced that I would have been an effective governor for my state, I had to admit that his assessment of my temperament had been accurate. As a legislator, I would have the freedom to be as tough or as cooperative as I chose in deciding what issues I wanted to bring to the table, who I was going to fight for, and why.

Even with these insights, on election night my defeat was a bitter pill to swallow. As I congratulated Linda Lingle on her historic win in my concession speech, I looked out at the somber faces of the local volunteers standing before me, men and women who had worked so hard on my behalf. I felt their disappointment keenly, but I also experienced a growing sense of calm. The campaign had been emotionally grueling, and I was not used to losing, but I was a stoic, much like my mother, and so what I remember feeling most of all that evening, along with disappointment, was a flood of relief that it was over, and knowing I had done my best in the hardest and most demanding race I had ever run. Now, all that was left was for me to graciously accept the will of the voters and move on.

It was long past midnight when Leighton, Mom, and I headed for home, all of us exhausted to the marrow of our bones. When we pulled into our garage, the headlights of our car illuminated the large Daruma doll that a friend had presented to me at the start of my gubernatorial campaign. The figure was almost as tall as I was, and I couldn't wrap my two arms around its girth. As Leighton and Mom exited the car and went into the house, I walked over to the large red-painted doll, staring into its reproachfully empty right eye.

As I stood there, seemingly out of nowhere I felt again the sensation of tumbling from the lofted second floor of my father's house at the age of three, banging the right side of my face on the edge of the stairs and almost losing that eye. I touched the small scar on the outer corner of my right eye and remembered Baachan tending my wound and watching over me as I healed. The thought came to me then that in all the races I had run while she was still with us, Baachan had only ever seen me win. At that moment my skin tingled as if touched by a soft breath, as if my grandmother were standing next to me whispering that my work was not done.

"When one door closes another will open," Mom had said to me earlier, after we all understood that I would end the night on the losing side. Now, I flicked off the garage light and went into the house, where I found Mom and Leighton seated at the kitchen table, both of them pretending not to be waiting for me. I felt such tenderness for the two of them, my unstinting allies, the people I could most count on to support me in any endeavor I undertook. I pictured Mom bent over her pressed flowers, creating the one-of-a-kind thank-you cards for me to send to supporters. And I thought of Leighton, a lone figure waiting in the deserted Honolulu airport terminal on so many nights when I caught the last flight home from campaigning on the neighbor islands. Seeing him there, waiting to greet me, had never failed to revive my weary spirit.

Now, I walked to the middle of the kitchen and met Mom's and Leighton's expectant eyes. "I think I have one more big race left in me," I told them. "I don't know if an opportunity will come again, but if it does, I will be ready."

They nodded as if what I was saying made sense to them. Then they rose from the table and went to get ready for bed. Even though neither one had spoken, I sensed they were reassured to see that the fire still burned in me. What I didn't yet know was that starting the next day Leighton would begin to quietly set aside money for my next campaign. None of us had any idea what that race would be, or that it would be more than three years before it presented itself. But I would recognize my moment at once when, in 2006, the seat Patsy Mink had once held opened up in the U.S. House of Representatives.

That spring, as I filed the paperwork for another contest, I silently promised the departed spirit of my baachan that on the morning after Election Day, November 7, 2006, I would color in the second eye of the enormous Daruma doll in my garage. Because in my bid for Congress, I fully intended to win.

Part Four

ONE THOUSAND CRANES

The other side of the anger is the hope.
We wouldn't be angry if we didn't still believe
that it could be better.

—*Jessica Morales Rocketto,*
As quoted in
GOOD AND MAD:
THE REVOLUTIONARY
POWER OF WOMEN'S ANGER
by Rebecca Traister

CHAPTER SIXTEEN

A Modern Campaign

For the first time in twenty-two years, I was not an elected official. "Enjoy yourself," Leighton told me. "You've been going nonstop." Ever generous, he added, "We'll be fine on what I bring in."

"I hope you're not expecting me to cook and clean, because if you are, I'm going out to get a job right now," I joked.

"Of course I don't expect that," he assured me in his soft-spoken way. "You act as if I don't know my wife. No, I want you to do whatever you want. You're always so busy trying to make sure everyone else is okay. Time to focus only on you."

You can see why some of my friends teasingly ask their husbands, "Why can't you be more like Leighton Oshima?" They say Leighton's motto is: "Whatever makes Mazie happy."

The truth is I had never been more appreciative of the man I had married than in the aftermath of defeat. The months immediately following election night are a blur; Leighton recalls that I appeared to be on autopilot, as if I had blunted all feeling so as to get on with the business of doing the next necessary thing. Without my really noticing it, my husband orchestrated a structure for my days, giving me time to make peace with losing. For weeks afterward, he drove me to my campaign office in the morning and picked me up in the evening; in between, I would sit at my desk writing thank-you notes and making calls to the people who had supported me. Leighton knew that despite the grit and resilience I projected, I was mourning the loss of the life I knew. For two decades I had proposed and tracked bills through the state legislature, drafted complaints, argued cases in court on behalf of injured parties, and been immersed in public life. Now, time slowed, the hours stretching out before me. On those interminable days after my first losing campaign, as I organized my papers and prepared to close my campaign office, I concentrated only on the tasks at hand and forced myself not to think too far beyond my final task before stepping down as lieutenant governor— my role in the formal swearing-in of Linda Lingle in January. After that ceremony, I would fully close the chapter on my governor's race.

One evening, I stood at my living-room window looking out over the city of Honolulu. From this distance, it glimmered like a spill of stars, and it occurred to me that for first time since I had become a state legislator, I was free to travel whenever I wanted, and for no reason other than the pure pleasure of seeing new places. In the moment I had the thought, the world shifted from muted grays and back to vivid color. I knew Leighton had several work trips to the mainland coming up, and I decided to join him. It was a new and enjoyable experience to travel to Seattle, San Francisco, and Los Angeles not as the working spouse, but as the free one.

I also took an assignment as guest lecturer for a month at a private university forty-five minutes outside of Tokyo by high-speed rail. I instructed students on American society and government during three sessions each week, and spent the rest of the time exploring the side streets of Tokyo, always an adventure given my laughable sense of direction. One day, when I was hopelessly lost, I stumbled onto a charming restaurant with ceramic pottery pieces in the window. I went in and, with my limited Japanese, told the owner, who was also the potter, how much I admired his work. Akito-san and I became friends, as yet unaware that his distinctive pottery would one day be displayed in my U.S. Senate office in Washington.

My love of art had been with me for as long as I could remember. Throughout my childhood I had enjoyed sketching comic book characters and scenes from nature, and as a teenager I had drawn portraits of movie stars. A frequent subject was Troy Donohue, the fifties and early sixties matinee idol whom I had watched on the TV detective series *Hawaiian Eye*, and whose blond, suntanned good looks had set the standard of cool for every haole surfer boy on Waikiki Beach. I no longer owned any of these drawings because every time we had moved to a new house, we had purged all but our most necessary belongings. Mom believed in traveling light.

I thought that I could always make new pictures, but at some point toward the end of high school, when working on the student newspaper took over my life, that part of my artistic expression ended, at least until my junior and senior years in college, when I took a number of art history and studio classes, including drawing, painting, and ceramics, and even considered becoming an art history major. Yet it never occurred to me to try to pursue art in any serious way. For one thing, I did not consider myself to be a good enough artist to "make it" in the field, and for another, our financially constrained circumstances didn't allow for such impractical dreams. Instead, I contented myself with spending hours in great art museums whenever I had the opportunity and studying the paintings of the masters, while channeling my creative impulse into my work as a state legislator.

Starting when I moved into my own tiny condo, I slowly began to build my art collection, though I didn't have enough space to display the artwork and could ill afford it on my paltry legislator's salary. I can still recall the first piece I purchased, a raku ceramic pot that cost me sixty dollars, which I paid for in installments of ten dollars a month. Later, after I married Leighton, became lieutenant governor, and moved to Waialae Nui Ridge, I was finally able to indulge my love of art, filling our walls with original works by well-known and lesser-known Hawaii artists, and acquiring large sculptures and furniture by local artisans, the more colorful and unusually crafted the better. Of course, nothing in my home matched, as I have a very eclectic eye.

I was also able to select artworks for my lieutenant governor's offices from the State Foundation on Culture and Arts' vast collection. When I discovered that a large distinctive portrait by Diego Rivera that I had once seen on display at the Art Academy on Beretania Street was housed in the state's collection, I requested it for my office. I was informed that, as the most valuable work in the collection, it had to be offered to the governor first. Fortunately for me, the governor declined the piece, and it remained installed in my inner office until it and two other pieces I had selected for my offices were later chosen for a state traveling exhibit.

Now, discovering Akito-san's pottery during my sojourn in Tokyo inspired me to seek out what would become the most restorative activity of my time away from politics, potting with my old friend Norma Yuskos, a ceramic artist who had lived and worked in Hawaii for decades before moving to California to be closer to her aging parents. Norma had been a fellow volunteer when I worked on our mutual friend Carl Takamura's district campaign in 1974, and in the early eighties, she had served as the clerk of the state legislature's Housing Committee when I was its chair. Soon after I returned from Japan, I was wandering through the house one day when my eye landed on a beautiful ceramic plate that Norma had made. The plate, which graced one of my handcrafted tables, had been glazed in a shimmery ombre of blues. I picked it up and turned it over, noticing that the underside was as meticulously finished as the top. Setting the plate back down, I decided to call my friend of twenty-five years.

"Norma," I said, "when can I come and pot with you? I have nothing but time on my hands now that my governor's race is done."

"How about next week?" she said.

Though Norma always held down a salaried day job, her true calling was art. She had dreamed of having her own studio for thirty years before she finally established one in Encinitas, about twenty-five miles north of San Diego, on a property that boasted stunning panoramas of wooded hillsides, beyond which lay the sparkling blue of the Pacific. Now part of a thriving artistic community, she hosted Friday Open Studios and weeklong guest-artist programs in her beautiful studio. The space featured a wall of windows that opened to allow in breezes flowing up the hillside, large worktables painted white, and lots of shelves for storage and display. Norma had thought of everything, even installing outlets in the ceiling so that the winding cords of potting tools, including mundane items like hair dryers, were neatly off the ground.

During what I have come to think of as my sabbatical from politics, I would spend at least a week each year in this serene, light-filled space, potting and claying with Norma. Whatever she happened to be working on when I got there, I would usually undertake as well. One time, she was in her mosaicking period, and I jumped right in to make a triptych of mirrors for my mantel. On another visit, after a trip Leighton and I made to London, during which a local had told us how pigs in London were happy and free, I made a large rectangular green platter with pig figures around the border. I dubbed it my "happy pig plate" because it reminded me of some of the best days of my childhood, reading Freddy the Pig books while perched in my favorite jacaranda tree, munching on dried squid.

I also crafted a series of square plates, which I glazed in vibrant colors. I called these my "envelope plates," because each dish had a design element on one edge that resembled the triangular flap of an envelope. When guests came to dinner at our house, I would serve dessert on them. "I made those," I would announce with not a shred of false modesty. I felt that it was important for people to know there were sides to me other than the political wonk they knew me to be. I had always believed that the creative right brain was just as important as the logical left brain, and this conviction was embodied by my art-filled home and office. It was why I would later install floating shelves in my Senate office, on which I would display my friends' artwork, as well as an egg-shaped dango piece that I made at Norma's studio after my trip to Japan.

My concentration as I potted was so complete that the world outside the studio fell away. In the evenings, Norma and I would make and eat dinner together, then lounge on couches in her living room, sipping wine and watching TV or reading. Other times, we would discuss Hawaii politics, as Norma knew the players and personalities well. I shared with her what I had told my mother and Leighton, that I had another big race in my future, and if the right opportunity presented itself, I would not hesitate to step back into the political fray. When we finally retired, I would sleep more soundly than I did anywhere else, and wake the next morning refreshed and ready for another day of claying.

During my weeks in Encinitas, Norma was a perfect art companion and muse. Patient by nature, she had a gentle way of teaching me about clay and pacing our days. And she was not without a sense of humor. Once, when I arrived to find her in the midst of creating ceramic roses for a series of garden planters, I decided to make some of the roses for my own garden back home. I watched as she instructed me on the process, and the first several roses I made were painstaking, almost up to Norma's standards. The next few were passable but they soon became less and less so until Norma walked over to me and put a hand over mine.

"Okay, Mazie, I think you're getting tired. You should stop now."

As I set aside the piece I had been working on, my eyes fell on the last two roses I had completed. I saw they were little more than misshapen blobs of clay. Norma, too, had noticed the precipitous decline in shape and form of my roses, and we both burst out laughing.

O ver the course of those three years, when I wasn't traveling with Leighton or recharging in Norma's studio, I made a point of strengthening connections I had made during my time as lieutenant governor with Asian American activists on the mainland. I knew that my experience as a lawmaker in Hawaii had been less racially charged than those of my counterparts in other states, where Asians were in the minority. As Jadine put it: "I wake up in the morning in California and nobody in power looks like me. I wake up in the morning in Hawaii, and almost everybody in power looks like me." I wanted to learn from the experiences of my mainland cohorts, and to nurture the alliances that would allow us to offer one another necessary support.

The importance of women supporting other women in politics was also top of mind, and I wanted to take a more active and intentional role in helping women candidates succeed. After my race for governor, it had become clearer than ever to me that women in Hawaii would have to build networks to combat the entrenched chauvinism or unconscious bias of politics in general, and of our state's Democratic leaders specifically. To this end, Jadine and I, along with a few other women we knew, decided to found the Patsy Mink Political Action Committee to support local women candidates from our party. We knew that for women to be competitive, they needed to be able to build campaign war chests that were as rich as the men's, a proposition that in Hawaii came with a few extra hurdles. As Jadine had explained to some of our sponsors, "It is tough for women to raise money for political races anywhere, but for an Asian American woman in Hawaii, a culture where men traditionally dominate, it's that much harder for women to be assertive in asking for money."

We modeled our political action committee on EMILY's List, the influential Washington, D.C., group founded by Ellen Malcolm and twenty-four other women in Malcolm's basement in 1985. Their goal was to help pro-choice Democratic women running for office by providing them with the resources needed to mount a winning campaign. The EMILY acronym, which stands for Early Money Is Like Yeast, was an acknowledgment of the fact that receiving strong donations early on in a political race went a long way toward attracting other influential donors. The group aimed to redistribute the balance of power within the halls of government by ensuring that progressive women who could make significant contributions in the areas of women's rights, reproductive freedom, education, health care, voting rights, and economic equality could compete with male candidates on an equal footing.

The Patsy Mink Political Action Committee adopted a similar mandate. We quickly understood why so few states had created similar PACs to assist women candidates: In the arena of politics, women had seldom been the askers or givers of contributions, and therefore had significantly fewer fundraising networks. While donors were increasingly recognizing the value of financially supporting pro-choice Democratic women by the time we formed our PAC, the money still didn't come easily. Jadine and I began by reaching out to our social contacts and asking them to contribute to our fund. It took a while for us to raise the inaugural twenty thousand dollars, but slowly the donations began coming in, and by 2004 we were able to formally launch our PAC. Thanks to an increasingly loyal donor network, we are now a player on Hawaii's political landscape, as progressive candidates solicit our PAC's endorsement. We are known for giving candidates in local races the maximum contribution allowed by law—two thousand dollars for a State House seat candidate and four thousand dollars for a State Senate seat candidate. And we write those checks early in the election season so that women contenders can gear up their campaign apparatus quickly—the yeast that helps them rise.

For three years, I raised money for our PAC and supported other women in their political races, while keeping an eye out for my own opportunity. Public service continued to be a noble cause for me, a chance to help Hawaii's workers and families remain strong. Then, in mid-2005, the news came that Ed Case planned to step down from the U.S. House of Representatives in order to challenge U.S. Senator Daniel Akaka for the seat he had held for the past fifteen years. Akaka, the first Native Hawaiian to serve in Congress, had been appointed by Governor John Waihee in 1990 after the death of Senator Spark Matsunaga. In the Senate, Akaka, a former music teacher who later led Hawaii's Office of Economic Opportunity, was known as a warm and principled legislator. He and elder statesman Daniel Inouye had been an effective team on behalf of our home state, and Hawaii's old-guard Democrats were not very happy with Ed Case trying to unseat the popular sitting senator.

I, on the other hand, appreciated the irony of my former primary opponent for governor creating an opening for me to embark on the "one big race left in me." Leighton often says that when the window of opportunity appears, one must be ready, because it might soon close and may never again become open to you. As always in politics, the right timing is key. As soon as I heard that the 2nd Congressional District seat that my friend Patsy Mink had held with distinction for the better part of thirty-seven years would be vacated, I knew it was the open window I had been waiting for. The decision to run was easy. My mother and Leighton were squarely behind me; there was no hesitation on their part as we discussed my entering the race. Mom understood my desire to keep being of service, while Leighton was excited by the prospect of me reentering the legislative arena in which I thrived, this time on the national stage, in a city where we had each lived as law students.

We all knew that winning would be a challenge, however, as I had been out of office and out of the public eye for more than three years. Heeding the lessons of my losing governor's race, this time I intended to mount a fully professional operation, with an experienced, paid campaign manager, paid full-time staffers, and seasoned media and polling teams. After I did the math, I had a very sobering discussion with my closest supporters about fundraising. Jadine pointed out that not only would I have to pull in enough donations to pay salaries for almost a full year of campaigning, I would also have to fund communications with voters through polling, media, and mailings in order to have full control of my messaging. We were beginning to grasp just how expensive my modern campaign was going to be, and how much of the money I would have to raise on my own.

Almost every political candidate will tell you that there is no more soul-crushing aspect of running for office than raising money. I personally found the experience of cold-calling potential donors—including perfect strangers, and people who hadn't heard from me in years—grueling, but there was no point in whining about it. I needed to overcome my reluctance to ask for money for myself instead of for other people. *Mind over matter*, I told myself. *You can do this.*

There is an art to the fundraising call. Start with those who support you unconditionally, and then move on to the people who share a common interest, or those who have a stake in your winning. Be as straightforward as possible: explain why you're calling and what makes you qualified, share your positions on issues that matter to your listeners, and then ask if they would be willing to write a check for one or two thousand dollars to support your candidacy. Keep it short. Keep going. Sounds simple enough, but when you're sitting there putting people on the line, believe me, it's very hard. Suddenly, your social contacts see you in a whole new light, and some will step up and some will step away.

Yet there was simply no way around making those calls myself. If I didn't pull out a victory in this race, it would probably be the end of my time as a public servant. That recognition had the effect of sharply focusing my mind, and so for week after week in the fall of 2005 I made calls all day long, from nine in the morning until five in the afternoon, asking for money. At six each evening, Jadine would call me to find out how much money I had managed to add to the coffers that day. She was a taskmaster I did not want to disappoint; just knowing that she would be on the other end of the line asking for an accounting of each day's effort helped me to stay motivated. As she never tired of reminding me, I would have to rise each morning with a gut-level determination to be "brave every day." And that was exactly what I did.

Nine other Democratic candidates had entered the race, all of them currently active in state government. I was the only contender who had been away from politics for years, and for that reason, people questioned my chances. I was gratified to learn, however, that I still had a deep well of support from former volunteers, influential friends, consumer groups, teachers, and the workers' unions. When the local paper made its first report on how much each of the candidates had raised, I was far in the lead, with a campaign war chest of three hundred thousand dollars. The candidate who came in second had raised seventy-five thousand dollars.

Everything changed after that article. Now, everyone saw me as the dark horse who had come out of nowhere to lead the pack. Throughout the race, I never lost that edge, though I never took anything for granted. EMILY's List took note of my fundraising advantage and sent their regional political director, Peggy Egan, to interview me and the one other woman in the race, Colleen Hanabusa, who was then the president of the State Senate, the first woman to serve in that role. Colleen was a formidable competitor, and I was deeply relieved when EMILY's List ultimately decided to throw their support to me in the hotly contested primary. I was quite sure that my superior war chest and the experienced team I had pledged to put together helped to tip the scales in my favor.

My stellar fundraising numbers, combined with the validation of EMILY's List, raised my national profile, and soon, more donations began flowing my way. It was exactly as Jadine had promised when I'd started out on my fundraising journey. "You have to be perceived as a player," she had said. "Build a war chest and the endorsements will come."

The next crucial step was to build a team that would help me succeed with a new kind of campaign. I was inclined to hire a woman with top-tier national experience, and after interviewing several prospects across the country, I settled on Julie Stauch, an Iowan who had worked on high-profile races. Julie had first entered campaign politics in 1984, when she caucused for Democratic candidates running against Ronald Reagan. Four years later she had phone banked for Democratic governor Michael Dukakis in his losing presidential bid against Reagan's vice president, George H. W. Bush.

Asked by *You Should Run* podcast host Tony Heyl in 2019 why she had kept going in politics after hard losses in her first two campaigns, Julie explained it this way: "In both cases the overall campaigns nationally lost, but locally where I was working, we won. For me that reinforced the difference that active individuals working together can make." Her answer reflects the collaborative roll-up-your-sleeves attitude that drew me to Julie. After those early experiences, she had gone on to rack up an impressive list of campaign victories. Now, with her as my campaign manager, I looked forward to joining that roster of wins.

I also hired a media team from Chicago, as well as a finance director, pollster, and other key personnel from the mainland. This meant finding local accommodations for a cadre of staffers. Thankfully, dear friends of mine stepped up to house the mainland transplants for the many months of my campaign, sparing us what could have been a prohibitive expense.

As it was, most of the money I had raised, fully two-thirds, would be diverted into an absentee ballot program, which Julie was convinced would give me the advantage. In Hawaii, county election officials sent absentee ballots to the homes of all registered voters who requested them. Our plan was to send mailers recapping my positions on the issues and my commitment to stand up for families and workers to homes in districts where I had polled strongly. These mailers would be timed to arrive around the same time as the absentee ballots. The program was a massive undertaking that relied on accurate readings of the issues constituents cared about and their feelings about me. Polling had shown that I benefited from a reservoir of goodwill based on voters' belief that I was honest, family focused, and willing to fight for them.

Now, through targeted mailings week after week, I was encouraging these constituents to vote early for me, using the absentee ballots that had been mailed to their households. This effort was completely under the radar, as it was a strategy that had not been undertaken to that extent in Hawaii before.

Many of my longtime supporters criticized me roundly for bringing in paid staffers from the mainland. "What's wrong with the way we've always done it?" they complained. "Aren't our local people good enough for you anymore?" Though most of them still came out to canvass and sign-hold for me, they resented Julie as an outsider and gave her a particularly hard time—especially about, of all things, the T-shirts that were a traditional part of local campaigns.

With so much money going to media spots and our absentee ballot program, the number of T-shirts we ordered for supporters had been greatly reduced, and just a few months into the race, they had all been given out. The subsequent lack of T-shirts led to constant carping among the different wings of my campaign. The local guard wanted us to print up more, and one of my sign-holding captains even came into the office to confront Julie about it.

"Sorry, you're going to have to make do without them," Julie told him. "It's not in the budget to order any more T-shirts."

"We can't sign-hold without T-shirts," my volunteer insisted.

"Well, the signs have Mazie's name in big bold letters," Julie said helpfully—or so she thought.

"That's not the point," the man shot back. As a local elder, he clearly resented taking direction from a blond, blue-eyed haole woman from Iowa. "This is not the way we do things here!"

"Look," Julie said, exasperated. "Do you want T-shirts or do you want to win?"

The man was silent for a moment, seriously considering the question.

"I want my T-shirts," he said finally. He was still grumbling about "these mainland types" as he walked away.

Similarly, some of my local campaign loyalists questioned the wisdom of spending by far the largest portion of my budget on the absentee ballot campaign, but I was banking on those ballots putting me ahead of the pack in the crowded ten-way Democratic primary. Besides, I had hired Julie for her expertise in running big congressional races, and it only made sense for me to implement the approaches she believed would bring us the win.

On primary night, when the polls closed at 6:00 and the Office of Elections gave their first readout, I was tens of thousands of votes ahead of everyone else. The other nine candidates in the race were stunned, but I knew that the absentee ballots had been included in this count and were responsible for my commanding lead. Predictably, when votes began to come in from the districts represented by my competitors, my lead dropped precipitously, but the absentee ballots had given me such a comfortable margin that I was able to squeak out the narrowest of victories over Colleen Hanabusa, with 21.84 percent of the vote to her 21.08 percent. I had won by a mere 844 votes.

Hawaii being an overwhelmingly Democratic state, I expected to do better in the general election, especially since the turmoil that had roiled my party four years before had receded, and enough time had passed that I was no longer tied to Ben Cayetano in the public's mind. My Republican opponent, Bob Hogue, was a popular sportscaster who had been elected to the State Senate and was then serving as its minority leader. As a Republican who was campaigning for national office in 2006, he was obliged to pledge allegiance to his party's leader, President George W. Bush, and to support Bush's war with Iraq, which was highly unpopular among voters in Hawaii. In this race, too, I would upset some of my supporters—this time thanks to a media spot we ran that spliced together numerous bits of footage of Bob Hogue saying George Bush's name. I thought the effect was somewhat comical, poking a little fun even as we drove home the deadly serious point that my competitor publicly approved of the warmongering president's actions. I believed it was important to challenge Hogue's nice-guy image and to distinguish between my opponent's position on the Iraq War and mine. I was satisfied the media spot accomplished that, but some of my supporters saw the ad as me going negative. Several volunteers from the Big Island called to rake me over the coals. "We don't do that in Hawaii," one scolded. "We don't attack each other." They demanded I pull the spot or lose their support. Many others whose opinions I valued also counseled me to take down the ad, but Jadine didn't agree.

"Everybody says they hate negative ads," she told me, "but *everyone* is persuaded by them." When she worked as the state director for California senator Alan Cranston's 1986 reelection campaign, she told me, he put out an ad about his opponent, Republican Ed Zschau, being a flip-flopper on the issues. Not long after the ad aired, one of Cranston's fundraisers reported that she'd overheard two women discussing the ad in a Safeway checkout line in San Francisco.

"Did you see Cranston's campaign ad about Zschau," one said. "I hate when politicians go negative like that."

"Oh, I know," the other woman replied. "It's so disrespectful."

"So are you going to vote for Zschau, then?" the first woman asked.

"Of course not," her friend replied. "He flip-flops!"

Alan Cranston had indeed won that race, and now Jadine assured me that a willingness to take on the opposition in so-called attack ads was a political reality with which I would simply have to grow comfortable. I trusted her instincts, and yet I was torn. Having grown up in Hawaii's aloha culture myself, one part of me understood why the Hogue-Bush media spot had rubbed some people the wrong way. I decided to put the question to two women outside the political firmament, whose sense of fairness and decency I felt I could count on: my mother and my mother-in-law. Should I pull the ad? I asked them. They both watched the commercial thoughtfully, and when it was done they both said, "No, don't pull it." Their response settled it for me, because if Laura Sato Hirono and Rosemary Kim Oshima thought the ad was okay, that was good enough for me. I confess I felt somewhat vindicated when Hogue put out a negative ad about me, which wasn't remotely as light in touch as my ad had been.

In the end, the Hogue-Bush media spot won me more votes than it cost me. When all of the general election ballots were tabulated, I won the U.S. House seat with 61 percent of the vote. As for Ed Case, he would lose to the incumbent Daniel Akaka in what would turn out to be the senator's final term. Senator Akaka's retirement six years later would offer me yet another open window, but that's getting ahead of the story.

Long after midnight on Election Night 2006, after I had thanked all my staff and volunteers and sent them home, I was walking with Leighton to the car and picturing the giant Daruma at the back of our garage that would greet us when we arrived home. I couldn't help smiling as the thought came to me that I had finally fulfilled my promise to Baachan to grant the Daruma doll its second eye.

CHAPTER SEVENTEEN

Roll Call

A week later, I flew to Washington, D.C., with Leighton to attend orientation for the newly elected U.S. representatives, and to find a place to live. Almost as soon as we freshmen arrived, the leading candidates for House majority leader, Steny Hoyer of Maryland and John Murtha of Pennsylvania, whom everyone called Jack, began lobbying us for our support. As had been expected, on November 16, 2006, House Democrats had unanimously chosen Nancy Pelosi of California to be the next Speaker of the House. The official vote wouldn't take place until the 110th Congress officially convened in early January, but with Democrats now in the majority, the Baltimore-born, tough-as-nails Pelosi was all but a lock to win the speakership, thereby becoming the first woman in history to serve as presiding officer and administrative leader of the House. But Democrats still had to decide who would become Speaker Pelosi's chief implementer and loyal right hand.

Hoyer had the inside track, as he had served as then–Minority Leader Pelosi's number two in the previous Congress, a role known as minority whip, and had actively stumped for many of the incoming freshmen, traveling to their states to assist their efforts and contributing more than a million dollars from his PAC on their behalf. Along with Pelosi, he had been unflagging in his determination to ensure a Democratic majority in the House after the 2006 midterms, and many of the newcomers now felt they owed him for the material aid he had given their campaigns. Hoyer had contributed to my race, too, and had called me regularly to find out if there was anything else I might need that he could provide. When I won, he had been one of the first to call to congratulate me.

"You know that I'm running for majority leader and I'd like to have your vote," he said, after I thanked him for supporting my campaign. I had been in politics long enough to know that the help he had offered was intended to serve his interests as much as my own, and that he now fully expected me to respond, "Of course." But in this, he would be disappointed.

"Steny," I replied, "I appreciate all that you did, but I'm not prepared to make that decision yet. I know that Jack Murtha is also going for the position."

Hoyer paused and then said pointedly, "You know that Jack Murtha is against abortion, don't you?" He knew that I was unequivocally pro-choice.

"I'll discuss that with Nancy Pelosi when I meet with her," I said.

I was well aware that Pelosi was backing Jack Murtha. The word was that she had never forgotten that Hoyer had contested her for the position of minority whip five years before, while Murtha had demonstrated his allegiance to Pelosi when he'd backed her in that leadership tussle. Murtha's strong antiwar stance was perhaps also a factor working in his favor. A former marine, he had initially supported military action in Iraq but had later become an outspoken opponent of the war. Some political commentators speculated that in elevating Murtha to majority leader now, Pelosi hoped to signal the anti-war shift within the party, in recognition of the fact that opposition to the war had been a pivotal issue for voters in the 2006 midterms, helping to deliver the House to Democratic control.

I was profoundly opposed to the Iraq War myself, convinced from the start that it had been entered into based on false information about the presence of weapons of mass destruction. During my race for Congress, even before I knew Jack Murtha would be in contention for majority leader, I had asked my campaign researchers to get me every speech he had ever given about the war. I thought it significant that a combat hawk from the party's conservative faction would come out so forcefully against military action, especially one who had originally supported it. To me, it was a testament to the man's independence and moral courage.

A few days into orientation week, Nancy Pelosi requested a meeting with me. I assumed she wanted to discuss my committee assignments as well as share her thinking about who should be the next majority leader. As this would be my first audience with the soon-to-be House Speaker, I thought carefully about what I would say to her and how I wanted the meeting to go.

We met in her spacious, light-filled office with its ornate gold chandelier, large gilt-framed mirror over a fireplace mantel, cream-colored couch and wing chairs, and gleaming dark wood accents. It was an elegant space, entirely fitting to the woman who occupied it. Pelosi greeted me with a clipped formality that still somehow managed to retain a dignified warmth. We got the committee talk out of the way first. I apprised her of my top choices—Transportation and Infrastructure, and Education and Labor—and she advised that since both were highly sought after, I should speak with the prospective chairs as soon as possible to ask for their support. Next, in her gracious way, Pelosi brought up a letter she had received that had been signed by a majority of the forty-one newly elected Democratic House members, indicating their support of Steny Hoyer. I pointed out that I had declined to add my name. "You are a wise woman," the presumptive Speaker said. Then suddenly, without further preamble, she posed the question that was clearly the real point of our meeting.

"Do you have any problems with Jack Murtha for majority leader?"

I appreciated her directness; I have always liked a straight shooter.

"I really like Jack's position on the war," I responded, "but he's also very conservative on social issues like reproductive choice—"

"I set the agenda," Pelosi cut in tersely. "Not him."

It signaled very clearly that she was going to be in charge, and I appreciated this tacit assurance that supporting Murtha would not negatively affect an issue that mattered greatly to me. Pelosi wasn't inviting a lengthy discussion, however. She merely wanted the bottom line. Yet it was important to me that she understand how I had made my decision, especially given the fact that Hoyer had helped my campaign. I wanted her to have a sense of how I operated in the political arena. I chose my next words carefully.

"When I was in state legislature and involved in leading organizational battles, I saw how critical it was for speakers to have the majority leader of their choice, so that they could work effectively as a team," I said. "So because I support you, Madame Speaker, I am prepared to support Jack Murtha. That's why I didn't sign the letter, even though I was strongly encouraged to do so."

This seemed to be enough for Pelosi, and we ended the meeting soon after. I went back to my newly occupied office in the Longworth House Office Building and immediately called Steny Hoyer to let him know that I planned to back Jack Murtha, and I explained why I had made that decision. That night, at a dinner hosted by Murtha and Hoyer for the new Democratic House members, I approached Murtha, whom I had never previously met, and told him the same thing. "You must sit right here beside me," he insisted, pulling out seats for Leighton and me. When the rest of the House members saw me seated next to him, they knew at once the decision I had made.

During dinner, I asked Jack why he had changed his position on the Iraq War. He explained that he had visited many severely injured veterans at Walter Reed hospital, men and women who had put their bodies on the line based on intelligence about stockpiles of WMDs that had since been discredited. Seeing the suffering of the wounded up close, he had concluded that he could no longer support an unjust war, and had begun to speak out against it. I shared with him that I, too, was against the conflict in Iraq, and that his writings had helped me to articulate my own position on what had been a core issue in my campaign.

The next day, my fellow representative from Hawaii, Neil Abercrombie, approached me, urging me to reconsider. "Steny already has the votes," he advised. "Why make an enemy of him?" I remember thinking: *If Steny Hoyer is the sort who would hold this vote against me, then I would certainly be justified in not choosing him.*

In the end, Steny won the secret ballot to serve as majority leader. After a closed-door meeting, he and Pelosi emerged to address the rank-and-file members of the House and the press and stood before us with hands joined together and raised in a show of unity. Watching them, I felt confident they would make their partnership work for the good of all.

To his credit, Steny never did hold my support of Jack Murtha against me. In fact, he would greet me warmly whenever we encountered each other, and I developed a respect and fondness for him as well. Hoyer had a cadre of people he would check in with on the issues, and he included me as part of that sounding board. To this day, he is a good friend and reliable contributor to my Senate campaigns. Certainly, he is a canny tactician who made a conscious decision to keep me close, but I also believe that in this arena, when you play it straight and make your decisions transparent, people respect you for it. Now that I was a member of Congress, the biggest political league of them all, I was determined to stay true to myself, even if that meant taking a loss now and then. Besides, as had been the case with Steny, sometimes short-term losses could turn into longer-term alliances.

I n the New Year, several of my family and friends—including my mother and mother-in-law, Malia, Roy's wife, Emi, and Leighton's sisters, Lynette and Lauren—arrived in Washington, D.C., to join Leighton and me for my official swearing in as a member of the 110th Congress. It would be my mother's first and only trip to the mainland in her lifetime. As I recall, January was bitterly cold that year. Leighton and I, both familiar with D.C. winters, had acclimatized easily, but Mom was continually chilly, accustomed as she was to the eternal summer in our home state. Bundling our mothers against the weather, we took them out to dinner and to visit some of the city's lauded museums, using rented wheelchairs and being careful not to tire them out. Despite the clanging congestion of cars and people and the overwhelming scale of the federal buildings, Mom carried on with her usual stoicism, even after she came down with a painful ear infection. When I left to attend orientation events on Capitol Hill, Emi, a nurse, stayed with Mom in her hotel room, trying to get her to rest and making sure she didn't miss a dose of the antibiotics that had been prescribed. In typical fashion, Mom waved off all the fussing and was back on her feet after a day.

I knew how much Mom and Leighton would miss me while I was in D.C., but they had remained determinedly upbeat. As always, they put me first, knowing that as much as I would hate not coming home to them every evening, my becoming an advocate for the people of Hawaii at the national level was deeply meaningful for me. Thankfully, I would still see them regularly, as House schedulers carved out time for members to travel to their home states for a week each month, so that they could remain in touch with the concerns of their constituents. I would also be able to spend the entire month of August back in Hawaii, during Congress's summer recess. This was comforting to each of us as we prepared to spend more time apart than we had in more than a decade.

At the official opening of Congress on January 2, 2007, the first item on the agenda was the formal poll of the entire House to elect the new Speaker. In a strict party-line vote, Nancy Pelosi defeated Ohio Republican John A. Boehner, 233 to 202. During the roll call, as I listened to the alphabetical recital of names, I remembered Nancy Pelosi telling me what our mutual friend Patsy Mink had said to her soon after Pelosi was first elected to Congress in 1987. As the two women served together, collaborating on legislation and wrangling votes for the bills they supported, the shrewd newcomer Pelosi had greatly impressed veteran lawmaker Mink. "One day, you will be the first woman Speaker of the House," Mink had told Pelosi then, and now, here I was, witnessing that prediction coming true. And so, when the Clerk of the House called my name—"Representative Mazie Hirono of Hawaii, how do you vote?"—I declared, "In memory of Patsy Mink, I proudly cast my vote for Nancy Pelosi." The new Speaker's head swiveled to stare at me with conspicuous surprise and an expansive smile, and I knew she was remembering Patsy Mink's words, too.

Later that morning, when I stood before Nancy Pelosi and raised my hand to take my oath of office, Leighton was at my side, along with our mothers, two beaming Asian American women with hands folded primly against their skirts, their quiet pride in me a palpable thing. I felt gratified that they were both there, one Japanese and the other Korean, representing two strands of our culture, united in their love and support for an immigrant daughter who had arrived at this improbable moment. When I stood apart and looked at my journey in this way, I could appreciate how unlikely it all seemed. I wondered, not for the first time, how my path might have been different if I'd had a more traditional Asian mother, one who had tried to steer me along an easier path. I was grateful then for the grace of having been raised by Laura Sato Hirono, who had never wavered in her faith that I could invent for myself any life I chose.

Among the new members being sworn in that year were Minnesota's Keith Ellison, an African American Muslim, and I, an Asian American Buddhist. Ellison had caused consternation among some of our red-state colleagues when he took his oath of office with his hand not on a Bible but on a Qur'an that had once been owned by Thomas Jefferson. Virginia Republican Virgil Goode had gone so far as to opine in *USA Today*, "If we do not stop illegal immigration totally, reduce legal immigration and end diversity visas, we are leaving ourselves vulnerable to infiltration by those who want to mold the United States into the image of their religion, rather than working with the Judeo-Christian principles that have made us a beacon for freedom-loving persons around the world."

As a Buddhist, I had used no book at all, a choice that did not escape the notice of the reporters, who peppered me with questions about my views on the Qur'an "controversy." The way I saw it, the outrage over Keith Ellison using a Qur'an instead of a Bible was nothing more than a cheap ploy by some Republicans to gin up xenophobic fear of "the other," and I did not hesitate to say so. "It's about time that we have people of other backgrounds and faiths in Congress," I told reporters, before asking rhetorically, "What happened to the separation of church and state and religious tolerance? I believe in those things."

would go on to serve in the U.S. House for six years, winning reelection by increasingly comfortable margins every two years. Fortuitously, I was able to secure positions on each of my first-choice committees during my inaugural term. First, I had approached Jim Oberstar, the Minnesota Democrat who chaired the Transportation and Infrastructure Committee. I explained to him that for Hawaii, the work of that committee was paramount, because airlines and sea lines were the Islands' only connection to the mainland and the rest of the world. Laughingly, I added that my husband was an avid Minnesota Vikings fan, one of maybe five in the entire state of Hawaii.

The other committee that interested me was Education and Labor, as schools and workers had long been two of my top priorities. The chair, George Miller, a California Democrat, noted that Patsy Mink had served with distinction on the committee, fighting for gender and racial equality, affordable childcare, and bilingual education. "There are only two spots left," he said after I shared my reasons for wanting to join his committee. "But with you being from Hawaii, I see there is a legacy issue here."

If Leighton liked to tease that his love of the Minnesota Vikings had tipped Jim Oberstar in my favor, I was sure that it was the love my colleagues had for Patsy Mink that had given me an edge with George Miller. Indeed, after I had voted for Nancy Pelosi for Speaker and invoked Patsy's name, many members had come up to me with tears in their eyes. They wanted me to know how painful it had been to learn that Patsy had died and they hadn't had a chance to say goodbye. I realized that I was now their closest link to the firecracker of a lawmaker who, as the first woman of color to serve in Congress, had made her mark not just on history but also on their hearts.

I was present in the House to witness history once again being made in 2008, after an electrifying campaign delivered Hawaii-born Barack Obama to the White House. As the world hailed the election of our first Black president, I shared in the nation's elation and wonder that we had arrived at a milestone that, one short year before, few of us could have imagined would be achieved in our lifetimes. Along with millions of African Americans, the people of Hawaii were bursting with pride that Obama was now our country's leader, and on the evening of January 20, 2009, we joyously celebrated our keiki o ka aina—son of the land—by staging our own state inaugural ball in Washington, D.C.

I will never forget how hopeful I felt for our country that night. I hoped that President Obama would bring to the White House his experience of growing up in Hawaii's multiethnic culture, which I believed would lead him to value more deeply than any past president the diversity of our nation. *Perhaps he would even raise the consciousness of some of my obstructionist red-state colleagues in Congress*, I thought wryly. We all knew who they were, a small cadre of economically secure straight white men who seemed incapable of legislating beyond the boundary of their self-interest and bedrock belief in their own entitlement.

Given how Obama's time in office actually unfolded—with the Republicans trying to block his initiatives at every turn—I suppose you could think me overly optimistic. Yet I have always believed in the potential of this country to live up to its highest ideals, and though my faith has been tested these past few years, I still do.

In the fall of 2008, our most pressing priority in Congress was to pass legislation that would shore up a national economy in crisis. The financial crash and housing market cataclysm that President Obama inherited on his first day in office had been driven largely by deregulation of the business sector over the previous decade, which had led to predatory lending practices on the part of investment bankers. Though Republicans in Congress tried to stymie his efforts at every turn, Obama ultimately managed to pass the

American Recovery and Reinvestment Act of 2009, a stimulus package that helped to rescue the failing economy and set the nation back on the road to economic health. Not a single House Republican voted for that massive relief bill, but that did not stop them from having their pictures taken back in their home states, posing in front of infrastructure projects funded by the bill. So much for my hope of bipartisan cooperation.

For me, working on the stimulus legislation had been meaningful, but perhaps most memorable during my six years in the House was the chance to help draft portions of the Affordable Care Act. My own state had led the nation in treating health care as a right rather than a privilege to be enjoyed by the few who could afford it. Hawaii's landmark Prepaid Health Care Act, adopted in 1974, had been the first in the country to require employers to provide subsidized health insurance to their full-time workers. Later, under Governor John Waihee in 1989, I had helped to pass the supplemental State Health Insurance Program, designed to create a safety net for poor children, the unemployed, and others unable to access employer-provided medical coverage. Now, I welcomed the opportunity to protect that right and extend similar coverage to a wider swath of Americans.

As the bill made its way through the House and the Senate, the right-wing fearmongering was at a fevered pitch. Republicans like Alaska governor Sarah Palin, who had risen to national prominence as the bottom half of Senator John McCain's ticket in his failed 2008 bid for the presidency, were running around the country making ridiculous claims, including spreading the lie that the ACA would create "death panels" for the elderly to deny them lifesaving medical care.

Despite such desperate attempts to quash the bill, after a hard-fought legislative battle, Obama signed the ACA into law on the morning of March 23, 2010, granting some twenty million previously unprotected Americans access to affordable health care. It was an emotional moment for me. I saw myself again at nine years old, climbing onto a step stool to wash my mother's work clothes because she was too sick to do it herself. I could still taste the fear curdling in my throat as I watched her tremble with fever under the covers, knowing we could not afford for her to see a doctor. The fear that my mother might die was too much to contemplate, but I did worry that her sickness could mean she might lose her meager paycheck, and then what would we do? Then there was the time when I was so sick myself that I lay shivering and hallucinating, alone in our rented boardinghouse room for two days, because Mom had to work and Roy had school. As awful as I felt, I knew there was nothing else to do but to survive, to ride out the fever without moaning about it, because Mom was doing her best, and the least I could do was to get better. These experiences did not fall away. Rather, they would inform my political choices for the rest of my life. Now, the passage of the ACA offered me a powerful affirmation that my desire to help people through public service was more than empty idealism, because I had played some small part in ensuring that millions of Americans would no longer have to face the fear that had plagued me as a child.

n the November 2010 midterm elections, Republicans won a majority of House seats, ending Democratic control of both branches of Congress. Democrats managed to retain a majority in the Senate, though red states picked up seven additional seats in that chamber. By that time, I had become familiar with House procedures, and as a member of the Congressional Asian Pacific American Caucus, or CAPAC, I had often partnered with members of the Congressional Black Caucus and the Hispanic Caucus to help push

through health-care initiatives and education programs to benefit marginalized communities, as well as bills to support minority-serving colleges and
universities.

As soon as the new Republican majority was sworn into the House in January 2011, they moved to end earmarks, which referred to the practice of
House and Senate members allocating funds for specific projects to benefit
their districts. Such earmarks constituted a tiny percentage of the appropriations budget; sometimes, they might be slipped into bills to help secure the
votes of particular members. Under Nancy Pelosi's speakership, substantial
earmark reforms had already been adopted, requiring transparency as to
who was getting an earmark, for what project, and the amount of its funding.
But now the Republican-controlled House was targeting even programs that
carried no actual funding, deeming them earmarks and slating them for elim-
ination. Among the so-called earmarks that were now on the chopping block
were authorized education programs for Native Hawaiians, Alaska Natives,
and American Indians.

Fortunately, one House member on the other side of the aisle was as passionate about retaining Native education projects as I was. Donald Young
was the Republicans' longest-serving representative, an Alaskan who had
first been elected to Congress in 1973. Don was married to an Alaska Native,
and had championed federal funding of indigenous programs throughout his
nineteen consecutive terms in the House. Now, he approached me to say that
he had convinced his caucus to support an amendment that would preserve Native education programs. He proposed that I sign on to a bipartisan
Young-Hirono amendment, which he hoped would ensure Democratic as
well as Republican votes, giving the provision a greater chance of being incorporated into the budget legislation currently being debated on the floor.

I was completely on board with this plan, and made sure the Democratic
leadership was aware that the bipartisan amendment would be offered with

my name attached, and that we should support it. But when the amendment came up for debate at close to midnight a few days later, word somehow had not reached Connecticut congresswoman Rosa DeLauro, who was managing the floor vote for Democrats that evening. Since Democrats were routinely voting down all the Republican amendments, and vice versa, Rosa remarked on the floor that Democrats would not support what she referred to as "the Young amendment." Most of the House members had already left for the evening, and because Rosa hadn't mentioned my name in connection with the provision, the few Democrats still in their seats failed to realize this was the amendment I had cosponsored, and the provision failed on a voice vote.

Don Young was apoplectic. He stormed up to me and started hollering in my face about the amendment not passing. "Why the hell didn't you talk to her?" he accused me, shaking his finger in Rosa's direction. But I wasn't focused on what he was saying right then. I was busy reviewing House procedures in my mind to come up with a plan to save the amendment. Beside me, Mike Honda, a California Democrat who, like me, was of Japanese descent, watched with interest to see what I would do next. I decided that my best opportunity lay in the fact that the provision had been put to a voice vote, with yeas and nays called out from the floor, and the presiding officer judging the winner. Since the votes of individual members aren't recorded in a voice vote, I could request a revote using the more formal roll call procedure, in which members' yeas or nays would be entered into the record with their names. I jumped to my feet and announced, "I call for a roll call vote!"—thereby ensuring that the measure would have a second chance the next day when a quorum would be present.

A red-faced Don Young was still berating me, but I pushed past him to go and talk to Rosa DeLauro, who was standing a few seats away. I asked Rosa why she had spoken against the amendment. "The Republicans are eliminating even nonearmarked programs," she said, "and we're going to hold them to it, because some of their programs are on the hit list, too. Why should we help them save this one program? What about all the other programs that won't be restored?" I explained to her that this was a measure that I was co-sponsoring with Don Young, and we had hoped it would garner bipartisan support.

Now, with less than twenty-four hours to ensure that the amendment would pass the second time around, I had my work cut out for me. I would have to reach out to as many of the 193 Democrats in the House as I could and convince them to support a revote on the amendment the next afternoon. The following morning, I spoke at our Democratic caucus meeting to explain why I was asking for everyone's commitment to vote yes on the Young-Hirono amendment. I reminded them how important Native education programs were to preserving and promoting the culture of indigenous Americans, including a large number of constituents in my home state. When we reconvened in the House chamber that afternoon, I was like a heat-seeking missile, finding members on the floor even as we continued to vote on dozens of other amendments every two minutes. I wanted to be absolutely sure that everyone knew I was cosponsoring the bipartisan amendment and that they would vote for it in the roll call.

After watching me on the floor, Rosa DeLauro told me that she would support my measure, and she would record her yea vote early to signal to our fellow Democrats that they should back the amendment, too. We both knew that with 435 representatives in the House, members often watched the massive digital monitor behind the Speaker's platform to see how a vote was going and whether their caucus was supporting a provision. The House was at almost full attendance by the time the Young-Hirono amendment was called, and right away the board lit up with Rosa's affirmative vote. I saw Mike Honda shake his head and chuckle appreciatively as the column of yes votes grew longer and longer on the huge screen. "You really know how to do this," he would say later. When all the votes were tallied, the provision had passed easily, with only four Democrats voting against it, because I hadn't been able to get to them in time and they had missed Rosa's signal.

Don Young was already making his way over to my desk, this time with a huge grin splitting his face. "You did it!" he exulted, throwing his arms around me in a bear hug. Grinning as enthusiastically as he was, I patted his shoulder and then stepped back from his embrace.

"You know, Don," I said, "when you came up to me last night, yelling in my face, I was too busy thinking how to save the amendment procedurally to really take it in. But if I'd had my wits about me, do you know what I would have said?"

"No, what?" he asked, his eyes still alight with our win.

"I would have said *fuck you*."

Don threw back his head and laughed uproariously. Though he and I would go on to disagree on just about every policy agenda other than indigenous issues, from then on the irascible Republican congressman from Alaska became my friend and champion, going so far as to draw heat from Mitch McConnell after he filmed a campaign ad in support of my Democratic primary bid for Senate two years later—but that race was not yet in my sights.

During my third term in Congress, I received sad news from home: Allison Lynde, whom everyone now knew as Allen or Al, had been found unresponsive on the morning of July 20, 2011, slumped on the floor by his desk at the Civil Rights Commission. Allison, as I still thought of him, had never kept fixed work hours; he must have stayed late the night before, a solitary worker in an empty office building.

Since we had parted ways, Allison had been dogged by personal and professional problems. After his theater ambitions failed to pan out, he had resumed making a living as a lawyer, but he was habitually disgruntled with his situation. He would often write to me in Washington, long letters detailing how mistreated he felt by bosses and coworkers who did not give him his due. He had developed a reputation in Hawaii's small legal circle for being difficult, and had quit or been asked to leave a number of jobs before landing at the Civil Rights Commission. After we broke up, I had often assisted him financially, while distancing myself from personal interaction with him, which in later years usually involved accusations of abandonment and requests for more help.

After I married Leighton, I had come to a much clearer understanding of my eighteen-year-long relationship with Allison. He had cared for me, that much I knew, and he had needed me, too, yet I had always suspected that he believed he could do better than me, and if I'm being honest, for a while I believed he could do better than me, too. I had never felt particularly attractive in Allison's eyes, perhaps because he was always criticizing my outfits and appearance. If I gained five pounds, he would say I was getting fat and was no longer appealing to him. Such comments kept me off balance. It was only after I refused his marriage proposal and moved on from our relationship that he began to understand what he had lost. A mutual friend told me years later that Allison had confided to her that I had been the love of his life, and that he had realized it too late.

Other friends had expressed relief on hearing that we had finally ended the romantic part of our relationship. "About time," one of them told me.

"Why didn't you say something?" I asked her.

"Like you would have listened," she retorted.

She was right. It had taken me a long time to understand that Allison and

I had shared an unhealthy codependency. Perhaps because I'd never known my father, or had a chance in childhood to observe a stable, mutually supportive romantic partnership in my own family, I hadn't fully realized how challenging my connection with Allison had been. In contrast, Leighton was so secure and supportive of me that he had agreed to help Allison on several occasions, even hiring him to work in his office, though that job didn't last long either. Once, when I asked if we could lend Allison a sum of money because he was going through another hard patch, Leighton replied, "Yes, because I know how important he was to you." Leighton would also take Allison's calls and meet with him in person to save me from the drain of dealing with him directly. If Allison and I had enabled in each other the parts of ourselves that needed to be healed, with Leighton I had found someone who was always on my side.

Until his very last day, Allison had remained troubled, too often blaming others for his downward spiral and relying on prescription pain medication to blunt his emotional pain. I would never know what had so abruptly ended his life, but when I heard he had died alone on the floor of his office, I thought: *What a sad fate.* Allison had possessed such talent, but he had also wrestled with many demons, and long-term happiness had eluded him.

Allison's mother had died some years before, and he had no remaining family other than a cousin and an elderly aunt who suffered from Alzheimer's, who lived with him in his condo and whom he supported. It pained me to learn that when the cousin went to break the news of Allison's death to her, before he could speak the aunt looked at him and said, "He's not coming back, is he?"

David Hagino took the lead in planning a memorial service, which would be held on the steps of the State Capitol. I had flown home to be among the small group of friends who gathered to pay our respects. Someone asked if I could provide an appropriate photograph for the gathering. As it happened, I had the perfect one.

Back when Allison and I were together, he had presented me with a huge framed portrait of himself as a birthday gift one year. This was back when he had recently discovered his love of the stage, and the photo was one of his theatrical headshots. There was no denying that Allison was handsome, but I had chuckled when I unwrapped the gift, because who gives a picture of himself for someone else's birthday? Allison had looked hurt and annoyed that I wasn't delighted by the gift, though I doubt he realized that his hold on me was already loosening. I never did display that picture on my wall, but I never got rid of it either. I thought that would have been bad karma for both Allison and me, and so I carried that framed photograph with me everyplace I lived, and for the past two decades it had remained tucked in a closet in the home I shared with Leighton. As I unwrapped the image for Allison's memorial service, I was glad that I had held on to it for so long.

In front of the State Capitol the next afternoon, noticing how the sunlight glinted off the frame of the photograph, I allowed my thoughts to roam back through the years, recalling another sunny afternoon, when Allison and I had stood in this very place, piles of lei around our necks, the two of us laughing in celebration of having just been sworn in as lawyers. Everything had felt so full of promise then. Now, with Leighton at my side, I listened as David spoke of the scores of young men Allison had saved from the hell of war as a conscientious objector, and of the many political campaigns we had run together. Taking some small consolation from this reminder of his successes, I silently bid my old friend a final farewell.

CHAPTER EIGHTEEN

Across the Aisle

After three terms in the House, I had a decision to make. Daniel Akaka, who had served in the Senate for twenty-two years, announced that he would not seek reelection in 2012. As soon as the news broke in Hawaii, Ed Case, my former primary opponent in the governor's race, declared that he would once again run for Senator Akaka's seat.

I spent several months assessing the pros and cons of entering the race. It was without a doubt the riskier path. Though nothing is sure in politics, I thought that as long as I continued to work hard to represent the people of my home state, voters would continue to reelect me to the House. If I ran for Senate, I would risk losing not only that race but my House seat as well. But I was Laura Sato Hirono's daughter: the safe proposition had never held any particular attraction for me. It seemed to me that in the Senate chamber I could be an even stronger advocate for my constituents. For one thing, the six-year term enjoyed by senators meant that I would no longer need to spend half of every two-year term in the House raising money to run for reelection. As a senator, I would also be charged with representing my entire state rather than just half of Hawaii as one of its two U.S. representatives. Further, in a legislative body with far fewer members, every voice would carry even more weight on issues of national concern. But what ultimately tipped the scales for me was the thought that I might look back on this open window and regret not running.

One doesn't get many do-overs in politics, but in significant ways, my Senate race in 2012 would turn out to be just that—an almost exact parallel to my race for governor ten years before, except this time, as a sitting member of the state's congressional delegation, I had the tacit support of Senator Daniel Inouye, who became more openly supportive as my campaign progressed. I would face the same Democratic opponent, Ed Case, in the primary, and I would once again beat him at the polls, this time by a decisive margin of 17 points. Victory tasted sweet as I advanced in the race to square off in the general election against my other former challenger in the governor's race, Republican Linda Lingle. The news media, catching the Republican National Committee's fervor at the possibility that this Senate seat could be a pickup for them, made much of our matchup, asking me in interview after interview why, having lost to Lingle before, I expected a different outcome. "I've learned a thing or two since my governor's race," I remember telling one reporter.

"Oh? What have your learned?" she asked.

I didn't hesitate. "I learned how to win."

As always, there were doubters. "How do you expect to beat Linda Lingle?" one friend demanded when I met with him to seek his endorsement. "She handed you your head on a platter last time." I refused to entertain his assessment. After all, I had almost pulled out a victory in the governor's race against long odds. "I only lost by four points last time," I reminded my naysayer, before pointing out that a win in the current race was well worth striving for, because if elected, I would bring new and much-needed perspectives into the Senate chamber. As I'd observed at my first big fundraising event in Hawaii, the Senate needed a lot more diversity.

"The good news is, I will bring a quadruple dose of diversity to the Senate," I told the crowd. I held up one hand and ticked them off on my fingers: "One, I am a woman. Two, I am Asian American, and if elected will become the first Asian woman ever to serve in the Senate. Three, I am an immigrant. And four, I am a Buddhist."

People began clapping enthusiastically, and then a lone voice shouted from the crowd, "Yeah, yeah, but are you gay?"

"Nobody's perfect," I shot back, and everyone erupted into laughter.

This exchange made the rounds on social media, eventually catching the attention of New York senator Chuck Schumer. Throughout that year, as I stumped nationally with several other Democratic candidates, Chuck never tired of asking me to repeat that story, which always provoked laughter and applause.

On election night that November, the mood at my campaign headquarters in Honolulu was especially jubilant. Early in the evening, it became clear that my rematch with Linda Lingle would have a vastly different outcome than our previous race. In the end, I won in a landslide, capturing fifty out of fifty-one districts in the Islands.

Having held my own in five grueling debates against Ed Case during the primary and five more against Linda Lingle during the general election, to beat both of them so decisively was gratifying. It can be strange and fortuitous how life turns, because if Ed Case had simply waited out Daniel Akaka's last term in the Senate, rather than running against him and thereby opening up his own seat for me, he would have been the congressional incumbent in 2012 and a strong favorite to win Akaka's seat. Had that happened, I might still have been at home on an extended sabbatical, perhaps never returning to politics. But Case had miscalculated, thus creating the vacancy that had allowed me to run for Congress, which put me in an advantageous position to win the Senate seat he had now failed to capture twice.

The other longtime member of Hawaii's Senate delegation, Daniel Inouye, then eighty-eight years old, would succumb to respiratory failure in December 2012, one month after my election to the Senate. When he realized he was dying, Inouye had written to Neil Abercrombie, then the governor of Hawaii, requesting that he appoint Representative Colleen Hanabusa to serve out the eighteen months left of his term. But Abercrombie ignored the senior senator's request and appointed his lieutenant governor, Brian Schatz, instead.

Without a doubt, political alliances were at play, though Abercrombie insisted he had chosen to appoint Schatz, who was in his midforties, to give him the chance to serve for more years and attain the kind of seniority and influence that Inouye had achieved. Although I had served with Colleen Hanabusa in the House and would have welcomed the opportunity to work with her again in the Senate, whatever Abercrombie's reasons for passing her over, I knew that Brian Schatz, too, was a bright and committed public servant. An interesting note was that Leighton's daughter, Malia, who was now an attorney, was Brian's extremely capable deputy chief of staff. Malia had previously volunteered on my campaigns and had exhibited strong people skills. Were it not for concerns about nepotism, I would have employed her myself.

A few weeks later, as I took my oath of office as a senator, I was humbled by the realization that Brian and I represented a new era in Hawaii politics, a changing of the guard, replacing a pair of old friends and elder statesmen who had championed the most diverse state in the union for seven decades combined.

⎯⎯⎯⎯

The Senate had a very different atmosphere from the House. With only one hundred members, less than a quarter of the 435 voting representatives in the lower chamber, everything moved at a more stately pace. The voting procedures, for example, at first seemed almost quaint. Unlike the electronic system in the House, where members stuck their cards into slots and saw their votes appear immediately on a giant monitor, and where scores of bills might be voted on in rapid succession, in the Senate a piece of legislation could be discussed for weeks on end, and the vote, when it was finally called, could take hours. Senators could also speak on the floor about issues of concern to them for extended periods of time, whether or not the concern was related to a bill currently being considered. In the early days, when I took my turn presiding over the Senate as a member of the Democratic majority, Alabama Republican Jeff Sessions would take to the floor almost weekly to rail against U.S. immigration policy. These floor speeches by individual senators were generally delivered to an almost empty chamber, but I always listened attentively, even to Sessions's repeated screeds. When major bills came to the floor, however, debate times were more strictly controlled, with party caucuses negotiating who would have an opportunity to speak.

Another way in which the Senate differed from the House was that, with so few members, senators served on more committees, which multiplied our workload. Incoming senators made their committee interests known to the leader of their party—for me in January 2013 that was Nevada Democrat Harry Reid—who would then parcel out assignments, often based on seniority. My first choice was the Senate Armed Services Committee. Given Hawaii's position at the crossroads of the Pacific and the large number of military personnel stationed there, I knew it was critically important for me to have a presence on that panel. I was also interested in Health, Education, Labor and Pensions—schools, health care, and workers—but as that committee was fully subscribed, I was granted my alternative choice: the Committee on the Judiciary. This was an auspicious assignment. It would allow me to have early input on the selection of judges and immigration policy, as both were under the subject matter jurisdiction of this committee. I was also appointed to Veteran Affairs, which would allow me to continue supporting active military as they moved to veteran status, as well as the Environment and Public Works Committee and Small Business and Entrepreneurship, which both offered prime opportunities to propose legislation and advance positions that could benefit my constituents back home.

The very first bill I introduced and got passed through the Senate required me to gain the support of none other than Jeff Sessions, whose views on issues such as voting rights and immigration were diametrically opposed to mine. And yet I needed the Alabama senator's help in getting a stalled bill to a vote on the floor via a process known as unanimous consent. The bill proposed a charitable tax contribution to help victims of a recent typhoon in the Philippines, and there was a deadline to get it passed. Apart from meeting a humanitarian need, the legislation was important to the large number of my constituents in Hawaii who were of Filipino descent and whose families had been devastated by the typhoon. I knew that the Republican caucus was against the provision, however, so when Sessions walked into the Senate chamber on the night I was trying to move the bill out of committee, I knew he was there to object. Since even one dissent would sink the bill's chances, I decided to appeal to Sessions directly.

I followed the elfin, silver-haired southerner into the Republican cloakroom, something rarely done by members of the opposite party. I wanted to explain to him why the bill was so important to the Philippines, one of our major allies.

"Why is your caucus against this bill?" I asked him.

Taken aback by my presence in the cloakroom, Sessions seemed ready to dismiss my question. "We have to be consistent in opposing this sort of tax provision," he said.

Lame, I thought. "Consistency is the hobgoblin of little minds," I quickly countered, and pointed out that this kind of legislation was not unprecedented. Then, looking directly into his eyes, I reached out and placed my palm gently on his heart. "I'm now speaking to this," I told him.

In the Senate, we seldom approached each other in such a personal way, yet my Republican colleague did not seem offended. In fact, his whole demeanor loosened, and when next he spoke his automatic formality was gone.

"Okay, Mazie," he said, his tone thoughtful. "I'm still going to object to the bill in the current form, but I think we might be able to reach a compromise we can support."

We put our heads together and worked things out on the spot, and the bill passed the Senate that evening. This type of bipartisan compromise on a unanimous consent matter was an extremely rare occurrence in the Senate, yet we had managed to get it done. President Obama signed the measure into law shortly after its passage in the House.

Even so, when Jeff Sessions became Donald Trump's nominee for attorney general five years later, I would vote against his confirmation, as I didn't believe a man with his restrictive views on American civil liberties should become the country's chief lawyer. Further, Sessions had managed to install his former aide Stephen Miller, a documented white nationalist, as an adviser in the Trump White House, which spoke volumes to me about what kind of an attorney general Sessions might be. Though I knew the Republican-led Senate would vote to appoint him anyway, his responses to my questions during his confirmation hearing had solidified my views about his willingness to implement Trump's racist agenda, which would be validated when he

cleared the way for Trump's "zero-tolerance" family separation policy just
months later.

I was reminded that even though my Republican colleagues and I could
sometimes meet on the same page, we remained far apart on many issues of
significance to the American people. And yet, after so many years in politics,
I knew the value of working across the aisle wherever we could find a sliver
of common ground, even if I found a colleague's views on other issues not
just disagreeable but outright repugnant. When it came to passing legislation, engaging in bipartisan consensus building with people whose views
might differ drastically from our own—both across the aisle and within
one's own party—was one of our greatest charges as lawmakers. For me, this
engagement had always felt deeply purposeful, which was why I had made
it my practice to find Republican cosponsors for many of the bills I introduced. I had even directed my staff to find issues of common concern with
members across the aisle, such as poor access to medical care in rural areas in
states like Iowa, which was also a problem for some on the neighbor islands
of my home state. Working on these issues in a bipartisan way could greatly
benefit constituents caught between conservatives and progressives, between
majority and minority caucuses, between red states and blue, so to truly
make life better for ordinary Americans, I had to be willing to work with
anyone who was willing to work with me.

In committee meetings and side conversations, however, members too often talked over one another, failing to listen attentively to the points a colleague was trying to make. North Dakota Democrat Heidi Heitkamp, one of
my closest friends in the Senate, came up with a novel idea to promote a more
thoughtful exchange among Democrats of differing views, using a lei that I
had given her.

On Tuesday mornings, visitors from Hawaii had a standing invitation to stop by my office for what we called Talk Story hour, an informal meet-and-greet over coffee and pastries during which constituents could share their concerns with me or simply say hello. They often brought me beautiful lei, which I would then wear on the Senate floor, and sometimes share with colleagues. One evening, in a gathering of moderate Democrats from conservative states, Heidi Heitkamp decreed that anyone who wanted to speak would have to wear a lei I had given her earlier that afternoon, with the proviso that the wearer could not be interrupted while speaking. Heidi had a musical laugh and dancing eyes, which probably helped convince her colleagues to go along with her unorthodox suggestion. "This lei is from Mazie," she told them cheerfully. "So when you wear it, be respectful. You have to become as Zen as she is." A number of our colleagues who were at the gathering later reported to me that Heidi's novel approach had worked surprisingly well.

While I would hardly have described myself as Zen—I was active and determined in committee meetings and on the Senate floor—my outward persona was still relatively reserved and polite back then. Until Trump was elected, that approach had usually worked well for me, and I saw no need to call upon my more contentious side as I pursued my goals. So I loved that Heidi had used my lei in this way. As I saw it, any approach that facilitated constructive communication and greater thoughtfulness—rather than each of us remaining locked in our own perspectives—was to be embraced. It was why, when I'd first arrived in the Senate, I had set up one-on-one introductory meetings with as many Republican senators as would allow me on their calendars. I wanted to make a human connection that might help us remain collegial later on, when our caucuses sparred on the floor.

I had started with the leaders, meeting with Mitch McConnell and six or seven other Republicans before the business of the Senate took over our time. In these informal sessions, I was particularly interested in what my colleagues did to relax, and thought a good way to connect would be to ask them about their hobbies or what they had chosen to hang on their walls. Orrin Hatch, the long-serving senator from Utah, who had crossed the aisle to help pass important legislation such as the Americans with Disabilities Act (ADA) and the Children's Health Insurance Program (CHIP), was a particular surprise. On his office walls were gold and platinum record albums. He explained that, in his spare time, he wrote religious and spiritual songs that had found a wide audience through the albums framed on his wall. Had I not visited him in his space, I would have had no idea that he possessed this gift. As I got up to leave after our meeting that afternoon, Hatch told me that if I ever needed his help, I should not hesitate to call on him.

The very next morning, he was graciously receptive when I took him at his word, approaching him on the floor to ask if he would cosponsor my proposed visa waiver for citizens of Hong Kong. I explained that such a waiver would allow travelers from Hong Kong—after an initial vetting—to enter our country multiple times without needing to obtain a visa each time, thus boosting visitors to states like my own with strong tourism economies. When I was done talking through the particulars, Hatch agreed to sign on. Though originally introduced as a bipartisan stand-alone bill, the Hong Kong visa waiver provision would later be incorporated into the comprehensive immigration reform legislation of 2013. I have no doubt that Hatch's support helped persuade my Republican colleagues to accept the measure.

Despite Republicans' knee-jerk opposition to many of President Obama's initiatives, back then, alliances across the aisle were easier to forge than they would be under Trump. Indeed, the 2013 immigration reform bill had been drafted by the bipartisan "Gang of Eight," a self-selected group that included four Democrats—Chuck Schumer of New York, Dick Durbin of Illinois, Michael Bennet of Colorado, and Bob Menendez of New Jersey—and four

Republicans—Lindsey Graham of South Carolina, John McCain and Jeff Flake of Arizona, and Marco Rubio of Florida.

Though I appreciated the Gang of Eight's effort to fix an immigration system that we all knew needed to be overhauled, I could not help feeling that the inclusion of women—especially me, the Senate's sole immigrant—early in the process could have improved the bill. I was glad that I would still have a chance to engage with the draft legislation before it went to the floor for debate, since immigration fell under the purview of the Judiciary Committee, on which I served. As it was, when the legislation came to our committee for markup, I noted with dismay that in revamping the U.S. visa program, the bill had eliminated certain long-standing categories of family visas.

The Gang of Eight's bill did not reflect an understanding of the real world challenges faced by immigrants in a new country and the importance of families remaining together. My own experience had shown me the importance of all generations rowing the boat together, everybody working to bring in money to support the family unit. This is how immigrants survive, and how they create a foundation on which subsequent generations might build. I also knew firsthand the devastation that results when families are kept apart, and so I became the lone voice on the committee pushing for family unity as a guiding principle, working doggedly to get amendments aimed at preserving family unity in the bill.

Unfortunately, the eight men drafting the legislation had made a pact to vote as a bloc on all proposed amendments that substantively changed their bill. They had also agreed to unanimously vote down any changes to the visa system they had devised as a signature part of the legislation. This often put the Gang's four Democrats in the unenviable position of having to oppose provisions with which they personally agreed. I'd spoken to Chuck Schumer about adding an amendment to support family reunification, for example,

and he implored me not to bring it up, as he would have to vote against it. "All
the advocacy groups you're working with will hate me," he said. "Well, I'll
make sure they don't hate you too much," I deadpanned, refusing to agree
not to raise an issue I knew to be vital to immigrants' well-being.

In the end, my family reunification amendment was not accepted, though
some of my other proposals, including one aimed at ensuring proper care for
unaccompanied minors at the border, forced the hand of the Gang's four Republicans and were adopted.

There was one important amendment that I had not completed drafting
while the bill was still in committee, as I had been working with several
different immigrant advocacy groups to ensure that the language of the
provision would correctly address our concerns. As originally written, the
comprehensive immigration reform bill disadvantaged women, in that it designated preferential categories for skilled workers in the areas of science and
technology, jobs that were disproportionately filled by men. There was no
preferred category covering jobs traditionally held by women, such as nurses,
home health aides, and teachers. I was banking on having the chance to argue for this additional category when the bill came up for debate in the wider
chamber.

Mine would be one of some two hundred additional amendments filed for
floor consideration. Now that the bill had moved out of committee to be considered by the full Senate, I assumed there would be an opportunity to debate
many of these proposed changes in turn. But I quickly realized that intense
negotiations were occurring behind the scenes about which provisions would
be taken up. Day after day I lobbied Chuck Schumer to get my amendment
to the floor. One day, he took me aside to let me know that for my one change,
our Republican colleagues wanted six of theirs. "If you want the Senate to
consider your amendment, you're going to have to get Lindsey Graham's
support," he told me.

I understood Chuck to mean that as a senior member of both the Judiciary Committee and the Gang of Eight, Lindsey could bring his fellow Republicans on board. I immediately reached out to Lindsey, and he agreed to meet with me, but for two weeks no meeting was scheduled. Finally, on the day before the bill was due to be put to a vote, I cornered him on the Senate floor and insisted we set a meeting for the following morning, before the vote was called. It had taken my staff and me a long time to draft this entire new category of immigrants, and Lindsey was our shot at giving the amendment a fighting chance.

My staff and I prepared for the meeting as if for a trial, anticipating all the arguments and identifying ahead of time the compromises we might be willing to make. We convened in Lindsey's office the next morning, and he listened to my proposal, politely at first, and then with increasing interest. He took issue with a couple of points, such as the timing for implementation; fortunately, they were items that I had already decided I would strategically concede. After Lindsey and I went back and forth on the language of the draft, making edits that would help minimize Republican resistance to the provision, he seemed satisfied. "You know, Mazie," he said when we were done, "you're very convincing. I'm going to support your amendment, and you have my word that I'll also support it when we negotiate the bill with the House."

With Lindsey Graham's backing, my amendment shot to the top of the list, and I had every hope that it would make it into the final bill. But now there was a new wrinkle: Chuck Schumer wanted the immigration reform bill to have as much bipartisan support as he could wrangle, and even though the four Republicans in the Gang of Eight had already pledged to back it, he wanted more Republicans to sign on. Working with Judiciary Committee chair Patrick Leahy, a Democrat from Vermont, Schumer engineered a late-breaking agreement to incorporate two additional provisions that would garner more Republican votes. After the inclusion of these provisions in what is known as a "manager's package," the further consideration of all other amendments, including mine, was effectively shut down.

This would be a powerful learning experience for me. I had seen that all sorts of political machinations could derail a proposed amendment once a bill came to the floor, and from then on, I would be relentless in getting my changes added to a bill while it was still in committee. Yet despite my disappointment, the experience had been a net positive: Eleven of the twenty-three provisions I had proposed during markup had been incorporated into the legislation, the second most amendments accepted from any member of our then eighteen-person Judiciary Committee, and I had worked with both Democrats and Republicans to get this done. I had also managed to forge a collegial bipartisan alliance with Lindsey Graham over one aspect of immigration reform, which I believed would serve us well as we debated other issues in the future.

Kirsten Gillibrand, a Democrat from New York who had become a friend, told me later that during the debate period for immigration reform, she had watched with amusement as I'd cornered Chuck Schumer day after day, several times a day, determined to get my amendment to the floor. Aware of my persistent nature, she had thought: *Chuck Schumer has no idea who he's dealing with in Mazie Hirono.* I smiled at Kirsten's insight. Never noisy in my approach, I had long thought of myself as a workhorse, not a show horse, which in the showboating arena of politics had led some to initially dismiss me as an undemanding Asian woman who would not challenge them. Perhaps because I seldom shared my perspective on pending legislation in the national press, some colleagues assumed I did not hold a strong position on the issue and therefore would not fight for my point of view. These colleagues realized soon enough how mistaken they were, and that in fact I was tenacious and strategic. But from my earliest days in the Hawaii State House, I had learned to take the long view, to assess the board and move my pieces into place accordingly.

Two years into my first term in the U.S. Senate, I had set my sights on getting onto the Appropriations Committee, which controlled the purse strings of the federal government. Hawaii's senior senator Daniel Inouye had served on the committee starting in 1971, and had chaired it for four years, until his death just one month before I was sworn in to the Senate. It was an incredibly powerful committee, and many members wanted to be on it.

In the fall of 2014, I approached the new Appropriations chair, Barbara Mikulski of Maryland, to make my interest in her committee known. The first woman to chair that influential panel, Barbara was a powerhouse among federal lawmakers. Her cherubic smile and lively eyes belied her toughness and resilience. She was the longest-serving woman in Congress, first elected to the House in 1977. Ten years later she became the first Democratic woman elected to the U.S. Senate in her own right. There had been women in the Senate before, but only those who had stepped in to finish a deceased husband's term. Born and raised in scrappy Baltimore, Barbara didn't need any man to push open the doors for her. She threw them open wide herself and marched through confidently, all four feet eleven inches of her.

Every woman in Congress owed a debt to Barbara Mikulski. For one thing, in the early nineties, she had challenged the Senate's outdated dress code for women, making it permissible for us to wear slacks. Until she and Senator Nancy Kassebaum, a Kansas Republican, showed up for a weekend session attired in pantsuits in 1993, Senate rules had dictated that women be dressed in skirts and stockings, with their arms covered, even though men were allowed to dress more casually on weekends. Barbara's and Nancy's nonregulation apparel that day caused a minor crisis, as the parliamentarian scurried to check the rules. Barbara was serenely unfazed. Indeed, she continued to wear pants in cheerful defiance of the dress code until the Senate finally voted a few months later to change the dress requirements for women.

Starting in 1992, Barbara also convened annual Women Power Workshops in her hideaway office to welcome incoming Senate women. Hideaway offices were handed out according to length of service; the main perk of hideaways was that lobbyists, reporters, and the public had no access to these secret spaces, to which lawmakers might escape to pore over briefing materials in peace, to hammer out difficult agreements with colleagues, or to share celebratory cocktails with friends. Not all hideaways were large, welcoming spaces, however. Tucked into the nooks of unmapped hallways and crannies of winding staircases, many were small and windowless. But given her seniority, Barbara's hideaway was a spacious room on an upper floor of the Capitol, attractively appointed with dark wood furniture, a ruby-red couch, an ornate, gilt-edged mirror opposite the entry, and a gallery wall of framed class portraits of Senate women from previous terms. As was the custom for hideaways, the outside door was unmarked except by a number, the room's location undisclosed to all but the guests Barbara invited into her sanctuary.

Over wine and cheese, the Maryland lawmaker offered new arrivals a crash course in committee rules and responsibilities, and the effective management of staffers. That first year, Barbara was one of only five women in the room. By the time I was elected to the Senate two decades later, there were twenty of us, with Barbara as our acknowledged dean. At her gatherings during my first term, I was surrounded by distinguished colleagues, women like Elizabeth Warren of Massachusetts, Amy Klobuchar of Minnesota, Claire McCaskill of Missouri, Kirsten Gillibrand of New York, Dianne Feinstein of California, Lisa Murkowski of Alaska, Heidi Heitkamp of North

Dakota, and many more. All were committed public servants, and the bonds we were forging had nothing to do with whether we were from a blue state or a red one.

Since I had gotten to know Barbara during these sessions, Barbara's response when I expressed my interest in joining the Appropriations Committee took me by surprise. We were on the floor of the Senate during a break in session. "If you want to get on this committee, Mazie," Barbara said, "you're going to have to be a lot more vocal and aggressive around here." Her criticism of how I conducted myself struck me as unwarranted, but I held my tongue, as I had no interest in discussing the matter on the Senate floor.

But a few days later, Barbara hit the same note during an after-hours meeting in her hideaway. Most of the women who had attended the bipartisan event had already left, but a number of the Democratic senators, including Amy Klobuchar and Kirsten Gillibrand, remained in the room. "As I was telling Mazie," Barbara started in, "she's going to have to learn to speak up. Mazie, we're going to have to hear your voice a lot more." This time, I set her straight. I realized that she, like so many of my colleagues, had misjudged my commitment, despite my six years in the House of Representatives and the two years I had already spent in the Senate, not to mention my years in the Hawaii state legislature and as lieutenant governor. Apparently she thought she was giving much-needed advice to a nice Japanese girl who did not like to make waves. It was mind-boggling to me that this groundbreaking, history-making feminist would hold what I saw as stereotypical notions of me as a demure and nonconfrontational Asian woman. Never mind that I had cannily steered a course through the rough-and-tumble of old-boy political networks for more than two decades, and had been duly elected to the nation's highest legislative chamber, just as she had been.

I faced her with a level gaze. "Excuse me, Barbara, but you don't know anything about me or my culture," I said. "You don't know anything about what I've had to overcome to get here, so I don't need lectures about how I should behave from you."

"Oh, I meant no offense," she assured me.

"So let's just move on, then," I replied.

Amy Klobuchar, then in her second term in the Senate, told me later that she had never heard anyone speak back to Barbara that way. Whether our dean of women felt affronted in the moment I cannot say, but after our little dustup, Barbara no longer doubted that I would speak my mind with her, and I welcomed her advice when it made sense to me. She was, after all, more experienced than any of the rest of the Senate women, and she was deeply invested in our success. Years later, after she left the Senate in 2017, we saw each other again at Hillary Clinton's seventieth birthday party in Washington, D.C. That night, Barbara made her way over to me.

"I still can't believe I spoke to you like that back when you first asked about Approps," she said, using shorthand for the committee name. "Mazie, I'm so sorry. I have no idea what I was thinking." It's worth noting that by then I had become one of the Senate's most outspoken critics of Donald Trump, and in on-air news interviews I didn't hesitate to voice my opinion of the way he was managing his presidency. I knew Barbara approved.

I never did get onto the Appropriations Committee. Brian Schatz, my colleague from Hawaii, who had been sworn in to the Senate five days before me, got the spot based on seniority—or so I was told. I was annoyed, because I had been in Congress far longer than Brian had, but I moved on and agreed to serve on the Intel Committee instead. What I learned in my two years there was invaluable and eye opening—though, of course, I can't discuss any of it.

The tendency of some Senate colleagues to underestimate me was one reason that I appreciated Lindsey Graham, who recognized my drive and determination. Though his politics and mine radically differed, after working with him on immigration reform and several other bills, I had come to see the South Carolinian as a conscientious public servant and a pragmatic consensus builder, a true believer fighting for the conservative cause alongside his closest friend in the Senate, maverick war hero John McCain.

All that changed with the 2016 election and the death of John McCain two years later. In the aftermath of these two shattering events, we would discover that Lindsey Graham had another side: that of a chameleon willing to remake himself in the image of the person in his orbit whom he had judged to be uniquely powerful. For decades, and to the benefit of us all, that person had been John McCain. But when a particularly virulent form of brain cancer claimed McCain's life on August 25, 2018, Lindsey lost not only a close friend but also an anchor. None of us had anticipated that he would begin to parrot the chaotic ramblings of the charlatan in chief, the pathologically unfit narcissist in the White House, a man whom Graham himself had throughout the 2016 primary claimed would destroy the Republican Party. "This is a fight for the heart and soul of the Republican Party," he had told CNN's Wolf Blitzer in March 2016, just two months before the New York con man became the presumptive Republican nominee. "If it's Donald Trump carrying the conservative banner," Graham had predicted, "we'll be unable in the future to grow the conservative cause."

Those of us who knew Lindsey before could hardly believe our eyes and ears as he was transformed into an uncritical groupie, underwriting the policies and cruelties of the most fraudulent president in modern history.

Political commentators struggled to explain Lindsey's conversion. Perhaps former Georgia gubernatorial candidate Stacey Abrams captured some kernel of psychological truth in a podcast interview she did with the *Washington Post*'s Jonathan Capehart. "Lindsey Graham has no other definition to his life," she reflected. "He lives in a time where fealty to Donald Trump is the only guarantee of his continued existence as the senator from South Carolina. And when your sole definition of who you are is the position you hold, then you will do anything not to lose that sense of who you are."

One of my colleagues on the Judiciary Committee expressed a similar idea when I shared my dismay at how completely under Trump's sway Graham had fallen. "Lindsey has always had a deep psychological need to attach himself to a stronger person," he said. "And for better or worse, he takes on the shading of that person."

"But Trump?" I moaned. "John McCain must be turning in his grave."

After the Arizona senator's funeral service, I was so concerned about the sense of loss that Lindsey must be feeling that I had picked some blooms from the churchyard where McCain's service was held and used them to make a card for Lindsey in remembrance of his longtime comrade. Just weeks later, I would lament the disappearance of the Lindsey Graham I had respected as a lawmaker and appreciated as a colleague. I missed the decency of the man who had huddled with me before a critical vote on immigration reform to figure out a way to get an amendment supporting immigrant women into the bill.

When Graham ascended to the chairmanship of the Senate Judiciary Committee in 2019, I pointedly commented to a reporter: "I hope the immigration Lindsey Graham, the person that I did bipartisan work with, will show up in that hearing room."

The next day, after Graham gaveled in for the first time as chair of the committee, he addressed the senators and the press people crowded into the room. "I want you to know that the immigration Lindsey Graham is here," he said in his opening remarks. The frowns and wrinkled brows around me revealed that people had no idea what on earth he was talking about, but I understood that his reference had been directed to me. He then added a strange coda: "But the other Lindsey Graham, the one I don't much like either, is also here."

Indeed, during the confirmation hearings for Justice Brett Kavanaugh the previous year, it wasn't the immigration Lindsey Graham who had shown his face. It was the other one. But by then I had learned to show my face in a new way, too.

CHAPTER NINETEEN

One Nation Under Siege

ong before the 2016 election, I had grappled with the truth that racism and sexism are never far below the surface in our country, and only eternal vigilance will keep their contagion in check. That contagion swept through our nation after November 8, 2016, the shocking night that Donald Trump was elected president.

Like much of the country, I felt pummeled by the results, unable to fully take in that a crude reality-TV pretender, whom the entire country had heard bragging about grabbing women's genitals, was now president. It made absolutely no sense to me that an extraordinarily qualified and committed public servant like Hillary Clinton had been unable to break through what she had referred to as "that highest, hardest glass ceiling." How could so many predictive polls have gotten the election outcome so wrong? What had befallen my country? Trump's campaign had unleashed on our country the

politics of white grievance, stoking the fires of hate and tribalism and escalating the violent "othering" of nonwhite Americans. As the world would
come to understand over the next four years, malign forces at home and
abroad had tampered with our electoral processes and essentially hijacked
the election. But on the night of November 8, this had not yet been proven
by a two-year-long special counsel investigation.

When I walked out to address the people gathered at the Japanese Cultural Center in Hawaii on election night, I refused to give a conciliatory
speech, as some had urged me to do. Instead, I spoke for only forty-five
seconds.

"It's clear that throughout this presidential campaign there's been a lot of
anger, fear, and feelings of frustration about the future of our country," I
began. "We need to acknowledge this anxiety, but this is not the time for our
country to allow fear to dictate our path forward. No matter who is sitting in
the Oval Office, we will continue to fight for the people who are getting
screwed every single second, minute, hour of the day. And if by our actions
we can decrease that number we will be making a difference and we will be
doing our jobs." With that, I left the stage.

People told me afterward that I had walked into a room filled with people
in bewildered despair, and I had shaken them awake, issuing a call to action
rather than admitting defeat. A switch had flipped in me, too. That night, I
vowed to fight for my country like I never had before. Just three months
later, I was at a rally in Washington, D.C., holding a bullhorn to my mouth
as I decried Trump's prohibition on travel from seven Muslim-majority
countries. He had instituted his so-called Muslim ban by executive order just
seven days after his inauguration. It was the first shot across the bow of racism. Soon, there would be many more.

My expectations of the most xenophobic, misogynistic, corrupt, and self-
dealing president in history could not have been lower, yet he would sink

beneath even that, plunging the nation into one crisis after another. There was no end to the cruelty, compulsive lies, and outright fraud perpetrated by Trump and his enablers. From the first days of his administration, most Americans suffered from a kind of whiplash, becoming almost catatonic with shock at the president's repeated assaults on our national norms. Equally as stupefying was the complete and utter abdication of oversight by the Republican majority in Congress.

Three months into the national trauma, during a congressional recess, I made arrangements to undergo elective cataract surgery, which would involve implanting a lens in my left eye. I had noticed a slow clouding of the vision in that eye, which made poring over hundreds of pages of fine print in legislative documents challenging. I had delayed scheduling the surgery, however. Though I had been assured that the procedure was straightforward and the incidence of complication rare, I secretly feared that I might be the botched exception that proved the rule.

My sight had already been compromised by a macular hole in the retina of my right eye, possibly connected to the injury sustained when I fell from the loft in my father's house as a three-year-old. Though my near-blind right eye caused depth perception problems when I descended stairs, it had not otherwise hindered me in my years as a legislator. But now the good eye needed to be shored up. I was intensely aware that if anything went wrong with the cataract surgery, I could go blind and would be unable to continue doing my job. It was why I had agonized for so many years about getting the procedure, and had instead devised work-arounds as my eyesight worsened. My staff helped me to deal with my sight issues in various ways. We would print out hard copies of my prepared remarks in ever-increasing font sizes, and I had also had a special riser built for use with the portable podium that senators used when giving speeches from their seats, to bring prepared texts closer to my one good eye. And when I was to address the Democratic National Convention with several other women senators in 2016, I spent the entire afternoon memorizing my remarks, as our rehearsal that morning had shown me that I would not be able to read from the giant teleprompter that the other speakers used. For me, that had been the last straw.

After finally screwing up my courage and setting a date for the eye surgery, I had to decide just how public to be about the procedure. There was no question that I would disclose it, but I was up for reelection the following year, and there had been indications that Tulsi Gabbard, the young congresswoman from Hawaii who had won my former House seat in 2012, was considering running against me. I considered the optics of our respective ages, Tulsi still in her thirties and me turning seventy later that year. And now I was about to undergo cataract surgery, which I knew could cause me to skew *old* in the minds of my constituents. I quickly realized I had to let this concern go. Voters had a right to full information as they decided who they wanted to represent them going forward. I would campaign as hard as I always did to hold my Senate seat, and then I would accept the will of the voters. With my communications team, I drafted a statement to be released the week before my procedure.

In preparation for the surgery, my physician at Johns Hopkins required a physical examination and chest X-ray to rule out underlying conditions that might affect my recovery. On April 7, 2017, I stopped by the office of the attending physician of the U.S. Congress, Dr. Brian Monahan, to have the tests performed, before heading to the Senate floor to cast my vote against the confirmation of Tenth Circuit Court of Appeals judge Neil Gorsuch to the Supreme Court. I knew that the Republican majority in the Senate would certainly confirm him, but it was important to register my opposition.

Like much of the country, I saw the impending appointment of Gorsuch as the theft of a Supreme Court seat by Senate majority leader Mitch McConnell. A month after Associate Justice Antonin Scalia's sudden death in February 2016, then-president Obama had nominated the moderate D.C. Circuit Court of Appeals judge Merrick Garland to replace him. But for almost an entire year, McConnell had refused to hold a confirmation hearing, insisting that since the court vacancy had come up in an election year, the nominee should be chosen by the next president. Predictably, Trump had selected a staunch conservative, but that was not my main reason for objecting to Gorsuch's confirmation. Gorsuch was known in legal circles to be a textualist, meaning he hewed to the literal meaning of the words that conveyed a law while ignoring the larger intent of the statute and the problem it had been crafted to address. The result was that his record showed a marked lack of empathy for the plight of ordinary people, with Gorsuch deciding almost always in favor of large corporations and organizational entities. His rigid literalism, combined with his conservative ideology, had led me to conclude he was not a nominee I could support.

With so much going on, I considered putting off my chest X-ray for another day, but ultimately decided that since I was already in the doctor's office, I might as well just get everything done. Early the next morning, a Saturday, Dr. Monahan called me at my home. "Have you ever sustained an injury to your right rib cage?" he asked. "Because I'm looking at your X-ray and there's a shadow here on your seventh rib and we don't know what it is."

"No, no injury," I replied. But then I recalled that I sometimes experienced a seizing sensation in that area. I had dismissed it as indigestion, not giving it a second thought. Indeed, my whole life I had paid little attention to my physical health. I was sixty-nine years old, yet I felt little different than I had when I was in my thirties. But now here was Dr. Monahan, who happened to also be a cancer specialist, calling me first thing on a Saturday morning and sounding as if he suspected something serious.

"We have to send you for a CT scan," he said. "I'll make an appointment for you with a specialist for Monday."

After hanging up with Dr. Monahan, even before I called Leighton and Mom, I called my communications director, Will Dempster, to let him know that we would need to hold off putting out the statement about my eye surgery, as I might now be facing a larger concern.

The CT scan was performed on Monday afternoon, right around the time that Gorsuch was being sworn in to the Supreme Court. By Tuesday afternoon, I was sitting across from Dr. Monahan in his office, listening as he pointed to my chest X-ray and explained that the shadow on my seventh rib was a metastasis from the stage-four cancer that had been detected in my right kidney by the CT scan.

So this is how I will go, I remember thinking.

Somehow, the conjecture did not frighten me. As Dr. Monahan kept talking, a sense of unreality crept in, and my thoughts wandered. Up to that point in my life, I had never been hospitalized. I considered myself to be in robust health and seldom gave any thought to the aches and pains I sometimes experienced. How could I now be facing what could very possibly be a fatal diagnosis? Surely Dr. Monahan must be mistaken, and this diagnosis applied to someone else. But no, it was my medical records and scans he had before him. With an effort, I brought my attention back to the present moment.

"Am I going to die anytime soon?" I asked, my voice steady.

"Not anytime soon," Dr. Monahan assured me.

"Good," I said, releasing the breath I hadn't even realized I was holding. "So what do we need to do?"

In the days following, I continued to feel strangely calm, a pragmatic re-solve growing inside me. My death might not be imminent, but now I ab-sorbed in a new way that my life was finite—something we all know but manage to put out of our minds in order to carry on. Now, the terminal na-ture of my illness lent an even greater urgency to my determination to con-front the ongoing crisis in government. But first, we needed to figure out whether I could go ahead with my eye surgery before treating the cancer, which Dr. Monahan had explained would require two major procedures, one to remove my right kidney and another to treat the metastasis on my seventh rib. We ultimately decided that I should undergo the cataract surgery the following week, and get that out of the way during the congressional recess. To my great relief, the procedure was an unqualified success. I could finally see again without double vision or a constant fog over my eyes, and I re-turned to work with the rest of my colleagues when the recess was over.

I had asked my staff to research how others in public life had handled the disclosure of serious health challenges, as I wanted to be careful in how I framed my own. I learned that approaches had varied from Maryland gover-nor Larry Hogan sharing every step of his treatment for non-Hodgkin's lym-phoma, to Senator Claire McCaskill posting a short note on social media that she would be home in Missouri undergoing treatment for breast cancer for the next three weeks. Also instructive was the experience of my close friend in the Senate, Heidi Heitkamp, who had run for governor of North Dakota in 2000. Diagnosed with breast cancer in the middle of the campaign, she had started chemo just three weeks before the election. Although she was widely liked and ahead in the polls, she ended up losing the race, as voters felt she needed to take care of her health first. I wondered if my own constituents might feel the same way. *What the heck is she doing running for reelection?* I imagined them thinking. *She needs to stay home and heal.*

Even so, I ultimately chose to be completely transparent about my own diagnosis. As I worked with my staff on a draft announcement, Will Dempster reflected, "You know, Senator, the politics will take care of itself. All you have to do is live. If you're alive, you will be fine, because you'll have put yourself out there in a way that people can connect with, and they will see that you're a fighter." I appreciated his take; it underscored my own instincts about how the news might be received. And so on May 16, 2017, I put out a press release sharing my full diagnosis and plan of care. "My doctor expects me to make a full recovery from these treatments," I stated. "I will continue working during my recovery, and look forward to returning to the Senate as soon as possible. I face this fight with the same determination I've fought for the people of Hawaii. And I never quit, especially when things get tough."

I underwent surgery to remove my right kidney the next day. When I woke from the anesthesia, I learned that the Justice Department had appointed Special Counsel Robert Mueller to investigate Russian interference in the 2016 election and possible wrongdoing by the president and his campaign team. I had barely opened my eyes after the operation when Leighton, who had flown from Hawaii to be with me, shared the news. Even before Trump had summarily fired FBI director James Comey on May 9 over his dissatisfaction with how Comey was handling the Russia probe (Trump himself admitted this motivation in a May 11 interview with NBC's Lester Holt), I had been calling for the appointment of a special prosecutor. The fact was, in firing Comey the president had effectively obstructed an ongoing investigation in plain sight of us all.

I asked Leighton to get my cell phone. I wanted to have my communications team put out a statement from me immediately on the critical importance of Mueller's appointment, and his being allowed to conduct his examination of the facts unfettered by a president bent on protecting his own flank. My team members had already drafted a statement but had hesitated to call to get my approval so soon after my surgery. One of my staffers read what they had composed; to my mind it needed to be stronger. "Let's toughen this up," I said. "I mean, I've been calling for this appointment for months." After dictating a new statement over the phone, I could feel the soreness from my surgery beginning to swamp the painkillers. "Okay, I have to stop now," I said. "I'm feeling nauseous, but it's not because of you guys," I added, with a groggy attempt at humor.

Though the news of my cancer had received very little coverage on the mainland, my diagnosis was front-page news in Hawaii for several days during the week of my surgery. Realizing that people in my home state needed to hear from me, I offered a popular local television news anchor, Paula Akana, an exclusive interview, and she flew from Honolulu to Washington, D.C., a few weeks later. I was still in pain, but I wanted people to see that I was not cowering in a corner somewhere, worrying that I might die. The cancer had not slowed me down. My constituents could still count on me to engage with the media, speak out at protests, and fight for them in Congress. "I'm definitely running for reelection," I assured Paula during our taped sit-down interview. "There's work to do." When the segment aired back home, it seemed to allay fears about my health. One measure of this was the fact that, on the day after it aired, Tulsi Gabbard endorsed my reelection bid, clearing a path for me to run in the Democratic primary unopposed.

Despite everything going on in the country, in the days after my surgery, my most pressing concern was my mother. I had told her of my cancer diagnosis as soon as it was confirmed, and now I imagined her lying awake at night, fretting about me. I decided to write her a letter. I knew the only way to convince her not to worry and agonize over me was to remind her that her concern would only make me anxious about her, which would complicate my healing. "The best thing you can do for me right now is to not worry," I wrote her. "I will be okay."

Leighton delivered my handwritten letter when he returned home. When next I called, Mom got on the phone. "Mazie, I promise I won't worry," she said simply.

As I recuperated in my Capitol Hill apartment after surgery, Heidi Heitkamp sent over a huge get-well card signed by all my Senate colleagues; even the curmudgeonly Mitch McConnell had written a get-well note. My friends in the Senate had also arranged for meals to be delivered to me, and a number of my Democratic colleagues kindly stood in for me at my fundraisers that had been previously scheduled—I was, after all, still running for reelection. I was touched and grateful for everyone's generosity, but I made it a point to be back at work only five days later.

When I walked through the double doors on the Republican side of the floor that first morning, John McCain rose from his seat and came over to me. "I love you, Mazie," he said as he enveloped me in a hug. I was surprised, as I had been among the many members who had at one point or another been on the receiving end of his famous wrath. The senator from Arizona would announce his own cancer diagnosis just two months later. When I heard the news, I belatedly wondered whether, on the day he so warmly welcomed me back to the Senate, he already knew that an aggressive glioblastoma was growing inside his brain.

In the early summer months of 2017, as John McCain and I faced our mortality, the health of millions of Americans was also being imperiled. Republicans were pressing to repeal critical aspects of the Affordable Care Act, including protections President Obama had put in place for people with preexisting conditions. On May 4, the Republican-led House had narrowly passed yet another bill to repeal the ACA, including slashing Medicaid funding to the tune of $839 billion by the end of the decade, a measure that would leave some twenty million Americans without health insurance. The sweeping cuts would reduce or eliminate access to care for poor people, the elderly, the disabled, health-care workers, and people with preexisting conditions, with no discernible purpose other than to offset tax breaks and other incentives to insurance companies, large corporations, medical industries, and high-income earners. Though doctors, hospitals, and patient advocacy groups had vociferously opposed the bill, Trump's enablers in Congress seemed intent on pleasing their president by plundering Obama's hard-won—and increasingly popular—achievement in health-care reform.

Nancy Pelosi, then the minority leader, had issued a dire warning to House Republicans after the bill passed. "You have every provision of this bill tattooed on your forehead," she had told them. "You will glow in the dark on this one." The provisions were so draconian that even the Senate Republicans knew they would have to tinker with the bill's language if they hoped to win passage in the higher chamber.

I had once been a child whose uninsured family could not afford routine, let alone crisis health care, and I was now among those Americans with preexisting conditions. Having so recently availed myself of the benefits of my own Medicare and other health insurance coverage, I was determined to pay my privilege forward. And so, on the night before I was to undergo my second surgery—this one to remove the cancerous seventh rib on my right side—I stepped up to the podium on the Senate floor to deliver my prepared remarks on the repeal bill.

"Mr. President," I began, addressing the Senate presiding officer. "We are all one diagnosis away from having a serious illness. Lots of us believe getting a serious illness is something that happens to other people. I was one of them. My moment of reckoning came two months ago." I went on to express my view that health care is not a privilege reserved only for those who could afford it. "It's why we are fighting so hard against Trumpcare," I said, using the term pointedly, in answer to the Republicans' insistence on derisively referring to the Affordable Care Act as Obamacare. "Thirteen of our male colleagues spent weeks sequestered away literally plotting how to deny millions of people in our country the health care they deserve. They spent these weeks figuring out how to squeeze as much as they could out of the poorest, sickest, and oldest members of our society so that they could give the richest people in our country a huge tax cut. This is not a health-care bill. This is a tax-cut-for-the-rich bill."

I pointed out that the Congressional Budget Office had estimated that twenty-two million people would lose their insurance if the bill passed, and I described the plight of three Americans I had met with that week, who would be catastrophically affected: a teenager who discovered he had bone cancer after sustaining a football injury; a twenty-seven-year-old father of three facing a lifetime of treatment for multiple sclerosis; and the mother of a daughter whose medication for cystic fibrosis would be prohibitively expensive if insurance companies were allowed to discriminate based on her child's preexisting condition. "Trumpcare will be a disaster for the American people and we will fight against it tooth and nail," I told my Senate colleagues. "Tomorrow I'm going in for surgery to remove the lesion I have on my rib, but I will be back as quickly as I can to keep up the fight against this mean, ugly bill. The stakes are too high to stay silent."

Though I had often addressed the Senate chamber on issues of concern to me, my tone in these speeches had lately become stronger, just as I was also becoming more outspoken in the press about Trump's repeated attacks on the rights of ordinary Americans. When I was done speaking from the floor that day, Chuck Schumer took the mic and thanked me for my remarks. "I want to salute on behalf of all of us the great senator from Hawaii," he said, using the flowery language of the chamber, but I believed his next words were sincere. "Her conviction to help those who need help is just inspiring to every one of us. We love you, we wish you well, and we can't wait for you to come back and rejoin the fight doubly invigorated." As I left the Senate chamber that night, my colleagues on both sides of the aisle wished me well with a care that felt outside of the usual politics. It was as if the gulf that existed between red states and blue states had, for a brief moment, been bridged by our common humanity.

The surgery the next day was particularly brutal, requiring my doctors to hack away five inches of my seventh rib and to anchor the remaining ribs by screwing them onto a 7-inch titanium plate. The operation, scheduled to last four hours, took almost six, leaving me with a deep gouge on the right side of my torso, which I thought would never fill in. As much as my doctors had tried to warn me about how hard the recovery would be, I had never undergone anything as painful as the removal of that rib. Complicating matters was the fact that my staff and I were worried that Mitch McConnell would call for a vote on the health-care repeal while I was still in the hospital, ensuring one less Democratic vote against the bill. We thought the call could come as soon as June 29, two days after my surgery.

What my Senate colleagues didn't know was that I had absolutely no intention of missing that vote. My team and I were fully prepared for me to be wheeled from my hospital bed to the door of the Senate chamber, at which point, no matter the condition of my postsurgery body, I would rise from the wheelchair and cast my vote. While I can laugh about this now, we were deadly serious. Fortunately, I was spared that particular act of bravery, because the ache of my healing rib cage was sharper than anything I could have imagined. In fact, on day two after my operation, the day we had imagined I'd be able to stand and vote, the pain was so intense that I had looked at the nurse with tears rolling down my face and blurted, "What the *fuck*?" I could hardly move my body for days, much less get out of bed without help, but Leighton was there, supporting me every step of the way.

My healing took longer this time, but I felt the great urgency of the moment, and so two weeks later I was back in my office on Capitol Hill. Wanting to reassure my constituents that I was up to doing my job, I did interview after interview with the media, and participated in protests opposing the health-care bill. On July 25, when the Senate voted to move ahead with a procedural vote on Trumpcare, I was in the chamber to cast my vote against it.

Afterward, I stood with several of my Democratic colleagues on the steps of the Capitol and vowed to a crowd of demonstrators that I would stay in the fight for as long as it took to stop the Republicans from stealing their health care. I held up a heavy bullhorn as I spoke, feeling the deep ache in my rib cage where the titanium plate met bone. The pain reminded me of exactly why I was there—to advocate for the right of each person in our country to meet a scary diagnosis and know they would be able to get the treatment they needed to live.

That evening a man by the name of Jim Becker posted a message on social media about the day's vote to proceed and my attendance at the rally that followed. "This is Senator Mazie Hirono of Hawaii," he had written, under my formal Senate photograph. "Senator Hirono is recovering from her second surgery for stage 4 kidney cancer. She showed up today to vote to protect the health insurance of 20+ million people. She stood up for people who aren't lucky enough to have gold-plated, taxpayer-funded coverage. She got no standing ovation, no time to make a speech with wall-to-wall cable news coverage, and no one is falling over themselves to talk about her courage. Real heroes walk their talk and honor their professed values when it actually matters."

By the time I saw the post the following morning, it had been shared hundreds of thousands of times. I felt gratified that Jim Becker had recognized my commitment, though I knew I was no more a hero than all the people marching in the streets to protect their fellow citizens. Yet he had gotten one thing exactly right: It was time for each of us to honor our professed values. It mattered because *we* mattered.

His post also underlined for me a growing realization that my journey had resonance for every person who had ever confronted a frightening diagnosis or felt their heart clench because a loved one's health was in jeopardy. Ever since we'd shared the news of my diagnosis, people had been stopping me on the street, in train stations, and at airports, thanking me for standing against the GOP effort to strip away their health care and sharing their own experiences of surviving critical illnesses. Sometimes tears spilled from their eyes as they told of loved ones unable to afford the necessary treatment and some who had passed away. As I listened to their stories and felt their pain, I saw that in opening up about my own cancer, I had become a kind of surrogate for people facing health challenges of their own. I felt humbled. So many people had placed a great trust in me to represent their experiences, and I intended to do nothing less.

On Thursday, July 27, Mitch McConnell finally set a vote on what the media was now referring to as the "Obamacare skinny repeal" bill. The Senate had been in a holding pattern all day, as members gave speeches for and against the legislation. In anticipation of the momentous vote, all the major news channels had been carrying the proceedings live. Well into the evening, there were more senators in the chamber than usual, as Senate minority leader Chuck Schumer had asked that all Democrats be in their seats or stay close to the floor so that there would be no chance of missing the vote when it was called. Every single one of the forty-eight Democrats would be needed, plus three Republicans, in order to defeat the bill. At that moment, we had some hope that Susan Collins of Maine and Lisa Murkowski of Alaska would cross party lines and vote against the bill, but that would put us at 50–50, which would give Vice President Mike Pence the opportunity to cast the tiebreaking vote—and there was no question which side he would come down on. To avoid that outcome, we needed one more Republican to vote with us for a clean 51–49 defeat of the legislation.

All afternoon, there had been whispers that Chuck Schumer was off somewhere talking to John McCain, who had been absent from the Senate for weeks, undergoing treatment for brain cancer. We nursed a brittle optimism that McCain might show up for the vote and save the day, but not a single Democrat breathed a word of this to the press. We barely even spoke of it to one another. Our hope was just too fragile.

I remember feeling unsettled as I sat in the chamber listening to senators debate the merits of the bill. At this late hour, almost 10:30 p.m., only Democrats were stepping up to speak, as the Republicans, apparently confident of victory, had conceded the rest of their allotted time. My colleagues were hitting many of the same talking points I had offered up myself a month before, yet I wondered if I might have something more to say. There was no time to craft a new speech, so I would have to address the chamber extemporaneously. In going on five years in the Senate, I had never spoken from the floor without prepared remarks. As much as I seemed always to have myself in hand, there were times when I would be churning inside but had restrained myself. I knew that an excess of emotion was not a good look for women in politics—at least, that had been the conventional wisdom during my three-plus decades as an elected official.

But that night, as I listened to my Democratic colleagues try to fend off the Republican effort to throw so many millions of Americans off the medical insurance rolls, I thought of my sister, Yuriko, who I knew with certainty did not have to die. It struck me then that I could bring a unique perspective to that chamber. I didn't think there was another senator who had watched a sister die of pneumonia at home because her family couldn't pay for the hospital care that might have saved her life.

I began jotting down notes where I sat. A block away, in an office on a high floor inside the Hart Senate Building, Will Dempster and my legislative director, Jeremy Horan, happened to notice me on live television, scribbling away. They decided to come and find me, in case I needed their input. I got a text from Will soon after, letting me know they were in the Lyndon B. Johnson Room, a small antechamber just off the Senate floor where the Democrats had set up our health-care war room.

For weeks now, outside of Congress, I had leaned into my personal story of undergoing treatment for kidney cancer in a way I never would have done before; I had seen that it humanized my connection to the issue of health care, and that people I encountered on my travels related powerfully to my story. But could I allow myself to be that vulnerable on the Senate floor? At this point, my floor speech linking Wayne's lifelong struggles to the family separation crisis was still several months in the future; nor had I ever explicitly expressed how my family's lack of health coverage during my childhood had made me a passionate advocate for affordable care. As a woman steeped in the emotional reticence of Japanese culture, this sort of public sharing of personal details didn't come easily to me. Yet I was American, too, and my fellow citizens who were most at risk were depending on me to tell my truth, because they couldn't be in this space to tell theirs.

I walked to the reception area to meet with Will and Jeremy. As we huddled around the conference table, a monitor on the wall above us was broadcasting the floor speeches live. Will confessed to me that he felt tapped out, and we agreed that I had already delivered every objective argument against

this skinny repeal bill in previous speeches. "However, if you have something personal to say, I think people would be open to hearing it," he suggested now. "But if you're going to speak, Senator, it would be good if you went
on by eleven p.m. so your remarks can be picked up live on the five p.m. news
back in Hawaii." Will was not my communications director for nothing.

"My pain meds will wear off around that time, too," I noted wryly, "so
yes, I will definitely need to speak before that happens."

As I left Will and Jeremy, I still hadn't made up my mind. But a few minutes later I made my way over to Patty Murray, the senator from Washington
who, as the ranking Democrat on the Health, Education, Labor and Pensions Committee, was in charge of scheduling Democratic speakers during
the debate period. I was not on the speaking roster, but now I requested a
spot and asked that it be as soon as possible, as I was on pain meds and feeling
a little woozy. It was the first and only time in my professional life that I have
ever used ill health as an excuse. Patty took one look at me and slotted me in
to speak after Cory Booker of New Jersey, who was currently addressing
the floor. Cory finished up his remarks just minutes before eleven.

Senators generally speak from a small portable podium set up at our desks
by the Senate pages. On this night, when a page brought the podium to me, I
shook my head. A podium felt wrong. For the first time, I would be addressing my colleagues from the floor without a written script, and I wanted to
speak to them without a barrier, physical or symbolic. As I stood in full view
of everyone, unprotected by the wooden gravitas of the speaker's podium, I
ignored the sharp sticking pain over my right rib cage, where the crevasse
left in my flesh by the surgeon's knife was continuing its invisible work of
knitting me back together. I decided it was a kind of metaphor: it was up to
me, in concert with every one of my Senate colleagues—from blue states *and*
red—to do the slow, painful work of knitting our traumatized country back
together.

I began to speak, noting, as each of my Democratic colleagues had done, that the proposed repeal would hurt millions of our most vulnerable citizens.

"I would say that I'm probably the only senator here who was not born in a hospital," I went on. "I was born at home in rural Japan. I lost a sister to pneumonia when she was only two years old in Japan. She died at home. Not in a hospital where maybe her life could have been saved." My voice broke then, and I stopped to collect myself. In the pause, Virginia Democrat Tim Kaine, who had been sitting with his back to me, turned his chair fully around so that he could see my face. Angus King later shared that he had wanted to turn his chair around, too, but thought better of it, suspecting that for me to have both him and Tim staring at me would have been too much, given the heightened emotion in the room.

When I resumed speaking, the kindness in Tim's face helped steady me, even as my heart tightened with remembered dread as I described being a poor child in Hawaii, worrying that my mother would fall ill, and understanding with clarity too sharp for one so young that if she couldn't work, we would be unprotected. "And now, here I am a United States senator," I continued. "I am fighting kidney cancer, and I'm just so grateful that I had health insurance so that I could concentrate on the care that I needed rather than how the heck I was going to afford the care that would probably save my life."

I reminded those in the room that when I had first received my diagnosis, they had shown me their concern, "including so many of my colleagues on the other side of the aisle who wrote me wonderful notes, sharing with me their own experience with major illness in their families or with their loved ones." I paused, looking around the Senate chamber, noticing that the usual conversational hum had given way to an attentive silence. "You showed me your care, you showed me your compassion," I said, and then, without quite realizing what I was about to do, I banged my fist on the table in front of me as I challenged them: "Where is that tonight!"

I yielded the floor with a plea to members to show the American people the compassion they had shown me. I had tears in my eyes as I finished, and Heidi Heitkamp, who sat next to me, wrapped me in her arms. As I walked from the Senate chamber afterward, I felt shaken by how exposed I had just allowed myself to be, but I knew that I had done the right thing, sharing my story in hopes that my fellow senators might be moved to see that night's critically important vote as a human calculus rather than a political one.

When I met with some of my team members in the reception room minutes later, they were excited. "That was incredible!" Will exclaimed. "You could hear a pin drop in there." I knew he was more aware than most of what those four minutes had demanded of me, and I wasn't even sure that what I'd said had made sense. But now, as people came up and thanked me for my remarks, I could feel that my words had touched them, even as they marveled that I had never before told them about my sister who died. They knew I had spoken from the heart, revealing myself in ways they had never heard me do before. Perhaps one measure of the impact of my speech was the fact that, immediately following it, Republicans rushed back into the Senate chamber to reclaim their time from the Democrats. Not wanting to risk more galvanizing human moments on the floor from other Democrats, they used up the rest of their debate time reading from and rehashing the bill until the vote was called.

When John McCain arrived around midnight, Vice President Mike Pence and Mitch McConnell took him aside repeatedly, trying to lobby his vote. In the end, their efforts were in vain, as the senator from Arizona voted his conscience. I felt jubilant when, sometime after midnight, the move to dismantle the Affordable Care Act was defeated by one vote, with John McCain giving his thumbs-down right in front of Mitch McConnell's face. Among the fifty-one nays were two senators battling serious cancer diagnoses. For each of us, this roll call could not have felt more critical. One of us would be fortunate enough to return to stable health in the weeks to come, while the other would pass from this world one year later.

I could not have predicted that the video of my health-care speech would go viral by morning, eventually garnering millions of views on social media, but I was beginning to understand that, in some ways, my diagnosis had been a gift. In the months that followed, it would take me on a journey of becoming more fully myself as I continued to set aside qualms about public spectacle rooted not just in my family's traditional Asian reserve but also in Hawaii's don't-rock-the-boat culture.

In the conflict-rich arena of politics, I had never sought the spotlight, never even referred to myself as a politician. I was a public servant. My work was to serve those who were vulnerable, and to do that, to pass the legislation that would help them and impede the bills that would hurt them, I had done what was necessary, but I had done it quietly. But now the time for quiet action was past. As I reflected to Rachel Maddow two months later, when she interviewed me about yet another Republican effort to eviscerate the ACA, "I think it's really important for people in our country to know that there are those of us who are fighting for them every single day." And so when the new, last-ditch Obamacare repeal bill drafted by Lindsey Graham of South Carolina and Bill Cassidy of Louisiana was introduced, Chuck Schumer tapped me to testify against the legislation on behalf of my Democratic caucus, and I willingly stepped forward once more. In the end, all the voices that had been raised against the gutting of health care would carry the day. Mitch McConnell failed to rustle up enough votes within his own caucus to pass the Graham-Cassidy bill, and it died before ever reaching the floor.

Having helped to beat back these unconscionable assaults on health care in the summer of 2017, I now resolved to express myself more forcefully, as well as more openly, to meet the myriad other dangers presented by the Trump administration, not just to our country but also to the world. Even if we did not yet have the needed majority in Congress to defeat the president legislatively, it was our duty to challenge the lies that slid off his tongue daily, and to fight tooth and nail against his cruel policies. Whether through public service, media, social advocacy, or the voting booth, it was incumbent on each of us to declare our resistance in the boldest terms. I had never been more convinced that the words and actions that we chose now would define our nation for generations.

n August 2017, I flew home to Hawaii for the first extended period of time since February. Had it been only seven months since the horrors of our forty-fifth president had been loosed on the country? During that time, my health challenges, as well as a packed Senate schedule, had kept me in Washington, D.C. Now, despite the unceasing threat that Trump's leadership posed to just about everyone, my trip home was restorative, a chance to sink into the comforts of being with my mother and Leighton, and to reconnect with my constituents. It helped Mom to see that I appeared as hearty as ever, and she finally relaxed into the assurance that my two surgeries had successfully treated my kidney cancer. But a month later, our world shifted again when, now back in D.C., I learned that spots of the slow-growing cancer had been found on my thyroid, and I would have to undergo a regimen of immunotherapy to keep it suppressed.

As I grappled with this news, Leighton called from Hawaii to say that my mother had suffered a stroke. I was shattered, even as he assured me that Mom had been given immediate attention and would also receive rehabilitative care. He promised to oversee her healing once she was discharged, and encouraged me to stay where I was and secure my own health while continuing to fight like hell against Trump. But Mom was now ninety-two, and frailer than she had ever been. It was hard to accept that I couldn't be with her during such a difficult time. As Leighton and I discussed hiring a home attendant to be with her during the hours he had to work, I felt doubly resolved to ensure that the right of health care would be preserved so that people like my mother would be protected.

A year later, my beloved mother would suffer a second stroke, which robbed her of much of her speech and mobility and left her largely bedridden. Although we had made alterations to the house to make it more accessible after her first stroke, now our split-level home became impossible for her to navigate, and we made the hard choice to move her to a skilled nursing facility a few minutes down the hill, with the home-care aide whom she had come to know still attending to her daily. I flew home to oversee my mother's transition to the care facility. I wanted to be sure she would be comfortable in the place that we had chosen. As painful as it was to see Mom so shrunken and ravaged by the incursions of age, my heart was eased somewhat by the flowering garden outside her room, where she could sit in her wheelchair under the blue sky she had always loved, watching koi fish swish and catch the sunlight in a glistening pond.

After I returned to Washington, D.C., Leighton was alone in our home on Waialae Nui Ridge for the first time. Though he and I still spoke by phone first thing each morning and last thing each night, he missed Mom's calm presence moving about the house, watering the yard, pruning her garden, pressing her flowers, and creating her sought-after greeting cards. He missed the daily calls he would make on his way home from work, asking Mom what he should pick up for dinner, and the gentle, unobtrusive ways in which she had always shown her care, like the orange she would peel and leave for him in the fridge every day.

Now, with me away for weeks at a time, once again Leighton would reveal the caring, compassionate man he truly was, as he took turns with Roy and Emi, one or the other of them stopping by to sit quietly with my mother every single day. At night, when he returned home, Leighton would peel an orange and sit on the lanai to eat it, looking out over the mountains and remembering all the good days he had shared with my mom.

CHAPTER TWENTY

Seeking Truth

Al Franken had been one of my favorites. So when in November 2017 a photo emerged of him on a USO plane laughingly pretending to grope a sleeping woman's breasts, I was faced with a difficult decision.

The Minnesota senator and I served together on the Judiciary Committee, and away from our professional duties, I considered him a friend. Franken had made a point of avoiding the national spotlight in favor of local media in his home state, so as to emphasize to his constituents that they were his first and foremost concern. I appreciated that about him, and until forced to reckon with the national nightmare that was our forty-fifth president, I had adopted the same approach. Franken was uniquely popular with his colleagues. As a former comedy writer and *Saturday Night Live* performer, he was perpetually armed with a dark-humored quip, which he delivered with merry eyes and pitch-perfect timing. Jokes aside, he was a dedicated public servant with an incisive mind and a relentless style of questioning. Many believed that it was his pointed examination of Jeff Sessions during his confirmation hearing for the post of attorney general in January 2017 that had led Sessions to later recuse himself from the Russia probe—which had paved the way for the appointment of Special Counsel Robert Mueller.

Franken had established himself as a ferocious adversary of the Trump administration, and so when the salacious picture emerged, many people protested that he was being set up. But the photograph was disturbing and hard to look away from. Taken in 2006, two years before Franken ran for the Senate, the image had been snapped during a USO tour on which Franken and the woman pictured, Leeann Tweeden, had performed comedy skits to boost the morale of troops stationed abroad. The photo dropped just before Thanksgiving, shortly after Hollywood mogul Harvey Weinstein had been accused by multiple women of rapes and sexual assaults that went back decades. Also that November, Republican Roy Moore was brazenly running for the Senate in a special election in Alabama, with the endorsement of the American president himself, despite reports that Moore had sexually assaulted three young women, two of them minors at the time of the attacks. Five more women had subsequently come forward with their own accusations of sexually coercive behavior by the former state judge, yet he refused to step out of the Senate race and denied all the allegations against him.

Of course, the year before, all of America had heard the infamous *Access Hollywood* tape, in which then–Republican nominee for president Donald Trump had been recorded boasting about grabbing women's genitals and crowing that "when you're a star they let you do it. You can do anything." In case anyone was left in doubt as to exactly what he meant, Trump further bragged, "Grab 'em by the pussy. You can do anything." Although scores of women had accused Trump of sexual assault, sexual harassment, and even

rape over the years, including during his presidential campaign, he had denied everything and had so far evaded all consequences for his actions. To
the further dismay of countless women, his "Grab 'em by the pussy" tape did
not cost him the election, though it did unleash a wave of anger that helped
to ignite a national #MeToo movement.

The phrase "me too" had originally been coined by sexual assault survivor Tarana Burke, a civil rights activist from the Bronx, New York, who a
decade before had started using it to support other survivors. Now, her man-
tra bloomed into a nationwide campaign, as all across the country women
and men broke their silence about the sexual violence and sexual misconduct
that had upended their lives, usually at the hands of predators who were overwhelmingly male. The tide was turning, because at last survivors were not
only being heard, they were also being believed when they told of their long-
buried experiences.

In the case of Leeann Tweeden, in addition to sharing the deeply troubling picture, she had written a damning account of feeling violated when
Franken grabbed her head and mashed his lips against hers during a kiss that
was called for in one of their comedy scripts. Privately, Franken was stunned.
He told friends that he recalled the events very differently. His first public
statement, put out the same day as Tweeden's post, reflected this: "I certainly
don't remember the rehearsal for the skit in the same way," he said, "but I
send my sincerest apologies to Leeann. As to the photo, it was clearly intended to be funny but wasn't. I shouldn't have done it."

The statement was a disaster: Franken had basically claimed that Tweeden
simply misinterpreted his actions in the rehearsal and that the photo of him
pretending to fondle her breasts was just a bad joke. The immediate backlash
on social media and in the press alerted him to the fact that he needed to take
more full-throated responsibility. Later that same day, Franken put out a second statement in which he apologized to Tweeden, and to "everyone else who

was part of that tour, to everyone who has worked for me, to everyone I represent, and to everyone who counts on me to be an ally and supporter and champion of women." He also wrote an apology letter to Tweeden in which he acknowledged that there was no excuse for his behavior in the photograph. But in the days following, seven more women accused the senator of having groped their bodies during photo ops or of having forcibly tried to kiss them. Three of the women went on record with their names, while four others chose to remain anonymous.

Shortly after the Tweeden photograph appeared, several Democratic senators had called for an ethics investigation of Franken's conduct. But now, with multiple new allegations, many of us felt it was time to ask our colleague to resign. In coming to this decision, I had engaged in searching conversations with the women on my staff as well as with my Senate colleagues and trusted friends and advisers back home in Hawaii. Many of Franken's supporters noted that the charges made against him were minor when compared to the alleged child molester in Alabama and the rapist movie mogul and the pussy grabber in the White House. Others pointed out that in cases of sexual assault, the claim of mitigating circumstances or misconstrued intent did not make a perpetrator less wrong. Either you had accorded another person's body the respect it deserved or you had unforgivably violated that social trust.

"This one really hurts," more than one woman told me. The truth was I struggled with the prospect of losing Al Franken, too. He had been a good senator, one of the best, and some believed he had a shot at successfully challenging Trump for the presidency in 2020. But how could we hope to hold Republican feet to the fire for sexual improprieties if we were willing to look the other way when one of our own had been accused of such acts?

By early December, Kirsten Gillibrand and I were discussing putting out a joint statement to request that Franken resign. We fully expected more

Senate women, including Kamala Harris of California and Claire McCaskill of Missouri, to speak out as well, but Kirsten surprised us when she decided to step out on her own, becoming the first to call for Franken's resignation after a reporter asked her directly what she thought about the allegations against him. I released my own statement moments later, and soon Kirsten and I were joined by most of the forty-eight Senate Democrats.

Al Franken announced his intention to step down on December 7, 2017. More than two dozen senators were present in the chamber as he made his farewell remarks, including many of the women who had led the calls for his resignation. Several of us had phoned Franken's office that morning, asking whether he would prefer that we not attend. The aide who had answered our call went to check with his boss and came back to the phone to say, "No, the senator would like his colleagues to be there." I shared this with Kirsten when she called me from her office, uncertain as to whether she should go. And so we were both on the floor that day, the air weighted with regret as more than one person in attendance wiped away tears.

"I, of all people, am aware that there is some irony in the fact that I am leaving while a man who has bragged on tape about his history of sexual assault sits in the Oval Office," Franken said that afternoon. "And a man who has repeatedly preyed on young girls campaigns for the Senate with the full support of his party. But this decision is not about me. It's about the people of Minnesota. It's become clear that I can't pursue the Ethics Committee process and at the same time remain an effective senator for them."

The next day, Joe Manchin, the moderate Democrat from West Virginia, confronted me on the Senate floor and said he thought it was hypocritical that Kirsten and I had shown up for Franken's farewell when we had called on him to resign. I explained calmly that Al had expressed the wish that we attend.

Franken would come to regret stepping down, later saying that he wished he had waited for the Ethics Committee investigation. Many of our colleagues, most of them men, would also go on record after the fact, saying they had made a mistake in calling for Franken's resignation before the Ethics Committee had had a chance to examine the allegations. No doubt they regretted losing such a capable colleague, and I did, too. On the other hand, I respected Franken's decision to resign and saw it as an indication that he was willing to take responsibility for his actions.

To this day, I am at peace with having called for his resignation, because there was no denying that incriminating photo and the allegations of the other women who came forward. I believed then, as I believe now, that when women tell their stories of being violated by men, we must first listen to the women, and we must be diligent in pursuing whatever evidence there is to be found to corroborate their allegations. Multiple credible accusations are one form of corroboration. What we should *not* do is disbelieve women's accusations from the outset, as has been the case for far too long.

Contrary to misleading arguments from some vociferous factions, the "believe women" dictate of the #MeToo movement does not ask that we blindly take the woman's word and refuse to investigate her claims. Rather it insists that once such accusations come to light, instead of dismissing them, we marshal all our efforts toward assembling the facts and working our way through to the truth, whatever the truth may turn out to be. Because it takes monumental courage for a sexual assault survivor to come forward and say: *You did this. This happened to me, too.*

Soon after Franken's resignation, I began asking two questions of every nominee, male and female, who appeared before any of the five committees on which I sat: "Since you became a legal adult, have you ever made unwanted requests for sexual favors or committed any verbal or physical harassment or assault of a sexual nature?" And: "Have you ever faced discipline or entered into a settlement related to this kind of conduct?" With sexual assault allegations proliferating across the country, I had concluded that we needed to get all nominees on record with answers to these questions. I reasoned that, should it later come to light that a nominee had engaged in sexually coercive behavior, and litigation was to be pursued, the fact that he or she had committed perjury before Congress would be documented in the transcript.

Many men, from the president on down, asserted—as indeed they always had—that women could easily fabricate sexual assault allegations. To hold the line against this effort to undermine the validity of women's #MeToo claims, I had decided, through my two questions, to help keep the movement in view and make sure that women's experiences would no longer be swept under the rug. These kinds of personal questions had never been asked in public nomination hearings and under oath before, but as far as I was concerned, now was the time to change that—especially given the vile misogynist and admitted sexual predator currently occupying the White House.

Though Democrats had called for the resignation of one of our own over sexual assault allegations less severe than the dozens that had been levied against the president, there was no indication that Trump would change his practice of flagrantly disrespecting and insulting women. On December 12, 2017, not even a week after Al Franken's resignation, Trump had tweeted that my friend Kirsten Gillibrand, who represented his home state of New York, "would come to my office 'begging' for campaign contributions not so long ago (and would do anything for them)." I had long bristled at his sexist and racist attacks on my fellow members of Congress, from Maxine Waters to Nancy Pelosi, and in this case the sexual innuendo made my skin crawl. On my way to a Judiciary Committee hearing the next day, I made a split-second decision to call the president out.

At this point, though I had begun to speak out more in the press and on cable news channels, I had never before stepped up to speak to a "spray"—as an assembly of reporters from dozens of different media outlets was referred to on Capitol Hill. Any House or Senate member could approach a spray and comment on whatever was on his or her mind, but like a handful of my colleagues, including Elizabeth Warren of Massachusetts and Tammy Baldwin of Wisconsin, I had made a point of avoiding the national media camped out in the Capitol. My chief concern was that the varied ideological perspectives within a spray might lead some reporters to decontextualize and reframe what I had said, until I didn't recognize my own message anymore.

But that afternoon, walking to my judiciary hearing in the Dirksen building, I had been discussing Trump's despicable tweet about Kirsten with Will Dempster and Katie Arita-Chang from my communications team, when we noticed the spray at the far end of the marbled hallway. Without thinking too hard about what I was about to say, I walked over to the thicket of microphones and became one of the first of my colleagues to openly call the president exactly what he was. "The only way to stop this president, who has a narcissistic need for attention—he's a misogynist and an admitted sexual predator and a liar," I began, "and the only thing that will stop him from attacking us—because nobody is safe—is his resignation." With that, I nodded to the reporters and continued on my way.

As straightforward as that moment might have seemed to viewers, it was a breakthrough for me. I had let down my guard and spoken plainly to a randomized spray of media outlets, without worrying too much about how others might receive my words. Sitting members of Congress didn't normally talk in such an unadorned way. We were more likely to use polite euphemisms to frame even the most egregious violations by government officials, the idea being, I suppose, to uphold the propriety of public office. And yet I had felt compelled to name the compulsive deceit and dishonor that Trump had brought to the White House, even if that meant doing so in a manner that was uncharacteristic not only of one in my position but also of the way I had previously expressed myself.

To my surprise, Lee Cataluna, a columnist for Hawaii's *Star-Advertiser* whose sharp pen had sliced and diced me on more than one occasion, was one of the first to take note: "I swear, icicles formed and broke in that D.C. hallway because she was so cold," she wrote of my remarks about Trump the very next day. "You could almost hear the frost crunching under her shoes as she walked away." Calling me an "ice-cold firebrand," she went on to praise me for being bolder than ever: "She's someone who got better with age, got stronger despite illness, became braver the more she became herself."

While I smiled at the arctic description of me, remembering my days in the Hawaii state legislature when I had been nicknamed the Ice Queen, I appreciated that Cataluna had also seen my fire. In the weeks that followed, as I continued calling out the president in the press, some reporters filed pieces about me "finding" my voice. Of course, I had always had a voice—and I had been using it for decades to advocate for my constituents. Still, I had to admit there was some truth in the stories claiming that my self-expression was evolving. The relentless assault on the nation by Trump and his enablers had demanded that I use my voice in a new way. It was not a question of *finding* my voice but of learning to trust the voice I had always had, to let the fire that had always been within me out.

To be perfectly honest, my preference for working behind the scenes, rather than declaring my positions in front of the cameras, had stemmed in part from the fact that I had never considered myself much of a public speaker. Certainly, I had never mastered what I thought of as "senatorial speak." Though I admired the silver tongues of some of my colleagues, for whom argument and rhetoric flowed fluently, I knew I wasn't like them. Perhaps because English had been my second language, my way of speaking was more direct, less flowery. While this plainspokenness was often the case for people who shared my racial and cultural background, as I started to speak out more in the national media, the immediate positive reinforcement I received helped me to become more comfortable doing so. I began to understand that I didn't have to use the same cadence as my colleagues for my voice to add value to the ongoing social conversation.

Indeed, the realization that I could just speak very naturally as myself, and that my comments would resonate, was a huge release for me. It was gratifying to hear people say: "You speak the way we think. You just stand there and say what you mean." It allowed me to acknowledge the fact that we don't all have to express ourselves in the same way for our message to be received. This was not to say that public speaking would ever come easily for me. But in such dangerous times, I knew that we would all have to push past what was easy and do what felt necessary and true.

The following fall, as I took my seat in the hearing room with the rest of the Senate Judiciary Committee to evaluate Trump's latest nominee to the U.S. Supreme Court, I could not have guessed how relevant my two questions aimed at uncovering past sexual assault allegations would turn out to be. It was September 4, 2018. On the committee were twenty-one members in all: ten Democrats and eleven Republicans; four women—all Democrats—and seventeen men. Before us sat Brett Kavanaugh, the federal appeals court judge who hoped to be confirmed to a lifetime appointment on the nation's highest court.

Early in the process, Kavanaugh had answered no to my two questions regarding sexual assault. At the time that I asked him those questions, I was more focused on weaknesses in his judicial history than on issues of personal conduct. Months earlier, I had observed in an NPR interview that I would vote to confirm the notoriously anti-choice jurist only if "he turns miraculously into a Sotomayor." My feelings about the man had been clear. To my mind, his previous judicial decisions suggested a judge who not only held views diametrically opposed to my own but who lacked the independence, temperament, and humanity required of a Supreme Court justice.

The stakes were astronomical. If confirmed, Kavanaugh would fill the vacancy left by Justice Anthony Kennedy's unexpected retirement in July. Kennedy had been a critical swing vote on the court, and his replacement by a right-wing ideologue just one year after confirming another conservative, Neil Gorsuch—to a seat that by rights should have been held by Merrick Garland—would tip the balance of the Supreme Court for generations. But Gorsuch had at least exhibited some intellectual heft. In my opinion, compared to both Garland and Gorsuch, Kavanaugh was a judicial lightweight, an ideologue wholly unsuited to a position on the nation's most hallowed tribunal.

Worse, the president had publicly expressed the idea that his nominee could be counted on to rule in his favor should any case involving his interests come before the court—which given Trump's messy self-dealing and corrupt policies seemed virtually inevitable. It was why I had decided not to be among the senators to meet privately with Kavanaugh in advance of the hearings. I had no intention of lending legitimacy to Trump's nominee in the same week that Michael Cohen, the president's personal lawyer, pleaded guilty on eight counts, including making an illegal campaign contribution in the form of hush money to an adult film star at the direction of the president himself. The same day that Cohen pled guilty, Trump's former campaign chairman, Paul Manafort, had been convicted on eight felony counts by a

Virginia jury in the case Robert Mueller's team had brought against him. "I have canceled my meeting with Judge Kavanaugh," I announced in a press statement, further noting that Trump, "an unindicted coconspirator in a criminal matter, did not deserve the courtesy of a meeting with his nominee—purposely selected to protect, as we say in Hawaii, his own okole." Whatever Kavanaugh had to say for himself, I wanted him to be under oath when he said it.

Perhaps the most disturbing aspect of Trump's Supreme Court nominations was the fact that anonymous donors had committed more than $20 million to getting Gorsuch and Kavanaugh onto the Supreme Court. They had funneled their dark money through secretive organizations like the Judicial Crisis Network, a D.C. nonprofit with ties to Trump, and the Federalist Society, a conservative legal network with which Gorsuch and Kavanaugh—as well as Chief Justice Roberts and Justices Alito and Thomas—were affiliated as past or present members.

In a *Washington Post Magazine* piece titled "Conquerors of the Courts," writer David Montgomery had observed that a "solidified conservative majority" on the Supreme Court would certainly end up deciding cases according to Federalist Society ideals. "In practice," he wrote, "this could mean fewer regulations of the environment and health care, more businesses allowed to refuse service to customers on religious grounds, and denial of protections claimed by newly vocal classes of minorities, such as transgender people." And this orchestrated takeover of the nation's highest court was only the most visible expression of what would likely turn out to be the Trump Republicans' most pernicious legacy—the packing of the nation's federal courts with scores of lifetime appointments of right-wing ideologues. Mitch McConnell had referred to this strategy as his "judges project," and many court watchers cited his free rein in this area as the reason for his obsequious support of the vile policies put forward by Trump.

"My goal," he would tell those gathered for the $200-a-plate annual Federalist Society gala in late 2018, "is to do everything we can for as long as we can to transform the federal judiciary, because everything else we do is transitory." As a member of the Judiciary Committee, I had seen firsthand that many of these nominees were woefully underqualified, while many others were simply bad judges who, like Kavanaugh, were deeply partisan and willing to twist the law to advance their ideological agendas. And yet the committee's Republican majority kept moving them into position across the American judicial system.

As the Kavanaugh hearing got underway on September 4, the three people of color on the Democratic side of the Judiciary Committee, Kamala Harris, Cory Booker, and I, resolved to do whatever we could to ensure fairness and transparency in the proceedings. The three of us had formed a bond rooted in our shared experience of the entitled and often unconscious expressions of white male privilege not only on the committee but also in society in general. During meetings, we often exchanged glances that spoke volumes, and generally supported one another's positions. As the three newest members of the committee, we also sat next to each other as seniority dictated, which had afforded us a good laugh when someone tweeted the question: "Do they make all the people of color sit together at the end of the row?"

We each understood that all of America would be watching the Kavanaugh hearings, and we felt gratified that so many of our constituents were already marching in the streets, making their objection to his confirmation heard. If some of the protesters were unaware of the degree to which conservative judges were being groomed and supported by well-financed networks like the Federalist Society, women and minority groups were absolutely clear on what a Kavanaugh confirmation would mean for their lives. It was why abortion rights groups, Women's March leaders, labor unionists, Black Lives Matter activists, and gun-reform advocates had organized intersectional demonstrations that swarmed into the Capitol and into the hearing room itself to engage in acts of civil disobedience during the proceedings. "This is a mockery and a travesty of justice," one woman shouted on the first morning. "Kavanaugh can't be trusted!" another woman yelled. The protesters also held nightly vigils on the Hill, writing letters to lawmakers, talking to the press, and planning the next day's actions. Some activists sported T-shirts proclaiming I AM WHAT'S AT STAKE, while a cluster of women staged a silent protest wearing long red robes and winged white bonnets to evoke author Margaret Atwood's dystopian novel *The Handmaid's Tale*, in which women are stripped of their human rights and become the chattel of a patriarchal state.

As an antiwar protester in my own youth, I welcomed the activism, despite the noisy tumult it created around an already tense proceeding. I hoped against hope that the wattage of so many media lights shining on our hearing would encourage my Senate colleagues, for once, to decline to rubber-stamp such a problematic nominee. Each member of the Judiciary Committee would have three rounds of up to thirty minutes in which to question Kavanaugh. My staff and I had spent long hours poring through his case histories and ultimately filling fourteen massive white binders with our research.

I was hardly alone in my opinion about Kavanaugh's legal record. A study of his cases by legal scholars had revealed that he tended to lean more on personal ideology than on applicable law. One court watcher, Adam Feldman, wrote in *Empirical SCOTUS* that in Kavanaugh's dozen years on the D.C. Circuit Court of Appeals, he had ruled "almost entirely in favor of big businesses, employers in employment disputes, and against defendants in criminal cases." He was hardly the kind of "workers first" jurist a populist like me might have wished for, but for me, the even greater issue was that in cases involving reproductive choice, Kavanaugh wasn't an impartial jurist but a blatant political operative, which, of course was part of why Trump had chosen him.

In the September 2017 case of *Garza v. Hargan*, for example, Kavanaugh had joined a D.C. Circuit Court of Appeals panel of judges in ruling that a seventeen-year-old undocumented immigrant in an Office of Refugee Resettlement shelter in Texas should not be allowed to leave detention to undergo an abortion. A Texas court had granted the unaccompanied minor permission to have the procedure without the parental consent required by state law, and the girl had secured private financing. But Kavanaugh, as part of a three-judge panel, vacated the lower court order that she be transported to her medical appointment. The American Civil Liberties Union appealed on the young woman's behalf, and the D.C. Circuit Court's full panel of judges overturned the earlier prohibition, allowing the teenager to end her pregnancy.

Kavanaugh dissented from that majority decision, arguing that it was "ultimately based on a constitutional principle as novel as it is wrong: a new right for unlawful immigrant minors in U.S. Government detention to obtain immediate abortion on demand." His absurd "new right" argument signaled to antiabortion ideologues, including members of the Federalist Society, that here was a jurist willing to twist and even misapply the law to achieve their ends. That November, Kavanaugh's name was added to Trump's list of potential Supreme Court nominees.

When Rochelle Garza, the attorney who had represented the undocumented teen, appeared before the Judiciary Committee as a witness against Kavanaugh, she testified that she believed the reason he felt it was permissible to make the decision he made was because of her client's immigration status. "Just because she was in detention, she should have still been able to go to her medical appointments," Garza said. "So really, in effect, his decision-making in this case is chipping away at the rights of immigrants in detention, but doing it through the lens of reproductive rights."

As a pro-choice woman and the only immigrant on the committee, I found her observation chilling. For me, it was just one more troubling example of Kavanaugh's ideologically driven rulings from the bench. Perhaps it was his penchant for such questionable judgments that had led the White House to intentionally obfuscate much of the nominee's legal record. Volumes of material pertaining to his tenure in the Office of the White House Counsel under George W. Bush were never disclosed, while more than a hundred thousand other documents were deemed Committee Confidential, meaning that members of the Judiciary Committee were allowed to review the huge volume of material, but we could not refer to its contents during the confirmation hearing without prior permission of the Judiciary Committee chair, Republican Chuck Grassley of Iowa.

Along with my team—which included Helaine Greenfeld, a veteran of judicial confirmation hearings, including that of Ruth Bader Ginsburg—I had already zeroed in on an amicus brief that Kavanaugh had written in connection with *Rice v. Cayetano*, a 2000 Supreme Court case involving voting for trustees to the Office of Hawaiian Affairs. OHA, a state agency, administered certain trust revenues for the benefit of Native Hawaiians. Ever since its creation during Hawaii's Constitutional Convention of 1978, its board had been elected through a process in which only Native Hawaiians were eligible to vote. In 1999, a Caucasian rancher named Harold Rice had sued to be allowed to cast a vote, and the case went to the U.S. Supreme Court. An interesting detail is that, prior to his appointment as chief justice, John Roberts had represented the State of Hawaii and Governor Ben Cayetano in the lawsuit, in support of OHA.

In his amicus brief—also called a friend-of-the-court brief, which can be filed by anyone not directly involved with a case who wishes to advise the court on the relevant subject matter—Kavanaugh had argued that Rice should be allowed to vote in the OHA board of trustees' election because Native Hawaiians were not entitled to protections granted to indigenous Americans. Kavanaugh based this conclusion on his assertion that Native Hawaiians came from Polynesia, and were not therefore indigenous to America. His brief consisted of a number of other erroneous assertions about Native Hawaiians, all intended to bolster his core argument. A simple Google search would have enlightened him on the correct history, namely the fact that Hawaii is a part of Polynesia, not separate from it, and so when Hawaii became a U.S. territory, and then a state, Native Hawaiians were, in fact, indigenous to the land.

The Supreme Court ultimately ruled that based on Fifteenth Amendment protections of the right to vote regardless of "race, color, or previous condition of servitude," OHA, as a state entity, could not limit its elections to Native Hawaiian voters only. However, the Supreme Court notably rejected Kavanaugh's core premise when it affirmed Hawaii's claim that "the native people who compose the OHA's electorate hold a position similar to Native American Indian tribes."

A search of the Committee Confidential Kavanaugh documents had revealed a 2002 email that Kavanaugh had written to President George W. Bush's Treasury Department, advising on a capital investment case on indigenous lands. Using the same flawed premise that the Supreme Court had clearly rejected in connection with *Rice v. Cayetano*, Kavanaugh had asserted that since Native Hawaiians did not share the legally protected status of indigenous people, "any programs targeting Native Hawaiians as a group are subject to strict scrutiny and of questionable validity under the Constitution."

I decided to reference the document in the hearing without first getting

Chairman Grassley's permission, as I saw no earthly reason why this particular item should have been deemed confidential. When my turn came to question the nominee on day two of the hearings, I began by reading from the email. With a goal of getting the nominee's views on the rights of indigenous people on the record, I asked him: "Do you think *Rice v. Cayetano* raises constitutional questions when Congress passes laws to benefit Native Hawaiians?"

Not surprisingly, Kavanaugh strove to be as noncommittal as possible in his response. "I think Congress's power, with respect to an issue like that, is substantial," he hedged. "I don't want to pre-commit to any particular program, but I understand that Congress has substantial power with respect to declaring, recognizing tribes."

"But you believe that any of these kinds of programs or laws passed by Congress should undergo strict scrutiny and raise constitutional questions?" I pressed him.

". . . I would listen to the arguments to your question," he said, stumbling over his words. "Congress has substantial power with respect to programs like this," he repeated. "I appreciate what you've said about Native Hawaiians. . . . I would want to hear the arguments on both sides."

After a few more similarly evasive sentences from the nominee, I summed up the crux of our exchange: "I think you have a problem here," I told Kavanaugh. "Your view is that Hawaiians don't deserve protections as indigenous people under the Constitution and your argument raises a serious question on how you would vote on the constitutionality of programs benefiting Alaska natives. I think that my colleague from Alaska should be deeply troubled by your views."

On her news program that week, Rachel Maddow astutely identified the overarching reason for my focus on the *Rice v. Cayetano* amicus brief and 2002 Kavanaugh email. She rightly understood that I hoped to encourage

Lisa Murkowski, the Republican from Alaska, to oppose confirmation of a jurist who might be inclined to gut the rights of Alaska Natives, a significant swath of her political support. Indeed, after I called out Kavanaugh on his views about the legal standing of indigenous people, Alaska Native leaders traveled to Washington, D.C., to meet with Murkowski, leaving her with complete clarity on the fact that if she voted to confirm Kavanaugh, she would lose their support in her next election. The Alaska senator ultimately announced that she would not be among the Republicans supporting Kavanaugh, but her single crossover vote would not be enough to block Trump's pick. Even if all Senate Democrats, including those from conservative states, voted not to confirm, we would still need at least one more Republican to cross party lines when the vote came to the floor.

What we didn't yet know as we questioned Kavanaugh that first week, and listened to testimony for and against his confirmation, was that the coming days would present us with a watershed moment in the history of the #MeToo movement, because as Brett Kavanaugh's legal record was held under scrutiny, multiple sexual assault allegations stretching back to his high school days were being leveled against him.

Rebel Women

We had had some inkling of the coming storm. The week before the Kavanaugh hearings were to begin, a reporter had called my deputy communications director, Katie Arita-Chang, to ask if she knew anything about allegations of sexual misconduct on the part of the nominee. Alerted to the possibility of such charges, Katie and the rest of my team made some inquiries to track down details. I finally asked that they stop pressing the matter. "Let's just deal with what we know," I told them. "We have other things to do to get ready for this confirmation hearing. The allegations will come out if there's anything there."

Rumors had continued to swirl in the background during the initial week of the hearing. The press seemed to be in a feeding frenzy to discover the truth behind the buzz about an accusation of sexual misconduct by Trump's nominee. Toward the end of the week, my communications staff received another call, this one much more specific: the reporter asked whether we had heard about a letter sent to California congresswoman Anna Eshoo, which had been passed on to the ranking Democrat on the Judiciary Committee, Senator Dianne Feinstein of California. Though the storm appeared to be gathering force, once again I encouraged my team to let the investigative reporters do their work while we did ours. We had reams of material to go through from the previous week's hearing, not to mention the other ongoing business of the Senate. But the sexual assault story kept percolating, leading the Democrats on the Judiciary Committee to ask Dianne Feinstein whether in fact she had received any such letter. It was then that she confirmed its existence.

Committee Democrats immediately urged a meeting so that we could all be apprised of the letter's contents. We convened in the ornate President's Room of the Capitol at 6:30 p.m. on Wednesday, September 12. Listening as Dianne read the letter aloud, we looked around at one another in shock. We soon discovered that Dianne had received the letter back in July, but had been asked to keep it confidential, which was why she had not disclosed it to the rest of us. And yet here was an actual, physical record alleging that the Supreme Court nominee currently before us might be guilty of sexual assault—a first-person account, no less—and no action had been taken. The atmosphere in that room was somber as the members took in the gravity of the situation. And then we all began weighing in on what needed to happen next. The prosecutors in the room, Kamala Harris and Amy Klobuchar, as well as Dick Durbin of Illinois, were adamant that the letter had to be turned over to the FBI. Dianne agreed to have her staff transmit the document the following morning, but that wasn't soon enough by anyone else's reckoning. "It has to be tonight," Dick Durbin insisted, and we all agreed.

Kamala Harris in particular was furious. As a former state attorney general, she was convinced that the letter should have been given to the FBI as soon as it had been received, even if the anonymity of the accuser had to be maintained. Worse, the woman accusing Kavanaugh lived in California, which made her Kamala's constituent, too, so why hadn't the document been shared with her? Instead, the committee Democrats now faced a scenario in which our Republican colleagues could—and would—accuse Dianne and the rest of us of waiting to release the damning letter until the very last moment, so as to damage Brett Kavanaugh's confirmation prospects. And yet I knew Dianne Feinstein; she was a person of integrity, and so even though I believed she should have handled the matter differently, I was convinced that she had simply been trying to honor the accuser's wish that the letter and the matter be kept confidential.

But now there was no holding back the news. Indeed, an hour before our meeting, the website the Intercept published a story headlined "Dianne Feinstein Withholding Brett Kavanaugh Document from Fellow Judiciary Committee Democrats." Four days later, on Sunday, September 16, 2018, an explosive *Washington Post* article revealed the contents of the letter in all its ugly detail. The piece alleged that as a seventeen-year-old student at Georgetown Prep, a prestigious boys' private school in North Bethesda, Maryland, Kavanaugh had sexually assaulted a fifteen-year-old girl at a house party. The accuser, identified as Dr. Christine Blasey Ford, was now a fifty-one-year-old research psychologist who lived with her husband and two sons in Northern California.

After the story broke nationally, other women came forward to describe a pattern of sexually assaultive behavior by an adult Kavanaugh, with one woman, Deborah Ramirez, claiming that he had slapped his penis against her at a Yale college party. Kavanaugh immediately released a document signed by sixty-five women who attested to his fine character. The quickness of this response suggested to me that he had known these accusations might surface.

The crush of protesters filling the atrium of the Hart Senate Office

Building and fanning out on the front steps of the Supreme Court became even more fevered and chaotic than it had been at the start of the hearing. So did the gauntlet of reporters camped out in the corridors of the Capitol. Given the latest turn of events, the media began replaying a clip of the two questions I had posed at the start of the hearings, when I had asked Kavanaugh if he had ever committed sexual assault, or settled or been disciplined in any such case against him. Although he had answered no to each of my questions, just as every other nominee had done, in his case, the question now arose as to whether he had lied under oath. The possibility that he might be disqualified for having perjured himself may be why the committee Republicans were now trying to push through a vote on the nominee without hearing from any of the women who had accused him.

In particular, Chuck Grassley's implication that suitable arrangements could not be made to have Dr. Ford testify infuriated me, as I knew from my own sources that she was doing everything she could to accommodate our committee's requests. I suspected that Grassley and the Republicans were purposely complicating and misrepresenting matters, and I was through holding my fire. When an ABC reporter asked how I felt about the Republicans' effort to—as I saw it—circumvent Dr. Ford's testimony, I sighed with all the exasperation I felt and responded, "That is such bullshit that I can hardly stand it."

"You just cursed on national TV," Will Dempster told me when the cameras stopped rolling.

"Did I?" I hadn't even realized how unclothed my disgust had been for the way the confirmation hearings were being handled. Still, I wondered if my swearing on national TV had been unseemly for a U.S. senator.

"Don't worry," Will said. "In these times, people get it."

I don't know whether Will was right, but swearing in public forums was new for me, though I had of late become increasingly unguarded with reporters. In interview after interview, though I tempered the profanity somewhat, I didn't hold back about my views on the Republican effort to silence Dr. Ford. "I think we all know when something is not fair," I told the press at one point. "We cannot continue the victimization and smearing of people like Dr. Ford." And when CBS News correspondent Nancy Cordes (who happens to be from Kauai) asked me at the weekly Democratic press conference whether the four women on the Judiciary Committee had a special responsibility to the public, I responded with some heat. "Guess who is perpetrating all of these kinds of actions?" I asked rhetorically. "It's the men in the country. I just want to say to the men of this country: Shut up and step up. Do the right thing for a change."

As I was walking away from the microphone, I ran into Mitch McConnell heading for his own press conference. Knowing that he would inevitably be asked about the allegations against Kavanaugh, and whether the nation would be allowed to hear from Dr. Ford, I pointed my finger at him and repeated, "Do the right thing."

By the time my staff and I got back to our office, the right-wing backlash to my comments, which had aired almost immediately on Fox News, was blowing up our phones. The clamor was deafening. The next morning, a reporter on CNN's *New Day* asked if I wanted to qualify my statement. I certainly did not. I doubled down, insisting I had meant exactly what I said: It was time for men to take responsibility for their disrespect and disregard for women's lived experiences, and to own up to the ways in which their attitudes had fueled the #MeToo movement. As I said to the CNN reporter: "For the men who are offended by this, you should ask yourself: Why are you offended? What about this offends you? We should all be holding together. We should all be treating each other like human beings."

When the video clip of me telling men to "Shut up and step up" went viral on social media that afternoon, we realized that not all the responses to my sentiment were critical. Women across the country applauded my bluntness, and some people even started merchandising cups, T-shirts, and bumper stickers bearing my words. It became a bit of a circus, but I concluded the uproar was worth it when two women I knew personally felt safe enough to reach out to me to tell their stories of being raped and sexually assaulted by men, and to describe their lasting trauma. They were among the scores of women who were now coming forward to share their own accounts of being sexually assaulted, and to demand that the Judiciary Committee make time to hear from the women who had accused Brett Kavanaugh.

Bowing to the pressure, the committee Republicans finally agreed to re-open the hearing and permit Dr. Ford to testify on September 27, 2018. The whole world was watching as the live proceedings were broadcast. My friend Jadine Nielsen later shared that she had watched on CNN from a restaurant in Brussels. Meanwhile, my longtime supporters Bob and Lynne Toyofuku were checking in to a hotel in Scotland when Dr. Ford began testifying. For the next two days, Bob and Lynne did not leave their hotel room, so immersed were they in what was unfolding back home. They later discovered that their hotel had set up televisions in public areas so that their fellow guests could follow the hearings in real time.

Dr. Ford's opening statement was compelling. "I believe it is my civic duty," she said of the decision to go public with her story. "The details that bring me here today are the ones I will never forget," she added. "They have been seared into my memory and haunted me." Dr. Ford subsequently detailed how, at a high school house party, a drunken Kavanaugh had ambushed her on her way to the bathroom, pushed her into a bedroom, and then climbed on top of her, pinning her to the bed. She testified that while fellow George-town Prep student Mark Judge watched, Kavanaugh fumbled to remove her clothes. She said she tried to scream, and that Kavanaugh responded by clamping a hand over her nose and mouth, almost suffocating her.

"I thought he might inadvertently kill me," she said. When the second boy in the room jumped on top of them, all three tumbled to the floor. At that point Ford pushed the boys off her, jumped to her feet, and fled the room. She locked herself in the bathroom, trying to gather herself. Then she opened the door and ran out of the house. Her keenest memory, she told the members of the Judiciary Committee, the one that would continue to plague her thoughts, was of Brett Kavanaugh and his friend laughing. A trained psy-chologist, she used the language of her profession to express just how deeply this aspect of the experience had marked her.

"Indelible in the hippocampus is the laughter," she told the room, her voice in that moment cracking. "The uproarious laughter between the two of them. They're having fun at my expense."

"You've never forgotten them laughing at you," Senator Patrick Leahy said.

"They were laughing with each other," Dr. Ford confirmed.

"And you were the object of that laughter?" Leahy pressed.

"I was underneath one of them," Dr. Ford said, "while the two laughed."

Listening to her testimony, I did not doubt that she was telling what was perhaps her most painful truth.

"Dr. Ford, with what degree of certainty do you believe Brett Kavanaugh assaulted you?" Dick Durbin asked her.

"One hundred percent," she replied.

In significant ways, Dr. Ford's appearance before the Senate Judiciary Committee felt like history repeating itself. Back in 1991, the committee had been poised to vote on another Supreme Court nominee, Clarence Thomas, without first hearing from attorney Anita Hill, the woman who had accused him of sexually harassing her when he had been her boss at the Equal Employment Opportunity Commission. A group of seven congresswomen, including Hawaii's Patsy Mink, had been so incensed at the attempt to silence Hill's voice that they had marched into the Senate and insisted that the vote be delayed. An iconic photograph shows the House women, led by California Democrat Barbara Boxer, rushing up the steps of the Capitol to demand that the fourteen men who then comprised the Judiciary Committee allow Anita Hill to be heard. Having previously received a letter signed by one hundred and twenty women law professors calling for a full investigation into Hill's allegations, the committee relented and Hill was allowed to testify.

Women across the country watched as a very accomplished and credible woman described how Thomas had subjected her to discourses on porn stars and pubic hair, and commented on the size of women's breasts. Anita Hill's experiences broadly reflected many of their own, and as they witnessed her being demeaned and dismissed by an all-white, all-male Senate Judiciary Committee, their anger grew. After the Senate confirmed Thomas anyway, America's women took their fury to the polls. One year after Hill's testimony, twenty-four women were voted into the House, more than doubling the number of women representatives, while in the Senate the number of women tripled from two to six with the election of four more women senators, including Illinois's Carol Moseley Braun, the first African American woman to serve in that chamber, and California's Dianne Feinstein. The referendum on men's conduct by voting women was so resounding that 1992 became known as the Year of the Woman.

And yet many of my colleagues appeared to have forgotten this particular lesson of history, because just as that previous panel had been closed to Anita Hill's testimony then, the Republican members of the current Judiciary

Committee, all of them men, seemed closed to Dr. Ford's testimony now. In the days before she appeared, the tone of discussions among these men had left the impression that they had agreed to hear her testimony to improve the optics of the proceedings, and not much more. And so, even before Dr. Ford told her story in that hearing room, I made the decision to state publicly that I believed she was telling the truth.

That evening, Leighton called me from Hawaii, expressing surprise that I had weighed in so strongly in advance of a full investigation into Dr. Ford's claims. As I explained to him, this was not a position I had come to lightly. A trained lawyer, I recognized the need to develop corroborating evidence before offering an opinion. In Dr. Ford's case, this evidence existed, and though I agreed that it needed to be further examined, my Republican colleagues were already closing ranks around their nominee by obstructing any further inquiry into Dr. Ford's claims. I felt it important for Dr. Ford to know that someone in that chamber, especially a woman, believed her, because years earlier, when the men on that previous panel had closed ranks around Clarence Thomas, no one in the room had spoken up for Anita Hill.

The vast majority of women who watched Dr. Ford's testimony had found her to be utterly credible, and her appearance before the committee would open the floodgates to long overdue #MeToo conversations across the country. Unfortunately, as happens far too often in these kinds of cases, Dr. Ford would be violated for a second time when committee Republicans insisted that while she may well have been assaulted, she was mistaken about the identity of her attacker. Susan Collins, the Republican from Maine, would go even further, telling CNN's Dana Bash, "I believe that she believes what she testified to," implying that Dr. Ford was somehow delusional. When

Bash asked me what I thought of this comment, I was forthright: "It's highly insulting to Dr. Ford," I said. Days later, in the lobby outside the Senate chamber, Susan Collins accused me of attacking *her*. "If you want to get back at me personally, Susan, you go right ahead," I responded, at which point she turned on her heel and walked away from me.

Dr. Ford's experiences, harrowing as they were, and the clarity with which she recounted them, did little to sway my Republican colleagues to take a more careful look at Kavanaugh's history. Indeed, Susan Collins would robustly defend the nominee in an address she made from the Senate floor on the day before the final confirmation vote. As I listened to her speech, I could not help feeling that she had been ill used by the men in her party, who had drafted her to be the face of their support for Kavanaugh, just as they had hidden behind another woman when they hired prosecutor Rachel Mitchell to put their questions to Dr. Ford during her testimony, making their discomfort in addressing her themselves crystal clear.

Not all potential swing votes in the larger Senate backed Kavanaugh, however. Among those who were disturbed by the nominee's record was Joe Donnelly, a moderate Democrat from Indiana. Despite the political daylight between us on some issues, Joe was one of my favorite colleagues. We had been elected to the House, and then the Senate, in the same years, and our spouses, too, had become warm friends. Now, after reviewing the Kavanaugh materials in the public domain, Joe felt strongly enough to call me.

"Have you looked at this guy's yearbook?" he asked me, the disgust clear in his voice. "You have to ask him about the yearbook, and don't let him lie to you."

Even though we were all obsessively counting and recounting how the full Senate vote would shake out, that night I refrained from asking Joe which way he was leaning. As the moderates in our party, Joe Donnelly, Heidi Heitkamp, and Joe Manchin had all been under intense scrutiny from media commentators trying to discern how they would vote. All three were up for reelection in 2018, and with the election coming just two months later, they were well aware that the way they voted on Kavanaugh could affect the outcomes. Everything in me wanted to know if we could count on Joe to help block the Kavanaugh confirmation, but not wanting to put my friend on the spot, I simply said, "From what you're telling me, Joe, I think you're going to make the right decision."

I was already aware that Kavanaugh's yearbook entry was replete with crude, misogynistic slang for lewd sexual acts, yet when Senator Sheldon Whitehouse, the Democrat from Rhode Island, asked him about the offensive terms, Kavanaugh offered up inoffensive meanings. No one was fooled—we all knew the nominee was lying—but we were less concerned by the high school braggadocio than with the issues of character they hinted at, which would be fully revealed when Kavanaugh finally took his place at the witness table after Dr. Ford's testimony. The man's arrogance, volatility, and utter lack of judicial temperament in responding to the charges against him would reveal him to be deeply unsuited to the nation's highest court in this regard, too.

And yet the very next day, Chairman Grassley proposed sending the nomination to the full Senate chamber, despite calls for a new FBI inquiry to assess the allegations against Kavanaugh by both Dr. Ford and Deborah Ramirez, the former Yale student whose testimony we would never get to hear. My Republican colleagues were poker-faced as they denied Connecticut Democrat Richard Blumenthal's motion to call Mark Judge as a witness who might be able to corroborate Dr. Ford's testimony. By the time my name was called on the question of whether to set a vote for that afternoon on moving the nomination out of committee, I was incensed. "I strongly object; this is totally ridiculous," I declared. "What a railroad job. The answer is no, no, no!"

Beside me, Cory Booker and Kamala Harris were so incredulous that

Grassley was trying to jam though a vote that they refused even to respond to the question. My eyes met Kamala's wordlessly, and we rose from our seats at the same moment that Dick Blumenthal, next to me, was rising from his. I saw that Sheldon Whitehouse, too, was getting to his feet. Moments later the four of us filed out of the packed hearing room in protest. Several women members of the House had been observing from the audience. They now rose, too, and followed us out, emerging into the marbled corridor en masse. They stood in solidarity with us as we gave an impromptu press conference to the media spray, each of the four senators in turn decrying the proceedings as a sham.

I went first. "I'm here standing with my colleagues because it's very clear that the Republicans will break every norm, every rule to get this person on the Supreme Court," I said. "He will weaken the court, and I'm not going to participate in this charade anymore."

Kamala Harris spoke next. "All we have asked for is that there be an FBI investigation," she declared, sounding every bit as incensed as I felt. "Dr. Ford came in and she poured out her heart. She gave the process dignity and respect, and the least we could do is give her the dignity and respect of a process that has credibility."

After Kamala, Sheldon Whitehouse stepped up to express how appalled he was by the partisanship we had all witnessed in the hearing room. "It was not right from my colleagues," he said, "and it was particularly not right from the nominee. I have never seen such a display of vengeful, partisan, conspiracy-theory behavior from someone seeking *any* judgeship, let alone a seat on the Supreme Court."

Then Dick Blumenthal took the mic. "Yesterday we heard from a powerfully credible sexual assault survivor," he said of Dr. Ford. He went on to characterize the ramming through of Kavanaugh's confirmation as "a betrayal" of all sexual assault survivors and of the American people.

Our disgust and dismay at the confirmation debacle that was unfolding in plain sight was shared by many. Indeed, the nominee's lack of self-control during his testimony—his aggressive, emotional responses to the senators' questions, his description of the proceedings as "a calculated and orchestrated political hit," and especially his invocation of the Clintons as longtime right-wing bogeymen—had been so egregious that it had prompted more than twenty-four hundred law professors to sign a letter imploring the Judiciary Committee not to confirm this man to the Supreme Court. As these legal scholars observed in their letter: "Judge Kavanaugh exhibited a lack of commitment to judicious inquiry" by not "being open to the necessary search for accuracy" regarding Dr. Ford; moreover, he was "intemperate, inflammatory and partial"—qualities at odds with the impartiality and dignity that are traditional prerequisites for confirmation to our highest court. Clearly, Kavanaugh had been speaking to an audience of one, the man who had nominated him.

In the end, the broad national outcry against confirming Trump's nominee would come to nothing. A last-minute call by Judiciary members Jeff Flake, a Republican from Arizona, and Chris Coons, a Democrat from Delaware, to reopen the FBI background investigation, depriving Grassley of a Republican vote he would need to ram the nomination through, had briefly fanned hopes that we would gain some clarity on the allegations against Kavanaugh. But the bogus inquiry that followed ultimately proved fruitless, as the White House set the parameters of the new probe so narrowly that not even Dr. Ford was interviewed. The frail hope that Jeff Flake might yet be a deciding vote against the nominee disappeared six days later with his comment that he believed the investigation to have been adequate. The die was now cast: Kavanaugh's nomination would be sent from the Judiciary Committee to the full Senate for consideration and a vote on his confirmation.

As I delivered my final remarks on Kavanaugh from the Senate floor on October 6, I was filled with a blistering anger. The nominee, I pointed out, had "twisted Ranking Member Feinstein's respect for Dr. Christine Blasey Ford's wish for privacy. He falsely claimed that Democrats had her accusation 'ready,' that Dr. Ford's accusation 'was held in secret for weeks,' because the Democrats, as Judge Kavanaugh put it, 'couldn't take me out on the merits.'

"What a paranoid fantasy," I observed dryly.

And I continued: "But this isn't a conspiracy, Judge Kavanaugh. It's reality. Look at what Dr. Ford's coming forward has triggered. People believe her for many reasons—her recall of the events is consistent with the way survivors of trauma remember things. Her demeanor was forthright and open; she had everything to lose and nothing to gain by coming forward, and despite what many are saying, there was quite a bit of corroboration of her story."

Appalled by all that had transpired in that hearing room over the past month, I then quoted at length from an article that social commentator Rebecca Traister had published in *The New York Times*. Titled "Fury Is a Political Weapon, and Women Need to Wield It," the piece had summed up the previous week of testimony so completely that I had decided to read excerpts of it into the record. Traister had written that "women were incandescent with rage and sorrow and horror" as they'd listened to Christine Blasey Ford testify. She had further noted that the calm, respectful tone of Dr. Ford's testimony, when contrasted with Kavanaugh's bellowing, sniveling contempt, had offered "an exceptionally clear distillation of who has historically been allowed to be angry on their own behalf, and who has not."

These observations were, for me, a searing indictment of the Republican majority in the Senate when they voted Kavanaugh onto the Supreme Court that same day. The nominee's appalling lack of self-control in the hearing alone should have been enough to disqualify him, yet the Republicans chose to ignore his truculent display and confirm him. Later, they excused his behavior as being righteously indignant in the face of his treatment by Democrats. One of my Republican colleagues even remarked to me after the vote, "I hope we can all get back to some compassion and civility." To which I replied: "How about showing some compassion for Dr. Ford?"

Another sad commentary on the entire proceeding was the fact that my friends Joe Donnelly, Claire McCaskill, and Heidi Heitkamp, all three of them Democrats from red states, had courageously voted against the nominee and subsequently lost their reelections. It was one more reason that I considered Kavanaugh's confirmation such a low point in the whole sick story of the Trump presidency.

A month later, I was seated next to Ruth Bader Ginsburg at a dinner party. Then eighty-five years old, the associate justice was widely viewed as anchoring the progressive wing of the Supreme Court. That night, troubled by the thought of where the newly solidified conservative majority on the court might lead our country, I had taken some small comfort from the continued presence on the bench of this brilliant and humane jurist. "You have to live forever," I whispered to the justice. She smiled at me before saying soberly, "There will be more five–four decisions now." We both agreed that we would not welcome many of them.

The Kavanaugh hearings would accelerate my emergence in the public's mind as an angry rebel woman of the resistance. Though some of my associates still considered me "nice," as I continued to call out hateful, dishonest, and obstructive behavior by the president, new labels were attached to me. Trump, with his usual contempt for women, now decried me as "that nasty senator," who had been "so vicious to Kavanaugh." The media commentary was much more appreciative, with one Hawaii columnist dubbing me a "badass" and a piece in *New York* magazine compiling "A Running List of Every Time Senator Mazie Hirono Has Called Bullsh*t." "Mazie Hirono, the junior senator from Hawaii, has made a name for herself as a giver of no fucks," the story began. Meanwhile, on the Facebook page for *Teen Vogue*, which under its first Black editor in chief, Elaine Welteroth, had become a bastion of millennial resistance to Trump, the comment "Mazie Hirono is a true hero" garnered thousands of likes and shares.

I had neither asked for nor anticipated my media makeover, but I did not shrink from the attention, because as Rebecca Traister had argued in her book *Good and Mad: The Revolutionary Power of Women's Anger*, women expressing righteous outrage needed to be encouraged. Too often when women show anger, we are criticized for being out of control. I no longer felt constrained by such conventions. I would speak my mind plainly, and if this meant expressing my outrage, I would do so.

I now found myself wondering whether Hillary Clinton might have connected more viscerally with voters had she been angrier as she campaigned against Trump. How might things have been different, I wondered, if she had ignored centuries of conventional wisdom insisting that women could not afford to show strong emotion in public forums, especially not justified rage, lest they be labeled as shrewish and summarily dismissed? Perhaps voters, especially women voters, would have understood more fully just how hard Hillary Clinton had always fought for them and their families, and how arduously she worked to find solutions to their challenges and concerns.

On one occasion, I had had cause to speculate that Hillary herself might have wished she had exhibited less restraint as a candidate. We were at her seventieth birthday party in Washington, D.C., in November 2017, a couple of months after the release of her memoir on the 2016 presidential race, *What Happened*. Before I left the party that night, I had asked her to sign my copy of her book, which I had brought with me. As she flipped it open to sign her name, I observed wryly, "You know, there are two words missing from your title."

Hillary didn't miss a beat.

"I know, right? What *the Fuck* Happened!"

We both laughed heartily, and I remember thinking this was the Hillary I would have wanted to see on the campaign trail, the woman who didn't mince words, whose wit was razor sharp, and whose anger was brilliant and necessary. That kind of electrifying outrage would have been a far more appropriate response to the ludicrous prospect of Donald Trump becoming president. The takeaway for me—as for the hundreds of thousands of women and their allies who had poured into the streets in the wake of Kavanaugh's confirmation to decry his elevation to the highest court—was this: To confront and defeat the toxic white masculinity of the current political moment, which the Kavanaugh hearing had revealed in all its mean entitlement, we women and our allies would have to give loud and persistent voice to our anger, and use it to lead the change.

One month later, we would do exactly that when women turned out in record numbers to vote in the 2018 midterm elections. "November is coming!" the women marching on Capitol Hill had warned when Kavanaugh was confirmed. True to their word, despite rampant and systematic voter suppression on the part of the Republicans, when all the ballots were tabulated, a historic slate of women and people of color had been elected to Congress. Nationally, voters had chosen Democratic over Republican candidates by a margin of 8 percentage points, the largest spread since the 1990s, with women favoring Democrats by a margin of 19 percentage points, the widest gender differential in at least two decades. And, just as in the aftermath of Anita Hill's 1991 testimony, during the November 2018 midterms, constituents' feelings about men's sexual conduct appeared to have also played a major role in the election, with 72 percent of those who saw sexual harassment as a serious problem voting blue.

When a record-breaking 132 women took their seats in the upper and lower chambers of the 116th Congress the following January, I was among them. After running unopposed in the Democratic primary, I had captured 71 percent of the vote in the Hawaii general election, earning a second Senate term. Crucially, the "blue wave" of the 2018 midterms had not only ushered in a second Year of the Woman, it had also restored the Democrats to a majority in the House. For the previous two years, both the Senate and the House had been under Republican control, but now we had gained a seat of power, at least in one chamber, from which to mount our opposition to the Trump administration's policies.

A couple of months after the Kavanaugh hearings concluded, I traveled home to be with Leighton for the Thanksgiving holiday and to spend as much time as I could sitting with Mom in the garden at the nursing facility where she had been living ever since her second stroke. Strolling through my own garden on Waialae Nui Ridge, I noticed that Mom's plants, once so lovingly tended, were becoming wilted, and one in particular, whose flowers Mom had often pressed for use in her card making, had all but expired. I grabbed a garden hose and began watering the plants myself, and when I went back inside the house, I asked Leighton to be sure to continue watering the garden in my absence. "Mom spent so many years planting all these beautiful flowers," I told him, "and we can't let them die just because she's not here to water them herself." Understanding how important this was to me, from then on Leighton would spend an hour each evening in the garden, watering Mom's beloved plants.

That visit home would be a memorable one in yet another way. Dr. Christine Blasey Ford reached out to me while she was visiting Oahu with her husband and sons, as her family often came to Hawaii on surfing vacations. Now, two months after her testimony before the Judiciary Committee during the Kavanaugh hearing, she called my state office to ask if she could see me. Rather than meet in a restaurant, where she might be recognized, we agreed she would come to my office in Honolulu.

As we spoke that afternoon, I was struck by Dr. Ford's warmth and decency. More than that, I was moved by it. She possessed the kind of fortitude in the face of adversity that my mother's example had taught me to admire. Sitting across from me in a long, loose skirt, white cotton top, and sandals, Dr. Ford appeared calm and settled, despite her recent ordeal. "I want to thank you," she told me early in our conversation. "I felt your support in that hearing room, and it strengthened me."

She went on to share that, as she sat there, answering our questions and reliving what was perhaps the most terrifying and humiliating moment of her life, she had made a conscious effort to meet the eyes of every senator who sat on the Judiciary Committee. "It was my effort to make a human connection," she explained. Only one person in that room had refused to meet her eyes, refused even to look her way. "Lindsey Graham was determined not to see me," she recalled. "But you supported me in that hearing room and outside of it, too. And I really appreciated that."

Unsurprised by Lindsey's behavior, I assured her that, even though Kavanaugh had been confirmed, I believed every word she had spoken, and so did the vast majority of people, especially women, who had heard her testimony. We all knew that had a proper FBI investigation into the allegations been allowed, there would have remained little doubt about what had transpired on that painful day.

"I knew even when I was in that hearing room that Brett Kavanaugh would be confirmed to the Supreme Court," Dr. Ford admitted then. "But I could not have lived with myself had I not come forward to share what I knew. At least my testimony is now a part of the public record. Really, I'm at peace."

I was heartened to hear this, and thanked her for her courage. "Our country owes you a debt of gratitude," I said. "I know that none of this has been easy."

She smiled graciously at my understatement, thinking perhaps of the threats of violence she had received, not only on social media but also through emails, phone calls, and strangers at her door. After Trump supporters published her home address and other personal details online, she and her family had been forced to move four times to escape harassment. Dr. Ford had also had to take a leave of absence from her positions as a psychology professor at Palo Alto University and as a research psychologist at Stanford University School of Medicine. She even had to hire a private security firm to ensure her family's safety. Through it all, she had remained fiercely private, refusing all requests from news editors eager to get her story.

She told me then that, alongside the threats, she had also received thousands of letters, cards, and emails thanking her for standing up for women everywhere. Those messages, she emphasized, had been the most meaningful to her. As Dr. Ford reported that her life was now slowly returning to normal, and that her family had recently been able to move back into their home, I felt a measure of relief. We hugged as we took our leave of each other, and as I watched this brave woman walk out of my office, I thought: *There goes a true patriot.*

CHAPTER TWENTY-TWO

Zombie Land

have been face-to-face with Trump only once during his presidency. On January 9, 2018, eight months before the Kavanaugh hearings would begin, I attended a bipartisan meeting at the White House to explore saving the Deferred Action for Childhood Arrivals program, or DACA. Trump had recently declared that he would end the program, which granted temporary legal status to some eight hundred thousand undocumented immigrants brought to the United States as children.

"I'm Senator Mazie Hirono of Hawaii," I said, but before I could go on to ask him about border wall funding being tied to continuing the DACA program, he replied curtly, "I know who you are." Given how obsessively he watched the news, no doubt he'd heard the harsh words I'd used to describe him on more than one occasion.

Week after week for the past years, as I had listened to Trump try to gaslight the nation with a new tranche of lies, or watched as he committed some new act of mindless cruelty, I had thought: *This is the nadir. Things can't possibly get any worse.* Always, I was wrong, because the next day Trump would outdo himself, escalating his attacks on our national norms and institutions, forcing new and necessary legal action against his unrelenting assault not just on fairness and decency but also on the rule of law itself.

One such moment had come in September 2017, when he ordered the termination of DACA. Starting with his characterization of Mexican immigrants as drug dealers, criminals, and rapists back when he first announced his run for the presidency, and even before that, with his fraudulent "birtherism" claims against President Obama, Trump had been viciously consistent in his efforts to keep nonwhites from being viewed as rightful American citizens. Immigration lawyers were still in court fighting against the newest iteration of his ban on travel from majority Muslim countries when Trump announced he was terminating DACA.

President Obama had created the program with the hope that Congress would ultimately pass the DREAM Act legislation long championed by Dick Durbin of Illinois. The DREAM Act aimed to create a pathway to citizenship for the DACA recipients, also called Dreamers. Now Trump had given Congress six months to reconsider the legislation, with DACA protections set to formally expire on March 5, 2018, if the bill failed to pass. That was how, on a Tuesday afternoon in January 2018, I found myself among the selected House and Senate members assembled in the Cabinet Room at the White House to discuss the policy. I had not been on the White House's initial list of invitees, but Minority Leader Chuck Schumer had insisted that as the only immigrant in the Senate, I should be present, along with a few other members for whom immigration was a key issue.

For weeks, thousands of protesters had flooded the hallways of the Senate office buildings, with the overflow gathering in front of the Capitol and the

Supreme Court, singing and chanting and demanding that the Dreamers be protected from deportation to countries they had never known. Enormously impressed by their engagement, I had opened my own suite of offices to the protesters as a place where they could charge their phones and get a drink of water. *When these young activists become citizens, they will run for office and make a difference*, I remember thinking. The idea filled me with hope.

Our meeting with Trump sorely challenged that sense of hopefulness, however. As TV cameras rolled, the conversation played out in typical form—at least for this administration. Grandiose statements from the president were quickly tempered by his Republican enablers and followed by reversals of any commitment he appeared to have made. Bring him a "clean, bipartisan DACA bill" and he would sign it, Trump declared at one point, but this would turn out to be just one more empty promise. Two days later, the president was already insisting via tweet that he would not sign any bill to preserve DACA unless it also allocated $18 billion for his vanity project (as I referred to it)—building an expensive, needless, and cruel wall along our border with Mexico.

"We have a president who tells you what you want to hear on Tuesday, and by Thursday everything he said is off the table," I remember telling a reporter. "How can anyone trust such a Tuesday-Thursday president?"

Fortunately, on the day after the White House immigration meeting, a federal judge issued an injunction against ending DACA, and two other district courts followed suit. This gave Congress an opportunity to finally act on the Dreamer legislation that had been before us since 2001. As of this writing, the bill has still not been passed. Under Mitch McConnell's majority leadership of the Senate, the legislation remains in limbo, as do the eight hundred thousand Dreamers it aims to protect.

As Democrats continually introduced bills that would constrain the president's worst impulses—bills that Mitch McConnell also refused to bring to the floor—the tornado of atrocities swirling out of the White House was escalating. Few policies caused me more personal anguish than the administration's border-control orders. In 2019, a year after the child separation crisis drove the nation to mobilize against Trump's inhumane directive, migrant children were still being removed from the custody of their asylum-seeking parents, despite the administration's claims to have ended the practice. And there were new cruelties: In some shelters, children were denied soap, toothbrushes, and other tools of basic human hygiene. They were also being poorly nourished, and girls in particular were at risk of being sexually trafficked. When I had visited the shelters myself, I had seen in the traumatized faces of the migrant children the ghost of my own brother Wayne. And in a truly farcical practice, detainees as young as three years old—the age Wayne had been when left with our grandparents—were being asked to represent themselves in immigration court without benefit of lawyers. I felt profound sorrow when, in June 2019, the American Civil Liberties Union's Border Rights Center reported that seven children had died as a result of the dire conditions of their detention.

My outrage reached a new crescendo in late June, when newspapers ran a heartrending photograph of twenty-five-year-old Oscar Alberto Ramirez Martinez and his twenty-three-month-old daughter, Angie Valeria, migrants from El Salvador who had drowned in the Rio Grande while trying to cross to America. The family, including Oscar's wife, Tania Vanessa Avalos, had left dire poverty in their home country to seek asylum in the United States. While waiting for their case to be called, they had spent months in a migrant camp in Mexico, a wilderness of tents and tarps and improvised shelters made from garbage bags, at the mercy of the elements, with unsanitary drinking water, overflowing ground toilets, and suffocating smoke from wood fires cooking fish from the river nearby. Losing hope, they decided to navigate the

Rio Grande, which runs along our southern border, on their own so that they could plead their case on the American side.

The child's mother waited on the bank of the river as her husband and little Angie waded into the rough currents just south of Brownsville, Texas. She told reporters that her husband had successfully delivered their daughter to the opposite shore and was returning to get his wife when he saw that little Angie, panicked at being left alone, was splashing back into the water, trying to reach her father. Oscar turned around and went back to his daughter, lifting her from the water and tucking her inside his black T-shirt to keep her from being swept out of his arms by the river currents. But he wasn't able to reach the shore a second time. The two were found some distance downriver, face-down in the water, the little girl's lifeless arms still circling her father's neck.

Of all the stories that emerged from Trump's immigration policies at our southern border, the migrant family drowned in the Rio Grande hit me hardest. I could not look at the photograph of that father and child without also imagining my brother Wayne, fighting for breath in raging waters. And this family's story was not so different from my own; Angie's parents had only been seeking safety and security for her future, just as my own mother had done for us.

Two weeks later, on July 11, 2019, which happened to be my mother's ninety-fifth birthday, I joined a press conference to encourage support of the Stop Cruelty to Migrant Children Act, a bill I had introduced along with several Democratic senators, including Chuck Schumer and Jeff Merkley of Oregon, to truly end child separations (except in cases where an adult was determined to be a danger to a child), and to establish health and safety minimums for children and families while they were in the custody of border agents. We wanted to ensure that children would be treated "with dignity, respect, and care," and to "minimize trauma, isolation, and conditions resembling prison" for migrant families. The bill also called for children to be granted legal representation in court hearings, and for them to be released into the custody of parents or other family members wherever possible.

As I waited for my turn at the podium, I held the photograph of Oscar and Angie Martinez in my mind. I was thinking about how brave the Martinez family had been to undertake such an arduous journey from their homeland, only to have all hope die in the unforgiving currents of the Rio Grande. I was thinking, too, about what this family might have encountered if they had successfully made it to the other side of the river. Would they have been deported back to El Salvador or sent back to Mexico to wait some more as their asylum petition made its interminable passage through the immigration court system? Or would the parents have been branded as criminals and incarcerated in a U.S. border prison, their daughter removed from their arms and sent who knows where?

I could feel the tears pooling behind my eyes as I stepped up to the mic. I tried to swallow the wave of emotion that was making it hard to catch my breath, to steady my voice. Yes, I was hurting for all the families our nation had so irrevocably broken, but I was angry, too. "Kids packed into detention facilities, a father and daughter drowned in the Rio Grande," I said to the reporters. "If you saw these pictures and felt no shame or pain, if you weren't appalled, then something is dead or dying in your hearts and in the heart of America. We have a crisis of conscience in our country. How can we call ourselves a nation that calls out to people like me to come to our country to seek a better life?" I continued. "I just want to say to all of you and to the American people: We better look to our hearts because if we do not then we are doing so much damage to our country that it will be hard for us to recover."

Sadly, this bill, too, would languish in the black hole of Mitch McConnell's inhumanity, never to be brought to the Senate floor.

Early in his tenure, I had come to see that the only thing Trump cared about was himself and money. It was clear to everyone that he had committed depredations in plain sight, often with cameras rolling, far too many of them to enumerate. And yet he kept getting away with everything, because as the nation reeled from the effort to process and respond to one offense—any one of which would have been enough to end the career of a prominent politician prior to the Trump era—he was busy committing several more. Knowing that the only thing that could save us would be to get this dangerous man out of office, I had been among the first in the Senate to publicly call for an impeachment inquiry after the release in April 2019 of Special Prosecutor Robert Mueller's damning report on Russian interference in our elections. While explicitly noting that his report did not clear the president of any wrongdoing, Mueller explained that since the special counsel's office was part of the Department of Justice, he did not have the option to charge the president with a crime. He seemed to suggest that it was up to the legislative branch to assess the evidence his team had gathered and determine how to move forward in holding a sitting president accountable.

By the fall, most of my Democratic colleagues were in full agreement that moral obligation, not to mention the oaths of office we had taken, demanded that we impeach the president. Though Speaker Pelosi had resisted going down the impeachment path for months—I suspected because the Mueller report had been so muddied and mischaracterized by the president's enablers, particularly the new attorney general, William Barr—Trump's call with President Volodymyr Zelensky of Ukraine had finally tipped the scales. On the call, heard by many officials who were conferenced in, Trump pressured Zelensky to dig up dirt on Joe Biden and his son Hunter; the younger Biden had previously served on the board of a Ukrainian natural gas company. For

Pelosi and the rest of the House Democrats, the spectacle of our president trying to blackmail a foreign leader into helping him smear a political rival by withholding congressionally appropriated military aid to the country was the last straw—a clear-cut and easily explained abuse of presidential power.

Trump made no attempt to deny his actions. His position seemed to be: *I did it. So what?* At rallies across the nation, he insisted that his call with Zelensky had been "perfect" and accused Democrats of trying to resurrect Special Counsel Robert Mueller's two-year-long "witch hunt"—which, it should be noted, had not "exonerated" him as the president claimed, and had ended with seven high-profile members of the Trump 2016 campaign being convicted and sent to jail.

Impeachment proceedings got under way in September, with the White House flagrantly ignoring witness and document subpoenas. By December, the House voted for articles of impeachment against Trump for abuse of power and obstruction of Congress. After the House impeaches a president, the case goes to the Senate to weigh the facts and decide if the president is guilty as charged. Everyone in America knew what the verdict would be. Mitch McConnell had made it abundantly clear that his Republican-led Senate had no intention of removing the corrupt president from office.

Sitting in the Senate chamber in late January 2020, listening as the House managers impeccably laid out their case, and while Trump's ill-prepared attorneys tried to obfuscate and distract, waves of outrage washed over me. How dare McConnell put the nation through this empty pretense of a trial? I was under no illusion that my Republican colleagues would show some guts or recognize the grave danger to our country that an acquittal would mean— an even more unfettered president. It was hard to believe they could not see the peril in encouraging the president's obvious feeling that he was above the law.

As Republicans voted repeatedly during the trial not to hear from witnesses or to require that pertinent documents be produced, I could not shake a sinking sense of unreality. I felt completely unmoored, my mind stubbornly refusing to accept that my country, the vaunted democracy that three short years before had been a respected world leader, was now subjecting its people to this mockery of an impeachment trial in defense of a lawless president.

Alan Dershowitz, one of Trump's lawyers, put forward what I considered to be the most ridiculous argument of all when he claimed that "the only thing that would make a quid pro quo unlawful is if the quo were in some way illegal. . . . If a president does something which he believes will help him get elected—in the public interest—that cannot be the kind of quid pro quo that results in impeachment." By that logic, even if a president cheats in an election, if his action doesn't actually violate the law, and he believes his election is in the public interest, then his action is unimpeachable. Though I knew that Dershowitz was merely licking Trump's boots, I still found his reasoning to be the most cynical and idiotic defense of executive power I had ever heard. During the break, I made a point of going to speak to reporters, whom McConnell had ordered to be sequestered in cordoned-off areas in distant corridors, thus limiting their ability to ask his Republican senators questions they did not want to answer. He knew full well there *were* no good answers that could begin to explain the willful determination of his party to turn a blind eye to the president's abuse of power. Here we were, in the midst of the most significant trial in decades, and the press—which normally had unfettered access to the Capitol and the ability to approach any legislator as we came and went—was being kept as far from the action as possible.

Clearly aiming to keep the public in the dark about the particulars of the mockery of a trial, McConnell had also banned electronic devices in the chamber, and was allowing senators to confer with one staff member only while inside the Capitol. Democratic senators' protests of these unreasonable conditions fell on McConnell's deaf ears, because he knew *he had the votes*. Determined to do my part to help inform the American people about the proceedings, instead of grabbing a bite to eat or a cup of coffee during the few short breaks we were granted during those very long days, I chose to go with my communications director to where the reporters had been penned. That week, I must have spoken to hundreds of reporters and appeared on cable news shows dozens of times to share my take on what was going on inside the chamber. Several other Democrats did the same. We all knew it was important for the American people to hear from us in real time.

Sharing my opinion of Dershowitz's bizarre argument with a spray of news outlets during a break, I was as blunt as I was now known to be. "It makes no sense at all," I said. "And this entire impeachment trial is a farce."

A week later, on February 5, 2020, Senate Republicans fell in line and voted to reject the charges against Trump. Only Utah senator Mitt Romney chose to heed his conscience, crossing party lines to vote yes on the abuse of power charge. While many other Republicans tried to cover themselves with floor speeches deeming the president's actions to be "inappropriate" and even "wrong," to a person they had concluded—absurdly—that his improprieties did not rise to the level of "high crimes and misdemeanors," and did not warrant his removal from office.

In the days that followed, I had the sensation that our nation had entered the Twilight Zone, a dark place filled with simpering Republican zombies who were sorely testing my faith in the checks and balances of American democracy. The con-man president had somehow managed to transform the members of his party into cowardly sycophants who had abdicated their responsibility to the American people by refusing to hold the rogue president accountable for his offenses. Worse, they had sent a dangerous message to Trump that, as president, he did not have to abide by the rule of law.

Why were the Republicans so beholden to Trump? People ask me this all the time. The question goes to the crux of everything, because without the Republicans' enabling of this president, his vile behavior might have been controlled. I can only surmise that my red-state colleagues feared losing the support of their party's base, which under Trump has become a cultist constituency, united by a shared vitriolic hatred of "the other"—people of color, immigrants, and LGBTQ people, as well as so-called coastal elites and libs. No doubt the Trump Republicans—bent on preserving their ability to legislate for the rich—were also afraid of losing the financial backing that Mitch McConnell could direct to their campaigns from corporate entities and wealthy donors who had benefited from the $1.5 trillion in tax cuts that the majority leader had pushed through the Senate in 2017, with not a single Democratic vote of support. As the president distracted us with his chaos and buffoonery, his red-state cronies had also loosened financial and environmental regulations on big business, installed judges whose corporate and antichoice biases were a flashing red light, and generally brought to the Senate floor those policies that would benefit big business rather than regular working people.

And yet even these explanations don't seem sufficient to explain the puppetlike abandonment of conscience by my colleagues across the aisle, men and women who appeared to have entered the same moral dead zone in which the con-man president existed. Still, it is the best I can come up with in the face of a legislative voting record among Trump Republicans that has been mean, self-serving, and unconscionable, and that has considered the needs of everyday Americans hardly at all.

CNN's Wolf Blitzer interviewed me the day after Republicans allowed Trump to once again shirk the consequences of his actions. I refused to concede that the president had been acquitted. "How do you acquit someone in a rigged trial where you don't get to hear from relevant witnesses or review documents?" I asked rhetorically. I had also predicted that "the petty, vindictive, spoiled brat" who was our president would soon be on newly emboldened display.

Trump didn't even wait twenty-four hours to prove me right. The very next day, he embarked on a chilling revenge tour, firing White House officials and career diplomats who had observed their legal duty to comply with the House investigation, including two decorated military men, Lieutenant Colonel Alexander Vindman and his twin brother, Lieutenant Colonel Yevgeny Vindman, who had served with distinction under both Republican and Democratic administrations. I watched the news footage aghast as Trump made unhinged boasts at fevered-up political rallies, vowing to make life hell for those who opposed him, and that no one could stop him. He churned out one furious tweet after another, threatening his critics with retaliatory investigations by the Department of Justice, as if Attorney General William Barr—who had succeeded Jeff Sessions after Trump essentially bullied him into leaving office for recusing himself in the Russia probe—were his own personal fixer and not the people's lawyer. The president appeared to have fully embraced the idea that he was untouchable, aided and abetted by Barr, who had already weaponized the Department of Justice by opening revenge probes into people who crossed his boss. This was not surprising coming from a man who had essentially auditioned for the attorney general's job with an unsolicited twenty-page memo in which he had presented an overly broad interpretation of executive powers and argued that Mueller "should not be permitted to demand that the president submit to interrogation about alleged obstruction."

In his infamous letter dated March 24, 2019, sent to the House and Senate Judiciary Committee leaders three weeks before the public release of the Mueller report, Barr blatantly distorted the top-line findings of the investigation in a calculated bid to get the headlines he wanted. Mueller himself had strongly refuted Barr's conclusions, yet the president and his henchman still managed to convince a swath of the American public that the president's hands had been declared clean. When the attorney general was called before the Senate Judiciary Committee on May 1, 2019, to answer for his distortion of the facts, he evaded, prevaricated, fudged, and dissembled in response to questions from Democratic committee members. I had anticipated this. It was why I had decided to use my time not to ask him more questions that would only draw more lies but rather to build a case against him.

When my turn came, I lit into Barr, accusing him of being one more enabler who had sacrificed a decent reputation "for the grifter and liar who sits in the Oval Office."

For posterity, I then read into the record exactly how Barr had misrepresented Mueller's findings. "You substituted your own political judgment for the Special Counsel's legal conclusions in a four-page letter to Congress," I said. "And now we know, thanks to a free press, that Mr. Mueller wrote you a letter objecting to your so-called summary. . . . He asked you to release the report summaries to correct the misimpression you created, but you refused. . . . When we read the report, we knew Robert Mueller's concerns were valid, and that your version of events was false. . . . Now we know more about your deep involvement in trying to cover up for Donald Trump.

"Being attorney general of the United States is a sacred trust," I concluded. "You have betrayed that trust. America deserves better. You should resign."

When my allotted time ended, Committee Chair Lindsey Graham was aggravated. "You've slandered this man," he said, raising his voice.

"I do not think that I'm slandering anyone, Mr. Chairman," I said, maintaining my composure.

Meanwhile, Barr was also speaking. "What I want to know is how did we get to this point?" he said, as if he were the victim rather than the American people, whom he had so deliberately deceived, and whose system of justice he was responsible for perverting.

With Lindsey Graham still banging his gavel and the three of us talking across one another, the cacophony of that moment reflected the general chaos and discord of the whole misbegotten Trump presidency. But Lindsey wasn't finished. "You have slandered this man from top to bottom," he declared, "so if you want more of this you're not going to get it." By "this," I believe he meant time. And then, completely undermining his prior statement, he added, "If you want to ask him questions, you can."

"Mr. Chairman," I interjected, "you clearly have your opinion and I have mine." And with that, the proceeding moved on.

Oddly, throughout our exchange, Lindsey Graham had refused to look in my direction despite the fact that he was addressing me. I recalled Dr. Christine Blasey Ford saying that during her testimony he would not meet her eyes either. I couldn't help wondering if Lindsey, like so many of his fellow Republican zombies, was merely putting on a show for the charlatan in chief, lately his golf buddy, who was almost certainly watching the proceedings live from the White House.

That night on *The Late Show*, Steven Colbert offered what I thought was the best summation of my questioning of Barr. "Hawaii senator Mazie Hirono took her whacks at this piñata of perjury," he said. I laughed out loud at this spot-on characterization of Barr's testimony, the humor a welcome moment of levity in the midst of such a deadly serious time.

CHAPTER TWENTY-THREE

Two Pandemics

t's hard to believe, looking back, that it was only a month after the conclusion of Trump's sham impeachment trial that the nation found itself in the crosshairs of a pandemic. First identified in Wuhan, China, the novel coronavirus, scientifically termed COVID-19, had traveled across borders and arrived on our shores from Europe sometime in late 2019. We began to understand just how deadly the virus could become when in March 2020 it swept through a nursing home in Washington state, taking the lives of thirty-five residents in less than a month.

I thought immediately of my own mother, who seldom left her bed anymore to sit in the garden. Perhaps fortuitously, we had recently moved her to a smaller nursing facility, where she now had her own bedroom in the more familial setting of a private home, and increased individual attention from the caregiving staff. But as the danger of the new virus to nursing home communities in particular became apparent, Leighton, Roy, and Emi could no longer visit and sit with Mom at her bedside; due to the necessary precautions, they were now obliged to wave at her through a window. It tore my heart when Leighton shared that Mom appeared confused to see him on the other side of a pane of glass, as if wondering why he didn't come inside. Though I knew the staff had explained the situation, Mom may not have grasped what they said.

I remembered the last time I had visited her. I had brought a branch of vibrant white flowers, and Mom's eyes sparkled at the sight of them. I suggested to Leighton now that he and Roy and Emi bring flowers every week for the staff to put in Mom's room. Her caregivers reported that the blooms had indeed made her happy, and they sent me pictures of Mom enjoying them, which never failed to make me cry. As the weeks went by, with Mom still unable to receive visitors in person, I began sending her videos of me being interviewed on the news, which the staff would load onto an iPad to share with her. Even though Mom could no longer fully comprehend what I was saying, I hoped that seeing her only daughter doing the work she loved would help her feel more connected to the life I was leading so far away.

As other families across the country suffered untold losses in the early months of 2020, Trump failed to act to protect the American people, despite urgent warnings and recommendations from scientists. An immune-compromised person myself, I shared the nation's dismay as the president refused to ramp up our nation's testing capacity or, as we learned more about the virus, to advise people to wear masks, wash hands, and avoid large public gatherings so as to limit community spread of the disease.

Thanks to Bob Woodward's tape-recorded conversations with the president for his latest book, *Rage*, everyone now knows that Trump understood from the start that the virus was airborne, highly contagious, and much more deadly than the flu. Yet he denied its severity, failed to institute federal safety guidelines, and refused to invoke the Defense Production Act to compel the manufacture of adequate medical supplies and personal protective equipment, while invoking it to force workers in crowded meatpacking plants, most of them immigrants and minorities, to continue operating without adequate safeguards. As the virus decimated the ranks of these workers, Trump insisted it posed no threat to Americans and would disappear "like a miracle." He also claimed that his political opponents' attempt to focus on his mishandling of the crisis was "a hoax," dreamed up to undermine his chance of being reelected in November 2020.

He continued to spread gross misinformation about COVID-19 on social media and through daily press briefings, at one point even suggesting that Americans inject themselves with bleach to cure the virus (he later insisted he was joking, a statement that very few people who had heard him advocate the snake oil remedy believed). In mid-March, when he brazenly declared, "I don't take responsibility at all," for his administration's fumbled response to testing early in the pandemic, it was perhaps the truest statement he had ever made, as he had left governors to grapple with the medical and economic crises brought by the virus on their own. The streets of blue states became eerily silent as nonessential businesses shut their doors and people sheltered in place to the degree they could. The scene was markedly different in many red states as residents, following the advice of governors who parroted the president's delusion, scoffed that the coronavirus was no more dangerous than the flu and argued that being asked to quarantine and wear masks in public was an infringement of their personal freedoms.

In April, vocal Trump supporters waving Nazi flags even stormed the Michigan State Capitol with assault rifles slung over their shoulders, ostensibly to show that they would not tolerate the government telling them what to do. Trump recklessly inflamed the already volatile situation by tweeting "Liberate Michigan!" in response. Months later, federal agents would disrupt a violent right-wing extremist plot to kidnap Michigan governor Gretchen

Whitmer, whose stay-at-home orders, issued to help slow the spread of the coronavirus, had drawn the ire of homegrown militias. Two of the six men arrested in connection with the planned act of domestic terrorism had been photographed with their long guns on the balcony of the State Capitol during the April demonstrations. Whitmer immediately called out the president as being "complicit" in the foiled kidnapping. "Our head of state has spent the past seven months denying science, ignoring his own health experts, stoking distrust, fomenting anger, and giving comfort to those who spread fear and hatred and division," she said. Trump, rather than unequivocally condemning the terrorist plot, further fueled the flames by criticizing Whitmer as a complainer and tweeting that she had done "a terrible job" in responding to COVID-19.

Meanwhile, confirmed cases of the virus in the United States rose to seven million by the fall, one of the worst infection rates in the world, and the death toll soared past two hundred thousand Americans—and counting. Amid the chaos, incompetence, and, in many cases, preventable death, Donald Trump would provoke fear, hatred, and division on yet another front by habitually referring to coronavirus as the "Chinese virus." While his intention was, of course, to shift the focus away from his failure to get ahead of the pandemic, he was also perilously "otherizing" Chinese people by associating their national heritage with a deadly and terrifying disease. Trump's intentional scapegoating was captured in a reporter's photo of the pages of a speech the president gave to the White House press corps, where the word "corona" could be seen scratched out, and written over it in Trump's jagged black Sharpie scrawl was the word "Chinese." As a result, Asian Americans across the country were increasingly targeted in hate crimes—spat on, cursed at, and physically assaulted. Even when the hostility did not rise to the level of physical violence, many Asian Americans felt themselves to be social pariahs, blamed by their neighbors for an illness to which they were as vulnerable as anyone.

In Philadelphia, soon after residents were asked to stay inside their homes and go out only for necessary food or pharmacy runs, David Kao, a friend of one of my staff members, made a pit stop at his usual organic grocery store. The mood inside was somber and tense, with shoppers standing six feet apart on the checkout line in observance of the city's new social-distancing guidelines. In front of David, a boy of maybe five years old was fidgeting and huddling against his mother.

"Mommy, scary, scary," he kept whimpering. David thought the child might be absorbing the anxious mood of the times.

And then the little boy said, "Danger, Mommy, danger."

That's when David looked up and saw that the little boy was pointing at him.

"Mommy, look, Chinese virus," the child said. "Danger."

David froze. He could feel everyone's eyes on him, waiting to see how he would respond. "Here I was in a fancy organic store, the only Asian in a sea of white, being outed by a child," he wrote on Facebook in mid-March. The child's mother mouthed, "I'm sorry," and David replied, "It's okay."

"But it's not okay," he admitted later. "I was gutted, and I'm still gutted."

Such stories made me grateful to be from a place like Hawaii, perhaps the only state in the union where Asians were not experiencing such overt Trump-fueled paranoia and hostility. Sadly, this resurgence of racism against Asians came on the heels of the Asian American community being newly energized by the dynamic runs of the first two candidates for president of Asian descent: Andrew Yang, the son of Taiwanese immigrants, and my friend Kamala Harris, whose mother, a scientist, had emigrated from India. Both candidates had eventually left the race, though Democratic nominee Joe Biden would later name Kamala as his running mate.

Now, in the wake of widespread antagonism toward our community, Kamala and I joined with the two other Asian American women in the 116th

Congress—Senator Tammy Duckworth of Illinois, who is Thai American, and Representative Grace Meng of New York, who is Chinese American—to introduce a resolution condemning discrimination against Asian Americans and immigrants and calling on public officials to denounce all its manifestations. "Inflammatory and racist rhetoric from officials at the highest level of our government has contributed to a disturbing rise in hate-crimes targeting Asian Americans," I wrote as part of our joint statement announcing the resolution. "Calling COVID-19 the 'Wuhan virus,' 'Kung flu,' or 'Chinese virus' isn't clever or funny, it's wrong and deeply harmful. This resolution sends a clear message that stoking racial divisions will only impede our efforts to overcome the immense challenges that this virus poses to our country."

Yet even when Trump was prevailed upon—temporarily, it turned out—to cease using the racially charged moniker for the virus, he still leaned on the language of "the other" when referring to Asians. "The spreading of the Virus is not their fault in any way, shape, or form," he tweeted on March 23, 2020. "They are working closely with us to get rid of it."

Yale sociology professor Dr. Grace Kao (no relation to David Kao) noted that Trump had used the words *us* and *they* in a manner that "very clearly marks that Asian Americans are not 'us.'" As a Chinese American, Kao had herself been on the receiving end of the antipathy toward Asians, but she did welcome one silver lining, namely the hope that the rampant xenophobia would bring home to Asians of different national origins that we must act in solidarity with one another, as well as with other marginalized ethnic groups. I would take her call to consciousness one step further: Every one of us needs to step forward to support the cause of *all* marginalized people, including immigrants, women, LGBTQ people, the disabled, poor people, and unprotected workers everywhere. This has always been our best hope for the security and uplift of all.

With the economy in free fall as a result of pandemic lockdowns and millions of Americans suddenly unemployed, Congress rushed to craft a relief bill that would provide a safety net for those who had been worst hit by the crisis. Unsurprisingly, Mitch McConnell put forward a draft that gave billions to corporate interests with no strings attached to how the money could be disbursed. As far as I was concerned, that was a nonstarter. I recalled keenly the painful lessons of the nation's last major economic meltdown in October 2008, a month before Barack Obama was elected president.

I had been in the House then, still in my first term, and even though Democrats had been in the majority, the Troubled Asset Relief Program, or TARP, had failed on the first pass. I was among a group of newer members who had voted against the bill, which we saw as a blank check to bail out banks, with no comparable relief offered to the hundreds of thousands of families whose homes had been foreclosed upon. I could imagine all too well what it must feel like to walk in the shoes of those homeowners—their fear of becoming homeless; the insecurity of not knowing if they would make it to the next payday. I remembered vividly my own mother working two jobs, coming home dead tired long after I was asleep and leaving the next morning before I opened my eyes. I could still see my grandmother's thin body covered in pain-relief patches at the end of a grueling day of manual labor, and my grandfather's silent exhaustion after his gardening shift at the Waialae Country Club. Then there was my brother Roy, heading to his after-school job as a stock boy as soon as he was legally old enough to work, so that he, too, could help to secure our family. As for me, I still carried with me the memory of the night when I shook my piggy bank and found it empty. I recalled Mom's sadness as she told me that she had used my saved dimes to buy groceries, the droop of her shoulders revealing how much she wished there had been another way. That particular image of my mother was so present for me as we debated the TARP bill that I was having trouble understanding why some of my colleagues weren't more concerned about people losing their homes. The struggling homeowners seemed almost like an abstraction to them, their legislative calculi devoid of the real world suffering that had been caused by the practices of the nation's biggest banks—who were now on our doorstep, hats in hand.

When the stock market tumbled some 700 points on the day the bill was voted down, though, I did wonder if I had been wrong not to sign on to it. Then-candidate Obama came to rally us in the House, expressing how urgently the American economy needed us to pass TARP. He and Nancy Pelosi, along with George W. Bush's treasury secretary, Henry Paulson, convinced us that we needed to go with the bill we had, which had started as a thin, three-page document from Paulson that by my lights was not nearly detailed or comprehensive enough to meet the scale of the problem. But after the Democratic House members made several changes and additions, I voted to pass it the second time, believing the assurances that once we had secured big finance, we'd have the opportunity to regroup and pass another bill to help homeowners.

We passed the bank bailout bill. However, to my great regret, we never did circle back to pass a comprehensive foreclosure relief bill. The banks and financial giants got theirs. The families they foreclosed on went under. This time, I was determined to hold the line with fellow Democrats by insisting on provisions for individuals who were feeling the most pain. I knew from experience that we needed to get such measures into the coronavirus relief bill from the start.

Nancy Pelosi apparently felt the same way. Rejecting McConnell's corporate bailout bill, she began crafting a House relief bill that was much more worker oriented. But we all very quickly realized that getting legislation from the Democratic-led House through the Republican-led Senate would lead to weeks of partisan wrangling, and the people of our country couldn't afford that. We ultimately decided that Senate minority leader Chuck Schumer would work with McConnell, along with Treasury Secretary Steven Mnuchin and ranking members of relevant committees, to modify the Senate relief bill and include aid for the millions of Americans who were once again under water. Chuck Schumer stayed in contact with Nancy Pelosi throughout the negotiations and held regular conference calls with Senate Democrats.

True to form, Mitch McConnell tried to apply pressure by accusing us in the press of delaying the coronavirus bill that people so sorely needed, but we simply refused to pass McConnell's version of "relief," which benefited corporate interests rather than the working people who were really hurting. Democrats stuck together, holding out for provisions like an extra six hundred dollars a week in unemployment benefits for those whose jobs had disappeared and the appointment of an inspector general to oversee how the corporate bailouts were administered. Our determination telegraphed to McConnell that his Republican members needed to compromise in order to come up with legislation that Democrats could sign on to.

We ultimately passed four relief bills, including the massive CARES Act, a $2 trillion emergency package that was approved unanimously by the Senate on March 25, 2020, and by the House two days later. The final legislation allotted $300 billion to cover onetime cash disbursements to qualifying individuals and households, and $260 billion to cover the nation's skyrocketing unemployment insurance claims. It was the first time in recent memory that the House and the Senate had demonstrated such unity of purpose on behalf of the American people. Even so, the CARES Act would have been very different had Senate Democrats not held firm in our resolve to focus on the individuals and families who were most in need. We knew, however, that further relief bills would be needed, and that the true referendum on our government's handling of the pandemic and its economic fallout would come on Election Day, November 3, 2020, when the nation would vote for either four more years of division and turmoil or the promise of restoration and change.

As if tensions were not already running high enough in the country, at the end of May the nation was jolted by the video of a Minneapolis cop kneeling for almost nine minutes on the neck of George Floyd, an unarmed Black man suspected of passing a forged $20 bill, ultimately killing him. Many Americans were finally awakening to a reality that the Black Lives Matter movement had been working to bring attention to since the killing of Michael Brown in 2014: that Black people in America are brutalized and murdered by police at disproportionate rates, often when doing nothing more than exercising their right to exist in public spaces. After months of isolation, anger, and fear, people of all races were now pouring out of their homes, face masks almost universally in place, to join protests against police violence and in support of Black lives. At demonstrations across the country and around the world, marchers chanted George Floyd's name and the names of other unarmed African Americans who had recently been killed by police or former law enforcement officers: Ahmaud Arbery, Breonna Taylor, Rayshard Brooks, and so many others.

People had filled the streets of American cities to protest excessive policing and systemic racism before, but this time seemed different. Where previous Black Lives Matter protests had been attended predominantly by Black people and people of color, now white allies linked arms to form a line at the front of marches, using their bodies as a buffer between demonstrators of color and police, hoping their whiteness would deter police clubs, rubber bullets, chemical gas, and pepper spray. Though police officers had managed to stand with equanimity when white nationalists waving Nazi flags and brandishing assault rifles had shouted in their faces at state capitols just weeks before, many now chose to wade into largely peaceful crowds, batons pummeling skulls and shoulders, tear gas causing people to cough and sputter in the middle of a pandemic spread by respiration droplets hovering in the air.

As disturbing as the police response was to witness, I was heartened by evidence that the protests were provoking a national acknowledgment of the racism woven through our institutions—65 percent of those polled now expressed support for the Black Lives Matter protests and two-thirds of Americans agreed that racism is "a big problem" in our country. In Congress, we debated bills to address systemic discrimination, curb police violence, and hold police forces accountable for the actions of so-called bad apples in their midst. Senator Elizabeth Warren was able to win bipartisan support for an amendment to the National Defense Authorization Act. The amendment called for the creation of a commission that would, within three years, recommend the removal of all symbols and monuments to the Confederacy from military bases and other properties, with the commission's proposals to be implemented by the secretary of defense. As one of the chief cosponsors of Elizabeth's amendment, I agreed wholeheartedly with what she said in June 2019 when she spoke for her amendment on the Senate floor. "This moment is about ending police brutality once and for all," she had stated. "It is also about ending systemic racism and dismantling white supremacy in every aspect of our economy and society. It is about building an America that lives up to its highest ideals."

I always say it's not enough to "get woke"; we have to "stay woke," which is why I found protests by people of all ages and backgrounds, which continued throughout the summer, so inspiring. In Portland, Oregon, demonstrators gathered for more than fifty nights in a row outside the courthouse. White grandparents who had never before marched against racism were turning out with their children and grandchildren night after night to keep the Black Lives Matter movement at the forefront of people's minds. Some of the protests took on an almost festive tone, as people of many different ethnicities and experiences found common ground, chanting and singing protest anthems as they marched in the cause of justice. Along the sidewalks, volunteers manned food and water stations in makeshift tents offering sustenance and places for marchers to rest when they needed to. Music blared from speakers set up in the streets as neighbors got to know neighbors. It was beautiful to watch these human connections being made. Even in my home state, thousands of people staged demonstrations in solidarity with the mainland protests, with ten thousand people showing up for a rally at the State Capitol in Honolulu in early June, and sign holders lining the highways and avenues on the neighbor islands, waving Black Lives Matter placards.

But with Trump's poll numbers sliding precipitously in the wake of his mishandling of the pandemic, our deepening economic woes, and the ongoing protests, the president did the unthinkable. In mid-July, he unleashed a force of militarized federal agents into the midst of peaceful demonstrators. As the unidentified agents lobbed tear-gas canisters into the crowd and snatched people off the streets of Portland and later, Chicago, without due process or cause, protesters began to turn out in ever-increasing numbers, vehemently pushing back against the un-American notion of a secret police force. Commentators suggested that the president had intended to provoke skirmishes and escalate violence to bolster his claim of being the law and order president. We had arrived at such an absurd political moment that no one doubted such dangerous and bad-faith actions on Trump's part to be true. Most of us understood the situation as exactly what it was, the bully president mimicking the tyrants and strongmen he so admired by attacking his own people for exercising their First Amendment rights.

The damage was incalculable. No longer was our country merely "flirting with fascism," as some had said. With Trump's deployment of his militarized federal force, we had definitively crossed over. In Portland, people with camera phones had captured footage of the camouflage-clad force kidnapping pedestrians and bundling them into unmarked black cars, brutally clubbing and breaking the arm of a navy veteran who tried to find out who they were, gassing and pepper-spraying a "wall of Moms" who had locked arms to protect other protesters, and shooting so-called nonlethal rounds at demonstrators at close range, shattering a young man's skull and leaving him fighting for his life in critical care.

Protesters then began to show up with helmets, gas masks, and leaf blowers to dissipate the tear gas, defaulting to an expectation of violence. Watching them, I had flashbacks to my own protest days, and I wondered: Had we really made so little progress since the sixties, when civil rights and antiwar protesters were met with water hoses, snarling dogs, police batons, and even gunfire? Had we learned nothing from the busloads of idealistic students who traveled south during 1964's Freedom Summer to register Blacks and poor whites to vote, only to be met with violent beatings from local officials and in some cases outright murder? Had we forgotten the thirteen students shot at Kent State, four of them killed by the Ohio National Guard during antiwar protests in May 1970? This was not the vision of America I had believed in during my relatively sheltered upbringing in Hawaii, the land I had pledged so many times to faithfully serve. Rather, this was a country careening off the rails, and all because Senate Republicans had failed to hold the petty tyrant in the Oval Office accountable for his actions. Now, the man was out of control, turning his seething malice on his own people with a flagrancy that revealed his utter contempt for the rule of law.

As the demonstrations persisted through the summer and into the fall of 2020, the nation began to recognize that right-wing citizen militias had been infiltrating the organized marches from the start, instigating riots, setting fire to buildings, and roughing up peaceful protesters. I condemned the violence and looting that had taken place at a small number of the protests, and was well aware that the imagery of buildings being burned and people fighting in the streets played right into Trump's divisive hands. His reelection campaign quickly began deploying the film footage in an attempt to scare white voters into believing that *they*—the people of color whom Trump had long "otherized" to stoke fear and division—would be coming for *us*, the real and true Americans, unless they reelected him. His racism now completely unveiled, he even threatened white suburban women that if the Democrats won, New Jersey senator Cory Booker would be put in charge of housing policy. Trump's clear implication was that they would not like who might then move into their neighborhoods.

With Trump explicitly fanning the flames of racial antagonism in order to help him win a second term, it became more evident than ever that as cruel, inept, and morally bankrupt as we had imagined a Trump presidency might be, it had been infinitely worse. And he would sink still lower.

After Ruth Bader Ginsburg succumbed to cancer on September 18, 2020, just six weeks before Election Day, he and his crony Mitch McConnell rushed to place yet another Federalist Society–backed ideologue on the Supreme Court. Amy Coney Barrett, a former law professor at Notre Dame, had been appointed by Trump to the Seventh Circuit Court in 2017. Now, despite McConnell having refused Merrick Garland a hearing in 2016, arguing that a Supreme Court justice should not be confirmed in an election year, and despite Justice Ginsburg's deathbed wish that her replacement be named by whomever the American people chose as their next president, Republicans were ramming through Barrett's confirmation. Their hypocrisy and crass opportunism infuriated me: not only were millions of Americans already engaged in early voting, but Trump had also insinuated that the conservative majority on the court would rule in his favor on the legal challenges he intended to bring before them should he lose the election.

Barrett, who would become the sixth right-wing justice on the nine-member court, had closely aligned herself with her mentor, the late Antonin Scalia, who for decades had led the court's conservative faction. Barrett's writings and rulings indicated that once seated on the bench, she would fall right in line with the ideological agenda of chipping away at LGBTQ rights, workers' rights, voting rights, reproductive rights, and the right to affordable health care. That was why when the confirmation vote was called on October 26, 2020, even though I knew the Republican majority would carry the day, my thumbs-down vote on her appointment was accompanied by a firm "Hell, no."

In a supreme irony, Trump and several top Republicans had been diagnosed with COVID-19 in the days following the White House ceremony at which Barrett's nomination was announced. Attendees had been packed shoulder-to-shoulder on chairs set up in the Rose Garden, and some had mingled indoors as well, with hardly a face mask in sight. The White House quickly became the country's most visible COVID-19 hot zone, despite its ready access to testing for anyone likely to come in contact with the president. Trump, of course, received expensive, experimental, top-of-the-line care at Walter Reed National Military Medical Center. Three days later, he returned to the White House by helicopter as night was falling. Despite still being contagious, he ripped off his mask and posed for a photo op on the White House balcony, preening in the dying light like a minor dictator drunk on his own grandiosity, even as he appeared to gasp for breath. Afterward, he entered the White House and conversed with staffers, still maskless and recklessly ignoring social distancing protocols.

In the final weeks of the 2020 election cycle, he behaved as if his own recovery from the virus proved that the disease was a trifle. He continued to hold campaign rallies in states where COVID-19 was surging, packing in supporters and sometimes even ridiculing people who chose to wear masks. I was hardly surprised when a Stanford University study found that the president's in-person rallies between June and September had spawned some thirty thousand new infections, leading to seven hundred deaths. By November 1, 2020, coronavirus cases in the United States had soared past nine million, with researchers at Johns Hopkins reporting that one American expired from the disease every 107 seconds. Trump's lack of empathy for the families of the dead was staggering, matched only by the man's utter lack of conscience, humanity, and shame.

As I said to Kamala Harris after Democratic presidential nominee Joe Biden chose her to be his running mate in what was widely characterized as a battle for the soul of America, "We are in a knife fight so don't bring a teaspoon." Standing on the threshold of history—if elected, the Oakland-born senator would become the first woman, the first Black woman, the first Asian American, and the first daughter of immigrants to serve in the White House—Kamala understood my metaphor exactly. We had all seen in the starkest terms that an absence of character, judgment, intellect, and compassion in a president could be deadly, and that democracy and good government could not be taken for granted.

And yet, even with the most depraved leader in our nation's history doing his worst, and two pandemics—COVID-19 and structural racism—plaguing our country, my fellow citizens had found ways to care for one another. They had delivered groceries to the sick and the elderly, donated to food banks, registered new voters, volunteered as poll workers, applauded essential workers, organized and marched for racial equality, and continued wearing masks to protect their fellow citizens. Their acts of kindness and courage had made clear to me that America's social contract, though frayed and battered by the Trump presidency, was stronger and more enduring than one bad man and his cult of followers would ever be. And so, throughout this difficult and unprecedented year, I continued to rise every morning, teleworking from home or my office as the virus still raged, or putting on my mask to make my way to the Capitol to cast votes or attend in-person committee hearings. I saw myself fully now as a fighter in the re- sistance, a citizen of this nation intent on doing all I could to stop the wrongs committed against the people I had pledged to serve. Always echoing in my mind was the promise that America's women had made in the run-up to the 2018 midterms. "November is coming," they had warned. *November is coming.*

The Paper Makers

n Japanese lore, the crane is said to live for one thousand years and to bring hope and healing. Japanese mothers pray, "O Flock of heavenly cranes, cover my child with your wings," asking for health and longevity for their young ones. It is also said that if a person folds one thousand origami cranes—an act known in Japan as senbazuru, which translates literally as "a thousand cranes"—a dearly held wish will be granted.

After my cancer diagnosis and surgeries in 2017, many people sent me origami cranes as an expression of their wish for my return to good health. A year later, my health now stable and my cancer controlled, my own wish for the healing of our sorely divided nation had led me to invite guests to my Senate office to fold paper cranes, which my staff and I would sew into long streamers using fishing line and hang from cherry branches mounted on a plain white wall. We had installed the colorful senbazuru behind my desk, where a slant of sunlight cast the winged paper chains in a mesmerizing dance of light and shade. One Tuesday morning, as I met with a group of DACA participants, one of them had presented me with a red origami heart instead of a crane. It was a thing of beauty, an exquisite and complex design, and it prompted me to begin folding hearts as well as cranes. It seemed to me that we would need courageous hearts as well as powerful wishes to get through our surreal new normal. How right I was—though none of us could have guessed just how surreal it would become.

After the 2018 midterms, I had felt a renewed hope that the forces of good might yet prevail, that enough of my Republican colleagues might come to their senses and help us to hold the corrupt president in check. That would require them to remember the oaths they had taken, and all of us to reach across a political chasm that, as time went on, began to feel more unbridgeable than ever. Yet for one hour each week, before the pandemic, a group of Democrats and Republicans did put aside the animus that too often marked our discourse on the floor and gathered in communion with one another. This single hour of scheduled bipartisanship occurred at 8:00 every Wednesday morning, when the Senate held its prayer breakfast in a room on the first floor of the Capitol, led by Senate chaplain Barry Black. Cochaired by a Democrat and a Republican, who shared organizational duties for a period of one year, the Senate prayer breakfast was a tradition that began around the time I was born, with the intention of fostering compassion and trust between lawmakers who might stand on opposite sides of the political map. As the inside joke among the attendees went, "It's much harder to stab someone in the back after you prayed for them in the morning."

While about two dozen senators attended the prayer breakfasts regularly, a few of the Senate Democrats were part of a more informal reflections group that met at the same 8:00 a.m. hour every other Wednesday. (Now, in the age of COVID-19, we gather weekly via Zoom.) Back when I had been a new congresswoman in 2006, I had been invited to join the House reflections group, which had been organized by the Faith and Politics Institute to give members a space for honest and introspective dialogue. It had been, for me, a soul-restoring hour, my version of church, in which we discussed readings on such subjects as moral courage, spiritual justice, kindness, and what love looks like in the public sphere.

I admired the Faith and Politics Institute, whose most famous program was an annual congressional pilgrimage to the Deep South, during which Democratic and Republican members of the House and Senate would travel together and reflect on the history of civil rights. The pilgrimage would culminate with a Sunday visit to the Edmund Pettus Bridge, which for years had been led by the late Georgia congressman John Lewis, one of the marchers beaten on that bridge during the seminal March 7, 1965, civil rights protest that became known as Bloody Sunday. I had participated in the pilgrimage twice, including during the fiftieth anniversary of Bloody Sunday in 2015, when President Obama had walked with us across the bridge, with the humble and heroic John Lewis still leading the way.

After I was elected to the Senate, Ohio Democrat Sherrod Brown and I had started a new reflections group for that chamber. For one hour every other week, we came together in Sherrod's office to exchange confidences, wishes, deep concerns. Often, we talked about our families and the work we hoped to achieve as lawmakers, relating to one another not as politicians but as fellow travelers on a path we all considered to be richly worthwhile. Over the years, this sort of sharing had helped us reach one another in a deeper way, and the regular participants in the group had become some of my best friends in Washington.

Over in the Capitol, where the weekly prayer breakfast was held, Senate colleagues were also giving their unguarded attention as they listened to whomever the group's chairs had chosen as the speaker for that week. There was some cross-pollination between the two groups, with a handful of reflections participants attending the prayer breakfast on the weeks we did not meet. In successive years, our reflections group lost the attendance of Delaware's Chris Coons and Virginia's Tim Kaine when each was drafted to serve as cochair of the prayer breakfast. Chris and Tim had each prevailed on me to be a guest speaker for the group.

My appearance before the prayer breakfast in 2015, the year when Chris Coons was cochair, was especially memorable. As the designated speaker, I was asked to choose the hymn for the gathering. A lifelong Buddhist, I knew very few hymns, and so I decided we would sing my favorite anthem, "We Shall Overcome," which I had long considered to be the most haunting yet hopeful protest song of all time. Chaplain Black would later share with me that in all his years of leading the prayer breakfast, not once had a guest speaker requested that particular song. I explained to those present that morning why the spiritual meant so much to me; how during my antiwar activism days, it had become the sound track for my political awakening. Then I joined in as Democrats and Republicans lifted up that beloved anthem of resistance movements everywhere, with Chaplain Black's resonant baritone leading the refrain.

Oh, deep in my heart
I do believe
We shall overcome, some day . . .

As I let myself be carried on the tide of our voices, I looked around the room and smiled with a secret, subversive pleasure at the sight of so many older white lawmakers singing a spiritual that evoked movements against racial injustice and other forms of oppression. I wagered that some of my colleagues had never before sung those poignant words, and I was happy to have afforded them the opportunity.

Afterward, I would often remember that moment with a feeling of stubborn optimism, because outside the halls of Congress, through the long dark night of a lawless presidency, amid a deadly and devastating pandemic, a huge swath of the American people had never stopped marching for justice and equality, and they had never stopped dreaming of the world that could be. Now, as I call back the memory of that chorus of voices from red states and purple states and blue states, singing in unison a spiritual that has never failed to move me, I can't help but imagine that the American people might yet make a senbazuru together, a winged chain of hope and healing, a wish for our nation coming true.

Tuesday, November 3, 2020—Election Day—fell on my seventy-third birthday. At home with Leighton on Waialae Nui Ridge, the two of us having voted early, I awoke that morning with a prayer on my lips, that decency and sanity would be restored to our nation. Throughout the day a number of my colleagues, including Kamala Harris, sent me birthday wishes. I texted back that my most fervent wish was that today, we would save our country. We had been warned that, with record-breaking voter turnouts and an unprecedented number of mail-in ballots, the outcome of the election might not be known for weeks. In the days following the election, as poll workers painstakingly tabulated the ballots and statisticians crunched the numbers, America watched anxiously, awaiting news of its fate.

On Friday night the election still had not been called, though Joe Biden and Kamala Harris had already won the key battleground states of Michigan and Wisconsin and were ahead in other crucial states, including the once reliably red Arizona; Georgia, which had not voted blue in nearly thirty years; and the all-important Pennsylvania with its twenty Electoral College votes. Pennsylvania alone, the state to which former vice president Joe Biden traced his working class roots, could put the Democratic ticket over the top of the required 270 electoral votes, but with frivolous legal challenges being filed by Trump's lawyers, the pace of ballot counting was deliberate, which is to say slow.

I spent most of Saturday, November 7, in airports and on planes, flying back to Washington, D.C., so that I would be present when Congress reopened the week after the election. I was in the air at 11:24 a.m. EST when CNN called Pennsylvania for Joe Biden and Kamala Harris, and then immediately announced that they were now our new president-elect and vice president–elect.

My joy when I landed at National Airport and learned that my birthday prayer would be answered was boundless. The sun seemed to shine brighter than it had the day before, and my heart felt lighter. In cities across America, people danced in the streets, face masks in place as they sang and cheered. Many people wept. I did, too, especially during Joe's magnanimous acceptance speech—and Kamala's history-making one—broadcast from Delaware later that night. I imagine we were all feeling a release from the heavy mental and emotional exhaustion we had carried for four long years.

The Biden-Harris ticket would go on to earn the most votes ever cast in a presidential race in the nation's history—upwards of eighty-one million when all the ballots were counted. The Republican ticket, too, garnered a large number of votes, some seventy-four million, but as I saw it, the more than seven-million-vote margin of victory represented a decisive repudiation of the Trump presidency by the American people, and a hefty mandate to restore the "soul of our nation." Though it concerned me that so many voters had sought a continuation of the politics of meanness, self-interest, and white grievance, it did not in any way dampen my readiness for the task at hand—rebuilding our besieged nation.

And yet, I could not have imagined just how besieged our nation would soon become. Few were surprised that Trump refused to concede, declaring the election stolen and suing for recount after recount in critical battleground states. His legal team brought more than sixty cases claiming voter fraud, to no avail. Judges all the way up to the Supreme Court rejected the lawsuits for lack of evidence or standing, effectively blocking the president's attempt to subvert the will of the voters. Trump even tried to reshuffle the leadership of the Justice Department to get them to petition the Supreme Court to invalidate the election in some states. The move was only foiled by the threat of mass resignations within the department.

Trump's delusion and desperation had reached a fever pitch by January 6, 2021, the day that Vice President Mike Pence was to preside over Congress's counting of the states' Electoral College votes as a last step in certifying the election results. For weeks, Trump had been calling on his base to come to Washington, D.C., for a massive "Stop the Steal" rally on that day. He had also been pressuring Pence to overturn the Electoral College results, refusing to accept that such an action would be unconstitutional. Trump had already convinced more than one hundred cravenly ambitious House and Senate Republicans to object to certifying the Electoral College count, even though their seditious spectacle had no chance whatsoever of changing the election outcome.

Ironically, Wednesday, January 6 had dawned full of hope, as America learned that Georgia Democrats Raphael Warnock and Jon Ossoff would win the previous day's Senatorial run-off races. Their victory meant Democrats and Republicans would now be equally represented with fifty members each in the Senate, with Vice President Kamala Harris casting the tie-breaking vote should it become necessary, thus giving the Democrats the majority. Given that Democrats had already secured a majority in the House, our new control of the Senate assured that President-elect Joe Biden's priorities and agendas would have a fighting chance. With Democrats leading both the executive and legislative branches of government, we could finally address pressing concerns like the pandemic, our flailing economy, climate change, immigration reform, voting rights, and equal justice for all.

Even so, as we gathered in the Capitol on January 6 to certify the election, the mood was somber. We had all been briefed about online threats from MAGA cultists and right-wing militia groups planning to show up for Trump's "Stop the Steal" rally, which the outgoing president himself had vowed via tweet would be "wild." In downtown Washington, D.C., merchants boarded up their shops in anticipation of trouble, and Capitol police asked lawmakers to use underground tunnels to access the House and Senate chambers that day to avoid interaction with hostile, pro-Trump extremists outside. The Capitol police had set up a perimeter some distance from the Capitol. We had every expectation they would be able to maintain that boundary, even with Trump whipping up the crowd during a speech that morning in which he explicitly exhorted his followers to march to the Capitol to stop the procedural certification of the votes. In that same speech, he also made clear his displeasure with Mike Pence, who despite four years of slavish allegiance to his boss, had resolved to do his constitutionally prescribed duty.

Vice President Pence opened the certification proceedings at 1 p.m. A little more than an hour later, a riotous mob crashed through police barriers and rushed toward the Capitol. Unknown to the lawmakers doing our jobs inside the nation's most sacred seat of democracy, a wooden gallows and noose had already been erected on the grounds outside the Capitol, and pipe bombs, presumably to distract attention, had been placed outside the Democratic National Committee and Republican National Committee headquarters. These instruments of death would fortunately be found and deactivated before doing damage. The same could not be said of the riled-up mob the president himself had incited.

By 2:15 p.m. the rioters were smashing windows and breaking down doors of the Capitol, using tire irons and long poles from which hung the American flags, Blue Lives Matter flags, Trump flags, and flags of the Confederacy. The surging mob, now chanting "Hang Mike Pence," would use those same flagpoles to beat and brutalize Capitol police, whom, it quickly became clear, were woefully outnumbered. One officer, bashed in the head by a fire extinguisher, would later die of his injuries. All told, five people would lose their lives as a result of that afternoon's violent siege of the Capitol.

On the Senate floor, to which we had adjourned to debate the Republican objection to certifying Arizona's election result, my first clue to the mayhem came when Capitol police suddenly swarmed around Mike Pence and whisked him out of the room. Senate staffers now poured into the chamber with the news that the Capitol had been breached, and rioting mobs were spreading through the building. Most of the one hundred Senators, and many of our staffers, were quickly escorted to safe quarters, where we remained for the next five hours. When TV monitors were finally wheeled into the room, we watched the news already being seen by the rest of the world, horrified by what was unfolding inside our citadel of democracy.

Everyone fielded calls and texts from family and friends wanting to know if we were safe. The Capitol police cautioned us not to send out photographs or share any details that might reveal our whereabouts. By then, rioters were charging down hallways inside the Capitol, banging on doors and yelling, "Where the fuck are they?" I did not doubt that if the insurrectionists found any of us, they would physically hurt us. The thought chilled me right through as we waited in our safe room, not knowing how or when the tumult might end. I later learned that a few of my Senate colleagues in other parts of the Capitol complex, and some of my House colleagues, had been terrifyingly close to being overrun by the mob and possibly taken hostage by rioters, who had come equipped with zip ties, homemade napalm, firearms, and handcuffs.

All that afternoon, as the nation's lawmakers huddled in secret rooms or crouched under tables in darkened offices with furniture barricading the doors, our resolve hardened: We knew that when the siege was over, when law enforcement was finally able to retake the building from insurrectionists ransacking both chambers of Congress, going through desks, and even vandalizing and stealing mail and a laptop from House Speaker Nancy Pelosi's office, when all was once again secured, no matter the hour, we would return to the business of certifying the election of Joe Biden and Kamala Harris. It mattered more intensely than ever that we show America and the world that our democracy would not be subverted—even if one hundred and thirty-nine House Republicans and eight Senate Republicans still went ahead with their baseless objections to the vote, utterly failing to grasp the lessons of the siege we had just lived through.

As we picked up the pieces of Trump's failed coup in the days that followed, and arrests of rioters climbed into the hundreds, Twitter, Facebook, and other social media sites suspended the accounts of the president and certain of his allies to limit their opportunity to foment more violence. "Gollum has lost his Precious," I tweeted in response to Trump's beloved Twitter account being shuttered; the *Lord of the Rings* reference immediately went viral. Within days, news reports indicated that online misinformation about election fraud had fallen by 73 percent—a stark illustration of the ability of tech companies to act as a check on the toxic lies that had infected our nation.

One week later, on January 13, 2021, the House voted to hold the instigator-in-chief accountable by impeaching him a second time, making him the only president in our history to bear the singular disgrace of being impeached twice, and the only president to have members of his own party vote in favor of indicting him. The sole article of impeachment—incitement of insurrection—would be turned over to the Senate on January 25, 2021, with the trial set to begin the week of February 8. If that body found Trump guilty as charged, he could be barred from running for political office ever again. As I contemplated the sorry end to what had been an unremittingly disastrous presidency, I lamented, not for the first time, how much carnage would have been avoided if only Republicans had been brave enough to remove the corrupt president from office during his first impeachment trial one year before.

Heartened by the thought that, in just one more week, Trump would no longer occupy the Oval Office, the country's attention now turned to ensuring a peaceful transfer of power to President-elect Biden and Vice President–elect Harris. With my own gaze determinedly cast toward the future, I took comfort in the fact that at our very darkest hour, our nation had succeeded in elevating a decent and deeply experienced man as the forty-sixth president of the United States, and a brilliant and resilient woman as his vice president. American voters—in particular people of color, suburban women, and young people dismayed by their leaders' abdication of all responsibility—had spoken loudly, ushering in a team that sought to unite us rather than divide us. Though we had been sorely buffeted and bruised, the enduring power of our democracy was affirmed; authoritarianism had been dealt a blow, and now we would have to find a way to bridge our tribal differences so our nation would never again be so imperiled.

I believe it will take time for truth and reconciliation to take hold in our country, but I remain ever hopeful, especially with a new generation of aware, enlightened, and principled leaders. As Joe Biden put it when he addressed a weary but deeply relieved and newly optimistic nation in his inaugural speech on January 20, 2021: "Through a crucible for the ages America has been tested anew and America has risen to the challenge. Today, we celebrate the triumph not of a candidate, but of a cause, the cause of democracy.

The will of the people has been heard and the will of the people has been heeded. We have learned again that democracy is precious. Democracy is fragile. And at this hour, my friends, democracy has prevailed."

Throughout my time in Congress, after a week of back-to-back committee meetings and floor debates, I have often spent Saturday or Sunday afternoons taking solitary walks along the Tidal Basin. It is a habit left over from my law school days when, instead of studying, I would wander among the cherry trees, daydreaming as I used to do as a child on my grandparents' farm back in Fukushima.

The Tidal Basin brings me peace in any season, but I have always loved it best in the spring, when the blossoms are at their peak. The park's 3,020 cherry trees were sent to Washington, D.C., as a gift from the city of Tokyo in 1912, the same year that my grandfather first arrived in this country as a sixteen-year-old farm laborer. I now see the trees as a lovely gesture of friendship between the two cultures that have shaped me. More than a century later, their fleecy blooms spilling along rich dark bark each spring never fail to transport me back to long-ago springs in Japan, when my mother and my baachan would take my brothers and me on trips to see the cherry blossoms.

In recent years, as the afternoon sun sets the glassy Potomac River ablaze, I will sometimes bend to retrieve a few of the tender pink petals from the ground. The pain from my missing seventh rib might flare, causing me to straighten up slowly, the blossoms tucked safely in my palm. Savoring the cool damp feel of them against my skin, I flash on a vision of my mother in years past, bending toward the earth as she tended the flower beds in our yard on Waialae Nui Ridge. I always feel a pang of longing, an aching wish for one more day of watching my mother in our garden, her hands working in the soil she loved. Now resting in a quiet room, mostly bedridden, Mom can no longer press the flowers she once grew to make her exquisite greeting cards. Her paper art, like so much else, is lost to her, her fingers unresponsive, her whispers indecipherable. And so I have begun to make my own greeting cards in homage to her life of patient labor.

Back in my apartment on Capitol Hill, I place the cherry blossoms in a ceramic bowl, mix in leaves and flowers gathered from outside the Capitol, and grind everything into slurry using as paper stock the cards on which my daily Senate schedules are printed. By evening, that long, slender card is always covered with my scrawled notations—names and numbers, committee speaking points, reminders of what I want to say when I am interviewed on the nightly news. But when all of that is behind me, when the people's work is done for another day, I stand in my tiny Washington, D.C., kitchen and mix bits of nature with the card stock that contains my very atoms, transforming the watery paste into rectangular sheets that I then air-dry to make cards—original, one-of-a-kind creations that I will send to friends and supporters, often with an origami crane or folded red heart tucked inside.

As I work, I picture my mother delicately arranging pressed flowers to make her own cards, and also my baachan, sitting beside me all those decades ago, the two of us using rice paste to fashion paper bags to cover the ripening green apples on my grandparents' farm. This ritual of making paper has become for me a kind of meditation, my way of staying connected to the spirits of these two steadfast women who so profoundly shaped my life, especially my mother, who crossed an ocean with hope for her children burning like a fire in her heart.

Mom made thousands of cards for me over the years, but when vendors approached her to sell her creations, she refused them. Her cards were a labor of love, intended to help me in my work, and for the enjoyment of those to whom I gave them. I remember when Mom offered to teach me her card-making methods, and I declined. At the time, my own artistic expression had been more focused on ceramics. Fortunately, I'd had the foresight to ask my mother to put together an album for me with some of her favorite card designs. How I cherish that album now.

Yet when I finally began to make my own cards many years later, it was in my own way. My greeting cards look nothing like my mother's. Mine are more rustic, because I make the paper from scratch, while she used precut commercial card stock. My creations are also more abstract; one series might bear no resemblance to the next. And yet every card I make is as much for my mother as it is for me. This is how it has always been between us, the two of us very different and yet so connected. Even now, with each new card I make, I imagine sharing it with my mother, and resting for a moment in the surpassing love that all my life has animated her gaze. *This is for you*, I will think but not say to the woman who already knows my reasons.

Acknowledgments

Like my life, this memoir has been a journey made possible by many people:

My heartfelt thanks to my agent, Will Lippincott of Aevitas Creative Management, and to Jeremy Paris, who first brought us together. From the start, Will believed I had a story to tell and convinced me that I should take the plunge and share it. He provided help and encouragement every step of the way with patience, warmth, and attention to detail.

A special mahalo to Rosemarie Robotham, an incredible collaborator whose commitment, patience, and talent brought my voice to life on the page. Rosemarie and I connected almost immediately over our shared immigrant experience, and her understanding, compassion, and empathy brought a richness to this manuscript. Through our many hours of conversation during the writing process, Rosemarie encouraged and pushed me to explore important life moments honestly and deeply. Her skills as a writer and collaborator can be seen throughout the pages of this book, and I am deeply grateful for her friendship and partnership over the past eighteen months.

To my editor, Lindsey Schwoeri, whose careful reading of the manuscript and thoughtful suggestions improved the tone and flow of this book. Her enthusiasm and faith in this project never wavered, and I am grateful to her and the entire Viking/Penguin publishing team, including Brian Tart, Andrea Schulz, Kate Stark, Mary Stone, Lindsay Prevette, Louise

Braverman, Kristina Fazzalaro, Britta Galanis, Bridget Gilleran, Claire
Leonard, and Allie Merola; production editor Nicole Celli; copy editor Jane
Cavolina; Nayon Cho for the beautiful cover; Alexis Farabaugh for the
book's interior design; and Claire Vaccaro, for the lovely renditions of my
mother's cards.

My abundant thanks also to Will Dempster, who read through every
page of the manuscript with me—several times—while keeping us all on
schedule and following up on the thousand and one things that needed to be
gathered and checked to bring the book to fruition.

To my colleagues in the U.S. House and Senate—especially my Faith
and Politics Institute Reflections ohana, including Doug Tanner, Liz
McCloskey, Joan Mooney, Jack Moline, former congressman and dear friend
Jim McDermott, and Senators Tammy Baldwin, Sherrod Brown, Chris
Coons, Tim Kaine, Tom Udall, and Sheldon Whitehouse—thank you for
your friendship and support.

To all the public-service–minded men and women who have worked with
me throughout my time in legislative politics and enabled me to be a voice for
the people of Hawaii, you have my enduring appreciation. I also wouldn't
be where I am today without the hundreds of volunteers on every campaign
I have run over the past forty years, who have had my back through thick
and thin.

My family and friends have been constant pillars of support for me
throughout my journey: my older brother, Roy, his wife, Emi, and her sister
Yuri Shimahara; my sister- and brother-in-law Lauren and Milton Miyashiro;
my sister-in-law Lynette Oshima; my stepdaughter, Malia Oshima Paul, and
her husband, Scott; and their families.

Thank you also to Ray Tam, who hired me to join his law firm and showed
me the importance of plaintiffs' law; Norma Yuskos, my ceramics muse; Steve
Carter, Amy Agbayani, David and Diane Lo, Mark and Ellen Borenstein,

Robert Toyofuku, Jadine Nielsen, Caryl Ito, Tim Johns, Alan Van Etten, Alan Yamamoto, Jill Tokuda, Elisa Yadao, Vincent Eng, and Rich Davis, longtime political advisers and friends. So many other wonderful people have lit the path for me, and I am grateful to them all.

Most important, I am thankful to my mother, Laura Chieko Hirono, the extraordinary and gifted woman to whom I have dedicated this memoir. She changed my life by bringing me to this country, and this is as much her story as it is mine.

Finally, my unending gratitude to my husband, Leighton Kim Oshima, whose unconditional love and support for over thirty years continues to be a stabilizing presence in my life, and whose enjoyment of reading and sharing a good laugh matches my own.

Notes

Chapter One: Tari and Chieko

5   **after ten hours in the field:** Teresa Bill, "Field Work & Family Work: Picture Brides on Hawaii's Sugar Plantations 1910–1920," University of Hawaii at Manoa, Department of Sociology, updated September 27, 1996.

8   **forcing Japan's surrender:** History.com editors, "Bombing of Hiroshima and Nagasaki," This Day in History, History.com, updated August 5, 2020, www.history.com/topics/world -war-ii/bombing-of-hiroshima-and-nagasaki.

Chapter Two: On Kewalo Street

21   **the Japanese emperor Meiji:** "Bunka No Hi: Celebrating Culture Day in Japan," Japanese Pod101.com, September 14, 2019, www.japanesepod101.com/blog/2019/09/24/culture-day/.

21   **diseases brought by the Europeans:** Gene Demby, "It Took Two Centuries, but the Native Hawaiian Population May Be Bouncing Back," Code Switch, NPR, April 18, 2015, www.npr.org/sections/codeswitch/2015/04/18/398578801/it-took-two-centuries-but -the-native-hawaii-ans-has-finally-bounced-back.

22   **Big Five, would control:** "Strikers, Scabs, and Sugar Mongers: How Immigrant Labor Struggle Shaped the Hawai'i We Know Today," *Densho Blog*, August 22, 2017, densho.org /strikers-scabs-sugar-mongers-immigrant-labor-struggle-shaped-hawaii-know-today/.

22   **immigration of Chinese laborers:** History.com staff, "Chinese Exclusion Act, History .com, Updated September 13, 2019, www.history.com/topics/immigration/chinese-exclusion -act-1882.

22   **shiploads of picture brides:** "Japanese Laborers Arrive," HawaiiHistory.org, www.ha waiihistory.org/index.cfm?fuseaction=ig.page&PageID=299.

22   **six cents an hour:** "Strikers, Scabs, and Sugar Mongers."

23   **labor strike in 1920:** "Strikers, Scabs, and Sugar Mongers."

23   **largest ethnic group:** Eleanor C. Nordyke and Y. Scott Matsumoto, "The Japanese in Ha-waii: A Historical and Demographic Perspective," *East-West Population Institute* 95 (1977), evols.library.manoa.hawaii.edu/bitstream/10524/528/2/JL11174.pdf.

23 in the census of 1960: "Table 1.03, the Population of Hawai'i by Race/Ethnicity: U.S. Census 1900–2010," Native Hawaiian Data Book, www.ohadatabook.com/T01-03-11u.pdf.

Chapter Three: Star Spangled

43 last reigning monarch: Jenny Ashcraft, "Hawaii Becomes a State: August 21, 1959," *Fishwrap* (blog), newspapers.com, August 1, 2019, blog.newspapers.com/hawaii-becomes-a -state/.

43 a resolution was passed annexing: Joint Resolution to Provide for Annexing the Hawaiian Islands to the United States, July 7, 1898; Enrolled Acts and Resolutions of Congress; General Records of the United States Government, 1778–1992; Record Group 11; National Archives.

43 denied the right to vote: Shiho Imai, "Naturalization Act of 1790," Densho Encyclopedia, encyclopedia.densho.org/Naturalization_Act_of_1790/.

44 *United States v. Wong Kim Ark*: History.com staff, "Chinese Exclusion Act, History.com, updated September 13, 2019, www.history.com/topics/immigration/chinese-exclusion-act -1882.

44 the Fourteenth Amendment: *United States v. Wong Kim Ark*, United States Supreme Court, March 29, 1898, Cornell Law School Legal Information Institute, www.law.cornell .edu/supremecourt/text/169/649.

45 recognition of their citizenship: Cherstin M. Lyon, "United States v. Wong Kim Ark," Densho Encyclopedia, encyclopedia.densho.org/United_States_v._Wong_Kim_Ark/.

45 profoundly discriminatory history: "The Immigration and Nationality Act of 1952 (the McCarran-Walter Act)," U.S. Department of State, Office of the Historian, Milestones, 1945–1952, history.state.gov/milestones/1945-1952/immigration-act.

45 interned in camps: "51e. Japanese-American Internment," USHistory.org, www.ushistory .org/us/51e.asp.

Chapter Six: Tinderbox

76 planned residential community: Chelsea Pferschy, "A Short History (and Cultural?) Lesson on Hawaii Kai," Kawaguchi Group, January 7, 2016, Alohatony.com, www.alohatony .com/blog/a-short-history-and-cultural-lesson-on-hawaii-kai-by-chelsea-pferschy-ra/.

83 The Bachman Hall protests: ilind.net/gallery_old/bachmangallery/source/bachman29 .htm.

84 The arrests further inflamed: Ibid.

Chapter Seven: Waimanalo

95 Bernice had described her art: Bernice Akamine, "Transcendients: Heroes at Borders," Taiji Terasaki website, https://www.taijiterasaki.com/bernice-akamine?rq=Bernice%20Akamine.

Chapter Eight: Rich Man's War

97 the suicide rate among veterans: John Ketwig, "Ketwig: More veterans commit suicide than were killed in Vietnam," *Roanoke Times*, November 10, 2017, www.roanoke.com/opin ion/commentary/ketwig-more-veterans-commit-suicide-than-were-killed-in-vietnam /article_2d841f24-c167-50bd-9e0b-02e42feb98d1.html.

98   **enemy deaths reported:** "Tet Offensive: Turning Point in Vietnam War," *New York Times*, January 31, 1988, www.nytimes.com/1988/01/31/world/tet-offensive-turning-point-in -vietnam-war.html.

98   **The allied losses, too, were devastating:** "Tet Offensive: Turning Point in Vietnam War."

99   **a photo essay in *Life* magazine:** Alex Ashlock, "'Look at These Beautiful Boys': In 1969, Life Magazine Published the Faces of Americans Killed in Vietnam," WBUR, *Here & Now*, June 27, 2019, www.wbur.org/hereandnow/2019/06/27/life-magazine-vietnam-american -dead.

100   **dopamine connections aren't fully mature:** "Success Story: Roy," VeteransInc.org, www.veteransinc.org/services/housing-programs/roy/.

100   **Others gained exemptions:** Blake Stilwell, "11 Ways People Dodged the Vietnam Draft," We Are the Mighty, July 3, 2018, www.wearethemighty.com/articles/vietnam-draft-dodger/.

101   **Inside each capsule:** Wesley Abney, "Live from Washington, It's Lottery Night 1969," HistoryNet.com, www.historynet.com/live-from-dc-its-lottery-night-1969.htm.

102   **the last scroll was unrolled:** Abney, "Live from Washington, It's Lottery Night 1969."

103   **young men were called:** Abney, "Live from Washington, It's Lottery Night 1969."

103   **the Defense Department announced:** "Draft Lowest Since 1964; 195 Likely Cutoff Number," *New York Times*, August 7, 1970, www.nytimes.com/1970/08/07/archives/draft -lowest-since-1964-195-likely-cutoff-number-70-draft-calls.html.

103   **American soldiers killed in action:** "Vietnam War Casualties (1955–1975)," Military Factory, www.militaryfactory.com/vietnam/casualties.asp.

103   **who went missing:** "MIA Facts Site," MIAFacts.org, www.miafacts.org/how_many _missing.htm.

Chapter Nine: Betty Friedan and Me

111   **Bill Clinton had stated:** Ryan Lizza, "Let's Be Friends," *New Yorker*, September 10, 2012, www.newyorker.com/magazine/2012/09/10/lets-be-friends.

114   **the election of a record number of women:** "Women in the 116th Congress," Quorum, Data Driven Insights, Quorum.us, www.quorum.us/data-driven-insights/women-in-116th -congress/401/.

Chapter Eleven: The Quiet Fisherman

139   **Other estimates ran much higher:** Kevin Sieff, "They Were One of the First Families Separated at the Border. Two and a Half Years Later, They're Still Apart," *Washington Post*, February 17, 2020, www.washingtonpost.com/world/the_americas/they-were-one-of-the -first-families-separated-at-the-border-two-and-a-half-years-later-theyre-still-apart /2020/02/17/38594c98-4152-11ea-99c7-1dfd4241a2fe_story.html.

139   **youngsters under the age of five sobbing:** Garance Burke and Martha Mendoza, "At Least 3 'Tender Age' Shelters Set Up for Child Migrants," Associated Press, June 20, 2018, apnews .com/dc0c9a5134d14862ba7c7ad9a811160e.

139   **Rachel Maddow breaking down:** "Rachel Maddow Breaks Down During Report on 'Tender Age' Shelters," *Guardian News*, June 19, 2018, www.youtube.com/watch?v=DKuIjT -k-C8.

140 **removed the laces from children's shoes:** Daniel Brown, "What It Looks Like at Every Stage When Migrant Families Get Separated at the US Border," *Business Insider*, June 19, 2018, www.businessinsider.com/photos-show-where-kids-go-when-separated-from-parents -at-the-us-border-2018-6#and-that-child-many-times-is-going-through-their-own -immigration-case-breislatt-said-10.

140 **referring to the migrants as "an infestation":** Gregory Korte and Alan Gomez, "Trump Ramps Up Rhetoric on Undocumented Immigrants: 'These Aren't People. These Are Animals,'" *USA Today*, May 16, 2018, www.usatoday.com/story/news/politics/2018/05/16 /trump-immigrants-animals-mexico-democrats-sanctuary-cities/617252002/.

141 **"I will continue to fight":** "Senator Hirono Speaks Out Against Family Separation & Detention," June 20, 2018, www.youtube.com/watch?v=3Am72gAdl6c.

141 **bowing to national outrage:** John Wagner, Nick Miroff, and Mike DeBonis, "Trump Reverses Course, Signs Order Ending His Policy of Separating Families at the Border," *Washington Post*, June 20, 2018, www.washingtonpost.com/powerpost/gop-leaders-voice-hope -that-bill-addressing-family-separations-will-pass-thursday/2018/06/20/cc79db9a-7480 -11e8-b4b7-308400242c2e_story.html.

142 **The hard truth was:** Christopher Sherman, Martha Mendoza, and Garance Burke, "US Held Record Number of Migrant Children in Custody in 2019," Associated Press, November 12, 2019, apnews.com/015702afdb4d4fbf85cf5070cd2c6824.

142 **"Stable and responsive relationships":** Sherman et al., "US Held Record Number of Migrant Children."

Chapter Thirteen: Lost and Found

164 **ties to the Nixon administration:** Lawrence Meyer, "Last Two Guilty in Watergate Plot," *Washington Post*, January 31, 1973, "Watergate25," www.washingtonpost.com/wp-srv/na tional/longterm/watergate/articles/013173-2.htm.

Chapter Fourteen: Made with Aloha

183 **fifteen thousand more votes:** "Primary Election—State of Hawaii—Statewide, September 17, 1994, Final Report," files.hawaii.gov/elections/files/results/1994/primary/histate wide.pdf.

185 **Hawaii Employers' Mutual Insurance Company:** "Our History," HEMIC.com, hemic .com/about-us/our-history/.

187 **shakkei, meaning "borrowed scenery":** Tom Oder, "The Art of Shakkei or 'Borrowed Scenery,'" Treehugger.com, updated May 31, 2017, www.treehugger.com/art-shakkei-or -borrowed-scenery-4863268.

Chapter Fifteen: Daruma Doll

194 **"Nothing I can do will ever be":** Rod Ohira, "Lieutenant Governor Reflects on the 'Bookends' of Her Life," *Honolulu Star-Bulletin*, May 8, 1999, archives.starbulletin.com/1999/05 /08/news/story5.html.

196 **Harris denied any wrongdoing:** B. Drummond Ayres Jr., "Top Democrat for Governor of Hawaii Withdraws," *New York Times*, June 1, 2002, www.nytimes.com/2002/06/01/us /top-democrat-for-governor-of-hawaii-withdraws.html.

203 **Kay Orr defeated:** Patrick Bigold, "Hawaii Awaits 1st Female Governor," *Chicago Tribune*, October 16, 2002, www.chicagotribune.com/news/ct-xpm-2002-10-16-0210160262-story .html.

205 **"The Democratic Party is imploding":** John M. Broder, "Hawaii Democrats Reeling After Scandals and a Death," *New York Times*, October 19, 2002, www.nytimes.com/2002/10 /19/us/2002-campaign-democrats-hawaii-democrats-reeling-after-scandals-death.html.

206 **Lingle would win:** "HI Governor," Race Details, Our Campaigns, www.ourcampaigns .com/RaceDetail.html?RaceID=36.

220 **The EMILY acronym:** "Our History," Emily's List, www.emilyslist.org/pages/entry /our-history.

225 *You Should Run* **podcast:** Tony Heyl, "You Should Organize . . . Julia Stauch," *You ShouldRunPodcast*, April 15, 2019, medium.com/@PodcastYou/you-should-organize-julie -stauch-f30354e00983.

227 **the narrowest of victories:** "HI District 2-D Primary," Race Details, Our Campaigns, www.ourcampaigns.com/RaceDetail.html?RaceID=277648.

Chapter Seventeen: Roll Call

231 **Hoyer had the inside track:** Susan Ferrechio, "In Rebuff to Pelosi, Democrats Elect Hoyer as Majority Leader," *New York Times*, November 16, 2006, archive.nytimes.com/www.ny times.com/cq/2006/11/16/cq_1955.html.

232 **the war had been a pivotal issue:** Carl Hulse, "Hoyer Beats Pelosi's Pick in Race for No. 2 House Post," *New York Times*, November 16, 2006, www.nytimes.com/2006/11/16/us/pol itics/16congcnd.html.

234 **he and Pelosi emerged:** Hulse, "Hoyer Beats Pelosi's Pick in Race for No. 2 House Post."

236 **Nancy Pelosi defeated Ohio Republican:** Bob Benenson, "Pelosi Officially Elected Speaker of the U.S. House," *New York Times*, January 4, 2007, archive.nytimes.com/www .nytimes.com/cq/2007/01/04/cq_2079.html.

237 **"If we do not stop illegal immigration":** Dennis Camire, "Buddhist Congresswoman Sworn In, Urges Tolerance," BuddhistChannel.tv, January 6, 2007, www.buddhistchannel .tv/index.php?id=60,3603,0,0,1,0.

237 **"What happened to the separation of church and state":** Camire, "Buddhist Congress-woman Sworn In."

240 **supplemental State Health Insurance Program:** Deane Neubauer, *Health Affairs* 12, no. 2 (Summer 1993), www.healthaffairs.org/doi/full/10.1377/hlthaff.12.2.31.

240 **Obama signed the ACA:** "Chart Book: Accomplishments of Affordable Care Act," Center on Budget and Policy Priorities, March 19, 2019, www.cbpp.org/research/health/chart -book-accomplishments-of-affordable-care-act.

Chapter Eighteen: Across the Aisle

255 **Stephen Miller, a documented white nationalist:** Paul Waldman, "Yes, Stephen Miller Is Absolutely a White Nationalist," *Washington Post*, November 13, 2019, www.washington post.com/opinions/2019/11/13/yes-stephen-miller-is-absolutely-white-nationalist/.

258 **Orrin Hatch, the long-serving senator:** Nicole Puglise, "Hatch Calls ADA One of His Most Important Achievements," *Roll Call*, August 4, 2015, www.rollcall.com/2015/08/04 /hatch-calls-ada-one-of-his-most-important-achievements/.

258 **Child Health Insurance Program:** Erik Neumann, "How Sen. Orrin Hatch Changed America's Health Care," Kaiser Health News, January 2, 2019, khn.org/news/how-sen -orrin-hatch-changed-americas-health-care/.

259 **revamping the U.S. visa program:** Liz Halloran, "Gang of 8 Champion Plan, Declare 'Year of Immigration Reform,'" NPR, April 18, 2013, www.npr.org/sections/itsallpolitics /2013/04/18/177780665/bipartisan-senate-gang-prepares-to-sell-immigration-plan.

264 **she continued to wear pants:** Nia-Malika Henderson, "Barbara Mikulski Made It Okay for Women to Wear Pants in the Senate," *Washington Post*, March 2, 2015, www.washingtonpost .com/news/the-fix/wp/2015/03/02/barbara-mikulski-made-it-ok-for-women-to-wear -pants-in-the-senate/.

264 **annual Women Power Workshops:** "Inside a Senate Hideaway," *Politico Magazine*, January 5, 2015, www.politico.com/magazine/gallery/2015/01/inside-a-senate-hideaway -000120?slide=5.

267 **Graham had predicted:** Nolan D. McCaskill, "Graham: We Should Have Kicked Trump Out of the Party," *Politico*, March 7, 2016, www.politico.com/blogs/2016-gop-primary-live -updates-and-results/2016/03/lindsey-graham-donald-trump-kicked-out-220402.

268 **"fealty to Donald Trump":** Jonathan Capehart, "The Deplorable Hypocrisy of Lindsey Graham and the Republican Party," *Washington Post*, December 16, 2019, www.washington post.com/opinions/2019/12/16/deplorable-hypocrisy-lindsey-graham-republican-party/.

Chapter Nineteen: One Nation Under Siege

276 **Although she was widely liked:** Simone Pathé, "Candidates Get Candid About Their Cancer Diagnoses in TV Ads," *Roll Call*, September 19, 2018, www.rollcall.com/2018/09/19 /candidates-get-candid-about-their-cancer-diagnoses-in-tv-ads/.

277 **"And I never quit":** Saba Hamedy, "Hawaii Sen. Mazie Hirono Diagnosed with Kidney Cancer," *CNN*, May 16, 2017, www.cnn.com/2017/05/16/politics/mazie-hirono-kidney -cancer/index.html.

278 **"There's work to do":** Paula Akana, "Interview with Sen. Mazie Hirono on Her Battle with Kidney Cancer," KITV4, June 22, 2017, updated July 13, 2017. www.kitv.com/story /35732007/exclusive-interview-with-sen-mazie-hirono-on-her-battle-with-kidney-cancer.

280 **another bill to repeal the ACA:** Benjy Sarlin, "Deep Medicaid Cuts Drive Backlash to House Health Care Bill," *NBC News*, May 5, 2017, www.nbcnews.com/politics/congress /deep-medicaid-cuts-drive-backlash-house-health-care-bill-n755626.

280 **The sweeping cuts:** Margot Sanger-Katz, "Who Wins and Who Loses in the Latest G.O.P. Health Care Bill," *New York Times*, May 4, 2017, www.nytimes.com/2017/05/04/upshot /who-wins-and-who-loses-in-the-latest-gop-health-care-bill.html.

280 **advocacy groups had vociferously opposed:** Thomas Kaplan and Robert Pear, "House Passes Measure to Repeal and Replace the Affordable Care Act," *New York Times*, May 4, 2017, www.nytimes.com/2017/05/04/us/politics/health-care-bill-vote.html.

280 **"You will glow in the dark":** Kaplan and Pear, "House Passes Measure to Repeal and Replace the Affordable Care Act."

281 **"This is a tax-cut-for-the-rich bill"**: "Sen. Mazie Hirono Debates Health Care Bill Late Night Session June 26, 2017," C-SPAN, June 26, 2017, www.c-span.org/video/?c4674995 /user-clip-sen-mazie-hirono-debates-health-care-bill-late-night-session-june-26-2017& start=8139.

281 **"The stakes are too high"**: "Sen. Mazie Hirono Debates Health Care Bill."

282 **"come back and rejoin the fight"**: "Sen. Mazie Hirono Debates Health Care Bill."

290 **yet another Republican effort to eviscerate**: *The Rachel Maddow Show*, transcript, September 18, 2017, www.msnbc.com/transcripts/rachel-maddow-show/2017-09-18.

Chapter Twenty: Seeking Truth

295 **Five more women had subsequently**: Samantha Cooney, "More Women Are Accusing Roy Moore of Sexual Misconduct. Here's Everything You Need to Know About the Scandal," *Time*, November 17, 2017, time.com/5029172/roy-moore-accusers/.

295 **Trump further bragged**: David A. Fahrenthold, "Trump Recorded Having Extremely Lewd Conversation About Women in 2005," *Washington Post*, October 8, 2016, www.wash ingtonpost.com/politics/trump-recorded-having-extremely-lewd-conversation-about -women-in-2005/2016/10/07/3b9ce776-8cb4-11e6-bf8a-3d26847eeed4_story.html.

296 **Tarana Burke, a civil rights activist**: Richard Feloni, "The Founder of #MeToo Explains Why Her Movement Isn't About 'Naming and Shaming,' and How She's Fighting to Reclaim Its Narrative," *Business Insider*, April 16, 2019, www.businessinsider.com/me-too-movement -founder-tarana-burke-says-it-needs-a-narrative-shift-2019-4.

296 **"I send my sincerest apologies"**: Chris Cillizza, "Al Franken's Absolutely Awful Apology," *CNN*, November 16, 2017, www.cnn.com/2017/11/16/politics/franken-apology/index.html.

297 **He also wrote an apology letter**: Meghan Keneally, "Sen. Al Franken's Accusers and Their Allegations Against Him," *ABC News*, December 6, 2017, abcnews.go.com/US/sen-al -frankens-accusers-accusations-made/story?id=51406862.

297 **Three of the women went on record**: Keneally, "Sen. Al Franken's Accusers and Their Allegations Against Him."

298 **"pursue the Ethics Committee process"**: Elana Schor and Seung Min Kim, "Franken Resigns," *Politico*, December 7, 2017, www.politico.com/story/2017/12/07/franken-resigns -285957.

300 **Trump had tweeted that my friend Kirsten Gillibrand**: Brian Bennett, "Trump Slams Sen. Kirsten Gillibrand, a Critic, with Sexually Suggestive Tweet," *Los Angeles Times*, Dececmber 12, 2017, www.latimes.com/politics/la-na-trump-gillibrand-20171212-story.html.

302 **"I swear, icicles formed"**: Lee Cataluna, "Amid Cancer Fight, Hirono's Force Seems to Grow," *Honolulu Star-Advertiser*, December 15, 2017, www.hirono.senate.gov/news/in-the -news/honolulu-star-advertiser-amid-cancer-fight-hironos-force-seems-to-grow.

304 **hush money to an adult film star**: Brett Samuels, "MichaelCohen Pleads Guilty to Eight Counts," *The Hill*, August 21, 2018, www.thehill.com/regulation/administration/402906 -cohen-pleads-guilty-to-federal-charges.

305 **the Federalist Society, a conservative**: Anna Massoglia and Andrew Perez, "Secretive Conservative Legal Group Funded by $17 Million Mystery Donor Before Kavanaugh Fight," OpenSecrets.org, May 17, 2019, www.opensecrets.org/news/2019/05/dark-money-group -funded-by-17million-mystery-donor-before-kavanaugh/.

305 **"Conquerors of the Courts":** David Montgomery, "Conqueror of the Courts," *Washington Post Magazine*, January 2, 2019, www.washingtonpost.com/news/magazine/wp/2019/01/02/feature/conquerors-of-the-courts/.

306 **$200-a-plate annual Federalist Society gala:** Montgomery, "Conqueror of the Courts."

307 **activists sported T-shirts:** Jason Breslow, "The Resistance at the Kavanaugh Hearings: More Than 200 Arrests," NPR, September 8, 2108, www.npr.org/2018/09/08/645497667/the-resistance-at-the-kavanaugh-hearings-more-than-200-arrests.

307 **Margaret Atwood's dystopian novel:** Cheyenne Haslett, "'The Handmaid's Tale Protesters Target Kavanaugh," *ABC News*, September 4, 2018, abcnews.go.com/Politics/handmaids-tale-protesters-target-kavanaugh/story?id=57592706.

307 **A study of his cases:** Stephanie Mencimer, "Trump's Supreme Court Frontrunner Is the 'Forrest Gump of Republican Politics,'" *Mother Jones*, June 29, 2018, www.motherjones.com/politics/2018/06/the-frontrunner-to-be-trumps-supreme-court-pick-is-the-forrest-gump-of-republican-politics/.

307 **One court watcher, Adam Feldman:** Carrie Johnson, "Brett Kavanaugh Supported Broad Leeway For Presidents Under Investigation," NPR, July 10, 2018, https://www.nhpr.org/post/brett-kavanaugh-supported-broad-leeway-presidents-under-investigation#stream/0.

308 **Kavanaugh dissented from:** Edith Roberts, "Potential Nominee Profile: Brett Kavanaugh," *Scotusblog*, June 28, 2018, www.scotusblog.com/2018/06/potential-nominee-profile-brett-kavanaugh/.

309 **"chipping away at the rights":** Grace Panetta, "'Your Decisions Affect Real People': The Lawyer Who Represented an Immigrant Teen in Her Fight to Get an Abortion Explains Why She Testified Against Brett Kavanaugh," *Business Insider*, September 8, 2018, www.businessinsider.com/rochelle-garza-immigration-abortion-case-testifies-against-kavanaugh-2018-9.

310 **it affirmed Hawaii's claim:** Ellen D. Katz, "Race and the Right to Vote After Rice v. Cayetano," *Michigan Law Review* 99, no. 3 (2000): 491–531, repository.law.umich.edu/cgi/viewcontent.cgi?article=2059&context=articles.

310 **"any programs targeting Native Hawaiians as a group":** Sophie Cocke, "Hirono releases confidential Kavanaugh email expressing views on Native Hawaiians," *Honolulu Star-Advertiser*, September 6, 2018, www.staradvertiser.com/2018/09/06/breaking-news/hirono-releases-confidential-kavanaugh-email-expressing-views-on-native-hawaiians/.

311 **"my colleague from Alaska should be deeply troubled":** Sophie Cocke "Hirono Calls Supreme Court Nominee's Views on Hawaiians 'Offensive,'" *Honolulu Star-Advertiser*, September 5, 2018, www.hawaiinewsnow.com/story/39034607/sen-hirono-releases-confidential-kavanaugh-documents/.

Chapter Twenty-One: Rebel Women

315 **After the story broke nationally:** Emily Stewart, "Brett Kavanaugh's Accuser, Christine Blasey Ford, Comes Forward in the Washington Post," *Vox*, September 16, 2018, www.vox.com/policy-and-politics/2018/9/16/17866988/brett-kavanaugh-christine-blasey-ford-washington-post.

317 **"Shut up and step up":** Eli Rosenberg and Lindsey Bever, "'Shut Up and Step Up': Sen. Hirono's Blunt Message to Men," *Washington Post*, September 19, 2018, www.washingtonpost.com/politics/2018/09/19/shut-up-step-up-this-senators-message-men-wake-kavanaugh-accusation/.

317 **"Why are you offended?":** Rosenberg and Bever, "'Shut Up and Step Up.'"

318 **Dr. Ford's opening statement:** Dylan Scott, "The 7 Most Important Moments from Christine Blasey Ford's Senate Testimony," *Vox*, September 27, 2018, www.vox.com/policy-and
-politics/2018/9/27/17910214/christine-blasey-ford-senate-testimony-brett-kavanaugh
-hearing.

319 **I thought he might inadvertently:** Emma Brown, "California Professor, Writer of Confidential Brett Kavanaugh Letter, Speaks Out About Her Allegation of Sexual Assault," *Washington Post*, September 16, 2018, www.washingtonpost.com/investigations/california-professor
-writer-of-confidential-brett-kavanaugh-letter-speaks-out-about-her-allegation-of-sexual
-assault/2018/09/16/46982194-b846-11e8-94eb-3bd52dfe917b_story.html.

319 **"I was underneath one of them":** Alex Shephard, "Indelible in the Hippocampus Is the
Laughter," *New Republic*, September 27, 2018, newrepublic.com/minutes/151423/christine
-blasey-ford-indelible-hippocampus-laughter.

319 **"One hundred percent," she replied:** Scott, "The 7 Most Important Moments from Christine Blasey Ford's Senate Testimony."

320 **women law professors calling for:** Judith Resnik, "This Question Changed the Face of the
Supreme Court," *CNN*, September 25, 2018, www.cnn.com/2018/09/25/opinions/anita
-hill-patsy-mink-changed-how-we-see-kavanaugh-judith-resnik/index.html.

320 **One year after Hill's testimony:** Sarah Pruitt, "How Anita Hill's Testimony Made America Cringe—and Change," History.com, updated April 2, 2019, www.history.com/news
/anita-hill-confirmation-hearings-impact.

324 **"I'm not going to participate in this charade":** "Senate and House Democrats on Brett
Kavanaugh Nomination," C-SPAN, September 28, 2018, www.c-span.org/video/?452225
-1/democrats-speak-walking-senate-judiciary-committee-hearing.

325 **imploring the Judiciary Committee not to confirm:** Max Brantley, "2,400 Law Professors, Including Six from Arkansas, Speak Out Against Kavanaugh," *Arkansas Times*, October
4, 2018, arktimes.com/arkansas-blog/2018/10/04/2400-law-professors-including-six-from
-arkansas-speak-out-against-kavanaugh.

326 **"who has historically been allowed to be angry":** Rebecca Traister, "Fury Is a Political
Weapon. And Women Need to Wield It," *New York Times*, September 29, 2018, www.ny
times.com/2018/09/29/opinion/sunday/fury-is-a-political-weapon-and-women-need
-to-wield-it.html.

327 **dubbing me a "badass":** Nina Totenberg, "The Quiet Rage of Mazie Hirono," NPR, June
7, 2018, www.npr.org/2018/06/07/617239314/the-quiet-rage-of-mazie-hirono.

327 **"A Running List of Every Time Senator Mazie Hirono":** Lisa Ryan, "A Running List
of Every Time Senator Mazie Hirono Has Called 'Bullsh*t,'" The Cut, *New York*, September
21, 2018, www.thecut.com/2018/09/senator-mazie-hirono-list-bull-kavanaugh.html.

329 **Nationally, voters had chosen Democratic:** "Women in the 116th Congress," Quorum,
Quorum.us, www.quorum.us/data-driven-insights/women-in-116th-congress/401/.

329 **during the November 2018 midterms:** Alec Tyson, "The 2018 Midterm Vote: Divisions
by Race, Gender, Education," Pew Research Center, November 8, 2018, www.pewresearch
.org/fact-tank/2018/11/08/the-2018-midterm-vote-divisions-by-race-gender-education/.

329 **132 women took their seats:** "Women in the 116th Congress."

Chapter Twenty-Two: Zombie Land

336 **reported that seven children had died:** Cynthia Pompa, "Immigrant Kids Keep Dying in CBP Detention Centers, and DHS Won't Take Accountability," ACLU, June 24, 2019, www.aclu.org/blog/immigrants-rights/immigrants-rights-and-detention/immigrant -kids-keep-dying-cbp-detention.

336 **waiting for their case to be called:** Nomaan Merchant, "Tents, Stench, Smoke: Health Risks Are Gripping Migrant Camp," Associated Press, November 14, 2019, apnews.com /337b139ed4fa4d208b93d491364e04da.

336 **Losing hope, they decided to navigate:** Bill Chappell, "A Father and Daughter Who Drowned at the Border Put Attention on Immigration," NPR, June 26, 2019, www .npr.org/2019/06/26/736177694/a-father-and-daughter-drowned-at-the-border-put -attention-on-immigration.

337 **found some distance downriver:** Chappell, "A Father and Daughter Who Drowned at the Border Put Attention on Immigration."

337 **treated "with dignity, respect, and care":** S.2113—Stop Cruelty to Migrant Children Act, 116th Congress, 1st Session, July 15, 2019, www.congress.gov/bill/116th-congress/senate -bill/2113/text.

338 **"We better look to our hearts":** Sophie Cocke, "Sen. Mazie Hirono Chokes Up as She Discusses Conditions for Children at the U.S.-Mexican Border," www.staradvertiser.com /2019/07/11/hawaii-news/sen-mazie-hirono-chokes-up-as-she-discusses-conditions-for -children-at-the-u-s-mexico-border/.

339 **up to the legislative branch to assess:** John Cassidy, "Robert Mueller Says It's Up to Congress to Indict a President," *New Yorker*, May 29, 2019, www.newyorker.com/news/our -columnists/robert-mueller-says-its-up-to-congress-to-indict-a-president.

341 **quid pro quo:** 166 Cong. Rec. S646 (daily ed. January 29, 2020), www.govinfo.gov/content /pkg/CREC-2020-01-29/pdf/CREC-2020-01-29-senate.pdf.

342 **"high crimes and misdemeanors":** Todd Ruger, "Out of the Impeachment, into the Fallout," *Roll Call*, February 5, 2020, www.rollcall.com/2020/02/05/out-of-the-impeachment -into-the-fallout/

344 **auditioned for the attorney general's job:** Jennifer Rubin, "What to Make of William Barr's Memo?" *Washington Post*, December 21, 2018, www.washingtonpost.com/opinions /2018/12/21/what-make-william-barrs-memo/

345 **Mueller himself had strongly refuted:** Devlin Barrett and Matt Zapotosky, "Mueller Complained That Barr's Letter Did Not Capture 'Context' of Trump Probe," *Washington Post*, April 30, 2019, www.washingtonpost.com/world/national-security/mueller-complained -that-barrs-letter-did-not-capture-context-of-trump-probe/2019/04/30/d3c8fdb6-6b7b -11e9-a66d-a82d3f3d96d5_story.html.

345 **"You should resign":** "Senator Hirono to Barr: 'You Knew and You Lied,'" C-SPAN, May 1, 2019, www.c-span.org/video/?c4795368/senator-hirono-barr-you-knew-lied.

346 **"you clearly have your opinion":** "Senator Hirono to Barr: 'You Knew and You Lied.'"

Chapter Twenty-Three: Two Pandemics

347 **nursing home in Washington state:** Jack Healy and Serge F. Kovaleski, "The Coronavirus's Rampage Through a Suburban Nursing Home," *New York Times*, March 21, 2020, www .nytimes.com/2020/03/21/us/coronavirus-nursing-home-kirkland-life-care.html.

349 **extremist plot to kidnap Michigan governor:** Alexandra Svokos, "The Alleged Kidnapping Plot Against Michigan Gov. Gretchen Whitmer, as Told in Photos," *ABC News*, October 9, 2020, abcnews.go.com/US/alleged-kidnapping-plot-michigan-gov-gretchen -whitmer-told/story?id=73523322.

350 **planned act of domestic terrorism:** Dan Mangan, "Six Men Charged with Conspiring to Kidnap Michigan Gov. Gretchen Whitmer, 7 Others Arrested Under State Anti-Terrorism Law," *CNBC*, October 8, 2020, www.cnbc.com/2020/10/08/michigan-gov-gretchen -whitmer-kidnap-plot-busted-by-fbi.html.

350 **fueled the flames by criticizing Whitmer:** Malachi Barrett, "Trump Criticizes Whitmer After FBI Foiled Plot to Kidnap Michigan Governor," *MLive*, October 8, 2020, www.mlive .com/public-interest/2020/10/trump-criticizes-whitmer-after-fbi-foiled-plot-to-kidnap -michigan-governor.html.

350 **jagged black Sharpie scrawl:** Austa Somvichian-Clause, "Trump's Use of the Term 'Chinese Virus' for Coronavirus Hurts Asian Americans, Says Expert," *The Hill*, March 25, 2020, thehill.com/changing-america/respect/diversity-inclusion/489464-trumps-use-of-the -term-chinese-virus-for.

352 **resolution condemning discrimination:** Resolution: Condemning All Forms of Anti-Asian Sentiment as Related to COVID–19, 116th Congress, 2d Session, March 25, 2020, Senate archives.

352 **"Calling COVID-19 the 'Wuhan virus,'":** "Harris, Duckworth, Hirono to Introduce Resolution Condemning Anti-Asian Racism Prompted by COVID-19," Kamala D. Harris, press release, March 25, 2020, Senate archives.

352 **"They are working closely with us":** Andrew Mark Miller, "Asian American CBS Reporter Rips Trump Tweet Urging the Public Not to Blame Asians for the Coronavirus," *Washington Examiner*, March 24, 2020, www.washingtonexaminer.com/news/asian-american-cbs -reporter-rips-trump-tweet-urging-the-public-not-to-blame-asians-for-the-coronavirus.

352 **sociology professor Dr. Grace Kao:** Somvichian-Clause, "Trump's Use of the Term 'Chinese Virus' for Coronavirus Hurts Asian Americans."

357 **support for the Black Lives Matter protests:** Savannah Behrmann, "Poll: Nearly Two-Thirds of Americans Support Protests Against Racial Injustice," *USA Today*, July 28, 2020, www.usatoday.com/story/news/politics/2020/07/28/poll-most-americans-support-black -lives-matter-protests/5532345002/.

357 **racism is "a big problem":** Eugene Scott, "Majority of Americans Say Race Discrimination Is a Big Problem in the U.S.," *Washington Post*, July 10, 2020, www.washingtonpost.com /politics/2020/07/10/majority-americans-say-race-discrimination-is-big-problem-us/.

357 **"an America that lives up to its highest ideals":** "Warren Delivers Floor Speech on Her Amendment to Rename All Bases and Other Military Assets Honoring the Confederacy," Elizabeth Warren, press release, June 30, 2020, www.warren.senate.gov/newsroom/press -releases/warren-delivers-floor-speech-on-her-amendment-to-rename-all-bases-and -other-military-assets-honoring-the-confederacy.

358 **rally at the State Capitol in Honolulu:** Dillon Ancheta and Rick Daysog, "Hawaii's Weekend Black Lives Matter Protests Drew Thousands Statewide," *Hawaii News Now*, June 6, 2020, www.hawaiinewsnow.com/2020/06/06/around-hawaii-thousands-take-streets -black-lives-matter-protests/.

362 **a Stanford University study found:** David Lim, "Study Links Trump Rallies to More Than 700 Covid Deaths," *Politico*, October 31, 2020, www.politico.com/news/2020/10/31 /trump-study-coronavirus-rallies-433760.

362 **soared past nine million:** "USA Coronovirus: News Summary for 1 November," *Diario AS English*, November 2, 2020, en.as.com/en/2020/11/01/latest_news/1604224661_012564 .html.

362 **every 107 seconds:** John Bacon, "'There's No Way to Sugarcoat It': COVID-19 Cases Are Surging; One American Dies Every 107 Seconds," *USA Today*, October 28, 2020, www .usatoday.com/story/news/health/2020/10/28/covid-cases-us-sees-surge-americans-tire -pandemic/6052710002/.

Epilogue: The Paper Makers

365 **if a person folds one thousand origami cranes:** "Meaning of the Origami Crane," JCCC Origami Project, Japanese Canadian Cultural Centre, hpsathome.com/wp-content /uploads/2020/05/meaning_of_the_origami_crane.pdf.

366 **"after you prayed for them":** Griffin Connolly, "Weekly Bipartisan Prayer Paying Dividends in Senate Negotiations," *Roll Call*, February 7, 2018, www.rollcall.com/2018/02/07 /weekly-bipartisan-prayer-paying-dividends-in-senate-negotiations/.

371 **more than sixty cases:** William Cummings, Joey Garrison, and Jim Sergent, "By the numbers: President Donald Trump's failed efforts to overturn the election," *USA Today*, January 6, 2021, https://www.usatoday.com/in-depth/news/politics/elections/2021/01/06/trumps -failed-efforts-overturn-election-numbers/4130307001/.

371 **the threat of mass resignations:** Jess Bravin and Sadie Gurman, "Trump Pressed Justice Department to Go Directly to the Supreme Court to Overturn Election Results," January 23, 2021, *The Wall Street Journal*, https://www.wsj.com/articles/trump-pressed-to-change-justice -department-leadership-to-boost-his-voter-fraud-claims-11611434369?st=tukbkyjihajqkxj &reflink=article_email_share.

371 **"Stop the Steal" rally:** Tina Nguyen, "MAGA Marchers Plot Final D.C. Stand on Jan. 6," *Politico*, January 4, 2021, https://www.politico.com/news/2021/01/04/maga-marchers -trump-last-stand-454382.

371 **certifying the Electoral College count:** Tina Nguyen, "MAGA Marchers Plot Final D.C. Stand on Jan. 6."

372 **vowed via tweet would be "wild":** Dan Barry and Sheera Frenkel, "'Be There. Will Be Wild!' Trump All But Circled the Date," *New York Times*, January 6, 2021, https://www .nytimes.com/2021/01/06/us/politics/capitol-mob-trump-supporters.html.

372 **his displeasure with Mike Pence:** Tom Foreman, "New Timeline Shows Just How Close Rioters Got to Pence and His Family," *CNN*, January 15, 2021, https://www.cnn.com /videos/politics/2021/01/15/mike-pence-close-call-capitol-riot-foreman-vpx.cnn.

372 **wooden gallows and noose:** Elaine Godfrey, "It Was Supposed to Be So Much Worse," *Atlantic*, January 9, 2021, https://www.theatlantic.com/politics/archive/2021/01/trump -rioters-wanted-more-violence-worse/617614.

373 **The surging mob:** Tom Foreman, "New Timeline Shows Just How Close Rioters Got to Pence and His Family."

373 **five people would lose their lives:** Jack Healy, "These Are the 5 People Who Died in the Capitol Riot," *New York Times*, https://www.nytimes.com/2021/01/11/us/who-died-in-capitol-building-attack.html.

374 **misinformation about election fraud:** Elizabeth Dwoskin and Craig Timberg, "Misinformation Dropped Dramatically the Week After Twitter Banned Trump and Some Allies," *Washington Post*, January 6, 2021, https://www.washingtonpost.com/technology/2021/01/16/misinformation-trump-twitter.

374 **the sole article of impeachment:** Mary Clare Jalonick and Lisa Mascaro, "Schumer: Trump Impeachment Trial to Begin Week of Feb. 8," Associated Press, January 22, 2021, https://apnews.com/article/joe-biden-donald-trump-capitol-siege-biden-cabinet-trials-462425af29b02c43e24913b6fd191b6f.

375 **"Through a crucible for the ages":** "Inaugural Address by President Joseph R. Biden, Jr.," The White House, January 20, 2021, https://www.whitehouse.gov/briefing-room/speeches-remarks/2021/01/20/inaugural-address-by-president-joseph-r-biden-jr/.